Major Soviet Writers

Major Soviet Writers

ESSAYS IN CRITICISM

Edited by
EDWARD J. BROWN
Stanford University

OXFORD UNIVERSITY PRESS
London   Oxford   New York
1973

OXFORD UNIVERSITY PRESS

Oxford   London   New York
Glasgow   Toronto   Melbourne   Wellington
Cape Town   Ibadan   Nairobi   Lusaka   Addis Ababa   Delhi
Bombay   Calcutta   Madras   Karachi   Lahore   Dacca
Kuala Lumpur   Hong Kong   Tokyo

Editor's Introduction

The present book offers a collection of what I believe to be the most useful critical essays—wherever written—on a number of important authors of the Soviet period. The book concentrates on "major authors" rather than on criticism as such, and the essays included do not represent any particular school or viewpoint, Soviet or non-Soviet. Their authors are American (fourteen essays), British (two essays), Swedish (two essays), Russian (six essays), and émigré Russian (two essays). The one requirement for selection was that each essay be concerned with critical analysis of the literary works involved. This necessarily eliminated much material, some of it excellent, dealing with historical, political, or simply biographical matters. For this reason we did not include the subtle and informative essays of Max Hayward on a number of contemporary writers, essays which could not have been omitted from a collection with a slightly different orientation. And Paustovsky's fascinating reminiscences of Babel were eliminated because their heaviest accent is on the personality of the man rather than on his works.

I submit that this approach to Soviet writers may even be a healthy innovation. Soviet criticism has tended to emphasize social background and social purpose in literature, and Western critics habitually experience a need to "explain" Soviet literary works in terms of political factors; this has led to a situation in which much writing about Soviet authors is implicitly (or even explicitly!) polemical, and tends to neglect literary values. But many Soviet writers present curious and fascinating problems for the literary analyst, even writers like Mayakovsky and Solzhenitsyn whose work is permeated with the events of the century. Jakobson's article on Mayakovsky is a classic example of an overall structural analysis, which takes full account of the author and his period, and the essays included here tend on the whole to follow that pattern.

The student of Soviet literature will naturally consult histories of literature for detailed information on particular writers, as well as for the social and political background of literature.[1]

By way of introduction to the collection it may be well to present here a brief statement concerning each of the authors treated and the essay or essays selected, along with some indication of other significant critical works.

Velimir Khlebnikov. Students of Russian poetry regard Khlebnikov as one of the greatest poets of the century, and there are some who place him above Pasternak and Mayakovsky. Those who know Western poetry as well as Russian consider that he is among the truly great poetic geniuses of the modern period, and one eminent Russian scholar describes him as "one of the greatest poets of all time." In spite of this he is very little known in the West, even by specialists, and articles about him are not numerous.[2] Khlebnikov's work is a prolonged poetic experiment in which the linguistic material is Russian; to appreciate that experiment fully requires intimate knowledge of the Russian language itself. Khlebnikov submits only with great reluctance to translation, and then only when image or formal device is central to a poem. Occasionally his language play can be imitated in English—the poem "Incantation by Laughter" is a case in point—and quite often the effect of a poem can be, if not translated, then described.

Jakobson's *Modern Russian Poetry* is the most perceptive study of Khlebnikov ever written, and it provides some acute observations on certain other modern poets, notably Mayakovsky. Moreover, the essay is a classic in the literature of the Russian formalist movement, and it contains an exposition of some of the most important ideas associated with that movement in its earliest period. Some readers will find the essay dense and difficult; it requires—and rewards—study. The analysis Jakobson offers is primarily linguistic: Khlebnikov's poetry is studied as the purest example of a poetic language practiced for its own sake.

The articles on Khlebnikov by Vladimir Mayakovsky and Yury Tynyanov are brief but illuminating appreciations of the poet, one of them by his close friend and collaborator, the other by a contemporary formalist critic, who, like Jakobson, witnessed at first hand the emergence of this original poetic phenomenon.

Boris Pasternak. One of the most important poets of the twentieth century, Pasternak was little known in the West until his novel *Doctor Zhivago*, which he regarded as the high point of his life's poetic endeavor, was published in 1958 outside the Soviet Union. After winning the Nobel Prize for this novel, he was severely harassed by the Soviet authorities. Since the time of the award a surfeit (I choose the word carefully) of articles and books about him has appeared in the West. Many of these have great merit and it was not easy to select among them.[3] Andrey Sinyavsky's essay was published in the Soviet Union as an introduction to a one-volume collection of Pasternak's poetry. Sinyavsky was arrested shortly after that as the author of stories and essays published in the West under the name Abram Tertz, and he was sentenced to a long term of hard labor. His essay is probably the best general statement on Pasternak's poetry.

Herbert Bowman's article on *Doctor Zhivago* is a lucid discussion which clarifies the novel's central meaning while reducing to proper perspective the widely preached political and religious-symbolical interpretation of Pasternak's great work.

Anna Akhmatova is the subject of two articles. The shorter of these, also by Sinyavsky, is a sensitive appreciation of her whole career as a poet and contains a number of valuable insights into formal features of her work. While critical essays on Akhmatova are not copious we should mention that the two-volume edition of her work published in the United States under the editorship of Gleb Struve and B. A. Filippov offers much valuable material, both in Russian and in English, along with an extremely useful bibliography.[4]

The second article on Akhmatova is an essay by Korney Chukovsky, who is widely known in the Soviet Union as an author of children's literature, critic, and translator of American poetry. Chukovsky contrasts Akhmatova with her great contemporary, Mayakovsky, and presents an original analysis of both poets.

Vladimir Mayakovsky is certainly the most eminent and the most honored poet of the modern period, and Soviet critics and scholars have produced an amazing number of books and articles about him. Only a small part of that vast product would warrant translation into English, and very little of it is concerned with critical analysis of verse forms, themes, and poetic structures. A useful collection of documentary materials about the poet's life appeared in 1966 in Poland and has been translated into English, but contains hardly any critical evaluation.[5] An excellent introduction to Mayakovsky is Patricia Blake's essay, "The Two Deaths of Vladimir Mayakovsky."[6]

Roman Jakobson's essay "On a Generation That Squandered Its Poets," which appeared in Berlin shortly after the poet's death in 1930, is a beautiful and moving statement on the fate of Mayakovsky and the group of poets to which he belonged. It also presents an analysis of the poet's central and persistent themes; anyone who has written on Mayakovsky since the appearance of that essay is to some extent in debt to it.

Osip Mandelshtam has always enjoyed esteem and popularity among sophisticated students of modern poetry, though he was persecuted during his lifetime and has been officially ignored since his death. The contemporary revival of interest in Mandelshtam has been due in large measure to the efforts of American scholars. The most complete edition of his works—in three volumes—is that produced in the United States under the editorship of Gleb Struve and Boris Filippov.[7] Clarence Brown's essay "On Reading Mandelshtam" was first published as an introduction to that collection, and, along with Nils Å. Nilsson's essay "Osip Mandelshtam and His Poetry," offers an unusually discerning statement of Mandelshtam's essential quality as a poet. Examples of Mandelshtam's poetry appeared in those essays in Russian, and have been translated for this edition by the editor. We offer one article on contemporary poetry: D. Merwyn Jones's original study of Andrey Voznesensky entitled "A Look Around."

Evgeny Zamyatin's career as a writer began shortly before the First World War with the publication of a number of stories dealing with life in the deep provinces of Russia and written in the mannered, language-conscious style of the Remizov school. He is well known in the west as the author of the antiutopian satire *We* (1920). Critical studies on Zamyatin, both Soviet and Western, have tended to emphasize the supposed political message of *We* and of some other works he wrote during the Soviet period. Richard Gregg and Christopher Collins both discuss Zamyatin's use of myth and symbol, and each makes an important contribution to the study of that author.

Boris Pilnyak and *Vsevolod Ivanov* may properly be called the "pioneers" since they were the writers who first clearly established themselves in Soviet prose of the 1920's, and they preserved at the same time many links with an earlier period. Robert Maguire's essay is a fine piece of literary criticism by a scholar who has a sensitive awareness of history and political background.

Yury Olesha wrote little, but the small body of his work deserves a high place in twentieth-century European literature as a whole. He has attracted the attention of numerous critics and scholars. Gleb Struve's long essay "A Writer of Unnecessary Themes" (*Pisatel nenuzhnykh tem*), not yet translated into English, presents a number of interesting facts and ideas concerning Olesha's career in the Soviet

Union. The Soviet critic Arkady Belinkov published some curious essays on Olesha in the Soviet provincial periodical *Baikal,* and Belinkov's lengthy work on him is currently being prepared for publication in the United States.[8] The essays reprinted here represent two different approaches to the work of Olesha. Nils Nilsson's "Through the Wrong End of Binoculars" is a model of analytic literary perception, investigating Olesha's way of seeing and presenting the world. William Harkins's essay is an exploration of a previously neglected aspect of Olesha: the evidence in his work of perverse and puzzling sexual attitudes. Harkins's "Freudian" analysis of *Envy* provides many insights that illuminate the symbolic structure of that novel.

Isaac Babel, like Olesha, had a small output, but the slender volume of his collected works offers an astonishing combination of verbal power and human insight. Shklovsky's essay is a virtuoso performance in criticism. It is deliberately impressionistic and subjective; it is an evocation not of Babel only but of the milieu and atmosphere from which Babel materialized; it contains a series of brilliant critical *bon mots,* each of which points to the essence of Babel's art. In addition, the essay succeeds in mimicking that lyrical-ironical note which is the cachet of Babel's own style. The second essay on Babel, by Sinyavsky, covers Babel's whole writing career.

Mikhail Zoshchenko is a magnificent satirist of Soviet life whose short stories have always been immensely popular in the Soviet Union. Hugh McLean's excellent introduction to the collection entitled *Nervous People* is readily available in paperback, and it seemed superfluous to reprint it here. I have included the same critic's essay on Zoshchenko's unfinished novel, *Before Sunrise,* a lucid and sophisticated treatment of an important, but involved and difficult, book.

Rufus Mathewson's essay "Four Novels" deals with authors whose work was characteristic of the 1930's: *Mikhail Sholokhov, Alexey Tolstoy, Leonid Leonov,* and *Nikolay Ostrovsky.* The novels which Mathewson analyzes were popular with the Soviet reader and also acceptable to the Stalinist authorities; this fine essay presents a panorama of the "full range of possibility in Soviet literature."

Yury Kazakov's writing provides an example of the impressionistic prose that was popular in the 1960's, and George Gibian's excellent essay on him interestingly analyzes Kazakov's own work and gives some attention also to the personal, intimate, and emotional prose that has characterized many young writers of the more recent period.

Alexander Solzhenitsyn is a powerful writer whose extraordinary gift has not been spoiled by his years in prison or by the harassment he suffered after his release. His special purpose as a writer is to reveal matters that are normally hidden from view, to break down the enforced segregation of the incarcerated and the cancerous, or to invade the privacy of a political dictator's study and rummage in the dark corners of his mind. He is, moreover, one of the most accomplished stylists now writing in Russian; unfortunately no translation can adequately represent the range and versatility he commands in his use of the spoken and written idiom. The present writer's essay on Solzhenitsyn is an examination of the characters he portrays, and the methods he uses in developing them.

Andrey Sinyavsky is represented in this collection by three superb critical articles, and indeed he was known as a critic in the Soviet Union until his arrest in 1965. The stories he had been publishing in the West under the name Abram Tertz mingled fantasy with social satire, and Deming Brown's article illuminates his procedures as an artist and examines his relationship to other writers, both Russian and Western.

Mikhail Bulgakov was one of many Russian writers whose careers were blighted by the dogmatism of the official literary establishment, but what strikes one is that his independent creative urge was so strong that he managed to write masterpieces in spite of the evil attacks which continued through most of his life, and although faced with the near certainty that much of what he wrote would not be published—at least not for a very long time. Perhaps he believed that, as the Devil put it in *The Master and Margarita*, "manuscripts don't burn" and no doubt he was confident that his thing of beauty would one day be a joy forever. And because he had this confidence we can now enjoy *The Master and Margarita*, which was first published in Moscow many years after his death.

Ellendea Proffer's essay is a study of Bulgakov's literary strategies in that novel, of his narrative techniques, and of the symbols he uses to tie together into a single whole the complex story lines he develops.

Obviously it was impossible to include every writer of the Soviet period who might be considered "major," and no doubt many readers will find omissions that they regret. Some will complain of the omission of Marina Tsvetaeva,[9] Nikolay Zabolotsky, Mikhail Kuzmin, Nikolay Gumilyov, Valentin Kataev, and many others in both prose and poetry. The field of émigré Russian poetry and prose is a rich expanse which might perhaps be dealt with in another book. In any case I hope very much that the critical essays assembled here under one cover will shed light on much of Soviet writing.

Contents

xi

Note on Transliteration

The transliteration systems in the previously published articles in English have been retained in this volume.

Major Soviet Writers

A Note on Soviet Poetry

Poetry in the immediate pre-Soviet period was dominated by two movements, acmeism and futurism. Both movements arose around 1910 and both represented a reaction against symbolism, which had been the dominant literary school. Each group strove in its own way to combat the metaphysical tendencies and the obscurities cultivated by the symbolists and to effect simplicity and clarity of style. The two movements were utterly opposed in their outlook and poetic methods, an opposition that is revealed in Chukovsky's essay on Akhmatova and Mayakovsky, which is included here. The acmeists revered poetic tradition and the accumulated values of artistic culture in all spheres; the futurists rejected the past and proclaimed the modern city as their theme. Along with Akhmatova and her husband Nikolay Gumilyov (who was executed in 1921) the third outstanding acmeist was Osip Mandelshtam. The leading futurists, in addition to Mayakovsky, were David Burliuk, the founder of the group and a well-known cubist painter, Alexey Kruchonykh, the author of dadalike "trans-sense" verse, Nikolay Aseev, a close follower of Mayakovsky, and Vassily Kamensky. Velimir Khlebnikov should also be included as a member of the futurist movement, but he was a case apart, and his poetry was a unique experiment with sense and sound. Boris Pasternak, one of the greatest poets of the century, was associated at one time with the futurists, but broke with them and, as Sinyavsky's essay points out, worked out in relative isolation his own poetic method and characteristic themes.

During the Soviet period the poets identified with acmeism continued to produce, but it can hardly be said that they prospered. The one literary group whose members as a whole supported the Bolsheviks were the Moscow futurists, who were installed in 1918 as editors of the official journal *Art of the Commune*, where they pressed their program of a "clean sweep" away from the old order in art and literature. Mayakovsky's statements of the program, both in prose and in poetry, betray the strident extremism that characterized both himself and the times. But the futurists soon found themselves in disharmony with the leaders of the Bolshevik party, and their pretensions to "dictatorship" were severely repulsed.

Under the aegis of the state, and sometimes with its support, a number of organizations developed which included poets who called themselves "proletarian." They claimed to speak for the "masses" and to eschew both individualism and effete modernism, and in their poetic methods they tended to be traditional, or to make use of lessons learned from the symbolists. They did not form a cohesive group but were broken up into many factions, such as the "Smithy" and the "Cosmos," and though their product in the earliest period consumed much paper, hardly any of them achieved real status as poets, though we might mention the names of Alexander Zharov, Alexey Gastev, Yosif Utkin, and Alexander Bezymensky.

A poet who was a deliberate contrast both to Mayakovsky and to the "proletarian" poets and who was probably more popular than either was Sergey Esenin. Esenin, moreover, fashioned for himself a biography intended to be appreciated along with his poems as commentary and supplement. Lost in what he called "Tavern Moscow," he instigated wild scenes, drank and fought in grand excess, and was frequently arrested. The city in Esenin's personal mythology is a labyrinth where men lose their souls, and he shrinks from the iron march of industry. The principal content of his melodious poetry is nostalgia for the old Russian rural way of life, something that was already disappearing. Esenin fashioned a body of poetry out of the childhood memories he brought with him from his native Ryazan, whose birches and cottages become brilliantly visible again in his lines.

Many talented poets celebrated the Russian peasant, and no doubt the greatest of them was Nikolay Klyuev, whose poetry draws heavily upon the linguistic and symbolic riches of the Russian religious schismatics. Others who wrote in the same vein were Pyotr Oreshin and Sergey Klychkov, both interesting poets who disappeared from view, like Klyuev, during the purges of the mid-thirties.

A number of poets with both talent and felicity of language managed to write and publish acceptable poetry throughout the Soviet period. Most of them never rose above the level of mediocrity, but we should mention as exceptions Nikolay Tikhonov, who was also a powerful figure in Soviet literary organizations, Eduard Bagritsky, a poet whose style is genuinely original, though he acknowledged the influence of Boris Pasternak, and Alexander Tvardovsky, a prolific poet who wrote on many themes—collectivization, the war, the excesses of Stalinism, and who until 1970 was the editor of the magazine *New World*. Such poets combine thematic tameness with a high degree of verbal skill, but they have added little to the history of Russian poetry. Another of this type is Margarita Aliger, who occasionally writes skillful lyrics giving the impression that she works at being honest.

In the post-Stalin literary revival of the sixties a prominent part was played by a number of poets. Evgeny Evtushenko is widely known both in the Soviet Union and abroad as a poet espousing liberal tendencies. In his poetry he shies away from verbal experiment or formal play and his work is replete with social mission, and with important ideas. On most issues he takes an honest stand, and one of his most famous poems is *Baby Yar*, in which he speaks out against anti-Semitism in the Soviet Union. He is an immensely successful platform poet, and his recitations are always well attended.

A number of relatively young poets developed during the sixties an individual lyrical accent, and among these we should mention Bella Akhmadulina, Boris Slutsky, Novella Matveeva, Viktor Sosnora, and Evgeny Vinokurov. Bulat Okudzhava is an enormously popular singer of his own songs, which he writes simply and without didacticism about intimate and personal things. Andrey Voznesensky, also well-known in the United States, is a gifted young poet whose great concern is with the texture of imagery and language, as Mr. Gareth Jones's article points out. Perhaps the most brilliant of contemporary Russian poets is Iosif Brodsky. Because he had no regular employment and worked only at the poet's trade he was tried in Leningrad in 1964 as a "parasite" and sentenced to a term at hard labor. His poems are distinct and individual lyrics which reveal a high level of sophistication concerning modern poetry as a whole, although he himself tends to be conservative in form. There is a deep religious strain in his work and he has clearly been influenced by the reading of the Bible. For the most part his work is published outside the Soviet Union, and it has not yet been the subject of a definitive study.

A group of poets known by the nonsense name of "oberiuty" revived during the late twenties the futurist play with language, adding in their product (some of which was in prose) a touch both of black humor and of the absurd. Daniel Kharms was the leader of the group, but perhaps its principal claim to fame is that it included among its members Zabolotsky, one of the leading poets of the century. His poetry ranges from complex and ingenious portrayal of nature, often in moments of seasonal change, to original and strange pictures of urban life. His verse techniques were at first subtle and experimental, though he tended to become conventional under the pressures of the Soviet regime. His work, too, is in need of a definitive critical study.

Soviet poetry has obviously been mutilated and its growth stunted by the repressions which characterized the Soviet regime, and it is truly remarkable that the harvest should be as rich as it is. The springs of poetry remain active in the Soviet Union, and there is reason to hope for future growth.[1]

The Editor

On a Generation That Squandered Its Poets

Mayakovsky's poetry—his imagery—his lyrical composition—I have written about these things and published some of my remarks. The idea of writing a monograph has never left me. Mayakovsky's poetry is qualitatively different from everything in Russian verse before him, however much one may establish the genetic links. This is what makes the subject particularly intriguing. The structure of his poetry is profoundly original and revolutionary. But how is it possible to write about Mayakovsky's poetry now, when the paramount subject is not the rhythm, but the death of the poet, when (if I may resort to Mayakovsky's own poetic phrase) "sudden grief is not yet ready to give in to a clearly realized pain."

During one of our meetings Mayakovsky, as was his custom, read me his last poems. Considering his creative potential I could not help comparing them with what he might have produced. "Very good," I said, "but not as good as Mayakovsky." But now the creative powers are canceled out, the inimitable stanzas can no longer be compared to anything else, the words "Mayakovsky's last poems" have suddenly taken on a tragic meaning. Sheer grief at his absence has overshadowed the absent one. Now it is more painful, but still easier, to write, not about the one we've lost but rather about our own loss and those of us who have suffered it.

It's our generation that has suffered the loss. Roughly, those of us who are now between thirty and forty-five years old. Those who, already fully formed, entered into the years of the Revolution not as unmolded clay, but still not hardened, still capable of adapting to ex-

From *Smert poeta*, copyright © 1931 Petropolis-Verlag (Berlin, 1931). Reprinted by permission of the author.

perience and change, still capable of taking a dynamic rather than a static view of our life.

It has been said more than once that the first poetic love of our generation was Alexander Blok. Velimir Khlebnikov gave us a new epos, the first genuinely epic creations after many decades of drought. Even his briefer verses create the impression of epic fragments and Khlebnikov easily combined them into narrative poems. Khlebnikov is epic in spite of our antiepic times, and therein lies one of the reasons for his alien aspect to the average reader. Other poets brought his poetry closer to the reader; they drew upon Khlebnikov, pouring out this "word ocean" into many lyrical streamlets. In contrast to Khlebnikov, Mayakovsky embodied within himself the lyrical urges of this generation. The broad epic canvas is deeply alien to him and unacceptable. Even when he attempts "a bloody Iliad of the Revolution," or "an Odyssey of the famine years," what appears is not an epic but a heroic lyric of vast range and variety of time, offered—"at the top of his voice." There was a point when symbolist poetry was in its decline and it was still not clear which of the two new mutually antagonistic trends, acmeism or futurism, would prevail. Khlebnikov and Mayakovsky gave the leitmotif of contemporaneity to literary art. The name of Gumilyov marks a secondary branch of modern Russian poetry—its characteristic overtone. For Khlebnikov and for Mayakovsky "the homeland of creative poetry is the future"; in contrast, Esenin is a lyrical glance backward. His verse expresses the weariness of a generation.

Modern Russian poetry after 1910 is largely defined by these names. The verse of Aseev and Selvinsky[1] is bright indeed, but it is a reflected light. They do not announce but reflect the spirit of the times. Their magnitude is a derivative quantity. Pasternak's books and perhaps those of Mandelshtam are remarkable, but theirs is a private[2] poetry: new creation will not be kindled by it. The heart of a generation cannot take fire with such verses because they do not shatter the boundaries of the present.

Gumilyov (1886-1921) was shot; after prolonged mental agony and in great pain, Blok (1880-1921) died; amid cruel privations and under circumstances of inhuman suffering, Khlebnikov (1885-1922) passed away; Esenin (1895-1925) and Mayakovsky (1894-1930) killed themselves. And so it happened that during the third decade of this century, those who inspired a generation perished between the ages of thirty and forty, and each one of them shared a sense of doom so vivid and sustained that it became unbearable.

And it was not just that they were killed or killed themselves; Blok and Khlebnikov, when they took to their beds with disease, had already perished. Zamyatin wrote in his reminiscences: "We are all to blame for this. . . . I remember that I could not stand it and I phoned Gorky: Blok is dead. We can't be forgiven for that." Shklovsky wrote in Khlebnikov's memory

> Forgive us for yourself and for others whom we will kill. The state is not responsible for the destruction of people. When Christ lived and spoke it did not understand his Aramaic, and it has never understood simple human speech. The Roman soldiers who pierced Christ's hands are no more to blame than the nails. Nevertheless, it is very painful for those whom they crucify.

Blok the poet fell silent and died long before the man, but his younger contemporaries snatched verses even from death. ("Whereever I die I'll die singing," wrote Mayakovsky.) Khlebnikov knew he was dying. His body decomposed while he lived. He asked for flowers in his room so that the stench would not be noticed, and he kept writing up to the end. A day before his suicide Esenin wrote a masterful poem about his impending death. Mayakovsky's farewell letter is full of poetry: we find the professional writer in every line of that document. He wrote it two nights before his death and in the interval there were to be conversations and conferences about the everyday business of literature; but in that letter we read: "Please don't gossip. The deceased hated gossip." We remember that Mayakovsky's long-standing demand upon himself was that the poet must "hurry time forward." And here he is, already looking at his suicide note through the eyes of someone reading it the day after tomorrow. The letter with its several literary motifs and with Mayakovsky's own death in it is so closely interrelated with his poetry that it can be understood only in the context of that poetry.

The poetry of Mayakovsky from his first verses to his last lines is one and indivisible. It represents the dialectical development of a single theme. It is an extraordinarily unified symbolic system. A symbol once thrown out only as a kind of hint will later be developed and presented in a totally new perspective. He himself underlines these links in his work by alluding to earlier works. In the poem *About That* (*Pro eto*) for instance, he recalls certain lines from the poem *Man* (*Chelovek*), written several years earlier, and in the latter poem he refers to lyrics of an even earlier period. An image at first offered humorously may later and in context lose its comic effect, or, conversely, a motif developed solemnly may be repeated in a parodistic vein. Nor does this mean that the beliefs of yesterday are necessarily held up to scorn; we have here, rather, two levels, the tragic and the comic, of a single symbolic system, as in the medieval theater. A single clear purpose directs the system of symbols. "We shall thunder out a new myth upon the world."

A mythology of Mayakovsky?

His first collection of poems was entitled *I*. Vladimir Mayakovsky is not only the hero of his first play, but his name is the title of that tragedy, as of his last collection of poems. His name is also the title of his last published volume of poetry. The author dedicates his verse "to his beloved self." When Mayakovsky was working on the poem *Man* he said, "I want to depict simply man, man in general, not an abstraction, à la Andreev,[3] but a genuine 'Ivan' who waves his arms, eats cabbage soup and can be directly felt." But Mayakovsky could directly feel only himself. This is said very well in Trotsky's article on him (an intelligent article, the poet said): "In order to raise man he elevates him to the level of Mayakovsky. The Greeks were anthropomorphists, naïvely likening the forces of nature to themselves; our poet is a Mayakomorphist, and he populates the squares, the streets, and the fields of the revolution only with himself." Even when the hero of Mayakovsky's poem appears as the 150-million-member collective, realized in one collective Ivan—a fantastic epic hero, the latter in turn assumes the familiar features of the poet's "ego." This "ego" asserts itself even more frankly in the rough drafts of that poem.

Empirical reality neither exhausts nor fully takes in the various shapes of the poet's "ego." Mayakovsky passes before us in one of his "innumerable souls. . . ." "The unbending spirit of eternal rebellion" has come to deck himself out in the poet's muscles, the irresponsible spirit without name or patronymic, "from future days, just a man." "And I feel that I am too small for myself. Someone obstinately bursts out of me." Weariness with fixed and narrow confines, the urge to transcend static boundaries—such is Mayakovsky's infinitely varied theme. No lair in the world can contain the poet and the unruly horde of his desires. "Driven into the earthly pen I drag a daily yoke." "The accursed world has me chained." The grief of Peter the Great is that of a "prisoner, held in chains in his own city." Hulks of districts crawl out from the "zones marked off by the governor." The poet's revolutionary call is directed at all of those "for whom life is cramped and unbearable," "who cry out because the nooses of noon are too tight."

The "ego" of the poet is a battering ram, thudding into a forbidden future; it is a mighty will "hurled over the last limit" toward the incarnation of the future, toward an absolute fullness of being: "one must rip joy from the days yet to come."

Opposed to this creative urge toward a transformed future is the stabilizing force of an immutable present, covered over, as this present is, by a stagnating slime, which stifles life in its tight, hard mold. The Russian name for this element is *byt*.[4] It is curious that this word and its derivatives should have such a prominent place in the Russian language (from which it spread even to the Komi),[5] while West European languages have no word that corresponds to it. Perhaps the reason is that in the European collective consciousness there is no concept of such a force as might oppose and break down the established norms of life. The revolt of the individual against the fixed forms of social convention presupposes the existence of such a force. The real antithesis of *byt* is, a slippage of social norms which is immediately sensed by those involved in social life. In Russia this sense of an unstable foundation has been present for a very long time, and not just as a historical generalization, but as a direct experience. We recall that in the early nineteenth century, during the time of Chaadaev,[6] there was the sense of a "dead and stagnant life," but at the same time a feeling of instability and uncertainty: "Everything is slipping away, everything is passing," wrote Chaadaev. "In our own homes we are as it were in temporary billets. In our family life we seem foreigners. In our cities we look like nomads." And as Mayakovsky put it:

> . . . laws/concepts/faiths
> The granite blocks of cities
> And even the very sun's reliable glow—
> Everything had become as it were fluid,
> Seemed to be sliding a little—
> A little bit thinned and watered down.

Only in the poem *About That* is the poet's desperate struggle with *byt* fully laid bare. There it is not personified as it is elsewhere in his work. On the contrary, the poet hammers his verbal attack directly into that moribund *byt* which he despises. And *byt* reacts by executing the rebel "with all rifles and batteries, from every Mauser and Browning." Elsewhere in Mayakovsky this phenomenon is, as we have said, personified, not however as a living person, but rather, in the poet's own phrase, as an animated tendency in things. In *Man* the poet's enemy is very broadly generalized as "Ruler of all, my rival, my invincible enemy." But it is also possible to localize this enemy and give him a particular shape. One may call him "Wilson," domicile him in Chicago and, in the language of fairy-tale hyperbole, outline his very portrait [as in 150,000,000]. But then the poet offers a "little footnote": "Those who draw the Wilsons, Lloyd Georges, and Clemenceaus sometimes show their mugs with moustaches, sometimes not; but that's beside the point since they're all one and the same thing." The enemy is a universal image. The forces of nature, people, metaphysical substances, are only its incidental aspects and disguises: "The same old bald fellow directs us unseen, the master of the earthly cancan. Sometimes in the shape of an idea, sometimes a kind of devil, or then again he glows as God, hidden behind a cloud." If we should try to translate the Mayakovskian mythology into the language of speculative philosophy, the exact equivalent for this enmity would be the antinomy "I" versus "not-I." A better designation for Mayakovsky's enemy could hardly be found.

Just as the creative "ego" of the poet is not coextensive with his actually existing self, so conversely the latter does not take in all of the former. In the faceless regiment of his acquaintances, all tangled in the "apartment-house spider web:"

> One of them/I recognized
> As like as a twin
> Myself/my very own self.

This terrible "double" of the poet is his conventional and commonplace "self," the purchaser and owner whom Khlebnikov once contrasted with the inventor and discoverer. That self has an emotional attachment to a safely selfish and stable life, to "*my* little place, and a household that's *mine*, with *my* little picture on the wall."

The poet is oppressed by the specter of an unchangeable world order, a universal appartment-house *byt:* "No sound. The universe is asleep."

> Revolutions shake up violently the bodies of kingdoms,
> The human herd changes its herdsmen.
> But *you*/uncrowned ruler of our hearts
> No rebellion ever touches.

Against this unbearable might of *byt* an uprising as yet unheard of and nameless must be contrived. The terms used in speaking of the class struggle are only conventional figures, only approximate symbols, only one of the levels: the *part for the whole*. Mayakovsky, who has witnessed "the sudden reversals of fortune in battles not yet fought," must give new meaning to the habitual terminology. In the rough draft of the poem 150,000,000 we find the following definitions:

> to be a bourgeois does not mean to own capital or squander gold. It means to be the heel of a corpse on the throat of the young. It means a mouth stopped up with fat. To be a proletarian doesn't mean to have a dirty face and work in a factory; it means to be in love with the future that's going to explode the filth of the cellars. . . . Believe me.

The basic fusion of Mayakovsky's poetry with the theme of the Revolution has often been pointed out. But another indissoluble combination of motifs in Mayakovsky's work has not so far been noticed: revolution and the destruction of the poet. This idea is suggested even as early as the *Tragedy* (1913), and afterwards the fact that the linkage of the two is not accidental becomes "clear to the point of hallucination." No mercy will be shown to the army of heroes, or to the doomed volunteers in the struggle. The poet himself is an expiatory offering in the name of that universal and real resurrection that is to come; that was the theme of the poem *War and the World* (*Voina i mir*, 1916). And in the poem *A Cloud in Pants* (*Oblako v Shtanakh*, 1915) the poet promises that when a certain year comes "in the thorny crown" of revolution, "for you I will tear out my soul and trample on it till it spread out, and I'll give it to you, a bloody banner." And in the poems written after the Revolution the same idea is there, but in the past tense. The poet, mobilized by the Revolution, has "stamped on the throat of his own song." (This line occurs in the last poem he published, an address to his "comrades-descendants" of the future, written in clear awareness of the coming end.) In the poem *About That* the poet is destroyed by *byt*. "The bloodletting is over. . . . Only high above the Kremlin the tatters of the poet shine in the wind—a little red flag." This image is plainly an echo of *A Cloud in Pants*.

The poet catches the music of the future in an insatiable ear, but he is not destined to enter the Promised Land. A vision of the future is present in all of the most essential pages in Mayakovsky's work. "And such a day dawned—Andersen's fairy tales crawled about like little pups at his feet"; "You can't tell whether it's air, or a flower, or a bird. It sings, and it's fragrant, and it's brightly colored all at once"; "Call us Cain or call us Abel, it doesn't matter. The future is here." For Mayakovsky the future is a dialectical synthesis. The removal of all contradictions finds its expression in the playful image of Christ playing at checkers with Cain, in the myth of the universe permeated by love, and in the proposition: "The commune is a place where bureaucrats will disappear and there will be many poems and songs." The present disharmony, the contradiction between poetry and building, "the delicate business of the poet's place in the working ranks," is one of Mayakovsky's most acute problems. "Why," he asked, "should literature occupy its own special little corner? Either it should appear in every newspaper, every day, on every page, or else it's totally useless. The kind of literature that's dished out as dessert can go to hell" (from the *Reminiscences of D. Lebedev*).

Mayakovsky always regarded ironically talk of the insignificance and early disappearance of poetry (really nonsense, he would say, but useful for the purpose of revolutionizing art). He planned to pose the question of the future of art in the *Fifth International* (*Pyaty International*, 1922), a poem which he worked on long and carefully but never finished. According to the plan of the piece, the first stage of the Revolution, a worldwide social transformation, has been completed, but humanity is bored. *Byt* still survives. So a new revolutionary act of world-shaking proportions is required: "a revolution of the spirit in the name of a new organization of life, a new art and a new science." The published introduction to the poem is an order to vacate the beauties of verse and introduce into poetry the brevity and accuracy of mathematical formulas. He offers an example of a poetic structure built on the model of a logical problem. When I reacted skeptically to this poetic program—the exortation in verse against verse—Mayakovsky smiled: "But didn't you notice that the solution of my logical problem is a trans-sense solution?"

The remarkable poem *Homeward!* (*Domoy!*, 1925) is devoted to the contradiction between the rational and the irrational. It is a dream about the fusion of the two elements, a kind of rationalization of the irrational:

> I feel/ like a Soviet factory
> Manufacturing happiness.
> I don't want/ to be plucked
> Like a flower/ after the day's work
>
> . . . .
>
> I want/ the heart to be paid
> Its wage of love/ at the specialist's rate
> I want/ the factory committee
> To put a lock on my lips
> When the work is done
> I want/ the pen to be equal to the bayonet
> And I want Stalin/ to report in the name of the Politburo

> About the production of verse
> As he does about pig iron and steel.
> "Thus, and so it is/ we've reached
> The topmost level/ up from the workers' hovels
> In the Union/ of Republics
> The appreciation of verse/ has exceeded the prewar level."

The idea of the acceptance of the irrational appears in Mayakovsky's work in various aspects, and each of the images he uses for this purpose tends to reappear in his poetry. The stars ("You know, if they light up the stars, that means, somebody needs them!"). The madness of spring ("Everything is clear concerning bread and concerning peace. But the prime question, the question of spring, must be elucidated.") And the heart, that changes winters to spring and water to wine ("It's that I'm going to raise my heart like a flag, a marvelous twentieth-century miracle.") And that hostile answer of the enemy in the poem *Man:* "If the heart is everything then why, why have I been gathering you, my dear money! How do they dare to sing? Who gave them the right? Who said the days could blossom into June? Lock the heavens in wires. Twist the earth into streets!"

But Mayakovsky's central irrational theme is the theme of love. It is a theme that cruelly punishes those who dare to forget it, whose storms toss us about violently and push everything else out of our ken. And like poetry itself this theme is inseparable from our present life; it is "closely mingled with "our jobs, our incomes, and all the rest." And love is crushed by *byt:*

> Omnipresent one
> You thought up a pair of hands
> Fixed it
> So that everyone has a head.
> Why couldn't you fix it
> So that without torment
> We could just kiss and kiss and kiss?

Eliminate the irrational? Mayakovsky draws a bitterly satirical picture: on the one hand, the heavy boredom of certain rational revelations: the usefulness of the cooperatives, the danger of liquor, political education, and on the other hand, an unashamed hooligan of planetary dimensions (in the poem *A Type* [*Tip,* 1926]). Here we have a satirical sharpening of the dialectical contradiction. Mayakovsky says "yes" to the rationalization of production, technology, and the planned economy if as a result of all this "the partially opened eye of the future sparkles with real earthly love." But he rejects it all if it means only a selfish clutching at the present. If that's the case then grandiose technology becomes only a "highly perfected apparatus of parochialism and gossip on a worldwide scale" (from *My Discovery of America*). Just such a planetary narrowness and parochialism permeates life in the year 1970, as shown in Mayakovsky's play about the future *The Bedbug* (*Klop,* 1928), where we see a rational organization without emotion, with no superfluous expenditure of energy, without dreams. A worldwide social revolution has been achieved, but the revolution of the spirit is still in the future. The play is a quiet protest against the spiritual inheritors of those languid judges who, in his early satirical poem "without knowing just why or wherefore, attacked Peru." Some of the characters in *The Bedbug* have a close affinity with the world of Zamyatin's *We* (*My,* 1920), although Mayakovsky bitterly ridicules not only the rational utopian community but the rebellion against it in the name of alcohol, the irrational and unregulated individual happiness. Zamyatin, however, idealizes that rebellion.

Mayakovsky has an unshakable faith that, beyond the mountain of suffering, beyond each rising plateau of revolutions, there does exist the "real heaven on earth," the only possible resolution of all contradictions. *Byt* is only a surrogate for the coming synthesis; it doesn't remove contradictions but only conceals them. The poet is unwilling to compromise with the dialectic; he rejects any mechanical softening of the contradictions. The objects of Mayakovsky's unsparing sarcasm are the "compromisers" (as in the play *Mystery-Bouffe*). Among the gallery of "bureaucrat-compromisers" portrayed in his agitational pieces, we have in *The Bathhouse* (*Banya,* 1930) the *glavnachpups* Pobedonosikov, whose very title is an acronym for "Chief Administrator for the Organizing of Compromises." Obstacles in the road to the future—such is the true nature of these "artificial people." The time machine will surely spew them out.

It seemed to him a criminal illusion to suppose that the essential and vital problem of building a worldwide "wonderful life" could be put aside for the sake of devising some kind of personal happiness. "It's early to rejoice," he wrote. The opening scenes of *The Bedbug* develop the idea that people are tired of a life full of struggle, tired of front-line equality, tired of military metaphors. "This is not nineteen-nineteen. People want to live." They build family nests for themselves: "Roses will bloom and be fragrant at the present juncture of time." "Such is the elegant fulfillment of our comrade's life of struggle." Oleg Bayan, the servant of beauty in *The Bedbug*, formulates this sentiment in the following words: "We have managed to compromise and control class and other contradictions, and in this you can't help seeing, if your eye is, so to speak, equipped with Marxism, as in a single drop of water, the future happiness of mankind, which the common people call socialism." (In an earlier, lyrical context the same idea took this form: "There he is in a soft bed, fruit beside him and wine on the night table.") Mayakovsky's sharply chiseled lines express unlimited contempt for all those who seek comfort and rest. All such people receive their answer from the mechanic in *The Bedbug:* "We'll never crawl out of our trenches with a white flag in our hands." And the poem *About That* develops the same theme in the form of an intimate personal experience. In that work Mayakovsky begs for the advent of love—his savior: "Confiscate my pain—take it away!" And Mayakovsky himself answers himself:

> Leave off!/ Don't/ not a word/ no requests,
> What's the point/ that you/ alone/ should succeed?
> I'll wait/ and together with the whole unloved earth
> With the whole/ human mass/ we'll win it.
> Seven years I stood/ and I'll stand two hundred
> Nailed here/ waiting for it.
> On the bridge of years/ derided/ scorned
> A redeemer of earthly love/ I must stand
> Stand for all/ for everyone I'll atone
> For everyone I'll weep.

But Mayakovsky knows very well that even if his youth should be four times renewed and he should four times again grow old, that would only mean a fourfold increase of his torment, a horror four times multiplied at the senseless daily grind and at premature celebrations of victory. In any case, he will never live to see the revelation all over the world of an absolute fullness of life, and the final count still stands: "I've not lived out my earthly lot; I've not lived through my earthly love." His destiny is to be an expiatory victim who never knew joy:

> A bullet for the rest
> For some a knife.
> But what about me?
> And when?

Mayakovsky has now given us the final answer to that question.

The Russian futurists believed in cutting themselves loose from the "classic generals," and yet they are vitally tied to the Russian literary tradition. It's interesting to note that Mayakovsky's famous line, so full of bravado (and it was also a tactical slogan): "But why don't we attack Pushkin?" was followed not long after by those mournful lines addressed to the same Pushkin: "You know I too will soon be dead and mute. And after my death we two will be quite close together." Mayakovsky's dreams of the future, which repeat the utopian visions of Dostoevsky's Versilov in A Raw Youth, the poet's frequent hymns to the "man-god," the "thirteenth" apostle's rejection of God—all of this is much closer to Russian literature of an earlier day than it is to official and regimented Soviet "godlessness." And Mayakovsky's belief in personal immortality has nothing to do with the official catechism of Yaroslavsky's "godless" movement. The poet's vision of the coming resurrection of the dead is vitally linked with the materialistic mysticism of the Russian philosopher Fyodorov.[7]

When in the spring of 1920 I returned to Moscow, which was tightly blockaded, I brought with me recent books and information about scientific developments in the West. Mayakovsky made me repeat several times my somewhat confused remarks on the general theory of relativity, and about the growing interest in that concept in Western Europe. The idea of the liberation of energy, the problem of the time dimension, and the idea that movement at the speed of light may actually be a reverse movement in time—all of these things fascinated Mayakovsky. I'd seldom seen him so interested and attentive. "Don't you think," he suddenly asked, "that we'll at last achieve immortality?" I was astonished, and I mumbled a skeptical comment. He thrust his jaw forward with that hypnotic insistence so familiar to anyone who knew Mayakovsky well: "I'm absolutely convinced," he said, "that one day there will be no more death. And the dead will be raised from the dead. I've got to find some scientist who'll give me a precise account of what's in Einstein's books. It's out of the question that I shouldn't understand it. I'll see to it that that scientist receives an academician's ration." At that point I became aware of a Mayakovsky that I'd never known before. The demand for victory over death had taken hold of him. He told me later that he was writing a poem called The Fourth International (he afterward changed it to The Fifth International) which would deal with such things. "Einstein will be a member of that International. The poem will be much more important than 150,000,000." Mayakovsky was at that time obsessed with the idea of sending Einstein a congratulatory telegram "from the art of the future to the science of the future." We never again returned to this matter in our conversations and he never finished The Fifth Interna-

tional. But in the epilogue to the poem *About That* we find the lines: "I see it, I see it clearly to the last sharp detail. . . . On the bright eminence of time, impervious to rot or destruction, the workshop of human resurrection."

The epilogue to the poem *About That* carries the following heading: "A request addressed to . . . (Please, comrade chemist, fill in the name yourself.") I haven't the slightest doubt that for Mayakovsky this was not just a literary device but a genuine and seriously offered request to some "quiet chemist with a domed forehead" living in the thirtieth century:

> Resurrect me!
> Even if only because I was a poet
> And waited for you,
> And put behind me prosaic nonsense.
> Resurrect me—
> Just for that!
> Do resurrect me—
> I want to live it all out.

The very same "Institute for Human Resurrections" reappears in the play *The Bedbug* but in a comic context. It is the insistent theme of Mayakovsky's last writings. Consider the situation in *The Bathhouse:* "A phosphorescent woman out of the future, empowered to select the best people for transfer into the future, appears in the time machine: "At the first signal we blast off, and smash through old decrepit time . . . Winged time will sweep away and cut loose the ballast, heavy with rubbish and ruined by lack of faith." Once again we see that the pledge of resurrection is faith. Moreover the people of the future must transform not only their own future, but also the past: "The fence of time our feet will trample. . . . As it has been written by us, so will the world be on Wednesday, in the past, and now and tomorrow and forever" (from *150,000,000*). The poem written in memory of Lenin offers the same idea, even though in a disguised form:

> Death will never dare
> To touch him.
> He stands
> In the total sum of what's to be!
> The young attend
> to these verses on his death
> But their hearts know
> That he's deathless.

In Mayakovsky's earliest things personal immortality is achieved in spite of science. "You students," he says, "all the stuff we know and study is rubbish. Physics, astronomy, and chemistry are all nonsense" (from the poem *Man*). At that time he regarded science as an idle occupation involving only the extraction of square roots or a kind of inhuman collection of fossilized fragments from the "epoch before last." His satirical *Hymn to the Scholar* turned into a genuine and fervent hymn only when he thought he'd found the miraculous instrument of human resurrection in Einstein's "futuristic brain" and in the physics and chemistry of the future. "Like logs thrown into a boom we are thrown at birth into the great river of human time; we toss about as we float downstream. But from now on that great river shall be submissive to us. I'll make time stand still, move in another direction and at a new rate of speed. People will be able to get out of the day like passengers getting out of a bus. . . ."

Whatever the means of achieving it, the vision of immortality in Mayakovsky's verse is unchangeable: there can be no resurrection of the spirit without the body, without the flesh itself. Immortality has nothing to do with any other world; it is indissolubly tied to this one. "I'm all for the heart," he wrote in *Man*, "but where can bodiless beings have a heart? . . . My eyes fixed earthward. . . . This herd of the bodiless, how they bore me!" "We want to live here on earth—no higher and no lower" (*Mystery-Bouffe*). "With the last measure of my heart I believe in this life, in this world, in all of it" (*About That*). Mayakovsky's dream is of an everlasting earth, and this earth is placed in sharp opposition to all superterrestrial, fleshless abstractions. In his poetry and in that of Khlebnikov the theme of earthly life is presented in a coarse physical incarnation (they even talk about the "meat" rather than the body). An extreme expression of this is the cult of tender feeling for the beast with his beastly wisdom.

"They will arise from the mounds of graves and their buried bones will grow flesh" (*War and the World*), wrote Mayakovsky. And those lines are not just a kind of literary verbalization. The vision of a future that resurrects people of the present is not just a poetic device that motivates the whimsical interweaving of two separate narrative levels. On the contrary—that vision is Mayakovsky's most cherished poetic myth.

This constant infatuation with a wonderful future is linked in Mayakovsky with a pronounced dislike of children, a fact which would seem at first sight to be hardly consonant with his fanatical belief in tomorrow. But just as we find in Dostoevsky an obtrusive and neurotic "father hatred" linked with great veneration for ancestors and reverence for tradition, so in Mayakovsky's spiritual world an abstract faith in the coming transformation of the world is joined quite properly with hatred for the evil continuum of specific tomorrows that only prolong today ("the calendar is nothing but the calendar!") and undying hostility to that "broody-hen" love that serves only to reproduce the present way of life. Mayakovsky was quite capable of giving full due to the creative mission of those "kids of the collective" in their unending quarrel with the old world, but at the same time he bristled whenever an actual "kid" ran into the room. Mayakovsky never recognized his own myth of the future in any concrete child; these he regarded simply as new offshoots of the hydra-headed enemy. That is why we find in the marvelous movie scenario *How Are You?* (*Kak pozhivaete?*) grotesques in the form of children which are the legitimate offspring of the Manilov pair Aristide and Themistocles in Gogol's *Dead Souls.* We recall that his youthful poem *A Few Words About Myself* (*Neskolko slov obo mne samom*, 1912) begins with the line "I love to watch children dying." And in the same poem child-murder is elevated to a cosmic theme: "Sun! My father! At least you have pity and torment me not! That's my blood you shed flowing along this low road." And surrounded by that same aura of sunshine the same "child complex" appears as an immemorial and at the same time personal motif in the poem *War and the World:*

> Listen—
> The sun just shed his first rays
> not yet knowing
> where he'll go when he's done his day's work;
> and that's me
> Mayakovsky,
> bringing as sacrifice to the idol's pedestal
> a beheaded infant.

There's no doubt that in Mayakovsky the theme of child-murder and self-murder are closely linked: these are simply two different ways of depriving the present of its immediate succession, of "tearing through decrepit time."

Mayakovsky's conception of the poet's role is clearly bound up with his belief in the possibility of conquering time and breaking its steady, slow step. He did not regard poetry as a mechanical superstructure added to the ready bases of existence (and it is no accident that he was so close to the formalist literary critics). A genuine poet is not one who feeds in the calm pastures of everyday life; his mug is not pointed at the ground. "The weak ones simply beat time and wait for something to happen that they can reflect; but the powerful rush far enough ahead so as to 'drag time along behind them!'" Mayakovsky's recurrent image of the poet is of one who overtakes and passes time, and we may say that this is the real image of Mayakovsky himself. Khlebnikov and Mayakovsky accurately forecast the Revolution (even including the date)—that is only a detail, but rather an important one. It would seem that the writer's fate has never until our day been laid bare with such pitiless candor in his own words. Impatient to know life, he recognizes it in his own story. The "godseeker" Blok and the Marxist Mayakovsky both understood clearly that verses are dictated to the poet by some primitive force the nature of which is not known. "We know not whence comes the basic beat of rhythm. . . ." We don't even know where this rhythm is located: "outside of me or within me? But most likely within me." The poet himself senses the necessity of his own verse, and his contemporaries feel that the poet's destiny is no accident. Is there anyone of us who doesn't share the impression that the poet's volumes are a kind of scenario in which he plays out the filmed story of his life? The poet is the principal character, and subordinate parts are also included; but the performers for these latter roles are recruited as the action develops, and to the extent that the plot requires them. And the plot has been laid out ahead of time right down to the details of the denouement.

The motif of suicide, so alien to the thematics of the futurist and "Left Front" groups, continually recurs in the work of Mayakovsky, from his earliest writings where madmen hang themselves in an unequal struggle with *byt* (the director, the "man with two kisses" in the *Tragedy* [*Tragedia*]), to the scenario *How Are You?* (*Kak pozhivaete?* 1928) in which a newspaper article about a girl's suicide induces horror in the poet. And when he tells about a young Communist who committed suicide he adds, "How like me that is. Horrors!" He tries on, so to speak, all possible varieties of suicide: "Rejoice now! He'll execute himself . . . The locomotive's wheel will embrace my neck . . . I'll run to the canal and there stick my head in the water's grinning mug . . . The heart bursts for a bullet, the throat raves for a razor . . . Beckons to the water, leads to the roof's slope . . . Druggist, give me the means to send my soul without any pain into the spacious beyond."

A simple résumé of Mayakovsky's poetic autobiography would be the following: the poet nurtured in his heart the unparalleled anguish of the present generation. That is why his verse is charged with hatred for the strongholds of the established order, and in his own work he finds "the alphabet of coming ages." Mayakovsky's earliest and most characteristic image is the one in which he "goes out through the city leaving his soul on the spears of houses, shred by shred." The hopelessness of his lonely struggle with the way things are became clearer to him at every turn. The brand of martyrdom is burned into him. There's no way to win an early victory. The poet is the doomed "outcast of the present."

> Mama!
> Tell my sisters, Lyuda and Olya,
> That there's no way out.

Gradually the idea that there's no way out (which appeared first in the lines from *A Cloud in Pants*) lost its purely literary character. From that poetic passage it found its way into prose, and "There's no way out" turns up as an author's remark on the margin of the manuscript of the poem *About That*. And from that prose context the same idea made its way into the poet's life: in his suicide note he said: "Mama, sisters, comrades, forgive me. This is not a good method (I don't recommend it to others), but for me there's no other way out."

The act was long in preparation. Fifteen years earlier in a prologue to a collection of poems, he wrote:

> Often I think
> Hadn't I better just
> Let a bullet mark the period of my sentence.
> Anyway, today
> I'm giving my farewell concert.

As time went on the theme of suicide became more and more pressing. Mayakovsky's most intense poems, *Man* (1916) and *About That* (1923), are dedicated to it. Each of these works is an ominous song of the victory of *byt* over the poet; their leitmotif is "Love's boat has smashed against the daily grind" (a line from his suicide note). The first is a detailed depiction of Mayakovsky's suicide. In the second there is already a clear sense that the suicide theme transcends literature and is already in the realm of "literature of fact." Once again—but even more disturbingly—the images of the first poem file past, the keenly observed stages of existence: the "half-death" in the vortex of the horrifyingly trivial, then the "final death"—"The lead in my heart! Not even a shudder!" This theme of suicide had become so real that it was out of the question to sketch the scene any more. It had to be exorcized. Propaganda pieces were necessary in order to slow down the inexorable movement of that theme. *About That* already initiates this long cycle of exorcism. "I won't give them the satisfaction of seeing me dead of a bullet." "I want to live on and on, moving through the years." The lines to Sergey Esenin are the apex of this cycle. To neutralize the impact of Esenin's death poem—such, in the words of Mayakovsky, was the salubrious aim of the lines addressed to him. But when you read them now, they sound even more sepulchral than Esenin's last lines. Esenin's lines equate life and death, but Mayakovsky in his poem can only say about life that it's harder than death. This is the same sort of enigmatic propaganda for life that occurs in Mayakovsky's earlier lines to the effect that only disquiet about the afterlife is a restraint upon the bullet. Such too are the farewell words in his suicide letter: "Be happy here."

In spite of all this the necrologists vie with each other in such comments as "One could expect anything of Mayakovsky, but not that he would kill himself" (Adamovich). And Lunacharsky: "The idea of suicide is simply incompatible with our image of the poet." And Malkin: "His death cannot be reconciled with his whole life which was that of a poet completely dedicated to the Revolution." And the newspaper *Pravda:* "His death is just as inconsistent with the life he led, as it is unmotivated by his poetry." And A. Khalatov: "Such a death was hardly proper for the Mayakovsky whom we knew." Or Koltsov: "It is not right for him. Can it be that none of us knew Mayakovsky?" And finally, the poet Demyan Bedny: "Incredible! What could he have lacked?"

Could these men of letters have so forgotten, or so misunderstood *All That Mayakovsky Composed?*[8] Or was there a general conviction that all of it was only "composed," only invented? Sound literary criticism rejects any direct or immediate conclusions about the biography of a poet when these are based only on the evidence of his works, but it does not at all follow from this that there is no connection whatsoever between the artist's biography and his art. Such an "antibiographical" position would be the equivalent, in reverse, of the simplistic biographical approach. Have we forgotten Mayakovsky's admiration for the "genuine heroism and martyrdom" of Khlebnikov, his teacher? "His life," wrote Mayakovsky, "matched his brilliant verbal constructs. That life is an example for poets and a reproach to poetizers." And it was Mayakovsky who wrote that even a poet's style of dress, even his intimate conversations with his wife should be determined by the whole of his poetic production. He understood very well the close interconnection of poetry and life.

After Esenin's suicide poem, said Mayakovsky, his death became a literary fact. "It was clear at once that those powerful verses, just those verses, would bring to the bullet or the noose many who had been hesitating." And when he approached the writing of his own autobiography, Mayakovsky remarked that the facts of a poet's life are interesting "only if they are borne out by his works." Who would dare assert that Mayakovsky's suicide is not borne out thus? "Don't gossip about my deed!" Mayakovsky adjured us just before his death. Yet those who stubbornly mark out a strict boundary between the "purely personal" fate of the poet and his literary biography create an atmosphere of low-grade, highly personal gossip—with those significant silences.

It is a historical fact that the people around Mayakovsky simply did not believe in his lyrical monologues. "They listened, all smiling, to the eminent clown." They took his various masquerade costumes for the true face of the man: first the pose of the fop ("It's good when the soul is shielded from inspection by a yellow blouse"); then the performance of an overeager journalist and agitator: "It's good, when you're in the teeth of the gallows, to cry out: 'Drink Van Houten's cocoa,' " Mayakovsky wrote in *A Cloud in Pants*. But then when he carried out that slogan in practice in his advertising jingles ("If you want good luck and good fortune buy a government lottery ticket") his readers and hearers saw the rhymed advertisement but missed the teeth of the gallows. As it turns out, it was easier to believe in the benefits of a lottery loan or the excellent quality of the pacifiers sold in the state stores than it was to believe that the poet had reached an extreme of despair, that he was in a state of misery and near death. The poem *About That* is a long and hopeless cry to the ages, but Moscow doesn't believe in tears. They stamped and whistled at this routine Mayakovskian artistic stunt, the latest of his "magnificent absurdities," but when the theatrical raspberry juice of the puppet show became real, genuine, thick blood, they were taken aback: Incredible! Inconsistent!

Mayakovsky himself often helped to spread illusions about himself. The record of a conversation we had in 1927 follows. I said, "The total sum of possible experience has been measured out to us. We might have predicted the early decline of our generation. But the symptoms of this are rapidly increasing in number. Take Aseev's line 'What about us, what about us, can it be we've lost our youth?' And consider Shklovsky's memento to himself!" And Mayakovsky answered, "Utter nonsense. The way I see it everything is ahead of us. If I ever thought that the best of me was in the past that would be the end for me." I reminded him of a recent poem in which the following lines occurred:

> I was born/ increased in size
> fed from the bottle—
> I lived/ worked/ grew oldish
> And life will pass
> As the Azores Islands
> Once passed into the distance.

"That's nothing," he said, "just a formal ending. An image only. My poem *Homeward* in the first version, ended with the lines:

> I want my country to understand me
> But if not—so what:
> I'll just pass my country by
> Like a slanting rain in summer.

But you know Brik told me to strike those lines out because they didn't go with the tone of the whole poem. So I struck them out."

The simplistic formalist literary credo professed by the Russian futurists inevitably drew their poetry toward the opposite of formalism: toward the cultivation of the heart's "unmasticated cry" and uninhibited frankness. Formalist literary theory placed the lyrical monologue in quotes and disguised the "ego" of the lyric poet under a pseudonym. But what unbounded horror results when suddenly you see through the pseudonym, and the phantoms of art invade life itself, just as in Mayakovsky's scenario *Bound in Film* a girl is captured from a film by a mad artist.

By the end of his life the satire and the laudatory ode had completely overshadowed his elegiac verse, which, by the way, he identified with the lyric in general. In the West the existence of this basic core in Mayakovsky's poetry was not even suspected. The West knew only the "drummer of the October Revolution." There are many explanations for this fact. In 1923 Mayakovsky had reached the end of the road as far as the elegiac mode was concerned. In an artistic sense the poem *About That* was a "repetition of the past," supersaturated and raised to perfection. His journalistic verse was a search for something new; it was an experiment in the production of new materials and in untested genres. To my skeptical comments about these poems Mayakovsky replied: "Later on you'll understand even them." And when *The Bedbug* and *The Bathhouse* appeared it became clear that his most recent poems had been a huge laboratory experiment in language and theme, a labor masterfully exploited in his first efforts in the area of prose drama, and offering a rich potential for future growth.

Finally, in connection with its social setting, the journalistic verse of Mayakovsky represented a shift from an unrestrained frontal attack in the direction of an enervating trench warfare. *Byt*, with its swarm of heartbreaking trivia, is still with him. And it is no longer "rubbish with its own proper face," but "petty, small, vulgar rubbish." You can't resist the pressure of such rubbish by grandiloquent pronouncements "in general and in toto," or by theses on communism, or by pure poetic devices. "Now you have to see the enemy and draw a bead upon him." You have to smash the "swarm of trivia" offered by *byt* "in a small way," and not grieve that the battle has been reduced to many minor engagements. The invention of strategies for describing "trifles which may also prove a sure step into the future"—this is how Mayakovsky understood the immediate task of the poet.

Just as one must not reduce Mayakovsky the propagandist to a single dimension, so, too, one-sided interpretations of the poet's death are shallow and opaque.

The newspaper *Pravda* on the morning after Mayakovsky's suicide announced that "the preliminary investigation indicates that his act was prompted by motives of a purely personal character." But the poet had already provided an answer to that in the subtitle of the poem *About That:* "From personal motives, but about the general way of life."

The late Bela Kun[9] advised us not to "subordinate the great cause to our own petty personal feelings." Mayakovsky had entered his objection in good time:

> With this petty/ and personal theme
> That's been sung so many times
> I've trod the poetical treadmill
> And I'm going to tread it again.
> This theme/ right now
> Is a prayer to Buddha
> And it sharpens a black man's knife for his master.
> If there's life on Mars/ and on it just one
> Human-hearted creature
> Then he too is writing now
> About that same thing.

The journalist Koltsov hastened to explain: "Mayakovsky himself was wholly absorbed in the business affairs of various literary groups and in political matters. Someone else fired that shot, some outsider who happened to be in control of a revolutionary poet's mind and will. It was the result of the temporary pressure of circumstances." And once again we recall the rebuke Mayakovsky delivered long before the fact:

> Dreams are a harm
> And it's useless to fantasize.
> You've got to bear the burden of service.
> But sometimes—
> Life appears to you in a new light
> And through the mess of trifles
> You catch sight of something great and good.

"We condemn this senseless, unforgivable act. It was a stupid and cowardly death. We cannot but protest most vigorously against his departure from life, against his barbarous end." (Such was the pronouncement of the Moscow Soviet and others.) But Mayakovsky had already parodied these very funeral speeches in *The Bedbug:* "Zoya Berezkin's shot herself"—"Aha! She'll catch it for that at her cell meeting." Says a doctor in the future world commune: "What is suicide? . . . You shot at yourself? . . . Was it an accident?" "No, it was from love." "Nonsense . . . Love makes you want to build bridges and have children. . . . But you . . . Yes, yes, yes!"

In general life has been imitating Mayakovsky's satirical lines with horrifying regularity. Pobedonosikov, the comic figure in *The Bathhouse,* who has many features that remind us of Lunacharsky, brags that "I have not time for boat rides. . . . Such petty entertainments are for various secretaries: 'Float on, gondola mine!' I have no gondola but a ship of state." And now Lunacharsky himself faithfully echoes his comic double. At a meeting called in memory of the poet the minister hastens to explain that the former's farewell lines about a "loveboat smashed on daily grind" have a pathetic sound: "We know very well that it was not on any love boat that he sailed our stormy seas. He was the captain of a mighty ship of state." These efforts to forget the "purely personal" tragedy of Mayakovsky sometimes take the form of conscious parody. A group of writers in a provincial town published a resolution in which they assure Soviet society that they will take very seriously the advice of the late poet not to follow his example.

It's very strange that on this occasion such terms as "accidental, personal" and so forth are used precisely by those who have always preached a strict social determinism. But how can one speak of a private episode in view of the fact that in a few years' time the whole bloom of Russian poetry has been swept away?

In one of Mayakovsky's longer poems each of the world's countries brings its best gift to the man of the future; Russia brings him poetry. "The power of their voices is most resoundingly woven into song." Western Europe is enraptured with Russian art: the medieval icon and the modern film, the classical ballet and the latest theatrical experiment, yesterday's novel and the latest music. And yet that art which is probably Russia's greatest achievement, her poetry, has never really been an export item. It is intimately Russian and closely linked to the Russian language and would probably not survive the rigors of translation. Russian poetry has witnessed two periods of high flowering: the beginning of the nineteenth century and the present century. And the earlier period as well as the later had as its epilogue the untimely destruction of very many great poets. If you can imagine how slight the contributions of Schiller, Hoffmann, Heine, and especially Goethe would have been if they had all disappeared in their thirties, then you will understand the following Russian statistics: Ryleev was executed when he was thirty-one. Batiushkov went mad when he was thirty. Venevitinov died at the age of twenty-two, Delvig at thirty-two. Griboyedov was killed when he was thirty-four, Pushkin when he was thirty-seven, Lermontov when he was twenty-six.[10] Their fate has more than once been characterized as a form of suicide. Mayakovsky himself compared his duel with *byt* to the fatal duels of Pushkin and Lermontov. There is much in common in the reactions of society in both periods to these untimely losses. Once again, a feeling of sudden and profound emptiness overwhelms one, an oppressive sense of an evil destiny lying heavily on Russian intellectual life. But now as then other notes are louder and more insistent.

The Western mind can hardly comprehend the stupid, unrestrained abuse of the dead poets. A certain Kikin expressed great disappointment that Martynov, the killer of that "cowardly scoundrel Lermontov," had been arrested. And Czar Nicholas I's final words on the same poet were: "He was a dog and he died a dog's death." And in the same spirit the contemporary newspaper *The Wheel* carried no obituary on the occasion of Mayakovsky's death, but instead a cluster of abusive remarks leading up to the following conclusion: "Mayakovsky's whole life gave off a bad smell. Is it possible that his tragic end could set all that right?"

．　．　．

Certain questions are particularly attractive to journalists. Who was responsible for the war? Who was to blame for the poet's death? Biographers are amateur private detectives and they will certainly be at great pains to establish the immediate reason for the suicide. They will add other names to that variegated assemblage of poet-killers, the "sonofabitch D'Anthès" who killed Pushkin, the "dashing Major Martynov" who killed Lermontov, and so forth. People who seek the explanation of various phenomena will, if they bear Russia a grudge, readily demonstrate, citing chapter, verse, and historical precedent, that it is dangerous to practice the trade of poet in Russia. And if their grudge is only against contemporary Russia it will also be quite easy to defend such a thesis with weighty arguments. But I'm of another mind. It seems to me that the one nearest the truth was the young Slovak poet who said: "Do you imagine that such things happen only there, in Russia? Why that's what our world is like nowadays." This is in answer to those phrases, which have, alas, become truisms, concerning the deadly absence of fresh air, certainly a fatal condition for poets. There are some countries where men kiss women's hands, and others where they only say, "I kiss your hand." There are countries where Marxist theory is answered by Leninist practice, and where the madness of the brave, the martyr's stake, and the poet's Golgotha are not just figurative expressions. . . .

In the last analysis what distinguishes Russia is not so much the fact that her great poets have ceased to be, but rather that not long ago she had so many of them. Since the time of the first symbolists Western Europe has had no great poetry.

The real question concerns not causes but consequences, however tempting it may be to protect oneself from a painful realization of what's happened by discussing the reasons for it.

> It's a small thing to build a locomotive:
> Wind up its wheels and off it goes.
> But if a song doesn't fill the railway station—
> Then why do we have alternating current?

Those lines are from Mayakovsky's *Order to the Army of Art* (*Prikaz po armii iskusstv*). We are living in what is called the "reconstruction period" and no doubt we will construct a great many locomotives and scientific hypotheses. But to our generation has been allotted the morose feat of building without song. And even if new songs should ring out they will belong to another generation and a different curve of time. Yet it's unlikely that there will be new songs. Russian poetry of our century is copying and it would seem outdoing the nineteenth century: "the fateful forties are approaching," the years, in other words, of lethargic inertia among poets.

The relationships between the biographies of a generation and the march of history are curious. Each age has its own inventory of requi sitions upon private holdings. Suddenly history finds a use for Beethoven's deafness and Cézanne's astigmatism. The age at which a generation's call to service in history's conscription comes, as well as the length of its service, are different for different periods. History mobilizes the youthful ardor of some generations and the tempered maturity or old wisdom of others. When their role is played out yesterday's rulers of men's minds and hearts depart from the proscenium to the backstage of history to live out their years in private, either on the profits from their intellectual investments, or else as paupers. But sometimes it happens otherwise. Our generation emerged at an extraordinarily young age: "We alone," as Mayakovsky put it, "are the face of our time. The trumpet of time blows for us." But up to the present moment there are not any replacements, nor even any partial reinforcements. Meanwhile the voice and the emotion of that generation have been cut short, and its allotted quota of feelings—joy and sadness, sarcasm and rapture—have been used up. And yet, the paroxysm of an irreplaceable generation turned out to be no private fate, but in fact the face of our time, the very breath of history.

We strained toward the future too impetuously and avidly to leave any past behind us. The connection of one period with another was broken. We lived too much for the future, thought about it, believed in it; the news of the day—sufficient unto itself—no longer existed for us. We lost a sense of the present. We were the witnesses of and participants in great social, scientific, and other cataclysms. *Byt* fell behind us, just as in the young Mayakovsky's splendid hyperbole: "One foot has already reached the next street." We knew that the plans of our fathers were already out of harmony with the facts of their lives. We read harsh lines alleging that our fathers had taken the old and musty way of life on a temporary lease. But our fathers still had left some remnant of faith in the idea that that way of life was both comfortable and obligatory upon all. Their children had only a singleminded, naked hatred for the ever more threadbare, ever more alien rubbish offered by the established order of things. And now the "efforts to organize a personal life are like attempts at reviving the dead."

As for the future, it doesn't belong to us either. In a few decades we shall be cruelly labeled as products of the nineteenth century. All we had were compelling songs of the future; and suddenly these songs are no longer part of the dynamic of history, but have been transformed into historico-literary facts. When singers have been killed and their song has been dragged into a museum and pinned to the wall of the past, the generation they represent is even more desolate, orphaned, and lost—impoverished in the most real sense of the word.

TRANSLATED BY E. J. BROWN

KORNEY CHUKOVSKY

Akhmatova and Mayakovsky

1

When I read Akhmatova's *White Flock* (*Beloe stado*)—her second book of poems—it seemed to me that she had perhaps already taken monastic vows. In her first book—*Rosary* (*Chotki*)—only the title had been monastic, but the second is permeated from start to finish with the aesthetic of the cloister.

In appearance Akhmatova is marked by a kind of rigid austerity; as she herself puts it, her lips now are "haughty," her eyes "oracular," her hands "waxen," "dry." I can almost see the black cowl over her prophetic visage.

> For a long time now my lips
> Do not kiss, but prophesy,

she says to her former sweetheart, as she reminds him of sin and of God. God is now constantly on her lips. It has been a long time since Russia has had a poet who uttered the name of the Lord so often.

When it rains, Akhmatova says:

> —The Lord is merciless with harvesters and gardeners.

When it is hot, she says:

> —The sun has become a sign of God's disfavor.

Seeing the sunlight, she says:

> —First ray, God's blessing.

Seeing the stars, she says:

> —Needle-pointed diamonds offered up to God.

From *Dom iskusstv*, No. 1 (Petrograd, 1920).

33

In her poetry all nature becomes a temple. Even a lake seems to her to resemble a church:

> And the deep lake shone blue,
> The baptist's temple not built by human hands.

Even to descriptions of winter she brings pure church imagery. Winter is, according to her expression, "whiter than the arches of Smolny cathedral." In any other poet these metaphors would seem pretentious affectation, but in the case of Akhmatova they are so in harmony with her entire monastic make-up as to emerge alive and authentic.

Depicting a Petersburg autumn, she says:

> . . . The air was not at all our own,
> Was like a gift of God, so splendid,

and it would seem that there is no object to which she would not attach the epithet "divine." The sun to her is divine, and the earth, and generosity, an army, birds, a garden, a lilac—"divine."

Church personages, functions, and objects appear more and more often in her poems: cross, ikon, holy picture, the liturgy, Bible, priest's stole, procession, altar, solea, Magdalene, Christ's shroud, apostle, Saint Eudoxia, King David, seraphim, archangels, angels, confession, Holy Week, Palm Sunday, Whit Monday—all these recur constantly.

It is not that she has become a clerical poet, singing exclusively of the church, on the contrary, she hardly has a word for churches. She deals with other subjects, but in dealing with them, makes use of crosses, shrouds, Bibles, and so on, whenever possible. Describing her pre-Spring, pre-Easter gladness, for example, she says:

> And in the Bible a red maple leaf,
> Marking the Song of Songs.

Describing her grief, she says:

> I have in me the sorrow which Kind David
> Kinglike bestowed upon the millennia.

But if church names and subjects are almost never the main themes in her poetry—they are mentioned rather only in passing—yet they have so impregnated her spiritual life that she will lyrically express the most varied of feelings through them. They figure in nature descriptions, and in love poems as well. There are, it must be said, few love poems in this book, but they have not disappeared altogether. In

them too we find the same monastic coloring: "How many genuflec-
tions in church were dedicated to the one who loved me?" she says in
one poem, and when in another her beloved scolds her, she piously
asks him to "Forgive me now. God taught us to forgive." Even her
words of love are religious:

> Because I have forgiven everyone
> everything, you will be my Angel. . . . I'll pray to God to
> forgive you, and all whom you love.

One senses in these words, intonations, and gestures a nun who
makes the sign of the cross as she kisses. And soon there are no longer
even kisses. Many of her latest poems speak of the death of this world
in her and how, buried alive, she awaits the Last Judgment. These
poems hint that she has become more incorporeal than the dead, that
silence has overcome her, that

> Like a burden, henceforth superfluous,
> The shadows of songs and passions have disappeared

from her memory. So that if in her latest book there had been neither
angels, nor shrouds, nor crosses, if there were no word in it about
God, we would still have guessed that these poems had issued from
a monastic cell that had renounced earthly vanity.

White Flock is characterized precisely by this removal from the
world: "Once again I live peacefully and austerely on the wild shores."
There is in this book a kind of afterlife wisdom and the calm of a soul
which has overcome suffering and earthly cares.

Leaving behind her former "levity"—a lightness of thought and feeling (which she now curses)—Akhmatova has become wholly transparent, transformed into an ikon, and she is often like one of Nesterov's[1] paintings, only more profound and prophetic. She seems
exhausted, with great round eyes, with the stigmata on her hands
and feet:

> Already accustomed to the high, pure bell,
> Already judged by nonterrestrial laws.

Her Orthodoxy is not of the rich Byzantine variety, but rather it is
of the Nesterov school and Northern: sad, spare, kin to the swamps
and scraggly, coniferous growth. She is our only remaining Orthodox
poet. There is something Old Russian, ancient about her. One can
easily picture a 16th- or 17th-century Novgorod woman whose entire
life is illuminated by an Orthodox aesthetic and who mingles kisses
with hymns. Never mind the references to Paris, to automobiles, and

literary cafés—this simply serves to accentuate Akhmatova's deeply Old Russian soul. Nowadays such subjects she treats as visions from a distant past; in the way that those who have renounced the world refer to their life in it:

> Yes, I loved them, those nighttime gatherings,
> Frosted glasses on a small table.

She loved them, but no longer; soon they will be forgotten altogether. Now her greatest pleasure lies in prayer. Strange, that no one has yet remarked on how often her verses turn into prayers. "Bless, O Lord, the rejoicing host of harvesters!" she beseeches in one poem; in another she pleads for God to destroy her inglorious fame. A third poem begs Him to return her squandered gift of song, and a fourth asks "that the storm cloud over darkened Russia become white in glorious rays of sunlight." In a fifth poem she prays, "Receive, O Lord, Thy slave."

All of this is still scarcely noticeable, it is done by stealth, and this lack of the demonstrative, the obtrusively loud is typical of Akhmatova's methods. In her work hints, words, barely audible, and barely noticed details dominate. And yet I would not be surprised if her next collection turns out to be a prayer book.

I must hasten to point out that anything one might say about her monasticism is no more than speculation. Personally, I prefer to construct the personality of a poet from almost imperceptible traits of style, from his instinctive (and often unconscious) predilections, from his often unsuspected inclination toward one or another particular epithet, image, or theme. For it seems to me that only in these unconscious traits is the underlying, individual personality of the poet revealed. Isn't it significant, for example, that Akhmatova should favor the epithets "meager," "wretched," "indigent"? Is it only by chance that she likes to think of herself as a beggar-woman with an empty knapsack?:

> Ah! empty knapsacks for the road,
> And tomorrow, foul weather and cold.

She says to her sweetheart: "Why do you knock on the door of a beggarly sinner?" She calls her soul not only beggarly but meager:

> —Pray a bit for the poor, for the lost, for my living soul.
> —How can I give you my beggarly soul as a rich gift?

Without this penchant for poverty and wretchedness, would she still be our age's most Christian lyricist? "Miserable bridge, a little bit warped," "bare land of Tver"—in general, all poverty and weakness is dear to her monastic muse. And, aptly, she wraps this muse in a beggarly shawl full of holes:

> And the muse in a torn shawl
> Sings long and doleful notes.

Her poems are saturated with material objects, but even here there is a tendency toward the wretched: armchairs are "worn," a rug is "frayed," a wall is dilapidated, a shawl full of holes, a knapsack empty, a flag faded, shoes worn out at heel, a statue smashed and overturned. All things turn out to be depreciated, damaged, but that is just what she cherishes.

II

To repeat: if there had been no mention of God in her books, we could still easily surmise that she is a deeply religious poet. This religiosity is expressed not only in words but in all things.

When in one of her earliest poems she wrote: "Glory be to Thee, inconsolable pain," we knew that this celebration of pain was not just an accidental trait. She would not be the most Christian of lyricists if she did not glorify pain. The eternal Russian attraction to self-effacement, humility, martyrdom, meekness, poverty, which had such allure for Tyutchev,[2] [Leo] Tolstoy, and Dostoevsky, fascinates her also. In this she is at one with the great spokesmen for the Russian soul. When in one poem she is told that she will fall ill, become homeless and unhappy, she gladdens and begins to sing a joyful song:

> From his cell the bishop surely heard me
> Singing on the road back,
> Singing of my indescribable gladness,
> Rejoicing, greatly astonished—

rejoicing in her future sorrow. For her, human happiness and fame are unattractive; she knows that "from happiness and fame hearts grow hopelessly old." She blesses her grief, for she sees in it the hand of God, pointing toward the angelic world beyond:

> Why did God punish me, each hour and every day?
> Or was it an angel instead, pointing to a heavenly
> world we ourselves cannot see?

Her Christian, evangelical, ascetic, spiritual make-up was foreshadowed in these earlier works. In her first book it was already evident that she was a poet of orphanhood and widowhood, evident that her lyrics fed on the feeling of lack of possessions, of separation and loss. And it is just from these orphanlike losses that Akhmatova created her finest songs: a voiceless nightingale, deprived of song; a dancer whose beloved has abandoned her; a woman losing her son; a woman who has lost her grey-eyed king, or whose tsarevich has died:

> He will never come for me . . .
> My tsarevich died today . . .

a woman who hears, "You'll have no more news of him"; a woman who cannot find her dear white house, although she looks everywhere for it and knows it's somewhere nearby. The poetess has come to love these orphaned souls who have lost that which is most dear to them, has come to love lyrically, sharing and enduring their losses:

> One less hope remaining—
> One more song to sing.

Such songs are even titled in kind: "Song of an Evening of Farewell," "Song of a Final Meeting," "Song of the Sorrow of Parting."

To be orphaned and weak, sonless, having no lover nor any white house, without a muse ("my Muse walked off along the road"), this is Akhmatova's whimsical artistic choice. And of all the torments of deprivation, she set her heart especially on one: the torment of hopeless love. "I love, but am not loved; I am loved, but love not"—this is highly descriptive of her work of the period. In this area there is no one who can be compared with her. She had a great talent for feeling unloved, no longer loved, unwanted, outcast. The very first lines of her *Rosary* told of this humiliating grief, and in so doing gave to our poetry a new theme.

She was the first to show through poetry what it means to be unloved and, having grown fond of this subject, created a whole line of sufferers, unrequited lovers, and the deathly melancholics, who either "wander like lost souls," or fall ill out of sadness, or else hang or drown themselves. Sometimes they curse their beloved ones as enemies and tormentors:

> . . . You are insolent and vicious . . .
> . . . Oh, how handsome you are, damn you . . .
> You're the cause of my illness . . .

But at the same time they love their pain, revel in it, cling to it as to something sacred, devoutly bless it.

III

In addition to being endowed with musical lyricism, Akhmatova has
the rare gift of the storyteller. Her verses are not merely songs, but
tales. Take a novella of Maupaussant, compress it into its most dis-
tilled form, and you have a poem by Akhmatova. Her lines on a tight-
rope-walker jilted by her lover, on a woman who threw herself into
a freezing pond, on a student who hanged himself out of hopeless
love, on a fisherman loved by a woman who was a fish-peddler—all
these are Maupaussant novellas, a thousand times compressed and
miraculously transformed into song. I've already remarked that Akhmatova's art is full of things, filled to the brim with objects. Her objects are not allegories or symbols; they are most commonplace: a
skirt, a muff, oysters, an umbrella. But she renders these small, banal
things unforgettable in powerfully bending them to fit her lyric. What,
for example, is a glove? And yet all Russia knows of the glove about
which a woman in Akhmatova's poem speaks as she leaves the man
who has rejected her:

> So helplessly my bosom grew cold,
> But my steps were light.
> I pulled onto my right hand
> My left hand glove.

Among Akhmatova's objects one finds, significantly, numerous
buildings and statues. She has an affinity for architecture and sculp-
ture. She herself in her poems can be found constructing more often
than singing. Many of her poems are buildings.

It is this abundance of concrete objects that distinguishes the poetry
of Akhmatova from the allegorical lyrics of such abstract poets as the
symbolists Jurgis Baltrushaitis, [K.D.] Balmont, and [Z.N.] Gippius.
One can traverse ten pages of their poems without once meeting a
skirt or an umbrella. (It should be said that the verses of Gippius, in
comparison with those of Akhmatova, often seem like algebraic formu-
lae, an enumeration of abstract categories.)

Akhmatova possesses something even surpassing her talent: an
implacable, ascetic spareness. She writes carefully and sparingly,
meticulously weighing each word, striving for that deceptive simplicity achieved only by great masters. Other poets seem by comparison mere pompous rhetoricians. I know of no one with a greater gift
for composition. The most difficult tasks involved in coupling narra-

tive with lyric are accomplished in her poems. Her rhythms are multiform and complex. An entire article could be written on her pyrrhics
and anacruses. . . . Her rhythmic breath was at first very short, lasting only for two lines at most. Now she has as much breath as she
needs. Her first verses were somewhat like mosaics, put together out
of separate pieces. Now she has overcome this. Today her name is
one of the most precious in our literature. Without Anna Akhmatova
we would be much the poorer. Only a great poet could create her
Right by the Sea (*U samogo morya*). The invisible presence of Pushkin is felt on every page. Each line is magnificently labored over, de-
finitively complete. Nothing is diffuse, slack; each word counts: "on a
rough spruce stump, an ant's highway." This striving for absolutely
finished, classical form can be seen throughout. If she had been a
British writer, her name would have been glorified on four continents,
her verses translated into every language of the world.

One must not forget, however, that she is a nun, that her world is
small and narrow—delightful, poetic, but small—so that practically the
biggest event in *Rosary* comes when

> He again touched my knees
> With an almost trembling hand.

For a shy and reserved woman a light touch of the hand has unforgettable meaning. Akhmatova has several poems on this light touching of
a hand:

> . . . How unlike embraces are the contact of these hands.
> . . . The contact through cloth of absently crossed hands.
> . . . Who, bringing flowers in unsure hands, touches my warm palm.

What intense sensitivity to every microscopic detail is needed so
that a hardly noticed contact of a hand should play such an important
role. Frantic kisses and embraces are almost nonexistent in Akhmatova's eroticism, which is produced almost without notice:

> He again touched my knees
> With an almost trembling hand.

Akhmatova's poetry is of the almost imperceptible, the barely
audible, the subtly elusive. What other poet would write, speaking of
her barely noticeable smile.

> I have a certain smile:
> A movement, barely visible, of the teeth.

And yet she devoted one of her best octaves to just this barely visible movement of the teeth. Her favorite words are "barely heard," "almost inaudible," "hardly visible":

> An almost inaudible, low conversation . . .
> And the muse's barely heard voice . . .
> And we will cherish this hardly audible rustle of feet for a
> thousand years. . . .

Soft, hardly audible sounds are unutterably delightful to her. The principal charm of her lyrics lies not in what is said, but in what is left unsaid. She is the master of silence, allusion, the significant pause. Her silences speak louder than words.

For the expression even of powerful emotions she makes use of tiny, almost indiscernible, microscopically minute images, and these in her work acquire singular suggestive power. When we read in one of her poems, for example, about a girl whose braids give off a barely perceptible scent of tobacco, we can guess that the girl has kissed someone she didn't love, that the smell of tobacco remained on her hair, that this smell fills her with disgust, and that she has been violated and is hopelessly unhappy. Inconspicuous sounds and smells in Akhmatova's poetry can be that revealing.

She cannot stand anything raucous. "Quiet" is always a word of praise in her vocabulary. Speaking of her sweetheart, she relates that people call him

> Quiet, quiet, asking no favors. . . .

"Quiet garden," "the quiet earth's breathing," "a quiet April day," "shine on me, quiet one," and the like, are to be found on every page.

Then suddenly, "at the silent twilight hour," this monastic silence—where the years quietly drift by, where "the voice of prayer is soft"—is broken by an inadmissible, frightening screech, a sort of rumbling, tramping, wailing, and howling:

> Drag the piano into the street!
> Crimson is the drum from the window!
> Split the piano open if you have to,
> But let's have noise, let's have thunder.

That's Mayakovsky bursting in, accompanied by thunder and lightning:

> Yell with rifles! Speak loud with cannons!
> We ourselves are both Christ and Savior!

And if Akhmatova should ask:

Why do you knock on the door of a beggarly sinner?

He gives this disrespectful and strange answer:

Hey you! *Allons enfants* into the water.

I can just imagine the commotion in Akhmatova's secluded monastery were this "inspired" ruffian to come barging in. One moment—silence, prayer, holiness . . . and then:

Strollers, pull your hands out of your pockets,
Take a rock, a knife, or a bomb,
And if one of you hasn't got any arms
Let him use his forehead to butt with.

He has no fondness for quiet or melancholy:

How can you call yourself a poet,
And then greyly chitter like a quail?
These days we've got to take brass knuckles
And split the world's skull open.

Every kind of violent slogan is in his armory. One minute he is yelling:

—Grab all these brilliant psychiatrists in our jaws
and toss them behind insane asylum bars!

And then again:

Come on, we'll paint Mondays and Tuesdays into holidays with blood.

It would be hard to imagine two human beings less alike than Akhmatova and Mayakovsky. Akhmatova is shrouded in silence, in whispered, almost inaudible words. Mayakovsky shouts like a thousand-throated public square. "The heart is our drum," he himself declares, and any page of his work will convince you of it. He is not only incapable of silence, but of any sort of measured conversation. He is ever shouting and raging.

Akhmatova is as devout as a prayer book. Angels, the Virgin, God are present in her every word. Mayakovsky cannot pass by God without hurling himself on Him with a shoemaker's knife:

I'll rip you, reeking of incense, wide open
From here to Alaska.

He has an old account to settle with God. Once long ago he'd appeared before God, peaceable and meek, and said amicably to Him:

—Listen, Mr. God, let's just build a merry-go-round on the
Tree of Knowledge of Good and Evil. Omnipresent, you'll be

> in each cupboard, and we'll lay out such great wines on the table that even grouchy Apostle Peter will feel like dancing the kickapoo!

God for some reason didn't go along with such felicities. Mayakovsky proposed some more:

> —We'll set up little Eves in Eden again—just say the word, and this very evening I'll round up all the most beautiful girls from the boulevards. Would you like that?

God shook his head and knit his grey brows. And it was then that Mayakovsky jumped on him with his shoemaker's knife. He didn't injure God, but the angels fared rather poorly. He cursed them as "winged scoundrels" and carried on in general. We are not told the results but know from subsequent poems that he offered some women "moulted angel wings" to adorn their hats. At times he has no objection to calling himself an angel, an apostle and even Jesus Christ, "the spat-upon Calvaryite" (as he puts it), and in his—new—Gospel describes his own Nativity and Ascension, and claims that pilgrims rush back from Christ's tomb to bow before him. "I am quite possibly the most beautiful of all your sons," he says in front of an icon of the Virgin Mary, and, as though foreseeing Blok's celebrated poem on the *twelve* new apostles, names himself as the thirteenth:

> In the day to day gospel,
> Having glorified the machine and England,
> I just might be
> The thirteenth apostle.

Entering a church, he smudges up an icon at the altar steps and *paints* an image of Stenka Razin over it.

> What do we have to do with God?
> Let's find peace with our own saints.

Hardly has he set foot in heaven, when all the gods run away from him, as from the devil.

> —Where are the gods? Took off all of them: Jehovah, Buddha, Allah.

Of course it would be easy to dismiss him as a blasphemer, a simple outrage—but let us try to get to like him instead. It will be difficult at first, but let us try. It will be especially hard for those like me who are so thankful for, and fond of, the poetry of Akhmatova. The two are really very different, and it's even strange that they should be living in the same century, walking the same earth. In actuality they are the opposite poles of Russian poetry, and never in its history has Russian poetry possessed such antipodes. It is as if they were on different planets, centuries apart. But let us attempt to embrace them both. Let us look at Mayakovsky closely and conscientiously, without prejudice.

IV

We have called Akhmatova the poet of microscopic trifles. The almost inaudible, the hardly seen, the barely noticed—this is the raw material for her work. She seems actually to look at the world through a microscope, and see that which is invisible to the naked eye. She has a heightened perception of the smallest speck of reality.

Mayakovsky, by contrast, is the poet of the colossal. In his world, the smallest speck of dust becomes Mount Ararat. His poetry operates on a gargantuan scale beyond the imagination of our previous poets. He appears always to be in front of a telescope, as when using stupendous augmentatives: portentous conversation, enormous Hell, colossal neck, huge step, great Babylon, massive tail. "Give me, give me a seventy-mile-wide superlanguage," one of his theatrical characters demands; it would appear that Mayakovsky himself already possesses such a language. Everything is blown up to such a size that words like "thousand," "million," and "billion" are commonplace.

Napoleon, for example, crossed only one single Arcole bridge, but Mayakovsky (so he tells it) crossed "a thousand Arcole bridges." Napoleon visited the pyramids, but in Mayakovsky's heart (so he says) loom a thousand thousand pyramids.

> You millions that go to dinner. . . .
> Set in million-foot type. . . .
> A million death-breeding sedges. . . .
> One hundred and fifty million speak through my lips. . . .
> I drag a million great and pure loves across a lifetime.
> And a million million little dirty loves.

Such is his hyperbolic style. Each of his poems is a great collection of exaggerations, and he can't do without them. Another poet might say that a flame burns in his heart; Mayakovsky asserts that his house is a roaring conflagration not to be extinguished even by forty-gallon barrels of tears (that's how he puts it—"barrels of tears"). Firemen bound up to him and pour water on his heart, but it's too late: his face is already burned, his mouth is in flames, his heat-cracked skull is split all the way open; his charred rib cage has collapsed.

Love caused this conflagration; such is Mayakovsky's love! Let Akhmatova, treating love, describe slight hand-touching and imperceptible lip movements—Mayakovsky needs a hundred-eyed flame, a ten-square-mile forest fire. And is it possible, for example, for him to say in the midst of all this giantism that he, like an ordinary mortal, has agitated nerves? No, he has to say that his nerves thrash and dance so desperately that

> The plaster fell from the ceiling below.
> Big nerves, tiny nerves, many nerves
> Leap madly, till soon
> Their legs give way.

We find here along with hyperbole another device: the concretization of everything abstract. His metaphorically flaming heart becomes an actual fire requiring hoses and fire chiefs.

His figuratively gyrating nerves turn into real dancers. This device of his is extremely interesting, but for the present we are concerned with giantism. Where did this ravenous need to aggrandize originate? Why does he describe himself as a towering titan, dwarfing other two-legged creatures, as though he saw even himself through a telescope? His verses continuously tell us that he is Don Quixote, Goliath, and Napoleon—in fact, who is Napoleon alongside him?

> —I walk Napoleon on a chain like a pug.

His gestures are correspondingly Brobdignagian:

> —Hey you, heaven, take off your hat: I'm coming . . .
> Sun, I challenge you to a duel. . . .

There are many people who simply laugh at this, but let us try to understand what is going on. Revolutions and wars have so accustomed our generation to large figures that it would be odd for poets reflective of the age *not* to pick up and use the thousands, millions, and billions now so clearly operative in life. War has summoned into the arena of history such countless hordes of people, things, events, words, money, deaths, biographies, from all corners of the globe, that a new, completely different arithmetic is needed—one on an unprecedented scale. Isn't it as the poet of this new, grandiose system of measurement that Mayakovsky deeply senses the great mass of humanity, senses her thousands of peoples swarming about on our planet, continually addresses himself to them, never for a minute forgetting their existence? "Parises, Berlins, Viennas" flash across his pages. On them one finds the Alps, the Balkans, Chicago, the Arctic Circle, London, the Sahara, Rome, the Atlantic Ocean, the English Channel, California—in fact the geography of the whole world.

Living in Moscow, he nonetheless (like anyone alive today) considers himself a citizen of the universe. This is a new feeling, heretofore unknown. At one time very few people had this feeling, but now it is quite common. The feeling, that is, that one's destiny depends on London, on Japan, on some out-of-the-way place that no one had heard of before yesterday . . . a feeling that it's enough to jab Kiev to make Moscow immediately give a start . . . a feeling that all life on our planet belongs to all of us. Our thinking has broken out of its closed circle and is expanding and growing.

And so a heightened awareness of great expanses is only natural to Mayakovsky's outsized scale of things. When he describes war in his poem *War and the World*, he doesn't single out a particular sector of war, a specific battle, but covers the whole worldwide field of slaughter, the million wrinkles of trenches that furrowed the earth, the thunder and lightning of billion-man armies—here blacks and Arabs, there Munich, Constantinople, the Marne—"the whole of blazing Europe" suspended in the skies like a chandelier. His telescope is such that, unresponsive to details and particulars, his vision takes in enormous distances. And to encompass these distances indeed requires a seventy-mile language.

> —My China has drowned, my Persia sank out of sight.
> Look, what's this? How's Alaska?
> Nothing left? Nothing! Goodbye!

How can this spectacle be captured in fine details, in units and tens? Only one standard is needed here—millions.

Such sweeping intercontinental feeling is completely unnatural to Akhmatova. Not for nothing is she a nun, as if walled in from the world. Not a single "million" is to be found in her verse. The grandiose does not suit her. When war broke out Akhmatova noticed neither Magyars nor blacks, nor greyheaded oceans, nor Europe lit up like a chandelier: she saw only Russia and in magnificent verses began selflessly praying for her, keenly attentive to prophecies promising that

> Our land no enemy will divide up
> For his amusement.
> The Virgin will spread over our great grief
> A pure white garment.

But Mayakovsky is unable to understand the meaning of "our land." For the motherland he has no feeling. "I'm not yours, snowy smotherland"—he said of Russia in that same 1915 and three years later declared through his favorite heroes that "we aren't nations at all. Work is our homeland!" which is all very real for a man who has traded patriotism for universality, felt on a worldwide scale.

V

But what is the essence of his work?

He is a poet of catastrophe and convulsion. Every word is earthshaking. In order to create a poem, he must first go mad. Only feverish and demented images are permitted on his pages. His skull is "inflamed," words are "frenzied," his face is more frightening than "sacrileges, killings, and slaughter." He says so himself. He has only to go out into the street, and the street collapses like a syphilitic nose and a crazed cathedral careens down the street, an insane god jumps out of a church icon and whirls about in the slush of the road, six-storied concrete giants break into a frantic dance:

> six-storied fauns broke out dancing . . .
> brothel upon brothel.

Even chimneys do the cancan on the roofs:

> Chimneys danced everywhere on the roofs,
> Each one kicking up a cancan.

All objects are torn up, sent reeling, spinning in a destructive whirlwind. The most inert, massive, and cumbrous things jump about in these verses like madmen. Even eighteen-ton monuments tear themselves from their pedestals. Letters jump off their signboards.

> The town suddenly came unscrewed. . . .
> Signboards gaped in horror, spitting out o's and s'es.

Mayakovsky is a poet of movement, of dynamics, whirlwinds. Since his first verses in 1910, his objects haven't stopped rushing and springing about. This bounding of massive objects is in fact Mayakovsky's favorite device. All his images are aimed at movement, action. It is positively impossible for him to describe something stationary, peaceful, quiet. On every page,

—Paris was ripped apart and sank into the abyss.
—The Nile reared up fierce, and Africa sank into it.
—The streets pour along, deluged houses dash down upon houses . . .
the whole world streams in a solid cascade.

Even the sun rushes about the sky:

> —The sun, mad house painter, dashed about.

Describing this cataclysmic convulsion of the universe, the poet indeed feels like a kind of madman, worked into a trancelike state by such a spectacle:

"I'm already half-crazy!" he cries out in one poem. "These are thoughts of a mad heap of things," he cries in another. "Now madness! There won't be anything," "Long live my madness!"

The war and the Revolution broke out, as it were, just for his sake alone. He could not live without them. What, after all, is a catastrophic poet without catastrophe? His entire literary being was exclusively geared to these subjects: just as a tiger is every inch a hunter, and an earthworm lives to burrow in the ground, so Mayakovsky's every particle and trait help make him a poet of war and revolution. It's just such subjects that require the hyperbolic style, that giantism and penchant for the massive that are organic to Mayakovsky. To deal with great events created by a mass of millions, a scale of millions is required.

In the second place, as we have seen, he is the poet of thunder and lightning, roars and screeches; he is incapable of maintaining any sort of quiet. Another obligatory trait: the Revolution can in no way be carried out in a whisper. For some time revolutionary cries had been heard in his poetry, and inhuman, inarticulate sounds—such as those that fill the streets of insurrection—characteristically burst from his pages:

> —O-o-o-o! O-xo-xo! EE-ee-ee-ee-ee! Oo-oo-oo-oo-oo! A-A-A-A-A! Aie! Aie!

Thirdly, as we have just seen, he is a poet of perpetual motion, cataclysmic convulsions, concussions between objects. This is another sine qua non: how can a poet of this cataclysmic era operate without such movement?

He was, in a word, expressly equipped by nature to sing of war and revolution. And, amazingly enough, he presaged and raved about the Revolution before it even began. As early as 1915, at the height of the war, I read with astonishment:

> —1916 is drawing near in the thorny crown of revolutions/. . . . And I am its harbinger, scouting it for you/ . . . like no other, I can see the future approaching,/over the mountains of time.

At that time no other poet had even *sensed* the revolution, but he even prophesied the year. True, in his impatience he erred slightly—the Revolution took place a year later—but his impatience was really very great.

VI

Akhmatova is not declamatory. She simply talks, hardly audibly, without gesture or pose. Or prays—almost to herself. In this effulgently clear atmosphere of her books, declamation would only come out false, unreal. I must admit, then, that I was deeply stung by two of her alexandrines, so different were they from the rest of her work:

> Thus does the dead man speak, troubling the murderer's sleep;
> Thus the angel of death lurks waiting at her fatal bed.

It seems to me that here Akhmatova was not herself, that she, in the solitude of her Tver residence, could have left these Parisian intonations and gestures to someone else.

I mention these lines because they are such an exception. In general her books must be read silently and alone. They lose much of their effect in public. But Mayakovsky is every inch a reciter. Each of his poems is meant for the soapbox. Earlier poets were read, but Mayakovsky writes for an imaginary assembled throng of listeners. By their very nature his poems are appeals to a crowd. He fancies himself a colossal madman, standing on some colossal stage, alone in front of a furious or exulting throng, staggering them with fierce howls:

> —Come, madmen from Russia and Poland!
> —Raise higher on blood-stained lampposts the bloody carcasses of
>   profiteers!

And note that the plural "you" can be found in almost every poem:

> —Hey, you. . . . —You, who . . . —Do you all understand?
>   —Look, —Listen, —Remember. . . .

He storms, rages; the crowd sobs, only rarely crying out in delight, "Mayakovsky, bravo," "What a wonderful scoundrel!" Sometimes he reviles the throng, calls it a "hundred-headed louse," "many-hammed snout," "massive-fleshed mass"; sometimes he spits in its face:

> —I'll burst out laughing and happily spit, spit in your face.

But all his work is nonetheless fit for the crowd only. He plays up to its appetites alone, and this is most important to him. In his best, most inspired works one senses the public speaker. I say this without pejorative connotations. He is a poet-brawler, a poet-screamer, a street poet, a public poet—that's what I particularly like about him. It would be silly to call him a writer—his calling is not writing, but yelling. His medium isn't paper, but his own throat—which is natural for a poet of the Revolution. He is Isaiah in the guise of a hooligan. The thousand-voiced roar of today's revolutionary streets emerges from his throat, and is it his fault if he is as vulgar as a mother oath, as simple as a pistol-shot? Street language must be fierce, scandalous, sensational. You have to strike the street dumb to get its attention. It needs fireworks and monstrously stunning words. These are perfect for it. And that is why it is somehow attractive to the contemporary soul. It despotically prescribes for art its own fantastic unprecedented laws. These laws have the same rights as the laws formerly prescribed for art by salons, country estates, feudal castles.

In every line Mayakovsky unconsciously serves this new street aesthetic:

> Streets are our paintbrushes,
> Public squares our palettes.

It is no accident that he plays nocturnes on drainpipes. He himself says that until he came along, the street was mute, that there was no way for it to cry out or converse, that there were only two words in its vocabulary: "bastard" and, apparently, some kind of "borscht." This street idiom first expressed itself in his rhythms. His verses, with few exceptions, are based not on those formal metric schemes which are so alien to contemporary ears, but on a living, conversational, street rhythm. He put together his own rhythms, those we hear in the marketplace, on trolley cars, at meetings, the rhythm of shouts, conversations, speeches, squabbles, agitators' exhortations, swearing. His only aim is to canonize his street rhythms in spite of all the laws of prosody. We read:

> "Well, Vladimir Vladimirovich, how do you
>   like the bottomless pit?"
> And I answer just as politely:
>   "Delightful abyss, charming."

These are the very intonations we might have just overheard at the corner of Basin and River streets. No anapests or iambs here, but the pounding of human blood, more precious, perhaps, than the most refined metric scheme.

Mayakovsky's book is like a public square. We constantly hear in it such things as:

> I'd have grabbed him and beat his head:
> I don't much go for him.

or,

> You're talking stupid! Cultured people!
> Really, it's almost insulting!

or else,

> I live on Great Presnya. No. 36, apt. 24.
> Kind of a quiet, peaceful spot, you know.
> So what's it to me if somewhere off in
>   some god-forsaken place
> They've been hatching up a war?

These conversational street rhythms are as much poetry as any that have been noted in schoolbooks.

Many poets aristocratically disdain them, just as in the 18th century the distinctive rhythms of peasant songs and popular epics were regarded as base and were prevented from coming in through the front door of literature. It is all the more to Mayakovsky's credit that he steadfastly reproduces in verse these scathing, energetic, vulgar rhythms of meeting hall orations, newspaper vendors' cries, exclamations, quarrels, and brawls:

> —No objections? Then it's decided? Comrades, this is a
>   knife in the back.
> —I didn't steal the silverware!
> —Hello, who's this—Mama? Mama!
> —You know Adelina Patti? She's here too!

Such rhythms are autonomous, and there's no point in measuring them in terms of poetic feet. They are a law unto themselves. And I think that in the near future all of our poetry will be moving in this direction: away from song and in the direction of a kind of conversational recitative, from meter to emotional rhythm.

·   ·   ·

VII

The most interesting feature of Mayakovsky's verse is contained in his profuse and pointed metaphors. His pages glow with the bold energy of the street, the sharpness of the marketplace, and the rough repartee of urban argument.

Mayakovsky in his similes is bold and effective. I remember how I liked the following:

—A woman as hackneyed as a proverb.
—I rushed out like a curse.
—I'll make you a gift of verses as gay as dolls and as sharp as toothpicks.
—The smile grew on his face broad and bold, his mouth spread to his ears; it was as though a troupe of Ukrainian dancers were giving a gala spectacle on his mug.

As a general thing all of these comparisons draw particular strength from the fact that they are so totally surprising.

Calm as a dead man's pulse. Midnight fell like the condemned man's head from the block. A night black as the traitor Azef. From the sky some kind of trash looked down, majestically, like Leo Tolstoy. A woman who calmly turns over pairs of lips, like a cook the pages of a cookbook. And so on, and so on, and so on.

.   .   .

IX

It is as though all of Russia is divided today between Akhmatovas and Mayakovskys. Between the two there are millennia. And they hate one another.

Akhmatova and Mayakovsky are just as antipathetic to each other as are the epochs that gave them birth. Akhmatova is the heir of all the precious riches of prerevolutionary Russian poetry; and she values her inheritance. She has many ancestors: Pushkin, Boratynsky, Annensky. She possesses that intellectual refinement and charm that are given to those who participate in a long cultural tradition. But Mayakovsky in every word and every line is the product of the present revolutionary epoch. The faith, the cry, the ecstasy, and the failures of that epoch are in his work. He has no ancestors. He is an ancestor himself and if he is strong in anything it is in his descendants. Behind Akhmatova there is a long and magnificent past. Before him there is a magnificent and distant future. She has long preserved the old Russian faith in God. He, as befits a revolutionary, is a blasphemer. For her the holy of holies is Russia, the motherland, "our earth." He, as is proper in a revolutionary bard, is an internationalist, a citizen of the whole universe, indifferent to his "snowy smotherland" and in love with the whole world. She is a lonely, silent one, forever in her cell and in the quiet:

How fine it is in my narrow abode.

He is a man of the street and the meeting; all for the crowd, he is himself a crowd. And while Akhmatova knows only the pronoun "thou" that a woman addresses to her beloved, or that other pronoun "Thou" that she addresses to God, Mayakovsky is constantly shouting "Hey, you," "You, those who . . . ," "you, you, you. . . ." That pronoun he shouts at the top of his voice to the many-faced mass.

As is proper for the heiress of an old and high culture, Akhmatova is sensitive to all "barely audible" and "barely visible" thoughts and sensations. Mayakovsky can see only what is grandiose and numerous and is deaf to whispers and rustles, and blind to religious effects à la Nesterov.

She practices at all times the famous Pushkinian restraint. She cannot stand hyperbole. He cannot get along for a moment without hyperbole. Each of his letters is a hyperbole.

In a word, we observe here not just a difference between two poets —who may be good, bad, or indifferent—but rather a contrast between two different worlds. Akhmatova and Mayakovsky are two incarnations of great historic forces, and each one of us must decide which of these opposites he will identify with, which he will reject and which accept.

For myself I can say that after a thorough examination of my literary conscience I find to my astonishment that I love them both equally. I regard myself as kin to both poets. For me there is no such question as "Akhmatova or Mayakovsky?" That Old Russia that Akhmatova stands for—so sensitive and so restrained—is very dear to me; as is the riotous and drumbeating element incarnated in Mayakovsky. As I see it, the two elements are not mutually exclusive; rather they complement one another, and both are equally necessary.

I think the time has come to bring about a synthesis of the two contrasting elements. The fact that Akhmatova's poetry should have taken rise from the Russia of the past surely must mean that that Russia is still alive today and that what is best and most spiritual in it has been preserved untouched for the purposes of art. And moreover not everything in Mayakovsky is darkness and chaos. He too has his own hurts, his own prayers, and his own thirst for justice. The synthesis of which I speak has long been clearly pointed to by history itself, and the sooner it takes place, the better. . . . All Russia yearns for it. There is no need for antagonism between the two cultural forces; they move irresistibly toward fusion. They can continue to exist only if they become reconciled. Otherwise both will perish.

TRANSLATED BY JOHN PEARSON

ANDREY SINYAVSKY

The Unshackled Voice: Anna Akhmatova

For years Akhmatova's poetry appeared locked, frozen within the limits set by her early books—*Evening, Rosary, White Flock*. Living in the past, in her private world and in her own poetic tradition, she seemed the prisoner of her own familiar themes, chosen intonations, long-discovered images from which she would never break away. That Akhmatova was "destined to repeat herself" was said by critics as early as the 1920s, and unfortunately this old impression still survives in the mind of the public.

Yet, if we turn to the Akhmatova of today and re-read what she has written in the past three decades, we are struck by many new, decisive notes, unexpected, bold developments, quite out of keeping with our long-established view of her character as a poet.

> The harsh epoch
> turned me back like a river.
> My life has been secretly changed,
> and flows
> along another course,
> past other landmarks,
> and I do not know my banks.

While remaining true to herself, this new Akhmatova forces us to discard the established image of her as merely a pre-revolutionary poet, narrow in scope and set in her ways. To begin with, this is glaringly disproved by the poems, full of tragic power and courage, written in the 1930s and in wartime. Akhmatova argues with those who would like to see her as an uncommitted person, estranged from the life of

From *Anna Akhmatova: Selected Poems*. (New York: Oxford University Press, 1969.) Translated from *Novy Mir*, no. 6, 1964. Reprinted by permission of Oxford University Press.

54

her own country and uninterested in the fate of the people. It is enough to take these lines about the years of the Yezhovshchina, years of personal tragedy for Akhmatova herself.[1]

> No—not under the vault of another sky,
> not under the shelter of other wings.
> I was with my people then,
> there where my people were doomed to be.

Her wartime poetry, where artist and citizen are so clearly at one, rings with high courage and compassion:

> We know what now lies on the scales
> and what is happening now.
> The hour of courage has struck for us
> and courage will not desert us.
> We have no fear in facing the bullets,
> no bitterness in being left without homes,
> and we will treasure you our Russian speech,
> the great Russian word.
> Pure and free we will uphold you
> and give you to our descendants,
> and save you from bondage forever.

Akhmatova's poetry has changed in its very structure, its very sound. We thought of it as muted, delicate, feminine and fragile, we followed the play of half-tones, of "motes," of barely audible, barely perceptible modulations. But who would have believed that this Royal Village Muse[2] could talk so loud, so big, in the language of the street and of the market place—and in speaking of the Royal Village itself, thrice sung and for so long the very symbol of the refined poetic language of the past?

> There the soldiers' jokes flow
> with undiminished venom.
> A striped sentry box,
> and a stream of tobacco smoke.
> They bawled out songs
> and swore at the priest's wife,
> drank vodka till late
> and ate honeyed sweets.
> The rook cawed and praised
> this ghostly world,
> and the giant cuirassier
> drove along on his sledge.

Unlike many of her contemporaries, Akhmatova, wary of sudden shifts and radical transformations of style, was attracted by traditional forms, by the clarity, precision and harmony of the language of Pushkin and Baratynsky. Today she still tends to poetic reminiscences, which at times have the effect of parallel mirrors deepening the perspective of the poem while bringing distant objects closer together ("The future matures in the past whose embers glow in the future . . ."). Literary names and associations, epigraphs, dedications, meetings and partings with the past ("As though I said goodbye again to what I said goodbye to long ago . . ."), the settling of accounts with herself and her memory—all this, so far from hindering her, lightens her task: to create, within the compass of a brief text, a sense of space and freely move about in it, calling out to other times and other spheres of being, communicating with them and recording their voices. So wide is the space that it can hold the universe, and if the communication is in whispers or in silence, this no longer matters. Silence in her verse is not a sign of solitude but of a presence of ineffable majesty.

> You and I are a mountain of grief . . .
> you and I will never meet.
> Only try at midnight to send me
> a greeting through the stars.

The new quality in Akhmatova's work compels us to look back and revise the conventional estimate of her early work. Did she, even in that first, muted period of her development, have in her as a hidden potential what later, matured and rejuvenated, was to become her strength?

Akhmatova was always recognized as a matter of the poetic self-portrait—a portrait so alive, alike and natural in gesture and expression that it almost leapt out of the framework of the poem. The small format proved astonishingly capacious. Akhmatova had the gift of putting a whole human life, with all its mysteries, its psychological twists, into a single quatrain.

> I am happy. But what I hold most dear
> are the sloping forest path,
> the simple crooked bridge,
> and that there are only a few days left to wait.

If her early poems are packed with meaning and images, equally striking at times are the range of her intonations and the power of her voice—a voice of which Mandelshtam once said, in a poem he dedicated to her, that it could "unshackle the soul." Such are the scope, the depth of feeling and tone that, in spite of the muted orchestration, they reveal a character of vast, massive, almost monumental stature. Everyone remembers her lines:

> Then be accursed. I will not touch
> your damned soul with a groan or a glance.
> But I swear to you by the garden of the angels,
> I swear by the miracle-working ikon,
> and by the fire and smoke of our nights
> that I will never return.

They are more than is usually assumed—the outcry of a hurt, humiliated and indignant woman: beyond the shrill tirade of the woman is the artist, the scope of whose personality it reveals.

Equally early Akhmatova showed her talents for civic and patriotic verse. A striking example is a poem written in 1917 as a rebuke to those who were about to leave the country at the moment when the revolution had set it ablaze. In the circumstances (though they are presented in a gloomy enough light) what is significant is the choice made by Akhmatova in favour of her own country. According to Kornei Chukovsky, Aleksandr Blok, who loved this poem and knew it by heart, considered it important on grounds of principle. "Akhmatova is right," he says, "these are shameful words. To run away from the Russian revolution is a disgrace."

> I heard a voice. It called me consolingly,
> 'Come here, leave
> your god-forsaken country,
> abandon Russia forever.
> I'll wash the blood from your hands,
> and rip black shame from your heart,
> and give you a new name to cover
> the pain of defeat and humiliation.'
> But I quite calmly
> put my hands over my ears,
> that my grieving soul
> should not be defiled by these shameful words.

From the barest whisper to fiery eloquence, from downcast eyes to lightning and thunderbolts—such is the range of Akhmatova's inspiration and voice. This, it seems, is what later developed and gave her strength to follow a new course, wide enough for anything from patriotic oratory to the silence of lofty metaphysical meditation, and the arguing voices of the living and the dead.

ROMAN JAKOBSON

Modern Russian Poetry:
Velimir Khlebnikov [Excerpts]

It is difficult to avoid schematization and a certain mechanical approach when we deal with the facts of a language spoken in the past. Even the specialist in language finds an everyday conversation more understandable than the *Stoglav*.[1] In just the same way Pushkin's verse—*as a poetic fact*—is less intelligible and more obscure than that of Mayakovsky or Khlebnikov.

We apprehend each new manifestation of the contemporary poetic language in its necessary relationship with three factors: the existing poetic tradition, the everyday language of the present time, and the developing poetic tendencies with which the given manifestation is confronted.

Khlebnikov describes the latter factor as follows: "When I observed how old poetry suddenly grew dim when the future that was hidden in it became the present day, I understood that the native land of creative work is the future. It is from the future that the wind of the gods of poetry blows."

When we deal with poets of the past, these factors must be reconstructed, and this can be done only partially and with great difficulty.

When Pushkin's poetry first appeared it was, in the expression of a journal of his time, "a phenomenon in the history of the Russian language and versification"; and at that time critics did not ponder over "the wisdom of Pushkin," but rather asked: "Why do these beautiful verses have meaning? Why do they affect more than just our hearing?"

Today Pushkin is a common household word, a repository of household philosophy. Pushkin's verse, as verse, is now simply taken on

From *Noveyshaya russkaya poeziya. Nabrosok pervy.* (Prague, 1921). Reprinted by permission of the author.

faith: having become the object of a kind of cult, it has petrified. It is not surprising that even experts on Pushkin such as Lerner and Shchegolev[2] fell for the bait when they took a clever counterfeit by a certain young poet as an authentic work of the great master.

Pushkin-like poems are now as easy to print as counterfeit Kerensky[3] bills; they lack any value of their own and circulate only in the absence of good hard cash.

We are inclined to speak of ease and unobtrusiveness of technique as the characteristic features of Pushkin. But this is an error of perspective. Pushkin's verse is for us an established form; our conclusion that it is simple follows from this. It was a quite different matter for Pushkin's contemporaries. Consider their reaction, and that of Pushkin himself. For example, an iambic pentameter without a caesura seems to us quite smooth and easy. But Pushkin had a special feeling for it, he sensed it as a difficult form and as a violent departure from earlier practice:

> To tell the truth, in a pentameter
> I love a caesura on the second foot.
> If not, the line moves from pit to knoll.
> Although now I'm lying comfortably on a soft bed,
> It seems to me I am speeding in a cart
> In a jolting dash across a frozen field.

Form exists for us only as long as it is difficult to perceive, as long as we sense the resistance of the material, as long as we waver as to whether what we read is prose or poetry, as long as our "cheekbones ache," as General Ermolov's cheekbones ached, according to Pushkin's report, during the reading of Griboyedov's[4] verse.

And yet even now scholarship deals only with deceased poets, or if now and then live ones are touched upon, it is only such as are firmly established in many volumes and by wide circulation. What has become a truism in the study of everyday language is still considered heresy by the students of poetic language who generally tag along far behind linguistics.

Students of the poetry of the past usually impose their own aesthetic attitudes on that past, project the contemporary methods of poetic production into the past. This is the reason for the scientific unsoundness of the studies in rhythm by the modernists, who read into Pushkin the current deformation of syllabo-tonic[5] verse. The past is examined —or rather, assessed—from the standpoint of the present, but scientific poetics will become possible only when it refuses to offer value judgments. Wouldn't it be absurd for a linguist to assess values to dialects according to their relative merits?

The development of a theory of poetic language will be possible only when poetry is treated as a social fact, when a kind of poetic dialectology is created.

From the point of view of this dialectology, Pushkin is the center of a poetic culture of a particular time, with a definite zone of influence. From this point of view, the poetic dialects of one zone, when they gravitate toward the cultural center of another, can be subdivided, like dialects of practical language, into: transitional dialects which have adopted a set of canons from the center of gravity; semitransitional dialects which adopt certain poetic tendencies from the center of gravity; and mixed dialects which adopt occasional alien elements or devices. Finally, it is essential to bear in mind the existence of archaic dialects with a conservative tendency, the center of gravity of which belongs to the past.

II

Khlebnikov is called a futurist; his poems are printed in futurist collections. Futurism is of course a new movement[6] in European art, and I shall not offer a more precise definition of the term now. Such definitions can only be arrived at inductively, through the analysis of many and complex artistic phenomena.

Any a priori formula suffers from dogmatism, since it sets up an artificial and premature distinction between real futurism and pseudofuturism, and the like. I should not like to repeat the methodological error of those contemporaries of romanticism, some of whom, according to Pushkin, considered romantic all works bearing the imprint of dreaminess and melancholy, while others regarded neologisms and grammatical mistakes as romantic.

I shall touch on just one feature which some experts on futurism, introducing extraneous factors into the study of poetry, have considered to be the essential component. I offer some excerpts from the manifestoes of Marinetti:[7]

> We shall sing of the great crowds tossed about by work, by pleasure, or revolt; the many-colored and polyphonic surf of revolutions in modern capitals; the nocturnal vibration of the arsenals and the yards under their violent electric moons; the gluttonous railway stations swallowing smoky serpents; the factories hung from the clouds by the ribbons of their smoke; the

bridges leaping like athletes hurled over the diabolical cutlery of sunny rivers; the adventurous steamers that sniff the horizon; the broad-chested locomotives, prancing on the rails like great steel horses curbed by long pipes, and the gliding flight of airplanes whose propellers snap like a flag in the wind, like the applause of an enthusiastic crowd.

Thus it appears that new material and new concepts in the poetry of the Italian futurists have led to a renewal of the devices of poetry and of artistic forms, and in this way, supposedly, the idea of *parole in libertà* (the free word) for instance, came into being. But this is a reform in the field of reportage, not in poetic language.

Let me say parenthetically that at the moment I'm only talking about Marinetti as a theoretician. As far as his poetry is concerned, all this may serve only as rationalization, as a particular application of a poetic fact.

We see that for Marinetti the impulse for innovation was the need to tell of new facts in the material and psychological worlds.

But the Russian futurists advanced a totally different thesis:

> Once there is new form, it follows that there is new content: form thus conditions content.
> Our creative shaping of speech throws everything into a new light.
> It is not new subject matter that defines genuine innovation.
> New light shed on the old world can yield the most fanciful play. (Kruchonykh[8] in the collection *The Three*)

The aim of poetry is here very clearly formulated, and it is precisely the Russian futurists who invented a poetry of the "self-developing, self-valuing word," as the established and clearly visible material of poetry. And so it is not surprising that Khlebnikov's poems sometimes deal with the depths of the Stone Age, sometimes with the Russo-Japanese War, sometimes with the days of Prince Vladimir . . . and then again with the future of the world.

. . .

In normal, everyday linguistic cerebration, according to Professor Shcherba's[9] formula, "the stimuli we receive and the results of their assimilation are not distinguished in our consciousness as two events separated in time. In other words we don't know the difference between the objectively given sensations and the result of a given perception."

In emotional language and poetic language, the verbal representations (phonetic as well as semantic) concentrate on themselves greater attention; the connection between the aspect of sound and that of meaning is tighter, more intimate, and language is accordingly more revolutionary, insofar as habitual associations by contiguity (*smezhnost*) retreat into the background. Note, for example, that appellative words—and hence personal names in general—undergo a rich variety of phonetic and formative modifications.

But beyond this there is no necessary affinity between emotional and poetic language. In emotional expression passionate outbursts govern the verbal mass, and precisely that "turbulent steam of emotion bursts the pipe of the sentence." But poetry—which is simply *utterance for the purpose of expression*—is governed, so to speak, by its own immanent laws; the communicative function, essential to both practical language and emotional language, has only minimal importance in poetry.[10] Poetry is indifferent to the subject of the utterance, while, on the other hand, practical or more exactly objective (*sachliche*) prose is indifferent—in Saran's[11] formulation—to rhythm.

Of course poetry can make use of the methods of emotional language, since the two are related in their purposes. Such utilization is characteristic of the opening stages of certain poetic movements, for instance romanticism. But poetic language is not composed of "*Affektträger*" (words that carry an emotional effect) in Sperber's[12] phrase, nor of the interjections and exclamations of hysterical discourse, as the Italian futurists have decreed.

The plastic arts involve the shaping of self-sufficient visual impressions, music the shaping of self-sufficient sound material, dance the organization of the self-sufficient gesture; and poetry is the formulation of the self-sufficient, "self-centered," word, as Khlebnikov puts it.

Poetry is language in its aesthetic function.

Thus the subject of literary scholarship is not literature but literariness (*literaturnost*), that is, that which makes of a given work a work of literature. And yet literary scholars up to now have often behaved like policemen who, in the course of arresting a particular person, would pick up, just in case, everybody and anybody who happened to be in the apartment, as well as people who happened to be passing on the street.

Similarly, the literary historian used anything that came to hand: biographical evidence, psychology, politics, philosophy. Instead of a literary science they created a conglomeration of homegrown disciplines. They seemed to forget that their articles deviated in the direction of those other disciplines—the history of philosophy, the history of culture, psychology, and so forth, and that while the latter may of course make use of literary works, these are for *their* purposes only defective, second-rate documents. If literary history wishes to become a science, it must recognize "device" as its sole concern. Then the fundamental problem will concern the uses and justification of device.

One of the commonest applications, or rather, in the given case, justifications of poetic language is emotional or mental experience, which serves as a kind of catchall where we may dispose of anything that can't be justified or explained in practical terms, or rationalized.

When Mayakovsky writes:

> I'll reveal for you, in words as simple as mooing,
> Your new souls that hum like arc lights,

it is the words "as simple as mooing" that interest us as poetic evidence, while the "soul" is secondary, ancillary, superimposed.

The romantics are often described as explorers of man's spiritual realm and poets of emotional experience, but as a matter of fact the contemporaries of the romantics thought of the movement exclusively in terms of its formal innovations. They observed first of all the destruction of the classical unities. And the testimony of contemporaries is the only valid evidence.

[We omit a fairly long excerpt from articles in the journals *Moscow Telegraph*, 1827, pt. 15, no. 10 and *Son of the Fatherland*, 1829, pt. 125, no. 15, which emphasize the formal innovations of the Byronic tale, but explain them as answering the needs of the "modern soul."]

Thus it is clear that a particular literary device was being logically justified by reference to the titanic and rebellious spirit, the free and arbitrary imagination.

The sentimentalists use the same device in embryonic form, where it is motivated by supposed "sentimental journeys." Similarly the mystical and "nature philosophy" elements of the romantic artistic credo simply serve as justification for an irrational poetic structure. The same is true for dreams, delirium, and other pathological phenomena, when they are used as poetic motifs. A typical illustration of the same sort of thing is symbolism.

Take a verbal joke of the type "I was walking along, and there's a hut. I stopped in, the dough-trough is kneading the woman. I smirked, but the trough did not like it, it grabbed the stove out of the shovel and was going to hit me; I leapt through my trousers and ripped out the threshold and ran away" (Onchukov, *Northern Tales—Severnye skazki*, p. 74), and compare it with an excerpt from Gogol:

> Everything in him turned into an undefined trembling, every feeling burned and everything before him appeared through a kind of fog; the sidewalk moved under him, carriages with galloping horses seemed immovable, a bridge was stretching and breaking in its arc, a house stood upside down, a sentry box was falling toward him, and a sentry's halberd, along with the golden words of a sign and the scissors drawn on it, seemed to sparkle on his very eyelashes. And all this was produced by one glance, one turn of a pretty little head (*Nevsky prospekt*).

The same device which in the verbal joke is motivated by humorous intent, is used by Gogol to evidence the sudden onset of passion.

In Khlebnikov's poem *The Crane* (*Zuravl*), a boy sees that the factory chimneys have begun to dance, that a revolt of things is going on:

> On the square in the damp of an entering corner
> Where the needle radiant with gold
> Covered the burial ground of tsars,
> There a boy whispered in horror—
> > hey! hey!
> Look how the chimneys started reeling around
> > drunk—there!
> The stuttering lips were pale with horror
> And his glance was riveted up high.
> What? Is the boy delirious in broad daylight?
> I call the boy.
> But he is silent and suddenly runs—
> > What a furious race!
> Slowly I get out my glasses.
> And it's really as though the chimneys
> > craned their necks.

Here we have the realization of the same trope, the projection of a literary device into artistic reality, the turning of a poetic trope into a poetic *fact*, into a plot element. Here, however, the image structure is still partly explained in logical fashion by reference to a pathological state of mind.

In another poem by Khlebnikov, however, *Marquise Desaix* (*Markiz Dezes*), even this motivation is lacking. Pictures at an exhibition simply come to life; then they bring the other things to life, while people turn to stone.

But why is a smile, with a schoolgirl's modesty,
about to answer, "I am of stone and of sky-blue, sir."
But why so ruthlessly and hopelessly did the clothes of
snow-covered bodies suddenly fall away.
The heart, accessible before to the full measure of
feelings,
Suddenly became a lump of mindless clay.
Laughing, grumbling, cackling,
Creatures rose against the rich,
Under an invisible shadow of a threat they lit up
the slaves' rebellion,
And who are their victims? We, the same people,
the same.
Dark-blue and red-green roosters
Come down from hats and peck at artifacts.
Gold patches on teeth
Standing like apparitions from the grave,
There baring their teeth a snowy pair of
ermine gallop, racing, throwing back their
shoulders and bright blue cocks.
There the rye forms ears in a luxuriant sheaf.
A young goldfinch builds a nest in someone's
dumbfounded mouth. Then everything approached a
mysterious line and limit.

There is a similar "realization of the device," laid bare of any logical
motivation, in Mayakovsky's *Tragedy* (a literary miracle):

Suddenly,
all things went rushing off, ripping
their voices,
and casting off tatters of outworn names.
Wineshop windows, all on their own,
splashed in the bottoms of bottles,
as though stirred by the finger of Satan.
From the shop of a tailor who'd fainted,
trousers escaped
and went walking along—
alone,
without human buttocks!
Out of a bedroom,
a drunken commode—
its black maw agape—
came stumbling.
Corsets wept, afraid of tumbling
down from signs reading "Robes et Modes."

The city offers material that fits neatly the structure of the verbal paradox and similar structures, as the examples we've seen from Gogol, Mayakovsky, and Khlebnikov clearly indicate. Urbanism offers opportunities for the application of a number of poetic devices: hence the urban verses of Mayakovsky and Khlebnikov.

Yet at the same time Mayakovsky says: "Abandon cities, you foolish people."

Or as Khlebnikov puts it:

> There's a certain fat gourmand who's fond of impaling human hearts on his spit, and who derives a mild enjoyment from the sound of hissing and breaking as he sees the bright red drops falling into the fire and flowing down—and the name of that fat man is—"the city."

What do we have here, a contradiction?

Let others superimpose upon the poet the thoughts expressed in his works! To incriminate the poet with ideas and emotions is as absurd as the behavior of the medieval audiences that beat the actor who played Judas and just as foolish as to blame Pushkin for the death of Lensky.

Why should the poet be held answerable for a clash of ideas but not for a duel with swords or pistols?

.   .   .

We have already characterized metamorphosis as the realization of a verbal construction: as a rule such a realization involves the development in time of a reverse parallelism (specifically an antithesis). If a negative parallelism rejects the category of metaphor in the name of the category of the real, then reverse parallelism denies the real in the name of metaphor.

For example:

> Those forests standing on the hill are not forests; they are the hair growing on the shaggy head of the forest grandfather. Beneath it, in the water, his beard is awash; under his beard and above his head is the high heaven. Those meadows are not meadows, but a green belt encircling the middle of the round sky.
>
> (Gogol, *Terrible Vengeance*)

> You think, on the cheeks of the café
> It's the sun that lovingly caresses?
> That's once again General Gallifet
> Coming to shoot down the rebels.
>
> (Mayakovsky, *A Cloud in Pants*)

(Incidentally erotic poetry is rich in examples of reverse parallelism.) Let us suppose we have a real image: a head. The metaphor: a beer mug. An example of negative paralellism would be "that's not a mug but a head." Logical reduction of the parallelism is a simile: "a head like a beer mug." And, finally, the development in time of a reverse parallel, a metamorphosis: "the head became a beer mug" ("the head is no longer a head but a beer mug").

.   .   .

There is an example of realized simile in Khlebnikov's play *Death's Mistake (Oshibka smerti)*. The lady death says that her head is as empty as a drinking glass. The guest asks for a drinking glass. Death unscrews her head.

.   .   .

And here is an example of realized hyperbole:

I flew off like a curse
My other foot was already in the next street[13] (Mayakovsky).

The realized oxymoron betrays its essentially verbal nature; though it has meaning, it does not have anything which could be called, in the terminology of contemporary philosophy, a *proper object* (as, for example, a "squared circle"). The character Kovalev in Gogol's story *The Nose* recognizes the nose as such even though it shrugs its shoulders, is in full uniform, and so forth.

.   .   .

Notice also the description of a miracle from one of the saints' lives in *The Brothers Karamazov* (in a humorous application): "The saint was tortured for his faith, and when they cut off his head at last, he got up, picked up the head, and politely kissed it."

In this case a human being is simply a traditional semantic unit which retains all of its attributes; in other words the semantic unit has become fixed.

The abrogation of the boundary between real and figurative meanings is characteristic of poetic language. Poetic language frequently operates with real images as though they were purely verbal figures (the device of reverse realization). Such is the case with puns.

.   .   .

1. In Dostoevsky's *Brothers Karamazov* there is a conversation between a marquis, who is ailing, and his spiritual father, a Jesuit: "Even

if a stern fate has deprived you of your nose, you may derive profit from this in that no one your whole life long will dare to tell you that your nose has been tweaked."[14] "Good father . . . . I would on the contrary be willing to have my nose tweaked every day of my life if only that nose were in its proper place."—"My son . . . since you proclaim that you would gladly have your nose tweaked all your life, then I must say that even in this your desire has been indirectly satisfied, since, because you've lost your nose, by that very fact you've had your nose tweaked."

2. And from *Anna Karenina*: "She brought back with her Vronsky's shadow," said the envoy's wife. "Well, what of it? There's a Grimm fairy tale: a man is without his *shadow*, it's been taken away from him as a punishment for something. I could never understand why it was a punishment. But it would be very unpleasant for a woman without her shadow." "Yes, but women *with shadows* usually end badly."

It is the conversion of real images into figures, their metaphorization, that forms the basis of symbolism as a poetic school.

The idea of space as a pictorial convention, a kind of ideograph of time, has penetrated the study of painting, but the problem of time and space as forms of poetic language is still a stranger to scholarship. The fact that language does violence to literary space is especially clear in the example of descriptions, where items that coexist spatially are arranged in temporal sequence. On this ground Lessing either rejects descriptive poetry or else fully accepts the violence done by language, insisting upon motivating narrative temporal sequence by actual temporal sequence, that is to say by describing an object as it comes into being, a suit as its pants are put on by the wearer, and so forth.

Concerning literary time, the device of temporal displacement offers a rich field for investigation. I've already cited the remark of a critic that "Byron began his stories either in the middle or at the end." Or consider Tolstoy's *The Death of Ivan Ilych*, where the denouement is given before the story begins; and Goncharov's *Oblomov*, where a temporal displacement is motivated by the hero's dream; and many other examples. There is a certain type of reader who foists this device on any literary work by starting to read at the end of the story. We find in Edgar Allan Poe's *The Raven* a kind of laboratory experiment in the device of temporal shift: only at the very end are things, as it were, turned inside out.

Khlebnikov offers an example of the *realization* of a temporal shift, and one, moreover, which is "laid bare" (*obnazhenny*), that is to say, not motivated, in his *World from the End* (*Mirskontsa*) . . . which has the effect of a motion picture film run backwards.

. . .

Another kind of temporal displacement favored by Khlebnikov is the anachronism. Take for example the poem *Uchimitsa* where the heroine is a student in the modern Bestuzhev Institute while the hero is the boyar's son Volodimirko. Or take *The Granddaughter of Malusha* (*Vnuchka Malushy*) which reminds us of Tolstoy's "Hero-Flood," with the sole exception that the temporal shift in Khlebnikov is not logically motivated (see below for unmotivated similes).

In the story *Ka* a whole series of time factors are woven together: "He has no outposts in time. Ka moves from dream to dream, intersects time and achieves bronzes (the bronzes of time). He disposes himself in the centuries as comfortably as in a swing. And isn't it so that the consciousness brings various times together just as an armchair and straight chairs are brought together by a drawingroom."

Certain of Khlebnikov's works are composed by arbitrarily stringing together various story elements. Such is *The Little Devil* (*Chortik*), and perhaps also *Children of Vydra* (*Deti Vydry*). (When story elements are arbitrarily arranged they don't follow one after another by logical necessity but are linked on the principle of formal likeness or contrast; we may compare the *Decameron*, where the stories of each day are linked only by similar plot situations.) This device has an ancient sanction, but in Khlebnikov's case it is "laid bare," that is, no line of justification is provided.

. . .

III

Colloquial speech provides the material for a major part of Khlebnikov's works. This reminds us of Mallarmé, who once said that he offered the bourgeois words which the latter reads every day in his newspapers but offered them in a startling context.

Only against the background of the familiar does the unfamiliar reach and impress us. There comes a time when the traditional poetic language hardens into stereotype and is no longer capable of being felt but is experienced rather as a ritual, as a holy text in which even the errors are considered sacred. The language of poetry is as it were covered by a veneer—and neither its tropes nor its poetic licenses any longer speak to the consciousness.

Form takes possession of the matter; the matter is totally dominated by the form. Then form becomes stereotype, and it is no longer alive. When this happens an access of new verbal material is required, an addition of fresh elements from the everyday language, to the end that the irrational structures of poetry may once again disturb us, may once again hit a vital spot.

Russian poetry has developed by way of constantly appropriating elements from the living language. This has been so from Simeon Polotsky[15] through Lomonosov,[16] Derzhavin, Pushkin, and Nekrasov[17] —and an example of the same process in our own day is Mayakovsky. The critics of Pushkin's day had reason to be horrified at his "skates loudly cutting the ice," and at that "awkward goose with its red pads," or at the "beaver collar silvered with frosty dust."

[We omit an example from Pushkin's poetry of lines of lines considered quite simple and clear by modern critics, but which seemed strained and difficult to contemporaries.]

The gradual wearing away of artistic form is characteristic of art forms other than poetry. Hanslick[18] offers examples of analogical developments in music:

> How many of Mozart's compositions were in their day considered the last word in the daring expression of fiery passion . . . Mozart's bursts of hot emotion, of fierce struggle, or of bitter and burning pain were at one time contrasted with that sense of a calm and pure enjoyment of life which supposedly flowed from the symphonies of Haydn. And twenty or thirty years later the same problem arose in comparing Mozart with Beethoven. The place of Mozart as a representative of violent impetuous emotion was taken by Beethoven, while Mozart was elevated to the Olympus of classical form occupied by Haydn. The well-known axiom that the "truly beautiful" (and who's to judge of that?) never, even over a long period, loses its charm has long since become an empty phrase if it is applied to music. Music is like nature, which each autumn sees hundreds of flowers wither, only to be replaced by new ones. A piece of music is a human thing, the product of a certain person, time, and cultural milieu, and therefore it always bears within itself the seeds of a more or less rapid death. . . . Both the performers and the audience feel a natural attraction to musical novelty. Critics who have learned how to honor what is old and established but haven't the heart to recognize what's new are guilty of destroying the productive forces (from *On the Beautiful in Music*).

Symbolist literary criticism in Russia at the present time suffers from just such an uneasiness about novelty. "Lyric poetry can be properly assessed only after the poet has passed away," they say (from *Works and Days* [*Trudy i dni*], No. 3, 1920).

And consider Bryusov's opinion that "it's hard to evaluate and judge a poet before his career is completed. Our opinion of Goethe's *Werther* is far different from that of his contemporaries who read it when it first appeared and could not know that Goethe would one day write the two parts of *Faust*" (from *Those Distant and Near* [*Dalekie i blizkie*], p. 54).

It follows as a natural conclusion that we should observe pictures only in museums, only after they've been covered with the moss of centuries. And the conclusion also follows that the poetic language of the past must be preserved; that the diction, syntax, and word usage of an earlier generation must be imposed as a norm.

Poetry makes use of "unusual words." Specific cases of "unusual words" are those which are in need of a gloss, a special explanation (*glossy*). In this class are archaisms, barbarisms, and provincialisms. But the symbolists forget something that was quite clear to Aristotle, namely that "one and the same word can be both a 'gloss' and in common use, but not for the same people"; they forget that what was a "gloss" for Pushkin is a stereotype in the contemporary poetic language. For instance Vyacheslav Ivanov[19] even goes so far as to recommend to beginning poets that they try to use in the main only Pushkinian words: if a word is in Pushkin that in itself is a criterion of its poetic quality.

IV

Khlebnikov's syntax (some observations). In the Russian language word order is almost never a determinant of meaning. The matter is somewhat different, however, in Russian poetry, where the regular intonation of everyday language is broken down. There is a sharp syntactic shift from the norms of everyday language even in the poetry of the Pushkin school, and in Mayakovsky's radical rhythmic reform we observe the same phenomenon. When we turn to the poetry of Khlebnikov, however, we find that in this respect it is atypical.

. . .

According to Peshkovsky[20] "Verb usage is the basic form of our linguistic cerebration. The predicate—the verb—is the most important member of the sentence and of our speech in general."

However in poetic language there is often a marked tendency toward verblessness. Fet's[21] verbless experiments immediately come to mind, and these inspired Khlebnikov to close imitation: "Whispering, muttering, rapture's groan, dark red of shame."

.   .   .

V

[We omit a brief section in which Jakobson deals with Khlebnikov's tendency to select epithets for euphonic rather than semantic reasons: for example, "strange fear"—*stranny strakh;* "full flame"—*polny plamen.*]

Often enough the function of an epithet is simply to emphasize an attribute as a syntactic fact; we have to do here with a "stripping bare of the attribute." O. M. Brik[22] has made the acute observation that the poets of the Pushkin "Pleiade" accomplished this in two ways: either by the use of what he calls "indifferent epithets," for instance *"pure* beauty," *"divine* head," or even "a *certain* czar in a *certain* year"; or by the use of strained epithets having, as one of Pushkin's contemporaries put it, "no concrete relationship to the noun they qualify," and which the critic proposed to call "adherent" rather than "adjective" forms. This latter type of epithet is quite characteristic of Khlebnikov. Examples:

> A crown of clever petals (khitrykh lepestkov)
> Wise petals (lepestki mudrye)
> In the wise woods (v umnykh lesakh).

Epithets in Khlebnikov's early (impressionistic) things are often created by a certain situation, for instance:

> And the evening wine (i vechernyee vino)
> And the evening women (i verchernye zhenshchiny)
> Woven into a single wreath (spletayutsya v yediny venok).

Similes. The problem of Khlebnikov's similes is extremely complicated. I offer here only certain guideposts. What is a poetic simile? If we ignore for the moment its function as a factor making for symmetry, we may characterize the simile as one of the methods for introducing into the poetic situation an order of facts not occasioned by the logical movement of the narration. Khlebnikov's similes are hardly ever motivated by any impression of real similarity of objects, but are simply compositional effects.

If we accept Khlebnikov's statement that there are words with which we see—"word-eyes"—and words with which we "do"—"word-hands"—and if we apply this formulation to similes we will see that Khlebnikov's similes are precisely "simile-hands."

Contamination of comparisons is common in his work:

"Like a black sail on the white sea its fierce pupils cut the eyes aslant: the frightening white eyes were raised toward the brows in the head of the dead one hanging by a braid" (from *Yesir*).

We have here a contamination of qualities: in color—white and black, and line—sail and sea.

.   .   .

Often enough the subject of a simile is selected not so much because of its similarity to the object of the simile, but rather in a different and larger context. . . . For instance:

> Dear city, there's something of an old lady in you:
> She seats herself on her box and would eat a bit,
> Shakes her babushka, and it's not a simple babushka,
> From one side to the other a flock of black birds flies.

The network of analogies Khlebnikov offers is very complex. Space and time are juxtaposed, visual and auditory perceptions, personages and action.

"Terrible is the hunt when the sedge is years—and the game—generations."

"And your eyes are a hut where two stepmother-spinners work the spindle."

.   .   .

VI

That focus upon expression, upon the verbal mass itself, which I have called the only essential characteristic of poetry, is directed not only to the form of the phrase, but also to the form of the word itself. Mechanical associations between sound and meaning are established more easily as they become more habitual. For this reason the everyday practical language is extremely conservative: the form of a word rapidly ceases to be felt.

In poetry, on the other hand, the operation of mechanical association is reduced to a minimum, while the dissociation of verbal elements acquires great importance. Dissociated fragments are readily combined into new formations. Dead affixes come to life.

Dissociation may be quite arbitrary, done simply for the purpose of devising new suffixes (a process familiar in everyday speech, take for example the form *golubchik* ["darling," based on *golub*–"dove"] but in poetry the process is greatly intensified). Take, for example, the invented forms used in children's language: sokh*run*, mok*run* (based on *sokh*–"dry," and *mokr*–"wet").

Poetry has from the earliest times engaged in play with suffixes; but only in modern poetry, and particularly in Khlebnikov, has this device become conscious, and as it were legitimate.

[Here Jakobson gives a number of examples from literature—Russian folklore, children's jingles, charms, and popular songs—which show the tendency in certain speech situations to augment and enrich the normal word forms by attaching various new suffixes. Most of these are untranslatable, though analogical processes in English might be found. Examples: *khleby–khlebisty, begunki–begut, skripulki–skripyat* (from *khleb*–"bread," *beg*–"speed," *skrip*–"squeak.")]

The possibility of isolating in a given word those parts which belong to the root and those forms which are appended to the root arises as a result of the mental association of these elements in the given word with corresponding elements in other combinations and in other words.

In the poems of Khlebnikov which give free reign to verbal creativity, we find juxtaposed as a rule either 1) neologisms with identical roots but different formants (prefixes, suffixes, and affixes), or 2) neologisms with identical formants and different roots. But in a poem the dissociation takes place not within the given structure of a language as a whole, as we have observed happening in the practical language, but within the framework of a particular poem, which as it were forms a closed linguistic system.

Let us see some examples.

1. First, we observe cases in which the root remains unchanged but the formants are different; in other words, we have a complex tautological construction, or a kind of "laying bare" of the "paregmenon" of classical rhetoric. Khlebnikov frequently uses productive extension of words without any logical justification, and this quite apart from the introduction of neologisms.

> O laugh it up you laughletes!
> O laugh it out you laughletes!
> That laugh with laughs, that laugherize laughily
> O laugh it out so laughily
> O of laughing at laughilies—
>   the laugh of laughish laugherators

Laughterly, laughterly
Outlaugh, downlaugh, laughlets, laughlets.
Laughulets, laughulets
O laugh it up you laughers!
O laugh it up you laughers!

(O rassmeytes smekhachi!
O zasmeytes smekhachi!
Chto smeyutsya smekhami, chto smeyanstvuyut smeyalno
    O zasmeytes usmeyalno
O rassmeshishch nadsmeyalnykh—
    smekh nadsmeynykh smekhachei, etc.)

2. The second type of example involves identical formants but with different root materials. Such forms often rhyme, as though in contradiction to the tendency of modern poetry not to rhyme identical parts of speech. The essence of rhyme according to Shcherba's formulation lies in the recognition of rhythmically repeated similar phonetic elements; but in the present case it consists in the segregation of identical formants, which facilitates dissociation.

[Jakobson here gives two sets of examples, in the first of which all of the words involved are neologisms, while in the second some are words used in the everyday language. The examples are not translatable, but the point is clear from a transliteration of some of them:

letaya nebu rad zorir
Sladok, dumaet gorir;
vezde presleduet mogun
vezde presleduet begun]

Economy of words is a virtue alien to poetry, except where it is justified by some special poetic purpose. Neologisms enrich poetry in three ways: 1. They create a bright euphonic interlude, while the established words become phonetically obsolete, being worn out by constant use, and, most important, because they are only partially apprehended in their phonetic patterns; 2. In the practical language the form of the word is no longer appreciated; it is dormant and petrified. However we cannot help apprehending the form of a poetic neologism, given so to speak *in statu nascendi;* 3. The meaning of a word at any given moment is more or less static, but the meaning of a neologism is to a significant extent defined by its context, while at the same time it may oblige the reader to a certain etymological cerebration. And incidentally etymology always plays a role in poetry. Two types of situations are possible in this connection:

A) *A renovation of meaning*, for instance in Derzhavin's *tuchnye tuchi*.[23] Such a renewal can be effected not only by the juxtaposition of words having one and the same root, but also by using a word in its literal meaning which the everyday language uses only figuratively that is, "the *great bulk* of bad weather," "a cloud *lightninglike* and black.[24]

B) Poetic etymology. This process is analogous to the popular etymology of practical language. Professor Zubaty[25] has offered some very interesting examples from Lithuanian folklore. Here is a Russian translation which approximates the original: *"Pyat volkov volka voloklo"* ("Five wolves dragged the wolf").

·   ·   ·

In the poem *To Madame Lenin* (*Gospozhe Lenin*) we find another type of fractional semantic unit. Here Khlebnikov has tried to find, as he himself put it, "infinitesimals" of artistic language. There is no complete character; instead he is split up into a number of constituent voices: the voice of sight, of hearing, of reason, of fear, and so on. What we have here is a kind of "realized synechdoche." Consider also the story *Ka*, where the soul is divided into constituent personages: Ka, Khu, and Ba.

Semantic deformation in poetry occurs in many different ways, and parallel to it we have also phonetic deformations. Take, for example, the splitting of words, A) for rhythmic purposes (in Horace, in Annensky,[26] and in Mayakovsky), or, B) the insertion of one word into another, a device not uncongenial to Khlebnikov (for instance his etymology *Po-do-l, ko-do-l*). That device was even used by the Latin poets, by Vergil, for instance; *"cere-*comminuit-*brum."*

Examples of this can be found in contemporary poetry, for instance in Mayakovsky, where there is however a measure of logical justification:

They were talking on the sidewalk	(Vygovorili na trottuare
"Pos-	"Poch-
And the car wheel turned again	Perekinulos na shinu
-toffice."	-ta")

Shifts of accent also come under the heading of phonetic deformation.

[Jakobson gives a number of untranslatable examples from folklore of words accented abnormally, as also of cases where poetry makes use of accentual "doublets," offering more than one accented form when more than one is possible.]

[We omit some untranslatable examples of phonetic and semantic deformation in which, as Jakobson puts it, the verbal form, both internal and external, is fully experienced, though the words are empty of content—ed.] . . .

. . .

VII

Poetic language possesses a certain rather elementary device: the rapprochement and commingling of distinct units of speech.

In the area of semantics varieties of this device are known as: the simile, which is a particular case of parallelism; the metamorphosis, in other words a parallelism developed in time; and metaphor, or a parallelism reduced to a single point.

In the area of euphony we find the following varieties of the device: rhyme, assonance, and alliteration (or sound repetition).

It is possible to produce verses characterized by an emphasis primarily on euphony. But is this sort of emphasis equivalent to the accentuation of pure sound? If the answer is yes then we have a species of vocal music, and vocal music of an inferior kind at that.

Euphony operates, however, not with sounds but with phonemes, that is, with acoustical impressions which are capable of being associated with meaning.

. . .

The form of a word can be apprehended only as it is a regular and repeated part of a given linguistic system. A totally isolated form dies out; and similarly a sound combination in a given poem (which is a kind of linguistic system *in statu nascendi*) becomes a kind of "sound image" (O. S. Brik's term[27]) and is apprehended only as a repeated part of a poem's system of "sound images."

In modern poetry special attention is given to consonants and, therefore, sound repetitions of the type AB, ABC, and so forth, are often illuminated by *poetic* etymology in such a way that the concept of basic meaning is linked with repeated clusters of consonants, while the differing vowel sounds come to seem as it were an inflection of the root, having the formal significance either of word-formants or of word-modifiers.

The following important statement of Khlebnikov characterizes poetic etymology as a fact of linguistic cerebration:

Have you ever heard of internal declension? Case forms within the word? If the genitive case answers the question "whence?" and the accusative and dative cases answer the question "whither?" and "where?" then the inflection of the root in those cases ought in the same way to give the resulting words opposite meanings. . . . Thus *bobr* (beaver) and *babr* (tiger) which mean respectively a harmless rodent and a fierce predator and which are formed by the accusative and genitive cases of the common root *bo-*, illustrate by their very structure that a *bobr-* should be hunted as a prize, while a *babr-* should be feared, since man himself might well become the object of the hunt. In this case the simplest form changes, by alteration of cases, the sense of the word structure. In the one word it is indicated that the action of struggle was directed at the beast (accusative case "whither?") and in the other word that the action arises from the beast (genitive case "whence?"). Similarly *beg* (flight) is occasioned by fear, while *Bog* (God) is a being toward whom fear ought to be directed. Thus the words *les* (forest) and *lysy* (bald), or take two words that are even more alike *lysina* (bald spot), and *lesina* (wooded spot), whose meaning involves the presence or absence of a certain kind of growth, you know what *lysaya gora* (bald mountain) means—bald mountains are hills or heads deprived of forest— these words arose through the alteration of the direction of a simple word by its declension in the accusative and the dative cases. . . . And so in other examples the sounds e and y are evidences of different cases of one and the same root. The area from which *les* has disappeared is called *lysina*. Similarly *byk* (bull) indicates that object from which a blow is to be expected, while *bok* (flank) indicates the place toward which the blow is to be directed. (*Union of Youth, Almanac No. 3*)

[We omit two pages of examples of "root inflection" taken from the works of Khlebnikov, Aseev, Mayakovsky, and Guro.[28] Some typical examples:

The girls are wondering (Devitsy divyatsya)
  On this night even the grave might love (V etu noch lyubit i mogila mogla)
Our god is speed (Nash bog beg).

We omit also two pages which give a wealth of examples of complex consonantal structure in Khlebnikov's poetry, which Jakobson analyzes according to the sound sequences that occur, for instance

N-G: I v utonnykh negakh snega (In the buried luxury of snow)
B-L, R-Z: bylykh belykh grez zari (The one-time white dreams of
dawn).]

The practical language offers examples of the substitution of an
initial consonant by analogy (for example, *devyat* [nine], a form
which arose on the analogy of *desyat* [ten]); this kind of development is even more common in slips of the tongue; for instance, the
anticipation of the first sound of a following word: *skap stoit* instead
of *shkap stoit* ("the cupboard stands"), where the initial sound "s" is
substituted for "sh." Or the reverse of that: *lesa lostut* in place of *lesa
rastut* ("the forests grow").

In the poetry of Khlebnikov this linguistic phenomenon is used as
a poetic device: an initial consonant is often replaced by another
drawn from other poetic roots. The word in question thus gains as it
were a new sound character. Its meaning wavers, and the word is
apprehended as an acquaintance with a suddenly unfamiliar face, or
as a stranger in whom we are able to see something familiar.

[We omit additional examples, along with a lengthy footnote in
which Jakobson outlines a method for a phonetic analysis of the paired
words, usually without definite meaning, that occur in various languages, for example in Russian, *gusli-musli*, *gogol mogol*; in English we
might suggest such pairs as *higgledy-piggledy*, *hurly-burly*.]

VIII

The play on synonyms is a kind of partial emancipation of words from
meaning, that is to say, the second word does not contribute a new
meaning, while, on the other hand, it offers the possibility of a differentiation of semantic nuances. Examples:

He is naked and bare (On gol i nag)
Know and realize (Znay i veday)
Who is our comrade and friend? (Kto nam tovarishch i drug)

The play on homonyms is exactly the opposite of the play on synonyms, but both are based on an incongruity between the unit of
meaning and the word itself. A parallel situation in painting is the
use of free-flowing color. Examples:

The braid (or scythe, another meaning of *kosa*—ed.) sometimes adorns
the head, hanging down to the shoulders, sometimes cuts the grass. (Kosa
to ukrashaet temya, spuskayas na plechi, to kosit travu).

[We omit two pages of examples of play on homonyms and synonyms taken from Russian folklore, children's songs, and from Bryusov and Khlebnikov. The last of these examples, from Khlebnikov, involves synonyms of opposite grammatical gender. Jakobson elucidates.]

The final example is interesting as an indicator of the compulsive influence of grammatical gender on the verbal image itself. When they are personified, words of feminine gender will be represented by female persons, and words of masculine gender by male persons. For example, when a Russian imagines the days of the week as persons he will see Monday and Sunday (masculine and neuter, respectively) as men, and Wednesday (feminine) as a woman. It is interesting that the Russian painter Repin should have been surprised that Stuck[29] represented sin (in German *die Sünde*, feminine, in Russian *grekh*, masculine) as a woman. . . .

Foreign and dialect words are sometimes favored for purposes of synonymic play:

There half-fearfully they moan: God (Tam poluboyazlivo stonut: Bog)
There they quietly whisper: *Gott* (Tam shepchut tikho: Gott)
There they moan briefly: *dieu* (Tam stonut kratko: de)

Foreign words in general are widely used in poetry because their sound patterns offer a surprise, while their meaning is muted.

. . .

IX

Just as semantic correspondences are weak in modern poetry, so rhyme, as a euphonic correspondence, is only approximate (similarities are experienced against a background of contrast). As concerns the sound pattern of Khlebnikov's rhymes, and indeed of rhyme in modern Russian poetry as a whole, the following features should be noted as characteristic:

1. Consonants have greater weight than vowels. This is true of modern euphonic patterns in general.

. . .

2. The distinction between hard and palatalized consonants is to a large extent lost for purposes of rhyme.

Vowels are characterized acoustically by variations in the height of their basic tones; similarly the distinction between palatalized and un-palatalized consonants is in their basic tone. Thus it would seem that the evolution of poetic euphony parallels the evolution of modern music: the deveolpment has been from emphasis on tone, in the direction of emphasis on sound.

3. Poets of the Pushkin school focused primarily upon the final sounds in making their rhymes, while modern poetry gives more importance to supporting sounds; agreement of the final sounds is not obligatory.

4. Consonants are not necessarily identical, but need only be similar in their acoustic effect.

5. The order of consonants in the rhyming words need not be identical (rhyme-metathesis is possible).

6. Accents in the rhyming words need not be identical.

. . . .

Khlebnikov to some extent "lays bare" the repetition of consonant sounds: often enough the word combinations that form the repetition have practically no logical justification:

> Polna soblazna i bela (Full of temptation and white)
> Ona zabyla pro belila (She forgot about the whiting).

[There follow a number of examples of sound repetition *for its own sake* from Pushkin, from Khlebnikov, and from popular jingles.]

Many examples could be given which show that in the poetry of Khlebnikov meaning is reduced in importance and euphonic constructions are created for their own sake. From this point it is only a step to the creation of a completely arbitrary language.

As Khlebnikov put it,

> My first idea in dealing with language is to find . . . a touchstone for the transformation of all Slavic words one into another, for the free fusion of all Slavic words. Such is the self-valuing word without relation to life or use. And seeing that all roots are simply phantoms behind which stand the living strings of the alphabet, the discovery of the general unity of all world languages, built out of the units of the alphabet—such is my second purpose. This is the way to the discovery of a worldwide trans-sense language.

Such arbitrary word-building may be associated in the forms it uses with the Russian language:

> Von tam na dorozhke bely vstal i stoit *vidennega*
> Vecher li derevo l prikhot moya?
> Akh, pozvolte mne eto slovo v vide negi.

Words of this type are as it were seeking a meaning for themselves. Here it is perhaps mistaken to speak of the complete absence of semantic sense. Such a word is rather an example of a negative internal form, as, for example, (according to Fortunatov[30]) the nominative case *dom* (where there is a *zero* case ending) is a word with negative external form.

The second type of arbitrary word-building avoids any correlation with a given poetic language. This is the case for example with the "talking in tongues" of religious sectarians: the creators of such speech believe that their words are related to foreign tongues. Khlebnikov's "trans-sense" (*zaumnye*) words are motivated by the idea, for example that they are written in bird language (*Mudroyat v silke*), apes' language (*Ka*), demons' language (*Noch v Galitsii*).

Even the motivation itself may be "trans-sense" in nature:

Bobeobi sang the lips	Bobeobi pelis guby
Veeomi sang the eyes	Veeomi pelis vzory
Lieeei sang the visage	Lieeei pelsya oblik
Gzi-gzi-gzeo sang the chain	Gzi-gzi gzeo pelas tsep
Thus on the canvas of certain correspondences	Tak na kholste kakikh-to sootvetstvii
Without extension lived the face	Vne protyazheniya zhilo litso.

We have seen in a number of examples how the word in Khlebnikov's poetry loses its concrete content and even loses its inner and finally even its outward form. It has been observed many times in the history of the poetry of all peoples and countries that, as Tredyakovsky[31] put it, for the poet "only sound" is important. The language of poetry strives to reach, as a final limit, the phonetic, or rather—to the extent that such a purpose may be present—the euphonic phrase—in other words, a trans-sense speech.

But concerning the limit of this striving Khlebnikov characteristically remarks: "When I wrote the words of Ikhnaton before his death, 'manch, manch,' they produced on me an unbearable effect. Now I hardly feel them anymore. I don't know why."

TRANSLATED BY E. J. BROWN

VLADIMIR MAYAKOVSKY

V. V. Khlebnikov

. . . Khlebnikov's poetical fame is immeasurably less than his significance.

For every hundred readers, fifty considered him simply a graphomaniac, forty read him for pleasure and were astonished that they found none, and only ten (futurist poets and philologists of the "OPOYAZ")[1] knew and loved this Columbus, this discoverer of new poetic continents that we now populate and cultivate.

Khlebnikov is not a poet for consumers—they can't read him. Khlebnikov is a poet for producers.

Khlebnikov never completed any extensive and finished poetic works. The apparent finished state of his published pieces is most often the work of his friends' hands. We chose from the pile of his discarded notebooks those that seemed most valuable to us and we published them. Often the tail of one draft was pasted to an extraneous head, to Khlebnikov's cheerful astonishment. You couldn't let him have anything to do with proofs: he would cross out everything completely and give you an entirely new text.

When bringing something in for publication, Khlebnikov usually remarked, "If something isn't right, change it." When he recited his poems he would sometimes break off in the middle of a sentence and indicate simply "et cetera."

In this "etc." is the whole of Khlebnikov: he posed a poetic task, provided the means for its solution, but the use of this solution for practical purposes, this he left to others.

The story of Khlebnikov's life is worthy of his brilliant literary constructions; it is an example to real poets and a reproach to hacks.

What about Khlebnikov and poetic language?

From "V. V. Khlebnikov," by V. Mayakovsky, in *Krasneya nov* (Moscow, July-August, 1922.)

83

For the so-called new poetry (our latest), and especially for the symbolists, the word is the raw material for the writing of verses (expressions of feelings and thoughts)—a raw material, the texture, resistance, and treatment of which was unknown. This raw material the new poets dealt with intuitively, first in one poem and then in another. The alliterative accidents of similar-sounding words were taken to be an internal cohesion, and to signify an unbreakable relationship. The established form of a word was considered to be permanent and some poets tried to fit it over things that went far beyond the verbal material itself.

For Khlebnikov, the word is an independent force which organizes the raw material of thoughts and feelings. Hence the delving into roots, into the source of the word, into the time when the name corresponded to things—when there were only ten root words, but new words appeared as case modifications of the root (declension of the root, according to Khlebnikov). For example, *byk* ("bull")—that which hits—*byot; bok* ("side")—the place *where* it hits. Or *lys* ("bald")—that which the forest (*les*) becomes; *los* ("elk"), *lis* ("fox")—those who live in the forest.

Take Khlebnikov's lines

> Lesa lysy.
> Lesa obezlosili. Lesa obezlisili.
> (The forests are bald/bare.
> The forests are elkless. The forests are foxless.)

These lines may not be broken apart. They are an iron chain.

·   ·   ·

The word as we think of it now is a completely arbitrary thing useful for practical purposes. But a word in its proper poetic function must express a wide variety of nuances of meaning.

Khlebnikov created an entire "periodic table of the word." Taking the word in its undeveloped unfamiliar forms, comparing these with the developed word, he demonstrated the necessity and inevitability of the emergence of new words.

If the existing word *plyas* ("dance") has a derivative *plyasunya* ("dancer"), then the growth of aviation, of "flying" (*lyot*), ought by analogy to yield the form *letunya* ("flier"). And if the day of christening is *krestiny*, then the day of flying is, of course, *letiny*. There is, of course, no trace here of cheap Slavophile slapping together of roots.

It is not important that the word *letunya* is for the present neither necessary nor established in usage. Khlebnikov is simply revealing the process of word formation.

Khlebnikov, however, is a master of verse.

I've already said that Khlebnikov did not have any finished compositions. In his last piece, *Zangezi,* for example, you clearly feel that two different variants have been published together. But in studying Khlebnikov you must take into account fragments of poems that contribute to the solution of poetic problems.

In all Khlebnikov's things you are struck by his unprecedented skill. He could not only quickly write a poem upon request (his mind worked on poetry twenty-four hours a day), but he could also give things the most unusual form. He wrote a very long poem, for instance, that's simply a palindrome; it may just as easily be read from right to left as from left to right:

> Koni Topot. Inok.
> No ne rech, a cheren on.
> (Horses, Clapping, Monk.
> But no speech, black he is.)

This, of course, is just a deliberate trick, the result of an excess of poetic inventiveness. But Khlebnikov was very little interested in trickery: he made things neither for self-display nor for the market.

Philological work brought Khlebnikov to a kind of poetry that develops a lyrical theme through variations on the root of a single word.

His best known poem, *Zaklyatie smekhom* (*Incantation by Laughter*), published in 1909, is a favorite of poets, innovators, and parodists, and of critics too:

> O laugh it up you laughletes! . . .
> That laugh with laughs
> That laugherize laughily.
> O laugh it out so laughily . . . the laugh
> of laughish laugherators.
> (O, zasmeytes, smekhachi,
> Chto smeyutsya smekhami,
> Chto smeyanstvuyut smeyalno,
> O, issmeysya rassmeyalno smekh
> Usmeynykh smeyachey. . . .)

Here the one word *smekh* ("laughter") yields *smeyevo,* the "country of laughter," and the sly *smeyunchiki* ("laughers"), and *smekhachi* (perhaps "laughletes")—by analogy with *silachi* ("athletes").

In comparison with Khlebnikov how verbally wretched is Balmont when he attempts to construct a poem using only the word *lyubit* ("to love"):

> Love, love, love, love,
> Madly love love itself.
> (Lyubite, lyubite, lyubite, lyubite,
> Bezumno lyubite, lyubite lyubov.)

This is mere tautology. Mere word poverty. And this is offered as a complete definition of love! Khlebnikov once submitted for publication six pages of derivations of the root *lyub* ("love"). It couldn't be published because the provincial typographer didn't have enough of the letter "l."

.   .   .

One other thing. I intentionally omit mention of those immense works of historical fantasy that Khlebnikov wrote, since their foundation is—poetry itself.

But what of Khlebnikov's life?

His own words describe that life better than anything else:

> Today again I will go there—
> Into the marketplace, to life,
> And a troop of songs I will lead
> In single combat with the market's roar.
> (Segodnya snova ya poydu
> Tuda—na zhizn, na torg, na rynok,
> I voysko pesen povedu
> S priboem rynka v poedinok.)

I knew Khlebnikov for twelve years. He came to Moscow often, and then, except for the last days, we met daily.

Khlebnikov's work never failed to amaze me. His empty room was always heaped with notebooks, paper, and scraps filled up with his minute handwriting. If there hadn't happened to occur, by chance, a publication at about this time of a collection of his pieces, and if someone had not extracted from the pile of manuscripts some publishable pages, then surely very much would have been lost. For Khlebnikov when he traveled stuffed his pillowcase with manuscripts, used them for a pillow, and then promptly lost the pillow.

Khlebnikov traveled often. The reason for these travels and their duration no one could ever hope to understand. Three years ago, after a great deal of difficulty, I succeeded in arranging a paying publication of some of his pieces (Khlebnikov had given me a rather large sheaf of confused manuscripts chosen in Prague by Jakobson, who had written a singularly excellent work on Khlebnikov).[2] On the evening of the day we had told Khlebnikov that permission would be granted and money received, I met him on Theatrical Square. He was carrying a small suitcase.

"Where are you going?"

"South. It's spring!" and he left.

He left riding the roof of a railway coach. He was gone two years. He retreated and attacked with our army in Persia, caught typhus several times, and then last winter returned again, this time in a coach for epileptics, exhausted and ragged, wearing nothing but a hospital robe.

He brought back with him not a single line. Of what he wrote during this period I know only the poem about hunger that was published in some Crimean newspaper, and two astonishing handwritten books, *Harmonious World* (*Ladomir*) and *A Scratch in the Clouds* (*Tsarapina po nebu*), which he had sent on earlier.

Harmonious World was submitted to the State Publishing House, but it never succeeded in being published. Could Khlebnikov ever have beaten that wall down with his head?

In practical matters Khlebnikov was an altogether disorganized person. He published not a single line on his own initiative. In his eulogy to Khlebnikov, Gorodetsky virtually attributes organizational talent to the poet: the creation of futurism, the publication of *A Slap in the Face of Public Taste* (*Poshchechina obshchestvennomu vkusu*), and so forth. This is completely false. Both *The Fishpond of Judges* (*Sadok sudey*, 1908),[3] in which appeared Khlebnikov's first poems, and the *Slap* were organized by David Burliuk. In order to involve Khlebnikov in anything you almost had to catch him with a snare. Of course, impracticality is detestable if it is the whim of a rich man, but with Khlebnikov, who hardly owned even his trousers, this indifference to his own advantage took on the character of genuine asceticism, a kind of martyrdom in the name of the poetic idea.

All who knew him loved Khlebnikov. But this was the love of the strong for a strong, extremely well-educated, and witty poet. He had no one of his own capable of caring for him. When he was ill he became very demanding and suspicious of people who did not give him their full attention. A sharp phrase, accidentally uttered without any reference to him, might be exaggerated and understood as disparagement of his poetry or disregard of him personally.

In the name of preserving a just literary perspective, I consider it my certain duty to publish in my own name and, I do not doubt, in the name of my friends the poets Aseev, Burliuk, Kruchonykh, Kamensky,[4] and Pasternak, the statement that we considered and do consider him one of our masters in the art of poetry, and a most magnificent knight in our poetic battles.

After Khlebnikov's death, there appeared in various journals and newspapers articles about him full of sympathy and understanding. I have read these articles with disgust. When will this comedy of posthumous kindness finally end? Where were those writers when Khlebnikov, abused by his critics, wandered about Russia alive? I know some still living who may not be his equals, but are neglected as much as he was.

Let us finally drop this reverence for hundred-year anniversaries, this honoring of posthumous publications! Let us have articles about the living! Let us have bread for the living! Let us have paper for the living!

TRANSLATED BY J. ROSENGRANT

On Khlebnikov

Speaking of Khlebnikov, you can avoid mentioning symbolism and futurism, and you don't have to mention trans-sense language (*zaum*) either. Because up till now such an approach has led not to a discussion of Khlebnikov, but of "something or someone and Khlebnikov": "Futurism and Khlebnikov," "Khlebnikov and Trans-Sense Language." "Khlebnikov and Mayakovsky" are rarely linked (but they have been), and "Khlebnikov and Kruchonykh" are often mentioned together.

This approach proves a false one. In the first place, both futurism and trans-sense language are not at all simple quantities, but rather complex names that cover a variety of phenomena, lexical units unifying various matters—something in the nature of a surname that serves not only people related to one another but others who happen to have the same last name.

After all, it's no accident Khlebnikov called himself *budetlyanin*[1] (not futurist), and it is no accident that this word has not stuck.

In the second place—and this is the main point—at different times generalizations will be made according to different indicators. Generally speaking, there is no such phenomenon as a personality "in general," a man "in general": in school his age is the standard; in a military company, his height. Military, medical, and class statistics will reckon the same person in different columns. Time passes—and time alters all generalization. And finally a time comes when there is a demand for the man himself. Writings on Pushkin treated him as a poet of romanticism, and Tyutchev[2] as a poet of the "German School." Reviewers could grasp this approach more readily, and textbooks found it more convenient.

Trends split up into schools; schools attenuate into groups.

"O Khlebnikove," in *Arkhaisty i novatory* (Leningrad, 1929).

89

But at this point Russian poetry and Russian literature must take a good look at Khlebnikov himself.

Why? Because suddenly a certain "and" of much greater proportions has come to light: "Modern Poetry *and* Khlebnikov" and a second "and" is already ripening: "Modern Literature *and* Khlebnikov."

II

When Khlebnikov died, one extremely cautious critic, perhaps just out of sheer caution, called all his work "clumsy attempts at revitalizing language and verse" and in the name "not only of literary conservatives" declared Khlebnikov's "unpoetic poetry" unnecessary. Of course, it all depends on what the critic understood by the word "literature." If by "literature" we should understand the periphery of literary and journalistic production and empty-headed, cautious ideas, he is correct. But there is a profound literature engaged in a harsh struggle for a new vision that has had its fruitless successes, made the conscious "mistakes" it needed to make, had its decisive uprisings, negotiations, battles, and deaths. And the deaths in this business are real, not metaphoric: the deaths of men and of generations.

III

It is a common notion that a teacher prepares for his students' acceptance. In point of fact just the opposite occurs: appreciation and acceptance of Tyutchev were prepared for by his pupil Fet and by the symbolists. What had seemed bold but unwarranted in Tyutchev in Pushkin's time, to Turgenev seemed illiterate, and Turgenev corrected Tyutchev. The poetic periphery was leveling the center. Only the symbolists restored the real meaning of Tyutchev's metrical "illiteracy." Likewise, Rimsky-Korsakov—musicians say—corrected the "illiterate" and "gawky" Moussorgsky whose music to this very day has been published only in part. Such "illiteracies" are illiterate, only in the sense that a phonetic transcription of language is "illiterate" when compared to Grot's[3] orthography. Many years pass while a principle ferments—subterranean and hidden—and at last it emerges onto the surface not as a "principle," but as a "phenomenon."

Khlebnikov's voice has already made itself heard in modern poetry: it has already created a ferment in the poetry of some; it has held private consultations with others. Students prepared the way for the acceptance of their teacher. The influence of his poetry is an accomplished fact. The influence of his lucid prose is a matter for the future.

IV

Verlaine distinguished between "poetry" and the "literature" of poetry. Perhaps there is "poetic poetry" and "literary poetry."

In this sense Khlebnikov's poetry, despite the fact that today's poetry secretly feeds on it, may be closest, not to that poetry, but, for instance, to today's painting. (Of course I'm not talking here about all of today's poetry, but about the mighty channel of the average poetry magazine that has suddenly come to claim attention.) At any rate, today's poetry prepared us for Khlebnikov's appearance in literature.

How does the process of literary materialization come about, the introduction into literary poetry of poetic poetry?

Baratynsky wrote:

> The thought first found embodiment
> In a poet's concentrated poem,
> Like a young maiden—obscure
> For an inattentive world;
> Later, emboldened, she has
> Already become evasive, talkative,
> She's plain to see on all sides,
> Like an experienced wife,
> In a novelist's unconstrained prose;
> Then, an old windbag, she,
> Giving forth an impudent shriek,
> Reproduces in journalistic polemics
> What has long been known to all.

If we toss out the reproachful and sarcastic tone of this poet-aristocrat, we are left with an accurate formula, one of the laws of literature.

The "young maiden" retains her youth, despite the novelist's prose and the journalistic polemics. Only she is no longer "obscure" to an inattentive world.

V

We are living in a great age; no one can have any doubts about it. But many use yesterday's criteria for various things; others—domestic criteria. A man's greatness is difficult to grasp. That is true in literature also. Dostoevsky wrote to Strakhov[4] apropos of the latter's book on Leo Tolstoy that he agreed with everything in this book except for one thing: that Tolstoy had uttered a new word in literature.

This was when *War and Peace* had already appeared. In Dostoevsky's opinion, neither Leo Tolstoy, nor he—Dostoevsky—nor Turgenev, had said anything new. Something new had been said earlier by Pushkin and Gogol. Dostoevsky did not say that out of humility. He had high standards; but then—and this is the main point—it is hard for a contemporary to see greatness in a contemporary, and it is even harder to see anything new in him. The issue of greatness is resolved through the centuries. Contemporaries always have a feeling of failure, a feeling that their literature is not successful, and a special failure is always something new in literature. Sumarokov,[5] a talented man of letters, said of Lomonosov, who was a literary genius: ". . . the poverty of his rhymes, the perplexing clusters of letters and pronunciation, the impurity of the verse composition, the ignorance of harmony, the breakdown of grammar and orthography, and all that is refractory to a delicate ear and abhorrent to unimpaired taste."

He chose as his motto the lines:

> Excess in poetry is always rot:
> Be skillful, artful, and diligent.

Lomonosov's verses were not understood and remained so: "nonsensical" in their "excess."

This was a failure.

With sap from Lomonosov, however, eighteenth-century literature retained its vitality in the person of Derzhavin. Russian poetry, including Pushkin, was reared on Lomonosov's struggle with Sumarokov. In the twenties Pushkin diplomatically spared him the "honors of a fashionable writer," but still studied him carefully. And Lomonosov's stanzas were still used by Lermontov. Lomonosovian flashes can be found quite frequently in the poetry of the nineteenth century.

Behind Lomonosov stood chemistry, a great science. Had he not been a chemist, he would probably have been held in contempt as a poet. There is no reason to fear your own vision: Khlebnikov's great failure as a poet turned out to be a new word in poetry. It is impossible now to predict the full extent of his fermenting influence.

·   ·   ·

VII

Khlebnikov said:

> It is for me, a butterfly, who has flown
> Into the room of a man's life,

> To leave the handwriting of my dust
> On the stern windows, like an inmate's autograph.

Khlebnikov's handwriting really resembled the dust a butterfly strews: the child's prism, the infantilism of the poetic word—revealed in his poetry not with "psychology," but in the very elementary, the briefest segments of words and phrases. The child and the savage were new poetic personalities who had suddenly mixed up the fixed "norms" of meter and word. A child's syntax, the infantile "look!," the sudden arbitrary shifts in the category and sense of certain words —all of this was part of a frank and outright struggle with the empty literary phrase, with literary clichés that were far removed from people and from the contemporary moment. It's useless to apply to Khlebnikov the seemingly very significant word "searches." He didn't "search," he "found."

Therefore, his individual verses have the quality of simple discoveries, just as simple and irreplaceable as certain lines of *Evgeny Onegin* were in their time:

> How often later we regret the loss of
> What we first discarded.

VIII

Khlebnikov's was a new vision. A new vision takes in various subjects simultaneously. Thus not only do these subjects "begin life in verse," according to Pasternak's remarkable formula, but they live also in the form of epic poetry.

And Khlebnikov is our only epic poet of the twentieth century. His short lyrical pieces are that same butterfly's handwriting, sudden, "infinite" notations that continue on into the distance, observations that enter into an epic, either themselves, or in a related form.

At the most crucial moments in an epic, the epic emerges out of the fairy tale. That's how *Ruslan and Lyudmila*[6] emerged, determining Pushkin's approach to the epic and to the versified tale of the nineteenth century; that's how Nekrasov's *Who is Happy in Russia?*, the democratic *Ruslan*, also emerged.

A pagan fairy tale was Khlebnikov's first narrative poem. Khlebnikov gave us a new "light poem" in the pre-Pushkin, eighteenth-century sense of this term, the almost anacreontic *Tale of the Stone Age* (*Skazka o kamennom veke*), a new bucolic idyl: *Shaman and Venus* (*Shaman i Venera*), *The Three Sisters* (*Tri sestry*), and *Sylvan Sadness* (*Les-*

naya toska). Of course, those who read *Harmonious World, Razin's Boat* (*Ustrug Razina*), *Night Before the Soviets* (*Nochyu pered sovetami*), and *Zangezi* will consider those other poems mere youthful things. But this doesn't lessen their importance. Such a pagan world—close at hand, bustling nearby, inconspicuously blending with our village and town—could be constructed only by an artist whose own verbal vision was new, childlike, and pagan:

> Sky-blue flowers
> Threaded by Lada into the buttonhole.

IX

Khlebnikov didn't collect themes assigned to him from outside himself. It's unlikely that such a term—assigned theme, an assignment—existed for him. An artist's method, his personality, and his vision grow into themes by themselves. Infantilism, a primeval pagan attitude toward the world, and an ignorance of modern man naturally lead to paganism as a theme. Khlebnikov himself "predicts" his own themes. You must give consideration to the strength and completeness of this relationship to grasp how Khlebnikov, a revolutionary of the word, "predicted" the Revolution of 1917 in his article on numbers.

X

Futurism's bitter word battles, which demolished any notion of a gradual, happy, and planned evolution of "the word," of poetic language, were, of course, no accident. Khlebnikov's new vision, like a pagan's and a child's mixing the big and the little, could not reconcile itself to the fact that the solid, confining literary language does not hit on the most important and intimate thing, that this important, incessant thing is driven off by the literary language's "wrappings" and declared accidental. Now for Khlebnikov, the accidental became art's primal element.

And so it is in science also. Small mistakes, "accidents," explained by the older scientists as errors due to imperfect experiments, serve as stimuli for new discoveries: what had been explained as an "imperfect experiment" turns out to be the action of unknown laws.

Khlebnikov the theoretician becomes the Lobachevsky[7] of the word: he does not find minor shortcomings in old systems, but discovers a new order, which results from the accidental displacement of those systems.

The new vision—very intimate, almost infantile (the "butterfly")—turned out to be a new order of words and of things.

People hastened to oversimplify his language theory—luckily it was called "trans-sense language"—reassuring themselves that Khlebnikov had created a "meaningless sound speech" (*zvukorech*). This is inaccurate. The whole essence of his theory is that he transferred the center of gravity in poetry from the issue of sound to that of meaning. For him no sound is uncolored by meaning, and the questions of "meter" and "theme" do not live separate existences. "Instrumentation," which had had the function of a kind of onomatopoeia, in his hands became a weapon to alter meaning, to revive a word's long-forgotten kinship with its near relatives, and to find new grounds for kinship with words that heretofore had been strangers.

XI

The "dreamer" did not separate his daily existence from dreaming, life from poetry. His vision became a new order, and he himself a "transport engineer of artistic language." "There are no transport engineers of language," he wrote. "Who would travel from Moscow to Kiev via New York? And yet what line of modern poetic language is free from such trips?" He preaches the "explosion of the language of silence, of the deaf-and-dumb layers of language." Those who think his language is "meaningless" do not see how a revolution is simultaneously a new order. Those who talk of Khlebnikov's "nonsense" should reconsider this question. It is not nonsense, but a new semantic system. Not only was Lomonosov "nonsensical" (this "nonsense" provoked Sumarokov's parodies), but there are parodies (many of them) of Zhukovsky in which this poet—whose work is now used as a primer for children—is ridiculed for his "nonsense." Fet was sheer nonsense to Dobrolyubov. All poets, even those who only partially altered the semantic system, have been declared nonsensical, but were later understood, not all by themselves, but because their readers rose to the level of the new semantic system. Blok's early verses were not easily "comprehensible," but who does not "comprehend" them now? But those who nevertheless wish to locate the Khlebnikov question's center of gravity precisely on the issue of poetic nonsense should read his prose: *Nikolay, The Hunter Usa Gali* (*Okhotnik Usa-Gali*), *Ka,* and so forth. This prose, semantically as clear as Pushkin's, will convince them that "nonsense" is not at all the issue, but a new semantic system, and that this system with different material yields different results—from Khlebnikov's trans-sense language, (meaningful, and not nonsensical) to the "logic" of his prose.

If you should write a line absolutely devoid of any meaning but in an impeccable iambic meter, it will turn out to be almost comprehensible. And how much of what was clearly considered Pushkin's formidable nonsense in his own day has lost its edge because we have gotten accustomed to his meter. For example:

> Two kindly shadows, two angels
> In bygone days given to me by Fate. . . .
> But both have wings and a flaming sword,
> Both stand guard and both take vengeance on me.

Very few readers have ever considered that the wings appear here quite improperly as a fearful attribute of angels, quite in contrast with their usual kindly import. Wings by themselves are not at all fearful and are a common attribute of angels in poetry. But how this "non-sense" deepens and broadens the associative movement of the lines!

And an exact, authentic transcript of human conversation, without any authorial elucidation, will seem meaningless. Khlebnikov's variable verse lines (first an iamb, then a trochee, a masculine ending followed by a feminine) contribute even to traditional verse language a variable semantic content, a special kind of sense.

Khlebnikov's verse is certainly not a linguistic collage. Rather it is modern man's intimate language, given as though accidentally overheard, with its abruptness, its mingling of a high style and domestic details, together with that sharp precision that modern science has given to language. At the same time it contains the infantilism of the modern city-dweller. We have commentaries on his poem *Gul-Mulla* by a man who knew Khlebnikov during his sojourn in Persia—and each fleeting image turns out to be perfectly exact, not "retold" in a literary fashion, but created afresh.

XII

Before the tribunal of Khlebnikov's new system literary traditions have been laid wide open. An enormous displacement of traditions results. Suddenly the ancient *Tale of Igor's Campaign* proves more modern than Bryusov. Pushkin enters the new system, not in hard, unchewed clumps that stylists like to flaunt, but transformed:

Apparently that's how the sky wished
To serve mysterious Fate,
So as to instill in all who exist
A cry for love and bread.

Lomonosov's and Pushkin's odes, the *Tale of Igor's Campaign,* and
the "Sobakevna" section from "The Night before the Soviets" that
echoes Nekrasov, are unrecognizable as "traditional": they have been
incorporated into a new system.

Khlebnikov was able to produce a revolution in literature for the
very reason that his system was not a closed literary one. His system
gives meaning to the language of verse and the language of numbers,
to chance conversations on the street, and to events from world history; for him the methods of literary revolution and historical revolution were similar. His long historical poem on numbers may not be
scientific, and his angle of vision may be only a poetic one, but *Harmonious World,* "Razin's Boat," "The Night before the Soviets," the
sixteenth fragment of *Zangezi,* and *The Night Search* (*Nochnoi obysk*)
may be the most important of all verses on the Revolution.

If the fist concealed a knife,
While vengeance dilated wide the pupils of her eyes,
It's Time that set up a howl: "Give!"
While dutiful Fate answered: "Aye, aye, sir!"

XIII

Poetry is similar to science in its methods—this is what Khlebnikov
teaches us.

It must be like a scientific discovery that meets the facts. And this
means that, when faced with the accidental, it must reorganize itself
so that the accidental ceases to be accidental.

The poet who regards the word and verse as objects, the importance and usage of which he has known for a long time (and so they
have begun to bore him), will regard an everyday object as a hopelessly old acquaintance however new the object may be. The role of
poet requires that a man regard things either looking down from
above (satire), or looking up from below (ode), or with his eyes
shut (song). Then, too, poets who write for magazines also have an
"aside" look, an "in general" look.

But Khlebnikov looks at things the way a scientist, penetrating into
a process and its movement, regards phenomena—he views them from
the same level. He has abandoned traditional poetic roles.

He finds nothing in poetry dilapidated (from the "ruble" to "nature"). He doesn't write of things "in general." He does have a personal thing. It courses on, correlated with the entire world, and is, therefore, valuable.

For him there are no "base" things.

His village poets don't view villages like a condescending urbanite sitting in his summer cottage. (How much smugness there is in our village lyric, in these village ditties about rye and blue-eyed homesteaders. They're not reminiscent of Karamzin—no chance of that. They're reminiscent of Volf's children's books: there the pictures of children presented them as pint-size little men with large heads, but without moustaches.) The same holds true for the East: the East in *Gul-mullah's Trumpet* (*Truba Gul-mully*) isn't European: there's no condescending interest, no exaggerated respect. On the same level—that's how the dimensions of themes change, and how they are reappraised.

This is possible only when the word itself is regarded as something like an atom, with its own processes and its own structure.

Khlebnikov is not a word collector, not a property owner, and not a wise guy seeking to startle. He looks upon words as a scientist, and he reappraises their dimensions.

.   .   .

XIV

And so Khlebnikov's poetic personality was constantly changing: the wise man of Zangezi, the pagan of the forest, the child-poet, Gul-mullah (the priest of flowers), and the Russian dervish, as they called him in Persia, was, at the same time, also an engineer of the word.

Khlebnikov's biography is the biography of a poet outside of the literature of books and magazines, happy in his own way, in his own way unhappy, complex, ironic, "unsociable," and amiable—a biography that came to a horrible end. It tied in with his poetic personality.

However strange and remarkable the life of this poet-wanderer was, however horrible his death, his biography must not overwhelm his poetry. There is no need to bury the man with his biography. In Russian literature there are too many examples of this. Venevitinov,[8] a complex and curious poet, died at twenty-two, and since then only one thing has been really remembered about him—that he died at twenty-two.

XV

No school and no trend can claim this man. His poetry is just as inimitable as that of any poet. And you can learn from him, only first
trace the paths of his development and his starting points, first study
his methods. Because in his methods is the ethic of the new poet. This
is the ethic of attention and fearlessness: attention to the "accidental"
(but actually characteristic and real), which is overwhelmed by rhet-
toric and blinded by habit; the fearlessness of the honest poetic word
which goes onto the paper without any literary "wrapping paper"—the
fearlessness of the right word that has no substitute, and is "not pan-
handled from the neighbors" as Vyazemsky[y] put it. And what if this
word is childish, if sometimes the most banal word is the most honest
of all? But this is precisely Khlebnikov's daring—and his freedom.
Without exception, all the literary schools of our time live by prohibi-
tion: you can't do this, you can't do that, this is banal, that is ludicrous. Khlebnikov existed in a state of poetic freedom which in every
given case was a matter of necessity.

TRANSLATED BY CHARLOTTE ROSENTHAL

ANDREY SINYAVSKY

The Poetry of Pasternak

Pasternak's work was known at first only to a relatively small circle of poetry connoisseurs. For many years critics pointed out his literary isolation and his singularity, and they tended to explain this by the fact that a reader opening his book for the first time would experience great difficulty in simply understanding the text. At the end of the twenties one of them wrote:

> Readers confront in him a poet of an original and totally individual cast of mind. In order to understand him one had to make a special effort and even alter the habitual process of perception. His manner of perceiving and even his vocabulary seem at first strange and astonishing. With the appearance of each book there were troubled questions about his unintelligibility, and what *could* this mean?

The heavily metaphorical style of Pasternak's early works was often taken as a kind of affectation, beyond which profound meanings were vaguely hinted at. His first books produced an impression of almost total alienation from contemporary life, and he acquired the reputation of a poet remote from social significance, locked in his own intimate, deeply personal world. But this negative and intolerant attitude toward Pasternak was not the sole critical reaction; at the beginning of the twenties Mayakovsky considered his works to be models of "a new poetry, magnificently sensitive to the present day." At the same time Bryusov remarked: "Pasternak does not have particular poems about the Revolution, but his verses, perhaps without his intent, are saturated with the spirit of the present day. Pasternak's psychology is not borrowed from old books; it expresses his own essence as a poet, and could have taken form only in the conditions of our life."

The nature of his genius, and his understanding of art, separated

From *Boris Pasternak, Stikhotvoreniya i Poemy* (Moscow, 1965), pp. 9-62.

Pasternak from the celebrants of revolution. Abstract ideals of moral perfection determined his attitude toward life, and his approach to reality, which were not always in accord with the demands of a concrete historical situation. The "eternal" categories of the good, of love, and of universal justice predominate in the world of Pasternak.

Yet many of his works, written at various times, do bear the imprint of the Revolution and of the new Soviet reality, and they are shown (as is usually his way) from the point of view of the moral changes brought into world history by our times and our people. He spoke of this very thing near the end of his life in a New Year's message to his foreign readers:

> . . . And there's something else you have to thank us for. Our Revolution, however great the differences were, set the tone for you too, filled the current century with sense and content. We are different, our young people are different—even the son of your banker is no longer what his father and grandfather were. . . . And for this new man, even in your old society, for the fact that he is more alive, more refined and more gifted than his corpulent, grandiloquent predecessors you should thank us because this child of the century is accepted in his maternal home called Russia. So now, isn't it best for us peacefully to wish one another a happy new year and to wish for one another that the peals of military thunder not be heard along with the popping of wine corks as we celebrate, and that they may never sound again during this or succeeding years. But if misfortune is fated to burst upon us, remember what events have taught us and in what a severe school we were tempered. There are no people more desperate than we; no people readier for the impossible and the fantastic. Any military challnge will convert us one and all into heroes, as did our recent terrible ordeal.

Even Pasternak's poems about nature, probably among the best of his work, are saturated with a significance that is important and necessary for people of our times. His landscapes with their enthusiasm for life and their fresh vision of the world are consonant with the mood of modern man. Not without reason did the poet himself link the creation of his book, *My Sister, Life* (*Sestra moya zhizn*), written in the summer of 1917, with a view of the world born of the new epoch: "I saw summer on the earth, as though not recognizing itself, both natural and prehistoric, as in a revelation. I left a book about it. In that book I expressed everything of a fantastic and elusive character that could be learned about the Revolution."

I

Boris Leonidovich Pasternak was born on February 10 (January 29), 1890 in Moscow. His father was the well-known artist Leonid Pasternak, his mother the pianist Rosa Kaufman. The childhood years of the poet passed in an atmosphere saturated with art, music, and literature. The many-sided cultural interests of his family affected his tastes and inclinations very early. When he was still a young boy the German poet Rainer Maria Rilke, Leo Tolstoy, and Scryabin all made a lasting impression on him. To these first encounters with artistic genius he later ascribed prime importance in the formation of his own cast of mind. Equally important was his later response to the poetry of Blok, an intensely personal, autobiographical experience, and of course his meeting with Mayakovsky.

Pasternak's first creative effort and interest were devoted entirely to music. At the age of thirteen he dedicated himself, under Scryabin's influence, to studying the theory of musical composition under the tutelage of Yury Engel and R. M. Glière.[1] After six years of persistent work he abandoned music forever. In 1909 he entered the Historicophilological Faculty of Moscow University, where he specialized in philosophy. To complete his philosophical education he went to Germany in 1912 and spent one semester at Marburg University. He also made a trip to Switzerland and Italy.

As early as 1908-1909 Pasternak had become interested in contemporary poetry and made friendships among poets. He became a member of the poetry circle of Yury P. Anisimov and tested his talent for the writing of verse. But only after his experience at Marburg did he realize what his true calling was. He then abandoned philosophy and gave himself up wholly to the writing of poetry, which, after 1913, became the main business of his life.

The same sudden breaks and eager shifts from one sphere of ideas and concerns to another—from music to philosophy and then to poetry—the same dissatisfaction with the self and creative perfectionism, the readiness to sacrifice years of work for the sake of a "second birth," all of these things characterize as well the literary biography of Pasternak. As he developed he boldly canceled out his past. The first period of his poetic search, marked by the combined influence of symbolism and futurism—he was a member of a group of moderate futurists "The Centrifuge"—he later thoroughly reassessed. Much of what he wrote before 1917 he omitted from later editions.

The publication of *My Sister, Life* in 1922 established Pasternak as one of the outstanding masters of contemporary poetry. This book, it may be said, marked him as a fully original phenomenon in Russian poetry. His earlier work—*A Twin in the Clouds* (*Bliznets v tuchakh*) and *Above the Barriers* (*Poverkh barerov*)—had the character of first trials: they were a preparation and a tuning of his instrument. The young poet was seeking his individual style, his own view of life, and his own place in the multiplicity of literary movements. A number of poems included in the earlier collections were later completely rewritten and were unrecognizable in their new form. Although the second collection of verse he published, *Above the Barriers*, reveals significant traits and settled tastes (the striving for unfettered verbal expression, the authentic recreation of a living picture, an excited, dynamic expressiveness) yet he considered it necessary to rework it radically when he prepared that book for a new edition in 1929. The poetic clichés peculiar to his early collections, which betrayed the influence of the symbolists, disappeared, as did abstractness and deliberate obscurity, along with futurist "trinkets," as he himself expressed it, that impart to verse an "irrelevant cleverness" to the detriment of its sense and meaning.

Dividing Pasternak's work into periods we may say that the years from 1912 to 1916 were a time of apprenticeship and accumulation of experience, a time when his poetic style was taking form but was not yet mature or fully independent. The most important landmark in Pasternak's literary development was the writing of *My Sister, Life* which appeared in 1922. His work on that book was energetic and impetuous and evidenced a sudden flight of poetic inspiration, a sudden access of creative energy. After *Themes and Variations* (*Temy i variatsii*), published in 1923, which was largely a byproduct and continuation of *My Sister, Life*, there followed a period during which the poet worked strenuously in the epic genre (1923-30). His work on *High Malady* (*Vysokaya bolezn*), *1905*, and *Lieutenant Schmidt*, and the novel in verse *Spektorsky* belongs to this period.

In the twenties Pasternak joined the literary group "Lef" (V. Mayakovsky, N. Aseev, S. Tretyakov, O. Brik, N. Chuzhak[2] and others). The "Lef" program with its emphasis on tendentious, agitational art and on sheer utility and technical mastery was alien to him. A brief and unstable connection with the "Lef" group he maintained because of his friendship with Mayakovsky and Aseev, and because of their common interest in poetic innovation and in the development of a new poetic language. But Pasternak was a stranger among the "Lef"-

ists, and this he announced publicly in 1928. Let us note in passing that group organization, adherence to any particular school or literary platform, were always alien to Pasternak. Even in the prerevolutionary period, when he joined his voice to the futurists, he had his own rather impressionistic interpretation of futurism, and he was alienated by the narrowness of the group to which he belonged.

At the beginning of the thirties, after working on the narrative poems, Pasternak again turned to lyric poetry with the publication of *Second Birth* (*Vtoroe rozhdenie*). Now he sharply altered the lyric tone and manner of expression, moving toward greater clarity and classical simplicity. This alteration of style was a long process and it was accompanied by temporary abatements of energy and prolonged interruptions in his creative work.

The thirties were a difficult and critical time for the poet. He wrote few original works, and instead devoted his energies to translation. Beginning in 1934 translation was his steady occupation and it continued until the end of his life: he translated Georgian poets, Shakespeare, Goethe, Kleist, Rilke, Verlaine and others.

Not until early in 1941, on the eve of the war, did he overcome his crisis and enter a new period of creative inspiration. A number of first-rate poems appeared in the volume *On Early Trains* (*Na rannikh poezdakh*, 1943). From this volume there is a direct thread leading to Pasternak's lyric poetry of the forties and the fifties, the work that crowned his poetic career. (Pasternak died May 30, 1960.)

Right up to the end of his life, Pasternak was constantly trying to re-examine and reappraise his literary career. It is well known, for example, that in 1956 he made the statement that he did not like his own style before 1940. Such modest self-appraisals, not always just, were in the nature of Pasternak, who preferred not to accumulate goods but to abandon what he had for the sake of future achievement. Art, in his understanding, was a constant gift of the self, a steady movement forward, concerned not with end results but with discoveries.

> The aim of creativity is self-giving
> And not sensations, not success.
> It's a disgrace, and signifies nothing,
> To be the story on everyone's lips.

. . .

The persistent lifelong need to renew one's style and approach did not, however, rule out a basic internal unity in his work from 1917 to 1960. His work is consistent in its principal tendencies of thought and style. After writing *My Sister, Life,* which affirmed the poet's credo on life and art, Pasternak altered the basic form of his lyrics without destroying it. He developed and completed what had first taken shape in that book and was his peculiar discovery.

We have outlined the development of Pasternak as a poet; now let us try to enter his world. This will demand close attention to his philosophy as well as to the verbal texture and figurative system of his poetry. To do this we will depart to some extent from a chronological account of his life and works to consider poems written at various times and often in different styles, all of them, however, part of a unified whole in that they echo one another in the stimuli they record and in the responses to those stimuli.

II

The central place in the lyric poems of Pasternak belongs to nature. There is much more in them than ordinary landscape description. Pasternak is dealing with life itself, with the reality of the world, in those poems which tell of springs and winters, of dawn and the rain. He is confessing, moreover, that faith in life which runs through all of his poetry and constitutes its moral foundation. Life in his view is something unconditional, eternal, absolute; it is an all-pervasive element and a great miracle. Wonder at the miracle of existence—this is the attitude in which Pasternak is fixed—always bewitched by his discovery that "it's spring again."

> Where have I heard snatches of this talk,
> Some time last year?
> Ah! There's no doubt of it, once again
> This night a stream came out of the grove.
> It's just that—and this has happened before—
> The mill pond moved its ice pack and swelled.
> It's actually a new miracle;
> It's spring again, just like the last time.
> She's here! She's here!

Freshness and health emanate from his landscapes. Osip Mandelshtam put this very well: "To read the verses of Pasternak is to cleanse the throat, to strengthen the breath, to renovate the lungs: such verses must be a curative for tuberculosis."

> Dawn will flutter the candle,
> Will light and send the martin to his goal
> As a reminder, in I fly:
> May life be always as fresh as this!

> Daybreak, like a shot in the dark.
> Bang!—and the rifle's blaze
> Dies out in midair.
> May life be always as fresh as this!

Day in and day out, in almost every poem Pasternak reiterates the vitality of nature, which is saving and triumphant. Trees, grass, clouds, streams are invested in his verse with the sacred right to speak in the name of life itself, to put us in the way of the good and the true. ("There's no grief anywhere that snow can't cure.") One sprig of willow may contain what's most precious, and most beautiful:

> When it fell to Desdemona to sing—
> And so little life was left her—
> Not about love, her guiding star,—
> But about a willow she sang, to a willow she wept.
>
> When it fell to Ophelia to sing—
> And choked she was with bitter dreams—
> What trophies did she take to her watery death?
> An armful of willow branches and some celandine.

A landscape in Pasternak is not just the object of description but the subject of the action, the main hero and the mover of events. The whole plenitude of life in the variety of its manifestations is contained in any scrap of nature which, as it seems, is capable of acting, feeling, and thinking. The likening of nature to man is common in poetry, but in Pasternak the landscape appears in the role of mentor and moral model. "The forest sheds its crimson dress"—such is the classical formula for autumn in Russian poetry. But in Pasternak we sometimes find a reversal of that image: "You throw off your dress just as the grove throws off its leaves . . ."; "Your thought, like the air, is pure of guile"—is the poet's remark to his beloved. Man is defined through nature; in relationship with nature he finds his own place. The power of nature, or more exactly her intercession, does not lower man; when he obeys and becomes like her he is hearing the voice of life itself. At the same time, nature in Pasternak's work is so close to man that, though pushed aside and replaced by the landscape, he comes to life in it once again. The world is so humanized that when we walk through forests and fields, we deal essentially, not with pictures of these forests and fields, but with their character and psychology.

Pasternak writes of his stay in Venice: "So this happiness touched me, too. I had the joy of learning that one may go day after day to an assignation with a piece of built-up space as with a living personality."

There is a meeting in his verse with a landscape perceived as a unique, distinctive personality:

> And now you enter a birch grove.
> And the two of you scrutinize one another.

Nature takes on all of the features of a person. We are used to hearing "The rain comes," but now we find out: "More from sleep than from the roof, more absent-minded than shy, the rain dallied at the door. . . ." Pasternak's landscapes have their own disposition, sympathies, pet diversions—clouds play catch, thunder engages in photography, streams sing sentimental songs. His landscapes are even endowed with the features of a portrait:

> And the forest sheds its raiment
> And drops streaming sweat.
>
> . . . .
>
> And shining, shining, like lips
> Not ever wiped by any hand
> Are the shoots of willow and the leaves of oak,
> And the tracks by the watering pond.

"Face of the azure," "face of the river," "face of the thunderstorm tearing the mask from itself"—such is the world of nature, a populous and many-faced gathering.

Pasternak's poetry is metaphorical through and through. But the metaphorical character of all of these comparisons we often do not perceive, so vivid is the action taking place before our eyes. The garden "cries" or a thunderstorm "rushes" not figuratively but literally—with the verisimilitude of authentic action:

> The thunderstorm's at the gate! in the yard!
> Transformed and stupefied,
> Now dark, now roaring, now silvery,
> It rushes along the glassed veranda.

The chief function of metaphor in the verse of Pasternak is to link one thing with another. Instantaneously and dynamically it gathers up into a single whole the separate strands of reality and thus embodies the unity of the world, the interaction and interpenetration of phenomena. Pasternak proceeds from the proposition that any two objects set side by side intimately interact and penetrate one another, and so he links them, not by their similarity but by their contiguity, using metaphor as the connection. The world is seen "whole," and the labor of re-unifying it is accomplished by the figurative meaning of words:

Spring. I'm in from the street where the poplar is astonished,
Where the distance is scared, where the house is afraid of falling,
Where the air is blue like the bundle of linen
Of a patient released from the hospital.

The landscape, indeed the whole world surrounding us, possesses in Pasternak a heightened sensitivity. It reacts sharply and instantaneously to the changes taking place in man; it does not merely respond to his feelings, thoughts, and moods (something quite common in literature), but becomes his complete likeness, an extension of him, his alter ego. There is a passage in the prose work *A Tale* which reveals the mechanics of such transformations. The hero, who is in love, suddenly observes:

> Of course the whole street, all full of dusky gloom, was utterly and entirely Anna. Seryozha was not alone in this and he knew it. And indeed, who had experienced it before him? However, his feeling was still vaster and more exact, and here the aid of friends and predecessors stopped. He saw how painful and difficult it was for Anna to be a city morning. She silently displayed herself in his presence and didn't call to him for help. And dying with grief for the real Arild . . . he watched her, cloaked in poplars as in icy towels, and engulfed in clouds, slowly throw back her Gothic brick towers.

Note this fact: the feeling that seized Seryozha was *vaster* and *more exact* than similar phenomena experienced by other people—friends and predecessors. Pasternak is in fact speaking of himself, of his divergence both from predecessors and contemporaries. His "correspondences" differ from the traditional ones (nature as an accompaniment to the experiences of man) precisely in the breadth and exactness of the image: everything—*entirely and wholly*—turns into Anna Arild.

In this, if you will, Pasternak is closest of all to the metaphorical leaps of Mayakovsky, where the world matches the hero's passion and agony: "From my weeping and my laughing the room's mug was raked with horror. . . ." But in him the diffusion of emotion into reality is motivated by restlessness drawn to an extreme degree of tension ("I cannot be calm"), by the force, by the grandeur of the poet's emotional experience. Pasternak is "calmer," "quieter," "more restrained," than Mayakovsky; in him such displacements are evoked not so much by the exclusiveness of passion as by the delicacy of his feeling for reflexes and resonances, by the sensitiveness of each object to its neighboring, adjacent object. The reciprocal reaction here does not achieve

Mayakovsky's hyperbolic dimensions but each drop of water reflects a spark of light; all objects, even the most insignificant, influence each other and each takes on the character of the other. In Pasternak's poetry it is impossible to distinguish between the man and the situation, the living feeling and dead matter. By means of metaphorical shorthand, reality is depicted in the confluence of heterogeneous parts, in the crossing of borders and contours, as an indivisible whole.

Pasternak was fascinated by the problem of creating within the limits of a short poem the all-encompassing atmosphere of being, of transmitting the "feeling of affinity with the universe" possessed by the poet. In his poems the lyrical narration does not develop consistently from one thing to the next but jumps "over the barriers," tending to a broad delineation, and a bold portrayal of the whole. Through allegory and the figurative meaning of words, things move from their long-accustomed places and enter into violent, chaotic movement whose purpose is to give the impression of reality in its natural disorder.

> I want to go home, to the enormity
> Of the apartment that inspires sadness.
> I'll go in, take off my coat, collect myself,
> I'll be lit by the streetlamps.

> The narrow ribbing of the partitions
> I'll pass through, I'll pass, like light.
> I'll pass as image enters into image
> And as one object cuts through another.

In this transparent space intersected by metaphors the image of the poet, of the artist, occupies a special place. In contrast to Blok, Tsvetaeva,[3] Mayakovsky, and Esenin, the lyrical voice is only rarely that of the poet himself. For those poets the personality of the poet was central and his work, unfolding as a diary of many years, as a story "about the times and about myself," was a kind of "Life," a dramatic biography played out before the eyes of the readers and surrounded by the aura of legend. Pasternak moves away from this conception, which he designated as a "romantic . . . notion of the poet's life as spectacle." He tells little about himself or from himself, assiduously removes and hides his own "ego." On reading his verses we sometimes have the illusion that there is no author at all, that he is absent even as a narrator, as the witness who observed what is described. Nature speaks for herself, in her own name:

> In through the open windows at their needlework
> The clouds settled down—lightly, like doves.

> They noted: the water made things finer:
> The fences—noticeably; the crosses—slightly.

The poet doesn't notice anything; "the clouds notice." And in another poem it is not the poet who reminisces about childhood but "the snow remembers just barely, just barely: beddy-bye it was called, with a whisper and like syrup the day would slowly sink behind the cradle. . . ." In one of his later poems, *First Frosts* (*Zamorozki*), we once again meet with this uncommon image, when the landscape and the viewer seem to have changed roles and the picture itself examines the man standing before it:

> On a cold morning the sun in the haze
> Stands as a pillar of fire in the smoke.
> And as in a bad snapshot
> The sun can't quite make me out.
> Until the sun comes out from the shadows,
> And flashes beyond the pond onto the meadow,
> The trees don't see me well
> Standing on the distant shore.

Mayakovsky and Tsvetaeva speak in their own person for the whole world; but Pasternak prefers that the world speak for him and in his place: "I don't speak of spring, it speaks of me."

> . . . By the fence
> Among the wet branches an argument was going on
> With the pale wind. I stood stock still. It was about me!

Nature herself is the main lyric hero. And the poet is everywhere and nowhere. He is not a detached glance at the spreading panorama, but rather its double, becoming now a sea, now a forest. In the poem *The Weeping Orchard* (*Plachushchy sad*), for instance, the usual parallel, "I and the orchard," is turned into an equation: "I am the orchard," and Pasternak in the same words speaks both "about it" and "about myself":

> Horrible!—It drips and listens:
> Does it all alone in the world
> Press the twig on the windowpane like lace,
> Or is there a witness?
> To my lips I'll raise it and lend an ear:
> Am I all alone in the world,
> Ready to weep on occasion,
> Or is there a witness?

This oneness with nature, without witnesses or watchers, makes Pasternak's verse especially intimate and authentic.

A garden is also the hero of his well-known poem *The Mirror* (*Zerkalo*), but a garden reflected in a large wall mirror, where it lives, so to speak, a second life, glimpsed in the mysterious mirror depth: "The enormous garden is pulled into the wall mirror in the hall—and doesn't break the glass!" It is interesting that in an earlier version this poem bore the significant title *I Myself* (*Ya sam*): even the story about the wall mirror that absorbs the garden was for the poet a story about himself. Pasternak thinks of himself as just such a mirror, a close relative of life, and its equal. But in the poem *The Little Girl* (*Devochka*), continuing the figurative line of *The Mirror*, the reverse relation is established—the wall mirror recognizes itself in a branch rushing in from the garden; the poet sees in nature his own likeness and repetition:

> My own, immense as the garden, but in character—
> My sister! Another mirror!

III

It was along these lines that Pasternak's poetic system took form, and in a book whose title sounds like a poetic manifesto: *My Sister, Life*. The oneness of the poet and nature was here asserted as his fundamental credo:

> It seemed the alpha and omega—
> Life and I are of the same stuff;
> And all year round, with snow or snowless,
> She was like my alter ego
> And "sister" was the name I called her.

Pasternak held the deep conviction that poetry was a direct consequence and product of life. The artist does not invent images, he collects them from the street, helping nature in her work of creation but never trying to replace her by his own interference.

.   .   .

The birth of art out of the womb of nature is Pasternak's favorite theme. The theme occurs in many variations, but it has one constant feature: life itself is the primary source of poetry, and the poet at best is only an accomplice, a coauthor, whose function it is to observe and be amazed, and to have a set of rhymes ready in his notebook. This accounts for the abundance of literary terms in Pasternak's nature descriptions.

> But now the days of blossoming come,
> And limetrees with their belt of fences
> Cast about them, together with their shade,
> An aroma that you can't resist.
> In those moments when it clutches
> At the heart, it composes
> The theme and content of a book
> Whose binding is the park and flower garden. . . .

This identification of art with life, of poetry with nature, and the remission of authorial rights to the landscape itself, serves one principal purpose: by offering us verses composed by nature herself the poet is assuring us of their authenticity. And authenticity—the truth of the image—is for Pasternak the highest criterion of art. In his views on literature and in his practice as a poet he is filled with the concern "not to distort the voice of life that speaks in us."

"The inability to find and tell the truth is a defect which no amount of skill in lying will ever conceal," Pasternak wrote. Realism as he understands it (the artist's sharpened receptivity and conscientious communication of real being, which like a living human person is always whole and unique) is present in any genuine art; we find it in the works of Tolstoy and Lermontov, of Chopin and Blok, of Shakespeare and Verlaine; while romanticism is for Pasternak on the whole a negative concept, inclined toward fantasy and tending to be less than faithful in its depiction of reality.

These aesthetic views are especially interesting since Pasternak was for a long time connected with the group of futurists, later called "Lef-ists," who accepted the so-called formal method, which treats the work of art as nothing but the sum of its technical devices. "Contemporary critics imagine," wrote Pasternak at the beginning of the 1920's,

> that art is like a fountain; as a matter of fact it is more like a
> sponge. They think that art should flow forth, whereas what it
> must do is absorb and become saturated. They imagine that it
> can be broken down into various means of depiction; as a mat-
> ter of fact it is formed by the organs of perception. It should
> always be a spectator and always see more purely, more sensi-
> tively, more truly than anyone else; but in our days it has made
> the acquaintance of face powder and the makeup room, and it
> is exhibited on the stage.

Pasternak regarded heightened perceptiveness as the decisive feature of his work, and we find this same image of poetry "as a sponge" developed in one of his early poems:

> Poetry! If you were an absorbent Greek sponge
> I would put you on the sticky verdure
> On the wet board
> Of some green garden bench.
> Grow yourself fine jabots and farthingales
> Absorb the clouds and the ravines
> Then at night, poetry, I'll squeeze you dry
> To the health of my greedy paper.

When we study the literary views of Pasternak we are struck by his insistent warning: "Don't interfere with me! don't frighten things away!" These warnings are largely directed at the adoption of preconceived attitudes toward nature, against the adoption of ready-made, stereotyped formulas, against cliché in the broadest sense of the word. For Pasternak strength, purity, and spontaneity of perception were the necessary condition of art, and innovation meant simply the search for the maximum possible naturalness and truth to life. That is why, for example, he remarked in his article on Chopin that this composer's work was "absolutely original, not because it is different from that of its rivals, but because it is so close to nature, from which he drew his musical compositions."

Such a view of art presupposes a fresh look at the world, which the artist perceives as though for the first time. Pasternak believed that creativity begins when "we cease to recognize the world" and endeavor to speak about it with the unconstrained ease of the first poet on earth. Hence the emphases and aspirations peculiar to his lyric poetry, the strangeness and fantastic quality in everyday things, which he prefers to all fairy tales and inventions, and the morning freshness of his vision. His characteristic pose is that of the man who has just awakened: "I wake. I'm enveloped by what's revealed." And hence also the sense of the first day of creation in everything that happens: "the whole steppe, just as it was before the Fall."

It is noteworthy that stylization found no place in his poetry. In Pasternak's style, in his vision of the world, there is no room for any imitation except the imitation of nature. When he deals with a historical figure, Balzac for example, he can create an original incarnation, something comparable, perhaps, to the Balzac of Rodin:

> He dreams of freedom like a lackey
> As an old man, a bookkeeper, dreams of a pension,
> But there's a weight in that fist
> Like a stonemason's sledgehammer.

A short poem dedicated to Anna Akhmatova begins in the following way:

> I think I shall pick out words
> Suited to your primeval, original gift.
> And if I'm wrong—that's a mere trifle.
> I'll still not part with my mistake.

He goes on then to reveal the essence of Akhmatova's poetry, but still remains himself, never attempting to write "in the style of Akhmatova." Unable to part with his "mistake," he selects words which remind us, not of someone else's style, but of the freshness and novelty of the world. That is why Pasternak is sometimes not afraid to approach very closely to the classics, and he ventures, without falling into banality, to use as an epigraph a frequently anthologized line such as "The golden cloud spent the night on the bosom of a cliff," or to begin a poem with the familiar lines of Pushkin: "On the shore of the desolate waves he stood, full of great thoughts." Meetings such as these with classical models hold no danger for him: his own freshness of vision and novelty of manner insure him against literary reminiscence, and he can even permit himself, as in *Themes and Variations*, to base his work on purely traditional images, since he treats them in a profoundly personal way.

In his life as a poet Pasternak gained close acquaintance with a broad variety of artistic work, both past and present. In spite of the sharply idiosyncratic character of his own outlook and style Pasternak believed not in a break with the cultural heritage but in continuous contact with it. He was a firm believer in the idea of historical succession in the development of art. This attachment to the past was another point of difference between Pasternak and the futurist milieu of the twenties and earlier, imbued as it was with the spirit of rejection and destruction of the past.

In answer to a questionnaire concerning the attitude of contemporary authors toward classical literature (1927), Pasternak wrote: "It seems to me that at the present time there are no grounds whatever for moving away from Pushkinian aesthetics. By the aesthetics of an artist I understand his notion of the nature of art, of the role of art in history, and of his own responsibility before it." And he explained just how, concretely, Pushkin had influenced his own work:

> Pushkinian aesthetics are so broad and elastic that they allow various interpretations at various periods of a man's life. His impetuous descriptiveness allows of an impressionistic interpretation, and that is how I understood him about fifteen years ago in line with my own tastes and the trends in literature that were current then. But now my understanding of Pushkin is broader and a moral element has entered into it.

Pasternak's early sojourn in the futurist group known as the "Centrifuge" has a special significance. The members of this group, in contradistinction to the more aggressive "cubofuturists," cultivated a tolerant attitude toward both traditional poetry and their immediate predecessors and teachers, the symbolists.

As far as the "legacy" of symbolism is concerned, Pasternak was sympathetic to Annensky, to Bely, and especially to Blok. In Blok's works he looked for that quality of "impetuous descriptiveness," understood in the spirit of impressionism, which then characterized his own style, a style in which there predominated "an instantaneous graphic depiction of movement." Many years later, in his autobiographical essay (1956), Pasternak confesses that among the various qualities of Blok it was precisely his "impetuosity," the "wandering attentiveness" of his gaze, the "fluency" of his observations that were closest to him and left the greatest imprint on his style.

> Adjectives without nouns, predicates without subjects, a game of hide and seek, much agitation, quickly flashing figures, abruptness of intonation—how suited this style was to the spirit of the time: secretive, underground, conspiratorial, hardly ever emerging from the cellar, couching its message in the language of conspiracy, its main character the city, its main event the street. . . . This city, this Petersburg of Blok, is the most real of the many Petersburgs. . . . At the same time the image of the city is composed of features chosen by such a nervous hand and subjected to such spiritualization that it is entirely transformed into a gripping expression of one of the rarest internal experiences.

It is clear that Blok receives here, so to speak, a typically Pasternakian orchestration. And in his interpretation of Shakespeare, Verlaine, Rilke, Tolstoy, Chekhov, Mayakovsky, and others who interested him Pasternak is equally distinct and individual. He is always biased and at times paradoxical in his aesthetic judgments and interpretations, and this often reveals the deep originality of his artistic nature, which combined a taste for tradition with the spirit of bold innovation. In *Safe Conduct* (*Okhrannaya gramota*) he tells of his youth and the influence of his immediate predecessors:

> What sort of art was it? It was the youthful art of Scryabin, Blok, Komissarzhevskaya,[4] Bely—progressive, thrilling, original art. And it was so striking that it not only did not provoke any thought of replacing it, but on the contrary, made you feel like repeating it from the very beginning in order to confirm it, but repeating it more swiftly, ardently, and completely. One felt

like retelling it in a single breath, and this was unthinkable
without passion; but passion leapt aside and thus something
new came into being. But the new arose not through nullifica-
tion of the old, as is usually thought, but on the contrary, in
the enraptured reproduction of a model.

In his efforts to look at reality and poetry with new eyes, to refresh the aesthetic perception of the world and recreate his poetic system accordingly, Pasternak had much in common with a number of
poets who, before and after the Revolution, fought for the liberation
of art from antiquated forms. In this broad movement, encompassing
in the twentieth century all spheres of art, there were many losses and
much empty affectation, but there was in it too that healthy force for
renewal without which no original, contemporary art can develop. And
that movement attended also to the demand of life itself, which would
simply not submit to formulation in a worn out idiom, or in clichés
that stick in one's teeth. As Mayakovsky put it:

> And suddenly
> all things
> rushed,
> rending the voice,
> to throw off the rage of their worn-out names.

The same cry is heard in Pasternak:

> What if the universe must wear a mask?
> What if there are no latitudes
> That don't ask to have their mouths puttied up
> For the winter?
> Yes, but things tear the mask from themselves,
> They lose their power, drop their honor,
> When they have a need to sing,
> When there's good cause for a downpour.

It is peculiar to Pasternak's view of things that the renovation of poetry consists in the liberation of things from verbal automatism, and
from the mask of literary clichés.

In the search for a new idiom capable of restoring individuality to
the world, Pasternak turned to the language of everyday conversation
and thus contributed to that decisive democratization of the poetic
language which affected the work of many poets of his time, and had
its most violent expression in the work of Mayakovsky. But whereas
Mayakovsky broadened the vocabulary in the direction of blatant
street language where vulgarisms jostle political slogans, and opened

the way for the inclusion in poetry of the themes of the city, war, and revolution, Pasternak long continued to use traditional themes, the common property of poets past and present. But he spoke of those hackneyed springs and sunsets in a new way. He described the beauty of nature not in the customary poetic banalities but using the common words of everyday life, in fact the language of prose. In this way he returned to it a lost freshness and gave it new meaning for art. He transformed a hackneyed subject into a vital event.

Pasternak does not disdain official jargon, colloquialisms, conversational idioms, but boldly introduces the low language of life into the high style of poetry. Such speech forms, worn out like common coins in our daily intercourse, suddenly sound new and fresh when he uses them. Thus the common idiom becomes itself a weapon in the struggle against literary cliché. Pasternak expresses the most elevated ideas in simple terms, without formality. He conveys the turbulent majesty of the Caucasus in the tone of an easygoing conversation: "The Caucasus was all spread out before you like the palm of your hand, and it looked like a rumpled bed." His originality lies in the faculty of lending poetry to the world by the use of prosaic language. He thus infuses verisimilitude into his verses and removes them from the sphere of invention to that of real poetry.

In the story *The Childhood of Luvers* (*Detstvo Luvers*), tracing the inward development of the heroine as she encounters reality, Pasternak remarks: "Life ceased to be a poetic trifle. And as it became prose and turned into fact, life was transformed into a dark and serious tale." The prose of actual fact is the source of his poetry: by means of that prose his images are made to partake of the real movement of things. It is in such a context that we may understand his paradoxical statement: "We drag the common event into prose for the sake of poetry. We draw prose into poetry for the sake of music." Speaking of Shakespeare's *Romeo and Juliet*, he once again declares that prose in poetry is the bearer of life: "The play is an example of the highest poetry, which in its best models is always impregnated with the simplicity and freshness of prose."

Prosaic idiom and popular vocabulary impart concreteness to Pasternak's images; they materialize abstract concepts and bring them closer to us. The syntactical and rhythmical structure of his verses serves the same purpose: the creation of an elastic poetic system whose tone reminds us (be it said, only reminds us) of conversation. He speaks in the language of poetry just as freely as we speak in our daily life. He develops his poetic phrase with great complexity of balance and subordination; he interrupts himself and omits connecting words, as happens regularly in ordinary speech. But the important effect he aims for is that of a free unfettered poetic line possessing a long breath and developing large and nicely balanced intonational periods. The faculty of thinking and speaking, not in separate lines but in whole stanzas, periods, turns of speech, is something that Pasternak especially valued in the work of other poets, and for this reason he had special praise for Tsvetaeva, whose verbal art was like his own.

However, it was not simply a matter of reducing verse to conversational form. A natural and unconstrained intonation he subordinates to a more general aesthetic demand, the demand for breadth and integrity of artistic perception, the re-creation in verse of a particular and single panoramic view of life and its atmosphere. This is clearly perceptible, for example, in the poem *Death of a Poet* (*Smert poeta*), dedicated to Mayakovsky. The life of a genius in the ages, his sudden death, the gossip and confusion of the witnesses to the catastrophe, and the clamorous, spring street—all are presented simultaneously as an excerpt from a bursting drama and its wretched accompaniment, and all of this is gathered together and set into motion by the irrepressible thrust of a voice which tears after the event, seizes, cleanses, and packs it into several powerful intonational periods developing one after the other.

.   .   .

Pasternak readily resorts to seeming digressions, for example, the rooks in the trees in the beginning of the poem about Mayakovsky. Such details, as a matter of fact, indicate the breadth and wide sweep of the poet's intonation, and they draw into the action all the surrounding environment, so that no part of the background is neutral. Sometimes he pretends to have lost track and seems to return to what he's already said, to begin it again from the beginning, and then, having marked time and tarried a bit, he continues his story. In this way he accommodates a fullness of portrayal with the apparently reflex movement of speech. Despite his enormous labor over their form, his verses do not produce the impression of finely finished artifacts. On the contrary, his line is sometimes awkward, difficult to the point of seeming tongue-tied. There are unexpected halts and repetitions; his speech is at times choked and almost sobbing, crowded with words that pile up on one another. Later it becomes light, winged, and transparent but retains the same spontaneity. In this naïve, unaffected outpouring of words, which seems at first not to be directed by the poet

but to carry him along after it, Pasternak attained the desired naturalness of the living Russian language. His own characterization of Paul
Verlaine might be applied to Pasternak himself:

> . . . He gave to the language in which he wrote that bound-
> less freedom which was actually his discovery in lyric poetry,
> and which we find only in the masters of prose dialogue in the
> novel and the drama. The Parisian idiom in all its freshness
> and enchanting acuity found its way in from the street and
> took its place in the poetic line as a whole and without the
> slightest embarrassment, as the melodic material of the verse
> structure. . . .

.   .   .

In the works of Pasternak the system of sounds of the verse line has
special significance. It is not just a question of rhyme, although that
feature of his verse is both novel and variegated (Bryusov, as a matter of fact, had good reason to consider Pasternak rather than Mayakovsky the creator of modern rhyme). In his poems not only the ends
of the lines but essentially any words in the text may rhyme. Words
are often assimilated to each other by their sound, whether they are
close together in the line or some distance apart:

> Parizh v zlatykh teltsakh, v deltsakh,
> V dozhdyakh, kak mshchenie dolgozhdannykh . . .
> (Paris in golden calves, in sharp dealers
> In rains, long awaited like vengeance. . . .)

This phenomenon is broader than mere sound effect and more significant than the usual melodic ordering of speech in poetry. Phonetic
connections arise as an expression of sense connections, the similarity
of sounds fastens together adjacent images, tells in the final analysis of
the harmony of different aspects of existence, interconnected and in-
terpenetrating. The sound instrumentation aids the transference of
sense from one object to another, a transfer realized through metaphor
and evoked by the poet's urge to reveal and to emphasize the internal
unity of the world. Rhyme, according to the picturesque definition of
Pasternak, is "not the echoing of lines," but immeasurably more: in it
is heard the "hum of roots and meadows," through it "the polyphony
of worlds enters as truth into our little world."

Such sharp attention to the "sound value" of words and their selection according to phonetic-semantic similarity reminds us of Khlebnikov. Khlebnikov invented a logical system of phonetics, linking every
sound with a definite abstract concept, with a precise "power scale"

by which to calculate the laws for his poetic cosmogony. This a priori assignment of a necessary meaning to certain sounds, this linguistic rationalism, is alien to Pasternak, as is Khlebnikov's emphasis on the hidden abstract meaning rather than the concrete sense of a word. No artificial, abstract bridges join words that are close in sound, but rather metaphor and association; and these are motivated by contiguity, or simply by the chance occurrence of sound similarity.

> The rowboat beats in the sleepy breast
> The willows hang down and kiss on collar bones,
> On elbows, oarlocks—oh, wait,
> After all, this might happen to anyone!

Here "oarlocks" (*uklyuchiny*) appear alongside of "collar bones" (*klyuchiny*) for the very same reason that the willows "kiss" and the boat "beats in the breast." What we have here is Pasternak's habitual interassimilation of nature, man, and things, supported and underlined by sound similarities.

In his poetry the frequent sound repetitions occur as it were unintentionally, as though involuntarily, and they do not vitiate the basic conversational intonation. These sound correspondences are like his metaphors in that they seem unforced and accidental, for, as he has said: "The more accidental the verse the more surely is it formed of sudden, sobbing speech."

In the verse of Pasternak, wrote Tynyanov, "chance turns out to be a stronger link than the closest logical connection." "You don't know the connection of the things he offers you, it is quite accidental, but once he has revealed it, you seem to remember and recognize it. It was really there all the time—and the image he has created turns out to be inevitable."

The explanation for this effect lies in the peculiarities of Pasternak's poetic idiom. In spite of their suddenness and surprise we believe in the links he sets up—through metaphoric or sound connections—just because they are expressed in everyday language naturally and without "straining," as though it all goes without saying. The accidental quality of his discoveries contributes to the effect of naturalness, and simplicity of intonation serves as a pledge that the lyrical experience is real.

Pasternak's poetic style of 1910-1929 was often complex and difficult to follow. One source of difficulty was an oversaturation with metaphor that resulted from the poet's effort to realize and reduce to language all of life's diverse interconnections. Pasternak knew full well that two objects placed side by side yield in their combination a third thing. Determined not to break up the world into its separate parts, he portrayed a unity in which things are whimsically and chaotically intermingled, and the poet never for a moment forgets "what happens to the visible world when you begin to see it." The complexity was thus a consequence of too many constituent items. Nevertheless when Pasternak catches nature in a flow of conversational language he shakes many concepts loose from their accustomed channels of association and provides them with new associations. And these, even though borrowed from everyday life, are quite unhackneyed in the totally new context. The simplest and most natural turn of phrase seems strange to an ear unaccustomed to hearing ordinary speech in a poem. In one of Edgar Allan Poe's stories, some clever detectives are thrown off the track in their search for a stolen document by a thief who hid it in the most obvious place. What is most obvious—the author explains —often eludes observation. It is something like that with Pasternak's images: they are "incomprehensible" because they are too near to us, too obvious.

For instance, in *Death of a Poet* Pasternak says of the deceased:

> You slept, pressing cheek to pillow,
> Slept—as sound as sound can be
> Cutting again and again in a swoop
> Into the category of young legends.

The subject is Mayakovsky's immortality, and it moves so vividly and literally into the future because Pasternak speaks of it in simple, conversational phrases, even bookkeeping expressions ("into the category"). In everyday use these words are hardly noticed, but in verse they are a great rarity, and they are a special surprise when they occur in a solemn and serious context.

· · ·

Pasternak's linguistic innovation was largely dictated by his search for a natural and unconstrained poetic idiom. This was fully revealed and confirmed in his work of the thirties and especially of the forties and fifties, to which we will soon turn. At that time his simplistic tendency, obscured in the earlier period by the peculiarly Pasternakian superflux of images, became clear and firm. At first this tendency escaped notice, though it produced its effect, so to speak, latently. The author was fully conscious of his purpose, though that purpose was not always accessible to the reader. On this subject Pasternak wrote the following lines in the early thirties:

Being kin with all that is, being sure of
And on easy terms with the future in everyday life,
You can't help, at last, falling into the heresy
Of an unusual simplicity.
But we won't be spared,
Since we don't hide it in any way.
It's what people need most,
But complexities are easier to grasp.

"Complexities" here stands for banality and stereotype. Simplicity
is announced as the inner basis, the stimulus and final goal of the explorations in poetry which at this time he had not yet fully completed.

IV

The central place in Pasternak's poetry belongs to the depiction of nature (it is clear that landscapes often reveal the soul of man, the feeling of love and so on). Now let us see how his artistic method operated in forming pictures of contemporary history. Here Pasternak
enjoyed several advantages: a keen ear for the "voice of life" and
freedom from pseudopoetic canons forbidding the use of the low language of reality. It is well known that many poets in the first years of
the Revolution experienced great difficulties precisely in this area, because they were limited in their language to a meager set of admis-
sible poetic adornments. " 'Nightingale' is allowed, but 'oil burner' is
impossible," as Mayakovsky remarked. It was a question of poetry's
right to use the vocabulary of the day.

On this score Pasternak was safe: "nightingale" did not exclude "oil
burner" for him, and the poisons of aestheticism had not contaminated
his mature poetic style. His problem was something else, namely his
understanding of the role and purpose of art, and his affinity with
those poetic types who by their nature and artistic makeup are disposed to apprehend life rather than work for its decisive revolutionary
change. Pasternak's view of art as an organ of perception, his idea of
the artist as an attentive and sensitive observer (but not a direct participant), limited his resources for the portrayal of our historical epoch
in images adequate to convey immediately its broad sweep. Here he
is the complete antipode of Mayakovsky, who once remarked that he
and Pasternak lived in the same house but in different rooms. The very
conception of poetry as an organ of perception, the striving to absorb,
to drink in the colors of living nature, is alien to Mayakovsky. Wholly
submerged in the events of history, affirming the active poetry of con-

flict, Mayakovsky sees even nature as material in need of processing ("And if Mt. Kazbek itself gets in the way—cut it down!"). He regards nature with disdainful condescension; any creation of human labor he values more highly than those "little ants," or "shreds of grass." Defining poetry, Mayakovsky likens it to a tool or a weapon, or to productive labor: the rioter's brass knuckles, the bayonet, the factory and the extraction of radium.

This differentiation of the functions of the poet and the public figure Pasternak formulated with great clarity in a prerevolutionary article, *The Black Goblet (Chyorny bokal)*. The poet and the hero, lyric poetry and history, eternity and time, are here seen as different and incompatible orders. "Both are a priori and absolute," he says and, rendering their due to "the soldiers of absolute history," the author reserves for poetry the right not to touch time, not to undertake the "preparation of history for tomorrow."

These ideas were expressed in an early and still rather immature period, and Pasternak abandoned them in practice. However, echoes and variations of such notions can be heard in one form or another even in his later work. He is capable of bestowing all the high titles of history upon a man of action or a hero, but he sharply distinguishes the "poet's vacant place" from all of them.

Pasternak called art "the farthest reach of the age" (not merely a resultant force) and he regarded works of art and historical events as related phenomena of different orders. Leo Tolstoy, according to his idea, had a clear affinity with the Revolution. And in his own book, *My Sister, Life*, he saw a certain parallel with the revolutionary spirit of the times. He even considered it to be a book about the Revolution, although it never speaks of social storms, but rather of very ordinary thunderstorms and dawns, and to treat it as allegory would be a crude mistake.

Nonetheless, history did enter the work of Pasternak, even during the period when he demonstratively refused to be drawn into it and pretended not to remember even "what millennium, my friends, it is outside." War and Revolution echo in some of his landscapes, and his picture of nature bears the stamp of history. Even in his early period, from 1915 to 1917, there are "skies on strike," and cavalry tracks on the ice. And in memory of 1905, the spirit of "soldiers' mutinies and

summer lightning flashes" is in the air, and clouds are likened to re-
cruits and prisoners of war:

> The clouds moved past a dusty market,
> Like recruits, early in the morning, passing a farm.
> They dragged along for an hour, for a century,
> Like captive Austrians,
> Like a quiet hoarse whisper.
> Like a whisper:
> "Some water,
> Sister."

Nature takes on alien signs, which it draws from the world of political disturbance and class conflict. This interpretation of historical reality and nature's realm was a perfectly normal thing, since Pasternak's
landscapes are given as a contemporary city-dweller perceives them,
and the latter takes with him on his strolls a chain of social and political associations. The groves and the meadows are drawn into the
crowd of events that make up his life.

After the Revolution these landscapes full of history are very common, and sometimes they grow into symbols of all revolutionary Russia. For instance, in the poem *The Kremlin in a Snowstorm at the End
of 1918* (*Kreml v buran kontsa 1918 goda*) the storm here is matched
with the immaterial whirlwind raging on the expanses of the new
epoch and rushing right on into the future. The times' elemental
quality and the weather of the Revolution are perceived here with
great excitement and sketched by a master of landscape depiction:

> On the last night of the year, incomparable,
> Looking strange, all in foam,
> Itself, the Kremlin, in the rigging of so many winters,
> Vented its hatred on this one.
> Grandiose, and full of age
> Like a mystic's vision
> Fearsome, it rushed right on
> Through the year not yet ended into the next not yet begun.

.   .   .

When in the twenties the poet turned to history, this was connected
with the unexpected appearance of narrative tendencies in his work.
In 1923 in *High Malady* (*Vysokaya bolezn*) he sent out a "reconnais-
sance into the narrative genre." After that came the long poems *1905*
and *Lieutenant Schmidt* (1925 to 1927) and in 1930 he completed
Spektorsky. The narrative form attracted Pasternak at that time to

such an extent that he, only recently a confirmed lyricist, declared, "I consider that narrative poetry is required by the times, and therefore in writing the book 1905 I turn from lyrical thought processes to narration, although this is very hard." At the same time he expressed the opinion that "lyric poetry has almost ceased to be heard in our time."

      .   .   .

His epic canvases are all dedicated to the period of Revolution. At first, in *High Malady*, Pasternak "presented an epic narrative without plot, as a slowly moving, gradually developing theme, which at the end is fully realized" (Tynyanov). The poet's speech is deliberately difficult and slow-moving, and it tries to convey the "moving enigma" of events: pictures of Revolution, war, and ruin are not developed in the form of consecutive narration but seem fused in the free-flowing current of the verse. The narrative "builds up" as the author plays his own part, "drags things out and hems and haws" and conveys the movement of life itself through various modulations in the flow of language:

> Although, as before, the ceiling,
> Serving as a support for a new closet
> Dragged the second floor onto the third
> And the fifth hauled up onto the sixth,
> Suggesting by a shift of ins and outs,
> That all is as it was before in the world,
> Yet this was a fake,
> And along the net of water pipes
> Clambers upward that empty,
> Sucking scream of hard times,
> That stench of laurel and soy beans,
> Burned on a fire of newspapers,
> More tiresome than these verses,
> And standing high like a milestone
> Sort of muttered: "Wait, now, really,
> Wasn't I thinking of eating something?"

Pasternak's *High Malady* is an attempt to approach the creation of epic by strictly linguistic means. We have to do essentially with a prolonged lyrical digression that, taking its departure from certain historical events, attempts to encompass those events and to reveal the face of the times by means which are outside the story proper—metaphors, syntactic peculiarities, varying vocal modulations, and so forth.

      .   .   .

In the poems following *High Malady* Pasternak turns to more direct forms of epic narration. But even in these the depiction of individual human fate and particular characters does not occupy much space. Even in *Lieutenant Schmidt* his attention is focused on the re-creation of the very spirit of the age, on unfolding a broad historical panorama. A sketchy dispersion of images, a bright ground of color that ties everything together and at the same time washes away the contours of individual characters, and which is in itself the essential thing— these are the distinctive features of Pasternak's poetry and prose.

> Can it be that, having lived in the scope of that
>   picture,
> He believes in the fact of an individual person?

the author questions the reader, constantly reminding him in *Spektorsky* that:

> Personalities are out of the question.
> Better forget about them right here and now.

He indicates that even the character whose name is the title of the poem actually interests us very little:

> I began to draw Spektorsky in blind
> Obedience to the power of my camera's lens.
> I wouldn't have given anything for my hero
> Nor would I readily have discussed him
> But I was writing about the net of rays
> In which he loomed before my eyes.

For Pasternak it is not Spektorsky but the broad scope of a historical perspective, the spectrum in which he is placed, a bit of history torn from the past by the rays of memory. In the structure of the poem a special role is played by the movement of memory. Individuals and episodes are interconnected by the logic of reminiscence, and step by step a grand historical canvas is unfolded.

One of the results of this unfolding of the theme in breadth is that the motif of space gains special significance. Broad horizons, the remoteness of time and distance, the urge to look about oneself and take in all that the eye sees, all of this is important. "Space sleeps, in love with space," such is the world revealed to the poet, the world of history turned into flat geometric surfaces. Space becomes a stimulus to creation ("The visibility of space around me called for a poem"), a motive force in the plot ("Through the visions of enamored space we move our tale back a year . . ."), both the hero of the work and a force that creates heroes. Lieutenant Schmidt learned how "amorous is homeless space," and space made of him a hero.

Broadening as much as possible the scope of the narration, Pasternak packs into his formed space images taken from a variety of sources. There are people, drawn with a few economical strokes, and landscapes which take on human passions and the feeling of the times, whole classes, estates, and groups, and a narrative of concrete historical events. Like nature, history too is drawn whole, as though in a single stroke, with a kaleidoscopic interaction of its rapidly moving events. Emphasis is placed on giving a total picture of life. In the poem *1905*, there pass in file fathers and children, peasants and factory workers, sailors and students. A storm at sea is transformed into the meeting on the *Potyomkin* and in the days of the December (1905) riots in Moscow "the sun looks through its binoculars and listens to the guns." Particular episodes are connected with the general condition of things, and the fortunes of the state itself:

> With every turn of the artillery wheels
> Someone fell
> From the gun crew,
> And with every
> Artillery horse
> Prestige fell.

Heterogeneous things and concepts are placed under a single token:

> Snow lay on the branches,
> In the wires,
> In the branchings of the parties,
> On the cockades of the dragoons
> And on the ties of the railroad track.

Pasternak is fond of presenting lists, sets, and enumerations that include objects drawn from various spheres of life and placed in a single series. In a few lines he sums up a whole situation while giving the concrete details of a picture, and it is all done as if by a single wave of the hand. . . . By this device he is able to give us broad historical panoramas along with particular episodes, as for example, in *Lieutenant Schmidt:*

> Benches, sabres, police braid,
> Faintings, shouts, sudden spasms of fighting,
> Reading, reading, reading, despite
> Dizziness, despite
> The fumes of sal ammoniac and the heady,

Drunken smell of tears and valerian,
Reading that's not a church chant,
A frame, and police veterans,
Pantaloons and the czar's sash,
And under the chandelier the sunrays' eight-faceted
reflection.

· · ·

Pasternak has a sharp eye for those "signs of the time" that are
scattered everywhere and communicate to every object a special significance. In his poems he is quick to develop the common denominator shared by human actions, sunsets, and city streets. And when in
Lieutenant Schmidt he speaks of the period of the Russo-Japanese
War, the eve of revolution, everything reiterates the uneasy state of
the world including even the Kiev hippodrome. History penetrates
into all the pores of life, turning the minutest details into its own
likeness.

Fields and distance sprawled in an ellipse.
The silks of umbrellas breathed the thirst for thunder.
The scorching day aimed through the bottomless sky
At the stands of the hippodrome.

The public sweated like bread *kvas* in a cooler,
Bewitched by the thawing of distances
Twirling in the sandstorm of hoofs and shank flaps,
The horses beat the open space like butter.

But behind it all, like the measured beating
From some sort of underground source
The war year climbed up behind the jockeys
Behind the horses and the spokes of the sulky wheels.

· · ·

. . . Pasternak is fond of defining things by way of their boundaries with other things; in a poem about the city he will sketch a sub-
urb, when dealing with the first of May he speaks of April 30.

How I love it in the first days
When there's still only talk of a Christmas tree.

In his lyrics of the period from the 1930's to the 1950's—a time when
narrative themes shifted from his poetry to his prose—this characteristic of Pasternak's artistic vision became especially marked. The lyrical
cycle entitled *Waves* (*Volny*), which opens the book *Second Birth*

(*Vtoroe rozhdenie*, 1932), is presented as an introduction to a theme, and it continues to develop until at last it becomes clear that the "introduction" itself is the real theme. The poet speaks of what he would like to write, and his very intention and promise turn into a story about the poet's world, moving on in succeeding waves into the future. That world is as yet unrealized, concealing within itself certain new possibilities and purposes similar to the plans that inspire the poet himself, and that, only half realized, also move on into the future. The very form of the introduction thus turns out to be pregnant with meaning and is in harmony with the ideas of inward historical growth and poetic development that are its central theme.

In Pasternak's next books—*On Early Trains* (*Na rannikh poezdakh*, 1943), *The Vast Earth* (*Zemnoy prostor*, 1945), *When It Clears Up* (*Kogda rezgulyaetsya*, 1957)—we once again observe the highly original way in which his poetry is linked to history. There are few direct comments on events. The important point is that poems written as a direct response to contemporary events, for example, some short poems about the Civil War (*Terrible Tale* [*Strashnaya skazka*], *Conqueror* [*Pobeditel*]), are markedly inferior in their artistic quality to others on the same theme written not as inspired propaganda but rather in his own original and intimately lyrical landscape-painting key (*Outpost* [*Zastava*], *Winter Nears* [*Zima priblizhaetsya*], and others). And it is noteworthy that the best verses, those permeated with the sense of history and of the present, often sound like an introduction or a foreword to the future. Usually they communicate a sense of the epoch through subtle movements in nature and in the soul of the poet, through details of the everyday routine. Thus, in the poem *Spring* (*Vesna*), when the end of the war is in the air, the poet strives to capture the voice of the time in the breath of ordinary life, now especially significant and full of promise:

> Everything this spring is special,
> Livelier than the sparrow's racket.
> I won't even try to tell
> How bright and quiet it is in my heart.
>
> One thinks in a different way, and writes.
> And as a loud octave in a chorus
> One hears the mighty earthlike voice
> Of the liberated lands.

In Pasternak's work of the period of the Revolution and of the twenties, the landscape itself takes on the signs of historical reality and is suffused with the Kremlin's storms, with the noisy talk of trees at their meetings. In his latest lyric poetry, however, history itself grows to resemble nature. Processes of growth and ripening predominate in it, and their outcome is astonishing but at the same time secret and imperceptible, like the slow growth of grass or the changes in the seasons (*Grass and Stones* [*Trava i kamni*], *After the Thunderstorm* [*Posle grozy*]). Of course this marks, not only the evolution of his style, but also a change in the poet's interests as an artist and in the life around him, which now reveals to him new facets and qualities. Phenomena of a moral nature concern Pasternak at this time, but not those whose focus is in the foreground of life. He is interested rather in processes taking place in the background, developing quietly and imperceptibly in the habits of everyday life, in the unsensational events in the life of the community and the individual. Here, he believed, was the kernel of history.

He was always attracted by "life without pomp and parade." Beginning with the thirties he more and more clearly prefers subjects lying as it were on the periphery of social life yet full of hidden historical significance (see further, for example, the poem *On Early Trains*). As he put it in one of his speeches, "Everything pompously elevated and rhetorical seems groundless, useless, and sometimes even morally suspect." He feels a special closeness now to the country roads, the cottages, the piers and ferries of the Russian province, as well as guileless feelings, and simple people doing humble work. Nature herself now seeks correspondences in such surroundings: fragrant tobacco is compared to a stoker at rest, spring puts on a padded jacket and finds a girl friend in the cattle yard. Prosaic and conversational idioms had already served him well as a source of poetry, but now they receive additional, ethical justification because they underline the author's democratic sympathies and his distaste for the magniloquent and vainglorious phrase.

. . .

Pasternak's later lyric poetry reveals his attitude to the world and the times in a perspective somewhat different from that of his early years. The idea of moral service becomes prevalent, although Pasternak does not cease to assert the perceptive force of poetry, its ability to catch living reality (and, of course, the moral element in the artistic apprehension of the world always was essential to him). At one time in his aesthetic system the image of poetry as a "sponge" was central, but now, without fully canceling that idea, another motif becomes dominant: "The purpose of artistic creation is to make a gift of the self." Toward the end of the poet's life, the sense of a realized historical mission rings out full and clear, and this is the source of the bright tonality of his late lyrics, notwithstanding the tragic notes in certain poems; and it is the source also of the dominant feeling of faith in the future.

.   .   .

Pasternak's peculiar view of the problems of art (in its relationship to nature, and to reality) is so organic to his vision of the world that we discover analogous attitudes and ideas even in his work on translation. That work is, of course, another chapter in his literary biography. Traits characteristic of his poetry reveal themselves even in this peripheral area, which as a matter of fact had, beginning with the thirties, a large and important place in his life. Pasternak as a translator strives above all to recreate the spirit of the original, disregarding the literal details of meaning. A work of genius is like living reality in that what it asks for is not a literal but a fully congenial rendition. And such a translation is, in principle and ideally, inspired by the original, takes its departure from the original, is in complete harmony with it, and yet is effective because of its own "uniqueness." According to Pasternak the translator should not merely make an accurate casting of the object he copies but should transmit its vital poetic force, thereby transforming his copy into an original creation on a level with the original even though in a different linguistic system.

It is clear that his reflections on the art of translation are very similar to his thoughts on art as such. He strives "above all for that deliberate freedom without which one can never come close to a great work of art." Comparing his work with that of other translators Pasternak said: "We are not in competition with anyone as to particular lines or passages. Rather we contend as to our total productions, and in their execution we are faithful to the great original, but at the same time bring it into consonance with our own speech system." "The relationship between the original and the translation should be one of root and derivation, of trunk and stem. A translation must come from an author who has long since experienced the original—long before his own effort to translate it. It should be the fruit of the original and its historical consequence."

Pasternak's best translations matured in him over a long period, while he prepared for them by the very process of his own inner growth. In a certain sense they are even autobiographical. For instance, his translations of Georgian lyric poetry were given special authenticity by his trips to Georgia in 1931 and 1936 and by his long friendship with a number of Georgian poets, as well as by that sensitive appreciation of the land and the people which inspired many of his own original poems. This might be called the Georgian "layer" in the creative work of Pasternak.

His translation of *Hamlet* appeared as a separate edition in 1941, initiating a series of translations of Shakespeare's tragedies. But in a poem written many years earlier we already find an idea that he later developed in his translations: "Ah! All of Shakespeare may be contained just in the fact that Hamlet chats quite unceremoniously with a ghost." "To chat unceremoniously," that is, to talk on the loftiest themes casually and colloquially, is, as we have already seen, Pasternak's habit. And indeed he has other traits that make him kin to Shakespeare's realism, freedom, pictorial quality, and so forth. "The influence of the original" (of course not alway direct but often complicated and refracted in diverse phenomena of world culture) in his case took effect long before he began his work on Shakespearean tragedy and to some extent was in harmony with his own interests and purposes. That is why Shakespeare took such deep root in the soil of Pasternak's own poetry. And his translating work, which was influenced by his own individual taste, manner, and predilections, in turn influenced his own original work. In this close and at the same time extraordinarily free communion with Shakespeare, whose majesty and power Pasternak strove to transmit "in all their uniqueness," he realized in practice his conviction that "translations are not simply a way of acquainting ourselves with particular literary works, but rather an instrumentality of the age-old intercourse between nations and cultures."

VI

The meaning of existence, the significance of man, the essence of the world—questions that agitated Pasternak for so many years—were especially absorbing to him near the end of his life, and at that time he devoted his lyric gift wholly to the search for basic principles, to the task of unraveling the mystery of first causes and final ends.

> In everything I feel like reaching
> Straight to the heart of the matter:
> In my work, in my search for a right path
> In my dark and troubled soul.

> Straight to the essence of the past,
> Straight to its cause,
> Straight to the basis, to the roots,
> Straight to the core.

The urge toward a philosophical formulation of life's problems is present in all the creative work of Pasternak. He is a poet-thinker, and he gravitates toward the art of broad generalization, and great spiritual saturation. He was always congenial to "that bottomless spirituality without which there is no originality, that infinity that opens up from any point in life in any direction and without which poetry is only a misunderstanding, temporarily unelucidated." In many of his works, of various periods, one senses the insistent desire "to dig down to the very essence." When telling about something he not only tries to show us what it is but to expose its primordial nature:

> My friend, you ask who commands
> That the speech of a pilgrim saint should burn?
> It was in the nature of lindens, and flagstones,
> And in the nature of summer to burn.

Not "The summer was hot," but "It was in the nature of summer to burn"—such is Pasternak's typical poetic method.

.   .   .

While the impressionist deliberately confines himself to asking the question "How is this object perceived at this moment?" Pasternak goes further and wishes to know what the object is. He looks into its depths, penetrates to its core, and frequently constructs an image that is a definition of its properties and essence. Thus he offers not only a first impression of an object, but a concept, an idea. Some of his poems are even called "definitions" (opredeleniya)—(Definition of Poetry [Opredelenie poezii], Definition of the Soul [Opredelenie dushi]), and the like. Other short poems have a structure that reminds us almost of a textbook or an explanatory dictionary:

> Poetry, I will swear
> By you, and will end up whispering hoarsely:
> Yours is not the bearing of a sweet singer. No,
> You are summer with a seat in third class,
> You are a suburb, not a refrain.

Pasternak is not afraid of such seemingly dry conclusions. He readily deduces formulas covering the nature of an object, works out its equations, investigates its properties and composition:

We were in Georgia. If you multiply
Destitution by tenderness, hell by paradise,
If you make a hothouse the base for glaciers,
The result you'll get will be this land.

And we'll understand in what exact doses
Success and labor and duty and air
Must be mixed with land and earth,
So as to produce men like these.

But even when he seeks the sense of a matter and delves into abstract realms, Pasternak's poems are always based on images, that is, they are whole and concrete. His "definitions" are only outwardly reminiscent of logical thought processes; actually they are reasoned out by means of the picture of life which is the basis of the composition.

In the poem quoted above, *In everything I feel like reaching* . . . (*Vo vsyom mne khochetsya doiti*), which has the character of an artistic program, Pasternak expresses the desire to write verses "about the properties of passion," to deduce its "law" and "principle." How then does he conceive this precious labor of investigating the essence of an object?

I would have laid out verses like a garden.
Trembling in all their veins,
Lindens would have flowered in them one after another—
Single file, one behind another.

I'd have brought the breath of roses into verse,
The scent of mint,
Of meadows, sedge, and haymaking,
The roll of thunder.

Just as Chopin once
Put the living miracle
Of farms, parks, groves, and graves,
Into his études.

Pasternak is a poet of the nearby and the concrete. He depicts only what he sees himself. But what he sees has an expansible significance and certain details are continually translated into a more general scheme. The ordinary objects surrounding us become the embodiment of good, of love, of beauty, and other eternal categories. Uniting the concrete and the abstract, the individual and the universal, the temporal and the eternal, the poet creates as it were an ideal portrayal of a real fact or person.

.   .   .

The war period understandably left its imprint on Pasternak's poetry and favored in particular the appearance of those archaic abstractions that came into wide literary use then. But actually such combinations of the highly abstract with the prosaically concrete were not so new for the poet as might seem at first. They did not involve a radical change in his stylistic system but rather a strengthening of what was already present in it. The ideal within the real was always more or less clearly visible in his images. To be convinced of this one need only turn to his love lyrics of the early thirties.

"My beauty, your whole bearing, your whole essence is near to my heart," the poet addresses his beloved and through her "bearing" discovers the "essence"—the laws of beauty:

> To you prayed Polycleitus.
> Your laws are long since published.
> Your laws are in the dim far-off of time.
> You have long been known to me.

He compares her with the future ("Measuring the silence with your steps, you enter like the future") and sees in her the embodiment of the "foundation" of life:

> To love some people is a heavy cross,
> But you are beautiful without a twist or turn,
> And the secret of your charm
> Is exactly the riddle of life.

Life, and this is characteristic of the world view of Pasternak, carries the "taste of great principles" into each of its manifestations. And the most insignificant objects become in its presence more ideal and are suffused with a light beating from within. A simple rest in a pine forest provides an occasion for generalization:

> And now we are immortal for a time,
> Here canonized as pine trees
> And freed from sickness, epidemic,
> And from death.

Once the gods were called "immortal," but now ordinary people coming into contact with eternal nature become eternal, for immortality, Pasternak believes, is poured out everywhere ("our daily immortality") and is only a synonym, another name, for life itself.

This intensity of poetic thought is especially noticeable in Pasternak from the thirties onward, and as his work developed the more conspicuous it became. It is somewhat more difficult to be aware of his thought in the early works, and the condensation of imagery was often taken as pretentiousness of form. As time passed Pasternak became more intelligible and that is why, naturally, the intellectual aspect of his poetry stood out more clearly. But his increasing clarity was itself largely due to the accelerated course of his thought, which became more ordered and more conscious of itself as an organizing principle of the verse.

In the early work of the poet the philosophical idea does not manifest itself outwardly, but is wholly concealed by the picture through which it is given. We almost never find explicit reflections and judgments offered in the author's name. The movement of thought is rather transferred to nature, which seems to become conscious of itself. Moreover, the author's idea is obscured by a superflux of impressions and associations that occur as though by accident, and it is complicated by the persistent effort to take into account all the interacting elements of life and tie them in a close net of metaphors. The early Pasternak is too consistent in his universal receptivity to be clear. And although, as we have seen, his idiom is basically natural and unforced, it has the natural quality of chaos bursting free and is in need of unraveling if it is to be wholly understood.

But the deep significance of Pasternak's poetry and the naturalness of his language could not forever remain behind the locked doors of "unintelligibility." The poet had always longed to be more accessible, to fuse the "bottomless spirituality" of his images and the "incredible simplicity" of their expression so fully that the reader might assimilate them effortlessly, as truth needing no explanation. This could be felt in certain works of the twenties and especially in *Second Birth*. Beginning with this book, and continuing in his lyrics of the thirties and forties, the poet moves toward simplicity and clarity.

.   .   .

Pasternak attained the simplicity he desired, but he still preserved the most valuable of his former achievements, the ability to perceive and depict the whole world. In his early work the barriers separating one thing from another, man from nature, time from eternity, were transcended through metaphor, which shifts objects and their qualities from one place to another but at the same time introduces confusion and a Babel of images. Now metaphor, continuing to play an important connective role, is no longer the only mediator between things. Their unity is achieved rather by a breadth and clarity in the poetic view of the world, a spiritual inspiration of feeling and thought before which all barriers fall, and life appears as one great whole where "nothing can perish," where a man lives and dies in the embrace of the Universal, and the wind—

> Agitates forest and cottage,
> Not each pine separately,
> But in their fulness all trees
> With all the boundless distance. . . .

In the late work of Pasternak, not only is the connection of one thing with another and the unity of the poet with the world given more simply and directly, but even the universe itself is "simpler than the sly ones think," and is founded on the primacy of a few simple, homogeneous realities that are clear to every man: land, love, bread, the sky. Sometimes a poem rests wholly on the affirmation of one such cornerstone of human existence. At the same time everyday life enters more and more into Pasternak's poetry, without, however, the complex allegory usually found in the early poems, but in the significance, clear to everyone, of everyday objects, habits, and occupations. The poetry of life's prose always inspired him, and in his later work it receives its full due.

During a half century of writing there were many changes and reconstructions in Pasternak's approach and style. But he remained true throughout his life to certain ideas, principles, and beliefs, which guided him in his work. One such deep conviction was that true art is always greater than itself, for it witnesses to the significance and greatness of life, and the immeasurable value of human existence. It is able to bear witness to these things without any declarations, profound symbols, or lofty allegories: the presence of greatness appears in the unfeigned reality of a story, in the hyperintense sensitivity and poetic inspiration of the artist, who, fascinated by the miracle of life, tells over and over again about just one thing, about its portentous presence, about life as such—even when his topic appears to be the snow falling or a noise in the forest.

This view of art is of course primarily applicable to the poetry of Pasternak himself. For him ordinary objects are marked by the fantastic presence of "life as such" and thus no less significant than, for example, Tyutchev's "primeval chaos" or Blok's "world music."

As always in Pasternak, what is most elevated turns out to be ultimately the most simple—life, filling everything and exhausting everything. "Poetry," said Pasternak, "will always remain that celebrated summit higher than any alp, which lies in the grass underfoot so that we need only bend down in order to see it and pick it up from the ground. . . ."

TRANSLATED BY THOMAS BERCZYNSKI

HERBERT E. BOWMAN

Postscript on Pasternak

The death of Boris Pasternak in 1960 can be taken to mark the end of an era in Russian literature. At least the chance is great that his work represents the last of the major survivals from a pre-Soviet literary world. For approximately a generation, one might say since the suicide of Mayakovsky in 1930, Soviet authority has imposed its controls upon a literary corporation that could always be suspected of concealing behind its official façade old creative currents of thought and old artistic traditions. But such survival as there has been, both in creation and in men, is surely at the point of becoming an event of the past. By and large, what happens from now on in Soviet literature will have to be viewed as truly indigenous to the Soviet world.

The death of Pasternak could hardly have suggested such significance if he had not succeeded in leaving *Doctor Zhivago* in our hands. His reputation as a poet was of course already secure, but he was a poet for the few. And it is remarkable how outspoken he became in dismissing his earlier work, as when he wrote: "I would never lift a finger to bring back from oblivion three-fourths of what I have written. . . . [*Doctor Zhivago* is] my chief and most important work, the only one I am not ashamed of and for which I can answer with the utmost confidence."[1] He seems to have been consciously joining that goodly company of Russian authors who have sought to enlarge the role of literary artist into the role of prophet.

Pasternak's quarrel with the editors of *Novy Mir*, the smuggled character of the publication of his novel in the West, the drama of the rejected Nobel Prize, the vast popular reading, or partial reading, of this unexpected consignment from the Soviet Russian world, all conspired to make of the appearance of the work an event in international

From *Survey*, No. 36 (1961), pp. 106-10. Reprinted by permission of *Survey*.

political life. It is hard to think of another literary work in the whole
history of literature that has aroused such a world-wide public stir.
Alas, we can never wash the finger marks of politics from anything
that comes to us from the Soviet Union. The political repercussions of
Doctor Zhivago certainly made most of the fame of the book. Even
in the years to come, it will remain impossible to read *Doctor Zhivago*
with completely undivided attention to it as a work of literary art, as
one can read *War and Peace* or *Madame Bovary*.

With such a *cause célèbre* at their disposal, Western critics were
urgently obliged to respond with commentaries. The result is that
Western commentary upon *Doctor Zhivago* has by this time expanded
into a considerable body of critical literature, almost a study in itself.
It is in fact becoming increasingly difficult to say anything new about
Doctor Zhivago, when so much has been said or at least hinted at.
But just because so much has been said, the reader of the many reviews becomes anxious, indeed almost belligerently determined, to
look again at the central meaning of the book.

If *Doctor Zhivago* could ever manage to clear the hurdles that
were set up in the reader's mind by politics, it had another great
hurdle to leap. This was the one erected by the knowledge that Pasternak's literary formation goes back to the age of Russian Symbolism
and post-Symbolism, and that he is a poet famous for the novelty of
his imagery. The very name "Doctor Zhivago," with its clear reference
to "live" and "life" in Russian roots, is enough to alert the scrupulous
critic to the presence of symbolic meanings and imaginative ambiguities. Similarly the first name of Yuri or George (St. George?). Similarly such a name as Evgraf. Lara or Larisa seems perhaps less promising. Unless one manages to discover a St. Larisa and works to make
something out of that. Indeed, such a book as this can be made to
provide grains for the mills of the most esoteric symbol-chopping.[2]
And beyond all the intricate minutiae, the reader cannot help but
notice the rich symbolic possibilities in the larger meanings of the
book. The two women in Yuri Zhivago's life, the wife Tonia and the
sweetheart Lara, suggest many possible meanings, all perhaps circling
around the image of Lara as the force in Russian life that draws
Zhivago—the feminine lure of Russia herself; and the opposite image
of Tonia as perhaps the more formal, more Westernising influence in
Russian life—Tonia the official wife, who will escape to France in the
end. The suspicion, however, that the book may have been intended
as a single long parable seems to seek in vain for its justification.
Edmund Wilson's argument, written at the beginning of the popular

discussion of the novel, that the theme of the whole work is really Death and Resurrection, is never really demonstrated.[3] Wilson leaves us with a few curious hints and presumably hopes that we will fill in the big picture for ourselves.

The dangers of too much sophistication in the interpretation of the work of literary art could hardly be better illustrated than by the case of *Doctor Zhivago*. What is especially disappointing in so much that has been written is that the major meaning of the book, far below or far beyond political strategy or literary tactics, has inspired so little genuine excitement. It is as if Pasternak had presented us with a gift, a great simple gift, and we spent all our time fussing with the wrappings. What is this gift? What was the author so anxious to convey? What inspires his book? For the greatness of *Doctor Zhivago* lies primarily in the revelation that, in the words of Rilke, "life is a glory." It is this great open secret, that only wisdom knows and that art is forever seeking to represent, that Pasternak has enshrined in his novel.

Against the constant background of political realities, the militant political realities of twentieth-century Russia, which almost seem to overwhelm human existence, Zhivago might have been expected to be nurturing some kind of relevant attitude, some theory. If not a political theory, then at least an apolitical one. Some direct answer, in any case, to the burning problems of life in Russia. But the arresting fact is that he has no such answer to offer. More than that: speculative of mind though he is, he never seems to be speculating directly upon the problems that appear to demand an answer most urgently. In this seeming weakness and non-engagement of Zhivago, Pasternak is in fact making a daring assertion: that the ultimate issues of life do not lie among what seem to be the momentous upheavals of history, but are revealed solely in that life-within-life that can be known only through the individual self. To call such an assertion daring is not to say that it is new. Pasternak is the first to insist that he is only rediscovering and reaffirming. For Zhivago or Pasternak, the eminent spokesman of his truth is Christ. But it is not "religion" that is being affirmed; it is that discovery of life out of which religion, or art, is made.

The disservice of over-sophisticated interpretations of Pasternak's novel is not in any one argument that is devised or any one point that is made. The great disservice is the creation of an attitude that is unreceptive to the lyrical simplicity of the book's major theme. To think of Zhivago as anything other than a suffering, exulting human person; to think of Lara as anything other than a Russian girl or Russian woman, is simply to lose touch at the outset with the solid reality in which Pasternak intends to work. Of course Lara will become for Zhivago something like the very embodiment of his beloved Russia, indeed of reality itself. But this is what every lover finds, this is the kind of rhapsody that every lover sings. Obviously, in a book so rich in imagery, in this poet's novel, there will be many imaginative hints and constructions. And we as readers are permitted to let our imaginations wander freely among the lights and shadows; but we are required first of all to see the real persons and the real objects that exist in the universe of this solid book.

The sense of life that quickens its pages draws all its power from Zhivago's dogged insistence upon remaining down to earth. This is what gives his story its triumphant meaning. If Zhivago did not inhabit the same world that we inhabit, he would lose his hold on us. But most of all he would not be able to say what Pasternak wants to tell us: that life lies not in some rarefied atmosphere, either of aesthetic daydreams or supernatural marvels or political abstractions, but among washtubs and hayfields, where these pure and humble things of common life are really recognised. It is in this spirit that Zhivago writes in praise of Pushkin in an entry in his diary:

> Air, light, the noise of life, reality burst into his poetry from the streets as though through an open window. The outside world, everyday things, nouns, crowded in and took possession of his lines, driving out the vaguer parts of speech. Things and more things lined up in rhymed columns on the page. . . . Only the familiar transformed by genius is truly great. The best object lesson in this is Pushkin.[4]

One of the sacred objects in Zhivago's world is a large, convenient table near the window of a well-furnished room. One keeps seeing that room in Varykino as if it were Zhivago's home in the world. And indeed in a delirium Zhivago had once dreamed of Moscow streets running over his desk, under the orange glow of the lamplight. Lara, too, in longing thoughts about returning home to her husband again, thinks mainly of Pasha's desk in the lamplight.

Lara is almost the ministering angel of common work and common tasks. She is eternally busy at the plain jobs of household life, and she becomes in this "prosaic, weekday aspect of her being . . . more breath-taking than if . . . [she were] going to a ball."[5] Silently watching her in the library at Yuriatin, Zhivago reflects: "She reads not as if reading were the highest human activity, but as if it were the simplest thing that even animals could do. As if she were carrying water from a well, or peeling potatoes."[6]

In a book that in itself has come to represent a kind of testament of human freedom, and in which the freedom of the person is everywhere asserted, it is remarkable how absent from its pages is the spirit of abandon, of excess. For all their animation, both Lara and Zhivago remain the very models of good sense. Not for a moment do they live together in a fool's paradise. Their deepest wish is to be able to live their lives sensibly, in the order and peace of good housekeeping and honest relationships. Even in the child Katenka, Lara observes the instincts of order and domesticity. In Lara's dissatisfaction with the gypsy life she must lead with Zhivago, she is only repeating in her more feminine way the reflection of one of Zhivago's old private thoughts: ". . . real life, meaningful experience, the actual goal of all quests, this was what art aimed at—homecoming, return to one's family, to oneself, to true existence."[7] The image of Lara and Zhivago seeking quiet domesticity in the abandoned home at Varykino becomes almost the central image of the book. They know they are living in a state of siege, barring off the rats and the cold inside, the wolves of evil omen outside, and beyond that the desolate expanse of winter and mortal danger. Within this fragile sanctuary at the end of the world, Lara busies herself with peeling potatoes and heating water, and Zhivago with writing poems. What setting could ever be devised to give greater poignancy to the sanctity of ordinary life? In the very midst of all the upheaval that surrounds them in the Russian world and threatens their very existence, Lara and Zhivago not only stay at home but seek home all the more desperately. Rather than seeking freedom in escape, they are bent on finding the stillness in the eye of the hurricane. It is part of the grim realism of the book that they will not be allowed to stand very long against the wind, which will finally blow them both into oblivion. But while they are able to endure, they stay fast. In all of Russian literature it would be hard to find a work that expresses more constant love of the Russian world that *Doctor Zhivago*. Russia is the place in which all the worst things are happening, a world that will finally drive both Lara and Zhivago to their death. But throughout their lives their greatest longing remains to find their home in it again. The love of life that permeates *Doctor Zhivago* is never abstract; it is always life as Zhivago and Lara know it, in the place they know. This is a love so great that it is willing to become martyrdom.

Russian nature is always invading. In the midst of life's cyclones, Zhivago is always being refreshed by a spring evening, the light from the sky, the smell of fields and trees, or woods in the setting sun. His sense of the world outdoors is so strong and lively that even in the bleakest times, as during his long walking journey back to Moscow, he is still capable of the old Pasternakian wit:

> The woods and the fields offered a complete contrast in those days. Deserted by man, the fields looked orphaned as if his absence had put them under a curse. The forest, however, well rid of him, flourished proudly in freedom as though released from captivity.[8]

This love of life was always visible in the work of Pasternak the poet, long before the writing of *Doctor Zhivago*. It is a love that now rises to pathos, because it must declare itself in the midst of hostile forces of so great a magnitude that it becomes the work of gallantry to speak, in the teeth of the gale, in the still, small voice of the poet. The significance of Pasternak's last work lies in his refusal to forsake the common earth; indeed, in his unaltered insistence that life resides only among common things, in unmannered relationships, in wholesome work and robust sanity. The pressure of dire events only forces Zhivago, like Pasternak, to draw closer to the plain sources of his being, to plant his feet all the more firmly on Russian earth.

Out of this momentous assertion that "the poetry of earth is never dead," all the major attitudes and thoughts of Zhivago and Lara can be deduced. And so the novel is filled with comment on many topics; but the comment can always be referred back to the stand that Zhivago and Lara have taken toward life.

No sharper judgment of political realities is made than by the observer who insists merely on remaining human. War, revolution, propaganda, terror—all the cruelties and defacements of political life are never more rudely exposed than by the look of a simple human eye. Pasternak's man with the right arm and left leg chopped off would never have been allowed to crawl into the pages of an official history of the Revolution. Pasternak's view of the Revolution, it has been said, would have been much less cruel if he had been a political writer.[9] Lara's lament over the falseness that had invaded her relations with Pasha-Strelnikov, her husband, is the most convincing condemnation of the falseness that corrupted Russian life generally after the Revolution. In this way, of course, *Doctor Zhivago* is a commentary

upon Russian history. Zhivago lives in the shadows of the flames of
twentieth-century Russia. But the verdict his life passes upon his world
never takes its bearings from political thinking. By remaining simply a
man, Zhivago passes his final judgment on the most critical historical
events of his time. In order to find its political significance, the reader
of *Doctor Zhivago* must first of all assimilate its sense of life, that
seems careless of politics.

Similarly, though there is religious discussion in the book, we are
always being reminded that Zhivago and Lara are not overtly religious, display no formal religiosity. What Zhivago is expressing is life,
not religion—but he finds thereby that he has achieved a fresh understanding of what Christ was talking about. Zhivago is the truly
religious person, who always seeks the place where life lies, and who
by so doing arrives at the intimate knowledge of religious meaning.
If one needed confirmation of this, Pasternak himself confirmed it in
an interview reported in 1958, in which he said:

> We have learned that we are the guests of existence, travellers
> between two stations. We must discover security within our-
> selves. During our short span of life we must find our own in-
> sights into our relationship with the existence in which we par-
> ticipate so briefly. Otherwise, we cannot live! This means, as I
> see it, a departure from the materialistic view of the nineteenth
> century. It means a reawakening of the spiritual world, of our
> inner life—of religion. I don't mean religion as a dogma or as a
> church, but as a vital feeling. Do you understand what I
> mean?[10]

In a recent discussion of *Doctor Zhivago,* John Strachey concludes
that the *"troika* of values" in Pasternak's novel consists of "aesthetic,
ethical, and religious experience."[11] Like so much of the literary criticism of the book, this brand of political and social criticism simply
submerges the inner excitement of Pasternak's message under a heavy
layer of thought. By finding only such colourless abstractions, Strachey
simply confesses that he can show us nothing in the book that would
justify our close attention—to say nothing of any quality in the work
that might excite our imagination or refresh our spirit. What originality can one possibly see in making the old sweeping gesture of pointing to "aesthetic, ethical, and religious experience," as if that were
all that Pasternak wished to do. Of course these are aspects of the
book. But they are, at the most, abstract aspects of a central lyrical
vitality. Pasternak is announcing a much more lively lesson than such
worn-out words suggest. He is saying that we must find life again.

And that out of the rediscovery of life, achieved in the midst of the battle of strident ideologies, that besieged and belittled hero, the single person, will find his centre again. Pasternak's hero is not a troika of values, which would be nothing for us, already gorged on "values." His hero is simply any one really living person. Yuri Zhivago is such a person. Lara also. If the book has a major weakness, it is that only Yuri and Lara are really alive in it. Around them come and go many lesser people; around them swirl some of the fiercest storms of the twentieth century. Just by remaining unalterably human and alive, sane and responsive, they embody the good news of Pasternak's testament.

The achievement of *Doctor Zhivago*, almost apart from its successes and failures as a novel, lies in extracting this joyful teaching out of the least promising circumstances of contemporary Soviet life. In *Doctor Zhivago*, Russian literature once again returns to its classic task of meditating upon the mystery of life—in an age of Socialist-Realism, when the political control of literature makes the work of genuine edification in art not only unpopular but illegitimate. For once in a long time, a literary work from Russia has succeeded in transcending politics and striking through to the reader's own centre of being. If out of this we insist on making just another political treatise or another literary fable, we simply reveal in ourselves the waning of that sense of life which Pasternak's novel was intended to restore.

CLARENCE BROWN

On Reading Mandelstam

I

In his imaginative and interesting article "On Freedom in Poetry" Vladimir Markov wittily constructs the following scale of values for contemporary Russian poetry. At the bottom is Esenin "for wide, general consumption"; in the middle are Gumilyev and, since recent times, Pasternak; and at the top, where he is available only to those who aspire to membership in a poetic elite, is Osip Mandelstam.[1] Whether this "unshakeable scale of values" . . . is likely to prove permanent in all its parts need not concern us now. But few would dispute that Mandelstam's position at the summit is an accurate image of the esteem in which he is held at this moment, and not only in the West. One could go further. Are there not signs here and there—see the reference to an "elite" above—that there is *in statu nascendi* a true cult of Mandelstam?

It is perhaps a natural and even an unavoidable development, and certainly it springs from impulses that are sympathetic and right. He has been these many years an underground, forbidden poet. He is both far from us and close to us in time: there are those who actually knew him, heard him read his poetry, walked the streets of Petersburg and Theodosia with him, and retain on the retina of their memory an image of the man in life. But their number grows smaller. Mandelstam met a fate of such savage injustice that its lightest word can harrow up the soul, and in the Soviet Union he has been waiting for nearly a decade in the anteroom of posthumous rehabilitation. There

From *Osip Mandelshtam. Sobranie sochinenii* (New York: Inter-Language Literary Associates, 1967), pp. i-xxvii. Reprinted by permission of Inter-Language Literary Associates and the author. The poems quoted in this article originally appeared in Russian and were translated for this edition by the editor.

146

is therefore a distinct cachet that attaches to knowing anything at all about him or about his difficult, demanding poetry. There is a natural outrage at what was done to him and this multiplies one's determination to see just homage paid to his legacy.

But a cult disadvantages no one so much as its own object. It requires its ikon and its vita, and these have already begun to take shape—final shape—and to freeze the living lineaments of a man into the standard image of an object of contemplation. The memoirists have begun to rely heavily on each other, and there can be little doubt that there are now certain itinerant motifs in the word-image of him that wander from one set of reminiscences to the other. When Vsevolod Roždestvenskij's memoirs began to appear in *Zvezda* there was little doubt that the unnamed poet described in the following phrases was Mandelstam: "quite short, rather puny, not much to look at . . . a huge head, grand, rather theatrical gestures . . . an almost childish naïveté . . . the bright, sharp eye of a bird."[2] (Any remaining doubt was removed when, in 1962, Roždestvenskij published his memoirs in book form and named Mandelstam—a hopeful sign). Virtually every one of these words can be found in several other notes on his appearance and character. One émigré writer, who never laid eyes on Mandelstam, furnishes more or less the same picture of him, citing as his authority a brother-in-law who had once (at the age of ten) heard the poet in Xarkov.

As a young man Mandelstam took frank pleasure in the evidence that his name had spread beyond the narrow limits of the literary circles of Petersburg. In Kiev he positively basked in the unexpected adulation with which he was met, and observed that many poets there knew his verse by heart. This reaction is so normal that only its absence would be remarkable. But the maturer poet had other and more complicated ideas about his audience. Some of these he put into one of the most brilliant of his critical essays, "O sobesednike." When I asked the poet N.[3] about this work and about Mandelstam's attitude toward his readers in general, I was told, "He was unhappy about the kind of people who read him. He thought them too refined, overly subtle in their reactions to poetry. He wanted to be read by simple people, by Komsomol youngsters, and not by poets alone." For him, poetry was at the center of life, not an ornament of its rarer and more sequestered moments, and he desired that it should be so for everyone. As he did not wish to be the exclusive property of a few, he could hardly have desired for himself a worse fate than to become the center of a cult.

But he will, I think, be spared this, for a cult derives all its seductive power from the distance and inaccessibility of the object. The publication by Gleb Struve and Boris Filippov of all of the known writings of Mandelstam will make him available to a wide audience of Russian readers both in the emigration and (though less conveniently) at home. Whether Mandelstam will achieve exactly the audience he desired—does any writer?—may be doubted, but he is, at least, now removed from the category of poets whose unpublished work is sedulously concealed by some, clandestinely circulated by others, and read by few.

As a glance at the bibliography in Volume III will disclose, the publication by the same editors of a sizable collection of Mandelstam's work in 1955 had as one of its more important consequences the introduction of his poetry to readers of Russian literature in the West. The translations made by poets of the stature of the American Robert Lowell and the German Paul Celan testify to the impact that Mandelstam has had outside of the bounds of his own literature. The great growth of Russian studies in recent years, particularly in England and America, has provided a very large audience for the brilliant poets and writers of Russia's "Silver Age." Among these Mandelstam has a reputation, exaggerated but not altogether groundless, for being extraordinarily difficult and opaque. The present brief introductory note aspires to nothing more than the function of a convenient English bridge by which, it is hoped, a good part of Mandelstam's audience will find an approach to the poetry and prose which await their more concentrated attention.

II

Mandelstam's earliest poetry is marked by an extraordinarily low temperature and a lack of movement that sometimes amounts to virtual stasis. It is characterized by quietude of manner, whiteness of color, elegance of form. The emotions are chaste, and there is a solemn ceremoniousness in the tones and attitudes of the speaker of the poems, whose presence is seldom felt. It is remarkable how often Mandelstam's diction is colored by negative words. Here are a few examples: nežiloj ("uninhabited") . . . nezvučnyj ("soundless") . . . nebogatyj ("poor") . . . nebyvalyj ("unprecedented") . . . nebytie ("nonexistence") . . . nevidimyj ("invisible") . . . neživoj ("lifeless") . . . nepodvižnyj ("motionless") . . . And so on. The list of such words could be a very long one, but these can serve to illustrate a frequent tendency of Mandelstam's: to summon up a quality or attribute only to deny it.

He was a master at describing emptiness, absence, vacancy, silence. I know of no equal to him in this regard, at least not in literature. In painting Andrew Wyeth often achieves a Mandelstamian feeling of emptiness, and I think the comparison is doubly apt since both Wyeth and Mandelstam lend poignancy to their "desert places" by including some reminder of human life. Both artists show us not the vacancies of the sea or the ininhabited steppe but the emptiness of rooms. I like to imagine to myself an illustration by Wyeth of a line that would seem peculiarly suited to his mood and talent:

> Silence, like a spinning-wheel, stood there in the white room.

This blankness is not altogether dead, as it never is in Mandelstam. It has a human nerve in it. The more we perceive that remarkable figure of the spinning wheel to betoken a now ended human activity, the more we sense the peculiar stillness of a thing whose function is to move, the more densely does that image gather the silence around it.

Here is a poem which has been published in different variants. I take the version that appeared in Mandelstam's first book of poetry *Kamen* (Stone) in 1913.

> Hearing stretches its sensitive sail,
> The widened gaze grows empty
> And through the silence floats
> A soundless chorus of midnight birds.

I think it is easy to appreciate, even across the years that separate us from this poem, the shock that was felt in the literary world of St. Petersburg when it made its appearance. The late Georgij Ivanov testified in his reminiscences of Mandelstam that his reaction on reading such poems as this was a sudden stabbing envy: "Why didn't I write that!"[4] And he quotes Gumilyev as having said that this poetic envy was far more accurate than any rational analysis to determine the true "weight" of someone else's poetry.

How extraordinary and how daring these images are! And not merely daring, but permanently daring. Time has not effaced their originality, and one recalls Ezra Pound's having defined literature as "news that *stays* news."

Nor have they anything to fear from analysis, which is durability of a sort that again argues the genius of their author. What is their effect? In the first line

Hearing stretches its sensitive sail

one is provided with a visual image which jolts the imagination through its equation of an abstraction (the sense of hearing) with a piece of maritime equipment. But the image is far more than visual. There is something tactile in our perception of the tautness of a sail stretched tight against the wind, and this sense is enhanced by the addition of the epithet *čutkij*, which means "delicately sensitive" in both the basic physical sense and in the transferred sense for which "tactful" is a common though not very satisfactory equivalent. And there is yet a third way in which this image strikes us, though I am not sure that I can find the words to express it (and I take such disability as the final proof that one is in the presence of poetic art of the highest calibre). "Auditory" is hardly the adequate description for a quality of sense perception which is not that of sound but of *silence* (it is later in the poem that one learns this particular aspect of the first image: the poem is about emptiness and silence). And the function of the sail metaphor is to make that silence almost palpable. This third way of perceiving the image is perhaps best expressed by calling it an intense, almost painful, *awareness* of the sense of hearing, but not of anything conveyed to the consciousness by that sense.

In the next image the sense of sight is treated in much the same way, and it has much the same sort of effect:

The widened gaze grows empty.

Here one finds not the word for sight itself (zrenie) but the word *vzor* "gaze," which is a sort of buried hypostatic image: a piece of sight, an instance of sight. This hypostasized sight is made more material by the epithet that is applied to it: *rassirennyj* "broadened, widened." And by the verb: it "becomes empty," which implies the condition of having been full, of having contained something.

This is a poem about emptiness so complete that it is hardly expressible, but obviously images and sounds must be found to convey the emptiness. That the dilemma can decidedly *not* be resolved by simple, declarative statement can be learned by looking at Milton's attempt to do something similar. In *Paradise Lost* (I/62–64) his purpose is to convey the absence of light, as Mandelstam's was to convey the absence of sound and vision:

. . . . yet from those flames
No light, but rather darkness visible
Served only to discover sights of woe.

The phrase "darkness visible" appeals uniquely to the intelligence, to purely rational perception and to no other.

And so it is an inevitable contradiction that after the two images which transmit the emptiness of hearing and sight, one is presented with an image that is visual and auditory:

> And through the silence sails
> A soundless chorus of midnight birds.

Silence itself is materialized as a medium through which these midnight birds fly, and the fundamental contradiction is emphasized by a device which is frequent in Mandelstam: the *contradictio in adjecto* —*nezvučnyj xor:* soundless chorus.

The tenaciousness of early reputations is well known. The poems that I have been talking about—the cool, quiet, laconic poetry bathed in the pale radiance of other worlds—is the poetry of Mandelstam's earliest youth. It is regarded by many as his best work (there are those who regularly prefer a poet's first poems and regard the changes wrought by maturity as a sort of betrayal), but it would be a great mistake to regard it as his only work.

In a poem of 1912 Mandelstam had exclaimed of some ball "thrown from a dim planet"

> So there it is, a genuine
> link with a mysterious world!

But one year later this Symbolist link with other worlds had been abruptly transformed into a tennis ball, batted about in a real tennis game between a "sportive girl" and an "ever-young Englishman." The pervading gloom of the Symbolist manner was replaced for a while by the Acmeist gaiety and delight in the things of this world. Mandelstam had written many poems filled with a longing for muteness—perhaps a remnant of the decadent *amor fati*—and this scheme was to return later in such superlatively moving poems as *To the German Language* but for the time being there was some delightfully witty poems to be written—poems about the cinema, about Carskoe Selo—perfectly empty little poems that reveal the poet disporting himself in his language and taking nonchalant delight in its consonants and vowels.

.   .   .

And the themes range over the whole world of art and all of Western culture. There are the famous poems in which the poet's vision caresses the immense perspectives and the classical architecture of his beloved Petersburg (to which he gave the Deržavinian and Hellenic name of Petropol), and the architecture of Paris (Notre Dame), of Moscow, where all the gentle churches lend their voices to a maidenly choir, and where Mandelstam was attracted as always by whatever seemed to him classical and Mediterranean in Russian culture:

> And the five-domed Moscow Cathedrals
> with their Italian and Russian soul
> remind me of the coming of Aurora
> but with a Russian name and in a coat of fur.

His poem about the Hagia Sophia in Istanbul is one of his most beautiful and beloved.

Other themes come from literature—all the way from the epic poems of Homer through the classical tragedies of Racine to the Victorian novels of Dickens and the weird tales of Edgar Allan Poe. Whatever one may think of the Soviet critic Selivanovskij's other opinions about Mandelstam, there is much truth in his remark that Mandelstam's poetry is not a reflection of life, but a reflection of its reflection in art.[5] And a critic who is far more well disposed toward Mandelstam, Viktor Žirmunskij, has applied to his work Schlegel's tag "die Poesie der Poesie."[6]

This brings us to two remarks that are perhaps repeated more often than others about the poetry of Osip Mandelstam: that it is impersonal and that it is impenetrable.

Certainly there is enough on the surface of his poetry, and especially of the early and better known poetry, that would seem to many people impersonal. Those who call it so generally have in mind the little *thing* poems with their nearly Japanese laconism (the nameless fruit falling from the tree in four brief lines) or the architectural poems, or the meditative poems. In other poems, though a *persona* may be present, it seems to matter so little, it seems to be so much a part of the patterned movement that it becomes lost, as in a trick picture, in the general composition. In the body of his work—by which I mean those of his poems that have been heretofore published and are known to the general reader—there are so few poems that concern themselves with anything outside of poetry and the other arts, there are so few that seem, for example, to point a moral, or advance a cause, or tell an entertaining story, or in fact to solicit our attention on any ground at all that is not in the strictest sense poetic ground, that there seems to be a certain lack of warmth, of humanness, about them. Hence the recurrent phrases: pure poetry, a poet's poet, rarefied atmosphere, museum-like, etc.

As for the charge of impenetrability, this is made by people who fail to understand Mandelstam because they are looking for the meaning in a place where he did not put it. This is the more to be regretted since Mandelstam himself, who had one of the clearest and most elevated conceptions of poetry of any Russian writer of his time, left in his critical writings explicit directions for reading his poetry. Those who use the word *meaningless* against him generally have in mind the notion that few of his poems can be paraphrased. The poet himself, meanwhile, regarded whatever is susceptible of paraphrase as belonging outside of poetry proper. It was not his concern to couch a prose meaning in the outward form of metered language.

Ultimately, of course, such charges are irrefutable because the terms "impersonal" and "impenetrable" are unspecifiable, relative, and subjective. But it has seemed to me that some light might be thrown on this matter by selecting a single poem of moderate length, one that already has a clear reputation for being a difficult, typically Mandelstamian poem, and examining it minutely with the aid of all that recent research into the life and work of this poet has unearthed. Such a poem is "Solominka, The Straw."[7]

You will doubtless not require the citation of authorities to know that this is a difficult, refractory work. Nevertheless, it is interesting to note that Georgij Adamovič has written of "Solominka": "This poem really represents a 'lofty muteness,' in the phrase of Gumilev. But can one illuminate this muteness? Hardly."[8]

Adamovič, a former Acmeist and a personal acquaintance of the poet, is a warm and generous admirer of Mandelstam. His remark is not a "charge"—far from it. Yet it is true that Adamovič's question, and his answer, can be found, *mutatis mutandis*, in all the standard attacks on Mandelstam's opacity.

I do not propose to assert that this is an easy poem or that it has a vividly recognizable personal element in it. It is, however, not so difficult that it cannot be made to yield a good deal of complexly articulated meaning. And it is by no means entirely divorced from the central concerns of the author's life. If we read it as closely as we can, if we follow all the clues to the end, and relate it to as much of Mandelstam's life as we can discover, I think we will conclude that it is more than a loose organization of hints and obliquities, clothed in gorgeous sound. If it proves to be more, perhaps it will appear that we must change our notions of how it is necessary to read him.

Our first impression is that we have here some of that mere *akustika* of which Mandelstam had accused the Symbolists. By the second stanza we are enmeshed in a dense web of phonic repetitions:

> Solómka zvónkaja, solomínka sukhája,
> Vsjú smért' ty výpila i sdélalas' nezhnéj,
> Slomálas' mílaja solómka nezhivája,
> Ne Saloméja, net, solomínka skoréj.

It does not require very intense investigation to see that two names are of primary importance. One is Solominka, the title, which means "a straw" but which is here sometimes capitalized and directly addressed as a person. The other is the name Salomeja. These two words, which closely resemble each other in sound, also provide the sound pattern for much of the poem. We see the near relatives of Solominka and Salomeja turning up everywhere: bessonnaja, bessonnicy, v ogromnoj spal'ne, solomka zvonkaja, v kruglom omute, v ogromnoj komnate, the verb slomalas, etc. Certainly, there is a good deal of obsessive toying with the basic phonic material.

What, in the plainest sense, is the poem about? It pictures a huge bedchamber in a house on the bank of the Neva in Petersburg. It is night in the month of December. The day is dead, the year is dying, and the subject of the poem seems to be death and the transformation that death brings. Throughout the poem, the speaker seems uneasy about a question of identity: Solominka or Salomeja? Toward the end of the first part, a new name enters, and there is a new question of identity:

> No, not Solominka—Ligeja, the dying—

Not Solominka (or Salomeja) but Ligeja, a name with the same ending as Salomeja. In the last line of the first part, the speaker himself enters with a line that reads like the happy conclusion of an effort— the blessed words have been found:

> I learned you, blessed words

These blessed words are names, the new one, Ligeja, and others:

> Lenore, Solominka, Ligeja, Serafita.

The identity of Solominka-Salomeja is left unclear to the end. But it can hardly matter now, since she is dead, whoever she is, and will return no more. Her place has been taken by the Decemberish Ligeja. This name, repeated three times in the poem, has assumed an importance that cannot be ignored. Was Mandelstam using this and the other blessed words for sound effects alone, or do they have some further significance?

Ligeja is one of the pale ladies of Edgar Allan Poe. She appears in a weird tale, which bears her name as the title, published in 1838. I will not go into detail here but will describe only those features of the story that bear on Mandelstam's poem.

Ligeja is an incredibly wise, ethereal creature. She is married to the narrator of Poe's tale, but she dies of some wasting disease and leaves her husband in an agony of remorse. He goes away, marries another woman, whom he cannot love since he is forever comparing her to the lost Ligeja. They live in a ruined abbey somewhere in England. The narrator begins to depend on opium, and finally his second wife falls ill and seems to be dying. Her bedchamber is in a turret of the abbey, and Poe lavishes his weirdest touches on the description of this dismal room. It is huge in size, the ceilings are immensely high, the walls are hung in some material covered with strange arabesque designs which assume fantastic shapes as the constant wind blows behind the hangings and causes them to shift about. There are sarcophagi with carved lids standing about in corners of the room. When the second wife of the narrator dies she is wrapped in her shroud and laid on the bed in this strange room. The narrator watches by her bed, where he is horrified to see her return to life. When the shroud is unwound, it turns out that the body of the narrator's second wife has been replaced by the resurrected Ligeja.

Limitations of space will prevent a step by step comparison of Mandelstam's poem with this story by Poe. But a close comparison would reveal how much of the tone, the atmosphere—and more importantly the specific details such as the sarcophagus, the high ceiling, the peculiar animation of the room—Mandelstam did derive from "Ligeja." The central moment of Poe's work involves the changed identity of the two female figures, the metamorphosis of one into the other, and the gradual revelation of this to the narrator, and this, as we have seen, is also the fundamental concern of "Solominka."

The suggestiveness of the line of "blessed words" does not stop here. The name Lenore recalls an even better known heroine of Poe, but it is the name Serafita which sheds more light on the creative processes at work in this poem.

Séraphita is the title of one of the philosophical novels of Balzac, published in 1835. Practically devoid of any novelistic events whatever, *Séraphita* is devoted mainly to an exposition of the mystical philosophy of Swedenborg. The character from whose name the title is derived is related to this philosophy by birth—she is the daughter of a disciple of the master—and also by being a veritable incarnation of Swedenborgian doctrine. The great interest which Séraphita presents for an interpretation of "Solominka" is to be seen in the fact of her disputed identity. To Minna, a young girl, she appears as a youth Séraphitus, but to Wilfrid and to Pastor Becker she appears in female form as Séraphita. Ultimately, the character is neither and both, for its essence is ethereal and angelic, but as one of the blessed names, it makes its contribution to the unified effect of Mandelstam's poem.

The poem is about death, the death of a beautiful, loved woman. The names from Poe—Lenore and Ligeja—are of two of his famous dead ladies. The name Séraphita is that of a love-ideal, a creature who in Balzac's novel is finally transfigured and taken into heaven.

But the death of the central character in Mandelstam's poem—whose name, Salomeja, deliberately left unexplained till now, engendered so much of the sound texture of this work—is happily only metaphorical. For the subject of the poem is still alive. Princess Salomeja Nikolaevna Andronikova, a famous Georgian beauty who was the toast of St. Petersburg and the object of more than one poet's attentions, left Russia after the Revolution. Her married name is Halpern, and she now resides in London. I am very grateful to her for the generous interest she has taken in my studies of Mandelstam, and for the memories of him which she has so kindly shared with me. It appears that the picture of the enormous bedchamber looking out on the black Neva derives not only from literature but also from life.

It is incidentally interesting to note that this reading of the poem "Solominka" by Mandel'štam serves to illuminate a much more recent poem by the last of the great trio of Acmeists, Anna Axmatova. The poem is entitled "Ten'" ("Shadow"), and it is clearly addressed to Axmatova's old friend, Princess Andronikova, for it contains the line

A poet called you "Solominka."

Most modern poetry demands much of its readers, but there are few modern Russian poets whose demands are so heavy as those of Mandelstam. "If you would read me, you must have my culture." He was proud to link himself to Dante and to require, as Dante did, that his reader possess that highest quality of the truly educated man: "dogadlivost," which means quickness of apprehension, the ability to take a hint.

·   ·   ·

III

The Silver Age of Russian literature, like its Golden Age, was for the greater part an age of poetry. Both were marked by an extraordinary renovation of verse technique and by a reawakening of poetic inspiration. But our concentration on the remarkable achievements in poetry has sometimes obscured for us the truly astonishing prose of the Russian modernist movements. This is the more to be wondered at when one considers that it was generally the same people who produced both. The Soviet critic N. Berkovskij, who wrote of Mandelstam's prose with great insight and sensitivity, if not with unqualified approval, declared in 1930 that the best Russian prose then being written was that of a reigning "triumvirate" of poets,—Tixonov, Pasternak, and Mandelstam.[9]

As a prosaist, Mandelstam did not emulate the example of Puškin, who strove to exclude from his prose whatever seemed ornamental and "poetic." Mandelstam's prose is distinctly and avowedly that of a poet. It is in fact so closely linked to his poetry in technique—and often by specific figures—that what we say of one can largely serve for the other. It reminds me rather of the prose of Wallace Stevens, if only in this: that it often seems on the very verge of becoming poetry. The essay "Language and Culture" for instance, is actually a sort of contrapuntal arrangement of prose and poetry. Abundant quotation is of course no novelty. In Mandelstam, however, the essential difference is that the verse—much of it, by the way, his own—is not so much illustration or interlude as it is a sequential development of the argument. It does not accompany the prose: it momentarily replaces it.

This is not, in our science-ridden age, to everyone's taste. An appetite for Mandelstam's prose takes longer to acquire, and there are those even among his greatest admirers, such as Georgij Adamovič, who have never acquired it. "Elegance" and "economy"—terms which humanists find to be the most seductive in the whole lexicon of scientific experiment—are widely supposed to legislate against mingling the procedures of poetry with those of prose within one body of discourse. Mandelstam was happily unconstrained by such considerations, and his prose is probably the most consistently joyous creation to come from his pen. His work as a whole is marked at all periods by a strong undercurrent of Pushkinian gaiety, but nowhere does this find such free and masterful expression as in his prose. Creative joy, an excess of inventive energy, is always disruptive of old boundaries and heedless of conventional prohibitions. It is—to use a word which Mandelstam found so many ways to approve in his chapter on Sergej Ivanyč—illegal, and we are reminded again of how well grounded are the impulses of all totalitarians, beginning with Plato, who would protect their unreal cities against poets. Surely he was among the wittiest writers of his generation, if by wit one understands the inevitable companion and lightener of high seriousness. His prose exhibits the best qualities of his poetry—concision, observation, surprise —but for those interested in the man behind the poems it brings another advantage: it reveals Mandelstam himself, or it is, at least, as far as he ever went in self-revelation. Most of it is plain autobiography, some of it is elaborately camouflaged autobiography, but all of it is to a remarkable degree personal and immediate.

Little that Mandelstam wrote in prose can be fitted into the ordinary categories. D. S. Mirsky, himself a redoubtable taxonomist of literature, admitted to a certain embarrassment when faced with the task of putting a label on *The Noise of Time*. "These chapters are not autobiography, they are not memoirs, although they do have to do with the author's milieu. Rather we might call them (if it didn't sound so highschoolish) cultural and historical scenes from the epoch of the dissolution of the monarchy."

In two senses it is rather like the autobiography of Maksim Gorkij. It is, in the first place, a book of characters, sharply observed and reproduced with a kindly objectivity. And in the second place, the figure of the author himself is curiously marginal. He is a kind of ambulatory recording instrument moving unobtrusively among the scenes of his childhood and youth, picking up the flavor of a conversation here, the sounds of a concert, audience and all, there. But we must bring this comparison to a halt, for nothing else in Mandelstam is like Gorkij. Leaving aside the huge question of style, we are struck most of all by the role which culture plays in Mandelstam's perception of the world. Precisely in his perception of the world, for the culture that I speak of is anything other than the merely superficial acquaintance with the arts which one might expect to find in any literate inhabitant of the Russian metropolis of St. Petersburg. His was not a culture of the nominative case: it had long ago spread obliquely down the paradigm, coloring all the peculiar syntax of his language-haunted vision. Nor was it narrowly aesthetic. It was above all historical, and Prince Mirsky, with his historian's appreciation of the matter, speaks in awed tones of "the daring, depth, and *truth* of the historical intuition" in Mandelstam's recollections. In whatever Mandelstam chooses to show us there is a compelling sense of relevance, of relatedness. Between the archeology of the family bookshelves, the sounds and odors of the railroad station in Pavlovsk, the chthonian delirium of a violin concert, the opening day exercises at the Tensev School, and the geography of a Jewish spa we make our way with pleasantly mingled feelings of astonishment and familiarity, for however sui generis these people and scenes may be, they are bound together by the silver thread of that historical intuition. It, more than mere chronology, is the principle of order and arrangement

The Noise of Time deals with Mandelstam's childhood and adolescence. Except for a brief but precious memoir by the late Mixail Karpovič, the years just following in Germany and Paris are surrounded by silence. Glimpses of Mandelstam the university student are also provided by others. In the autobiographical vein, we have only two more writings of any extent from his own hand. The first, Theodosia, comes nearer to being a continuation of The Noise of Time, from which it was not separated when the two appeared under the latter title in 1925. It is a record of certain people and impressions which Mandelstam encountered in the Crimea during the latter days of the Civil War when it was occupied by the dispirited Volunteer Army of Denikin and Wrangel. Everything about the situation—the desperate political collapse, the hopeless apprehension of disaster, the very topography of the little peninsula itself, protruding into the Black Sea like a springboard into exile—imparts to Theodosia a kind of ultimate refinement of that fin de siècle atmosphere which Mandelstam had portrayed in his earlier work. In the Crimea and on his return trip to the north of Russia he found himself in serio-comic difficulties with both sides. Ilya Érenburg provides, in his memoirs People, Years, Life (Lyudi, gody, žizn'), more circumstantial information than Mandelstam himself about the latter's sojourn in a Crimean prison, but the return journey also contained encounters of this sort, and these Mandelstam describes in a brief article written for Ogonek, "The Mensheviks in Georgia." In 1930 Mandelstam traveled about the south again, this time in Armenia, and his account of this appeared in Zvezda under the title "A Journey to Armenia." It is, one need hardly point out, about as much like ordinary "travel writing" as his autobiography is like normal autobiography. The great Formalist critic Viktor Šklovskij called it "a trip among grammatical forms, libraries, words, and quotations."[10] He might have added "picture galleries," for it is characteristic that Mandelstam's keenest observations of nature come not from the surrounding country but from an exhibit of French Impressionists. The people he meets are portrayed with the humane irony that always attended his drawing of the human figure. As in Gogol, some of the most memorable are those who appear for scarcely more than a second and leave us with an ache to know more about them. One such is the man, a certain Dr. Gercberg, who struck Mandelstam as "the pale shadow of an Ibsen problem."

There is, to the best of our present knowledge, only one work of fiction among Mandelstam's prose writings. This is the fascinating surrealistic novella entitled *The Egyptian Stamp*. It reminds one strongly of a much more extensive—but equally neglected—body of imaginative prose, that of the Futurist poet Velimir Xlebnikov, by which it was clearly influenced. But Mandelstam's novella had an added dimension, or dimensions, and if we call it fiction it is only to avoid some more cumbersome designation of its true nature, for it is about equally fiction, autobiography, and criticism. The plot is the merest nothing. A little man named Parnok runs about Petersburg during the Kerenskij summer between the two revolutions of 1917 trying to accomplish two things, to retrieve certain items of his clothing and to prevent a lynch murder, and he fails in both. On this frail narrative Mandelstam hangs a dream-like swarm of portraiture, cityscape, reminiscence, word-play, and cultured jottings of extraordinary variety. It is in part a strange little inventory of the interior museum in which his life was largely passed. There is a kind of contrapuntal rhythm among passages of hallucinatory nonchalance and passages thick with the smell of actuality. Some of the characters come straight from the circle of Mandelstam's acquaintances without so much as the perfunctory uniliteral camouflage of Tolstoys, Bolkonskijs and Drubeckojs: Parnok, the hero, and Father Bruni have the real names of real people.

But Parnok's ancestry (of which, by the way, much is made in the story) is far more complex than the discovery of his real namesake would indicate. For Parnok is also Puškin's mad Evgenij, running headlong from the colossus of the State. He is Gogol's Akakij Akakievič, devoting his very life to a search for a symbolic cloak. He is Dostoevsky's Mr. Goljadkin, confronted with a hateful image of the self. And he is, finally, Osip Mandelstam. I crave the reader's indulgence for the nakedness of these assertions. In a forthcoming book of translations of Mandelstam's prose, I shall elaborate on these two elements—the critical comment on one of the central traditions of Russian prose and the latent autobiography.[11]

Like all genuine originals, Mandelstam was always himself. His criticism is conveyed to us by the same instrument that produced the memoirs and the fiction. That is to say, he does not assume a manner of talking depending on the subject-matter. He talks about everything in his own manner. In this, he reminds one of e.e. cummings, another authentic rarity, who lectured to Harvard audiences in the same voice that he used to write introductions to Krazy Kat or to write an outraged note to people who had botched a recording. It might as well be said at the outset that his being utterly true to his own nature is not always a good thing for his criticism. Some of it is too private for me, at least, to understand. Some of it, to use a distinction which he himself makes in "The Morning of Acmeism," seems to be written not with the consciousness but with the word. I have said that his prose closely resembles his poetry. In the essay on Dante he presents us with a figure for the movement of a poem, and this figure is an example of how vividly and memorably Mandelstam can convey to his reader a critical notion and also an example of the procedures which render some parts of his criticism *not* vivid or even comprehensible. The figure is of a swarm of Chinese junks moving about in various directions on a river. The sense of a poem leaps from junk to junk in making its way across the river. As the junks continue to move this way and that, it is pointless even to try to reestablish the thought's hectic itinerary from one to the other. Poetry written in the spirit of this image is alive with a sense of daring enterprise and constant, unfailing amazement, but if critical prose makes its way thus eccentrically through a restless flotilla of associations, the result will sometimes be vague.

Having broached Mandelstam's criticism with these negative reservations, I now feel free to state that in spite of occasional baffling passages I find his little book *On poetry* and his other scattered essays on literary art to be laden with some of the most startling, impressive, and brilliant observations that I have ever read.

The word "surprise" crops up sooner or later in nearly everything said about his work as a critic. This would please Mandelstam, who put the very highest estimate on surprise as a quality of art in general. Part of the surprise is certainly occasioned (at least for those who knew him) by an unwillingness to believe that anyone so scatterbrained and frivolous as Mandelstam is often reported to have been in life could possibly have written anything with the magisterial authority that informs his criticism. But a more substantial part of the surprise derives from the news that anyone at all should write about poetry as he did.

I have just been turning through the pages of Mandelstam's critical essays, confident in the expectation of finding many brief passages that would lend themselves to quotation, but I must confess to a certain disappointment. I do not think that he is really very quotable, and the reason for this disability is a measure of one of his strongest qualities as a critic. There must be few who rely so heavily on context. Mandelstam's sharpest perceptions are so thickly interwoven with the fabric of his argument (and of his Argument) that they are extricated only at their, and the reader's, peril. His criticism is impressionistic (I do not think he would approve my saying this) and like all impressionism it demands to be taken whole. This is true even of the longest and most ambitious work, such as the "Razgovor o Dante," ("Conversation about Dante") an essay of rare intellectual passion and beauty. Here he moves over the vast range of his subject, from canto to canto of the great poem, attracted now by this, now by that quality, quoting, translating, bodying forth his thought with metaphor and imaginatively recreating the physical and mental world of the great Italian. The result is continuous excitement that arises from one's almost palpable sense of the *Divina Commedia* not as a finished monument but as a poem in the process of becoming.

.   .   .

And here, finally, is one of the most remarkable things ever said about Anna Axmatova, for whom, as a person and as a poet, Mandelstam always entertained the most perfectly unblemished devotion:

> Axmatova possessed the purest literary language of her day, but at the same time she constantly employed the traditional devices of the Russian folk song; and not only of Russian but of all folk songs. In her poems there is not any intellectual affectation, but rather the typical parallelism of the folk song where there is a striking asymmetry of two contiguous statements, on the model: "an alder tree in the garden, and in Kiev an old man." It is this kind of thing that gives us those characteristic diptych stanzas with a sudden twist at the end. And her poems are close to the folk song not only in their structure but in their essence, since they are always and without fail lamentations. Considering Axmatova's purely literary vocabulary, spoken as it were through her clenched teeth, the folk quality renders her especially interesting. We discern in a sophisticated Russian lady of the twentieth century a woman of the village, a peasant.

There is one category of Mandelstam's prose of which we have scarcely any information at all: his letters.[12] It is known that there exists a sizable collection of letters written over a period of years to his wife, and I have been told of a touching letter written to his wife's mother before their marriage. One of the greatest living Russian writers said to me that these letters, taken together, "constitute a unique document of the XXth century." For this epistolary fund Mandelstam's readers, well schooled in the art of patient expectation, must wait still longer. It is comforting to recall the words of the same writer: "Don't worry if you don't have everything of Mandelstam. If we were speaking of some small poet, there would be good reason to fear that you might never find everything. But we are speaking of Osip Emilevič Mandelstam. He is one of the greatest poets of our time. Everything, absolutely everything—the poems, the prose, the letters—every single thing will be published." It would not become us to have less faith than this.

NILS ÅKE NILSSON

Osip Mandel'štam and His Poetry

I

Osip Mandel'štam published his first collection of poems in 1913. It came out under the patronage of the new poetic group known as the Acmeists which had issued its first manifestoes the very same year.

The title, *Stone* (*Kamen*), sounded very much like a challenge, a slogan for the new movement. It was quite in accordance with the demands for "hardness" of verse made by the young poets. But it seems as if it might also be a hint at the choice of patrons selected by Nikolaj Gumilev, the organizer and leader of the group. One of them was the French poet Théophile Gautier, chosen by the Acmeists as a master of poetic craftmanship. It may be that Mandel'štam designated his collection under the influence of Gautier's wellknown collection *Emaux et camées,* and yet at the same time also in conscious contrast to it (a translation of *Emaux et camées* was published in 1914). The Romantic Gautier chose refined symbols (enamels and cameos) in his demand for precision and clarity in poetry; Mandel'štam, sixty years later, embraced a coarse, everyday material, the simple stone. It is obviously a prosaic symbol, yet timeless and in a way sacred—the material of which streets and cathedrals are made.[1]

The title seems to indicate a uniformity in motives and mood. Matters, however, are not as simple as they might seem at the first glance. On the contrary, Mandel'štam's first book is rather heterogeneous and ambiguous. The first thing to strike us is the fact that each poem is dated and included in the collection chronologically. This arrangement is not made unintentionally. What the poet wishes to say

From *Scando-Slavica,* IX (1963), pp. 37-52. Reprinted by permission of *Scando-Slavica* and the author. The poems quoted here originally appeared in Russian and were translated for this edition by the editor.

by this is obviously that the collection is intended to show some kind of development, the development of a poet or, possibly, of a form of poetics. This gives us, I think, a starting-point to an understanding of it.

There is, to be sure, a cycle of poems about stone buildings which forms, in a way, the centre of the collection—they all seem to fit the theme of the title. There are poems about Notre Dame, Sophia Cathedral in Constantinople, the Admiralty Building in Petersburg and of Roman architecture in Italy. Even landscapes are often considered architectonically; fields are compared to Roman forums and trees to colonnades.

The vocabulary too, contains many words which emphasize the concept of hardness suggested by the title. Most frequent, as might be expected, are the words "stone" and "stony" (*kamen, kamennyj*). Next follow "crystal" and "crystallic" (*xrustal', xrustal'nyj*), "heavy" (*tiaželyj*), "coarse" (*grubyj*). There are also isolated examples of more precious stones, especially in earlier poems, revealing a certain influence of Symbolist poetry: "diamond" (*almaz*), "gold" (*zoloto*), "mother-of-pearl" (*perlamutr*), "enamel" (*emal'*), "porcelain" (*farfor*).

Coupled with this vocabulary indicating heavy, solid objects, there is, however, a quite different one in exact opposition to it: a vocabulary of airy, weightless objects and concepts. There are adjectives like "tender" (*nežnyj*), "fragile" (*xrupkij*), "delicate" (*lomkij, tonenkij*), nouns like "foam" (*pena*), "reed" (*trostinka*), "straw" (*solominka*), "mist" (*tuman*), "cobweb" (*pautina*), "lace" (*kruževo*) and so on.

These contrasting elements of the vocabulary are most interesting. They seem to reveal a certain dualism in the poet's outlook on life. This world is not, as the title of the collection would seem to indicate, a solid world where all objects stand firmly in place. It is rather a dualistic world, a world in which a fatal and uncertain balance reigns.

This impression is stressed by a motif which is also built up on contrasts and introduced at the very beginning of the collection. It is a contrast between the fragility and shortness of human existence on the one hand, and the eternity of time and life in general on the other. This motif is a crucial one in Mandel'štam's poetry. Let us begin by examining it.

II

The first part of the collection has, without a doubt, much in common with the poetry of the Symbolists. The dominant mood is one of nostalgia, sadness, depression; *pechal'* (sadness) is, in fact, a dominant word in the collection. The setting often emphasizes the impression of something unreal. It is, to be sure, our earth which is discussed but we can hardly discern any palpable details. People and objects are wrapped in a dreamlike, misty or bizarre fairytale atmosphere, creating thereby an impression of fear and emptiness. The world is empty, but the poet must nevertheless accept and love it, for this is the only world given to him:

> I'm mortally tired of life
> I take nothing from it
> But I love my poor earth
> Since I know no other.[2] (4)

What Mandel'štam is concerned with in the first part of his collection may be described as the poet's return to earth after dwelling in the Symbolist realm of abstract, metaphysical speculation. Although the return is necessary it is by no means easy to make. It is a return to a bare world and the poet is at first frightened by its nakedness and meaninglessness. What is worldly reality without the promise of a greater reality? Life without God seems to him as impalpable as mist, and he feels himself to be an empty cage from which God has flown like a bird:

> I could not make out your vague and fearful image
> In the deep fog.
> "Lord!"—I said in error,
> I hadn't intended to say that.
> God's name, like a great bird
> Flew out of my breast.
> Ahead the thick fog rolls,
> Behind, an empty cage. (30)

Thus Man must live on earth without God. The skies above are silent; church bells no longer ring:

> The skies are silent.
> From the misted belfry
> Someone has taken the bells,
> There stands an orphaned
> And dumb eminence
> Like an empty tower, white
> And nothing but silence and fog. (21)

But Man cannot live without reflecting on the mystery of life and death. He cannot live without the perspective of eternity. Eternity (*vechnost*) is, in fact, another frequent and important word in the collection. This point of view is actually not opposed to the tenets of Acmeism. It is true that Gumilev accused the Symbolists of preoccupation with the problem of how to attain knowledge of the unknown, of a preoccupation with mysticism, theosophy and occultism, of "flirting with eternity." But even in stressing his loyalty "to Thee, O Mother Earth" the Acmeist poet could not liberate himself from the impact of the mysteries of life and death. The poet, Gumilev said, must always be aware of the unknown without corrupting its images with likely or unlikely guesses; this was, he stressed, a tenet of Acmeism.

This problem certainly was of crucial moment for the Acmeists. Lacking this background the world of senses they were praising finally became tedious and superficial. As we know, poets like Axmatova and Gumilev himself were to reconsider it in the further development of their poetry. Mandel'štam was concerned with this question from the very beginning.

One of the first poems by Mandel'štam treating the problem of eternity is dated as early as 1909. The world is presented here, as often in Symbolist poetry, as a jail (*v temnice mira*) which holds Man fettered. Outside its window stands eternity. What can Man do? He breathes on the glass and his breath forms a pattern there: his hope is now that this his pattern on the glass will remain even after time and rain have washed away the dust on it:

> A body is given to me
> What am I to do with it—so whole, and so much mine?
>
> For the quiet joy of living and breathing
> Tell me, to whom should I offer thanks?
>
> I am the gardener and also the flower,
> In the jail of the world I am not alone.
>
> On eternity's great glass
> My breath and my warmth have left a mark
>
> A pattern I shall print upon it
> Unrecognizable till now.
>
> Let the moment's murk float away
> But that sweet pattern cannot be destroyed. (8)

Without this hope of eternity man is frightened and this fear "is the awareness of emptiness" (*samy strax est' čuvstvo pustoty*). Therefore there is no choice, he must try to live for eternity:

> Some few live for eternity,
> But if you are concerned for the moment
> Your lot is fearful and your house infirm. (34)

In his search for a symbol of eternity within the realm of reality the poet introduces the symbol of stone, i.e. the building, the tower, primarily as contrast to the old image of the stars:

> I hate the light
> Of monotonous stars.
> Greetings, my old vision
> The tower's pointed height! (29)

This poem which is dated 1912 introduces the poems on Notre Dame and Sophia Cathedral in Constantinople where the symbol of earthly eternity finds its clear expression:

> And the wise spherical building
> Will outlive nations and centuries. (38)

To be sure, this sounds very much like a paraphrase of Gautier's well-known lines: "Tout passe. L'art robuste seul a l'éternité." But Mandel'štam does not stop here. He is, as we shall see, to develop the idea in a quite new direction. This is clearly demonstrated in one of the central poems of the collection, the poem on the Admiralty Building in Petersburg (*Admiraltejstvo*).

At first Mandel'štam presents the building to us in daring imagery. Now it is a frigate, now an acropolis, glowering at us through the leaves of a tree on a tiresome Petersburg summer's day. The building belongs, he says, to two elements, to water and to air. This idea is very concretely suggested by its situation on the shores of the Neva and because of its tall spire:

> A frigate or an acropolis
> It shines from afar, kin to water and to sky. (48)

It has the appearence of an airy bark; its spire seems unapproachable. In bold comparisons Mandel'štam calls forth the picture of a glorious work of art. But then he suddenly makes a halt; we must not think that art is something supernatural, metaphysical in the Symbolist sense of the term. The building is created by man, is a part of our everyday life; a carpenter might use the spire as an ocular yardstick in his daily work:

> It teaches us: beauty is no demigod's whim,
> But a simple carpenter's measuring stick.

This, however, is not meant to diminish the importance of art, to reduce it to the dimensions of the petty-bourgeois. It is only meant to set art in its proper place, in this world of Man. Art means more to Man than that. In the following two stanzas Mandel'štam again returns to the bold metaphors of the beginning. Art, he says, is a new element (free man created a fifth element). This element embodies immense strength: it transforms reality, loosens the bonds of the three dimensions which fetter Man and it makes the wonder, the miracle of eternity occur here, on this earth. A new freedom is given to Man, as he says in the concluding lines, using the sea imagery so skilfully exploited in the poem:

> Our three-dimensional bonds are broken
> And worldwide seas are opened to us.

This led Mandel'štam to an idea which at first glance seems somewhat unexpected but, in fact, is a logical development of his ideas. Finally it is not buildings or cities or works of art that survive, that create in us this feeling of "beautiful permanence" which Man needs in his fragile and changing world. What survives is Man himself, Man as a creative force in the universe:

> Let the names of fine cities
> Caress the ear with their ephemeral importance.
> It isn't Rome that lives through the ages
> But man's place in the universe. (66)

This, as we see, is something more than the Parnassians' "l'art robuste seul a l'éternité." It seems even, at first glance, somewhat contradictory to what he himself had said in the earlier poems just quoted about the wise spheric buildings which will "survive people and centuries." But Mandel'štam goes further; the beautiful poem on the Admiralty Building in Petersburg contains still another important point leading to the very heart of his poetics.

The dualism of the vocabulary of the whole collection, which I have already mentioned, is clearly demonstrated in the poem: there is everywhere this contrast between words indicating solid, heavy concepts and words associated with lightness, fragility, movement. The Admiralty Building is akin to both water and the skies. It seems to be placed firmly on the shores of the Neva but at the same time it gives the impression of conquering solidity, immobility, the laws of nature. It gives the impression of movement, of flight upwards, of liberation from the law of gravity.

Thus, a solid, earthbound object of art finally creates an impression quite opposite to what one would expect: an impression of lightness, of liberation. Art breaks down the inflexible physical nature surrounding Man, threatening to bind him in a deterministic ring.

Here I think we are approaching the essential point of Mandel'štam's view of poetry in his first collection. The same idea is clearly expressed in the other poems about stone buildings too. In *Notre Dame* the poet observes exactly this wonderful play of contrasts, of solidity struggling with lightness, of immobility with flight, creating the wonderful tension of great art:

> An elemental labyrinth,
>   a forest unknowable
> A reasoned chasm of the Gothic spirit
> Egyptian power and Christian shyness
> Reeds beside oaks, and, always czar—
>   the plumb. (39)

Thus the cathedral is also a model for himself, the poet, as well as for poetry in general. It teaches how to write poetry, how to transform the earthbound objects of reality into an impression of weightless beauty:

> And so the more carefully I studied
> O fortress Notre Dame, thy monstrous ribs
> The more I thought: and I too out of
> Crude weight will someday create a thing of beauty.

In the earlier poems the contrasts of reality created a feeling of fear in the poet, an impression of something unreal. Now he knows: through art a certain balance can be attained, a new feeling of freedom. It is a fragile, an uncertain balance but it is the only one Man can attain. Facing a world in flux, a dynamic reality of contradictions and tensions, the artist is able in his art, by stones or words, to create an illusion of harmony and eternity.

The important thing is not the stability or the indestructibility but the transformation of the material. The "heaviness," reality as it is, is "no good" (*nedobraja*). It must be transformed into the artist's personal vision of the world. This, however, has a double danger. Reality is often transformed into something almost weightless, clear and transparent, a structure of glass (we have observed how frequently "crystal" and "crystalline" are met with beside "stone" and "stony"; a frequent word is also "transparent" [*prozračnyj*], getting still more frequent in the next collection) which can easily break down if the balance is upset, if the pressure of reality on art becomes too hard—and this, as we shall see, is exactly what happens with Mandel'štam's balance. The other point is that there is no real place for the poet himself in the harmony created by him. Art is a means by which the poet tries to bind chaos. It stands between him and reality. To attain the illusion of order and harmony he must remain something of an outsider, he must, as Mandel'-štam says, "keep his distance."

If we now try to approach Mandel'štam's poetic style for some few general observations (a more detailed analysis lies outside this brief introduction) we cannot expect to find a complete uniformity. In my opinion the first collection above all bears witness of a development towards a poetics and a view of the world. There is, without a doubt, a certain difference between the first poems and the last. Many of the earlier poems are, for instance, written in stanzas of two lines; they often seem to be something like miniatures, sketches, exercises. One is often given the impression of something unexpressed, something un-accomplished. This is stressed by the fact that he concludes by no means few poems with three dots (. . .). It is easy for us to notice a difference in the later poems. Not only are they built up more care-fully, but also contain an often repeated device of more self-confident expression; in fact, many poems end with an exclamation mark, stress-ing the impression of something finished, definitive—or, at least, the impression that the poet tries to make himself believe in the definitive-ness of his interpretation of reality.

But still the collection as a whole has many important points in com-mon. The architecture of cathedrals being Mandel'štam's model, we are able to understand his interest in the structure of the poems. He starts with the smallest units; more than any one of the other Acmeists his main concern is the word, the word *per se,* as it was at the same time for the Futurists. Perhaps the title of his collection has still another significance, suggesting the word as the basic element of poetry as the stone is that of architecture.

It is here not only a question of the careful choice of "the right word," the right syntagmas and their arrangement in the sentence. The important thing is the tension between the words, just as the secret of a building of stone lies in the tension between contrasting structural elements. There are many different devices of tension to be found in Mandel'štam's poetry; still they are not permitted to be an end in them-selves. Reigning in the cathedral with its many contrasting elements is the plumb (see *Notre Dame*); reigning in poetry is the balance—this is the main feature of Mandel'štam's neo-classicism.

III

We find these principles wholly at work in the central poems of the collection *Stone*. In his next collection they are developed into mature craftmanship but also, as we shall see, in yet another direction. This collection he called *Tristia* and it appeared in 1923. The title seems to indicate that he is here continuing the mood of melancholy and sadness of the first collection. But there is more to the title: apparently Mandel'-štam has taken it from Ovid. He evokes a parallel to the banished Roman poet's lamentations from the coast of the Black Sea (*Flebilis ut noster status est, ita flebile carmen . . .*).

The background to this new tone of sadness is the appearance of a new element of reality contrasting with the order and harmony finally created in the first book: this is the revolution and the civil war which the poet was forced to witness at first hand. He tries to keep these experiences at a poetic distance by clothing what happens in a garb of classical history and mythology. He sees them as a classical tragedy, as a part of world history's perpetual circulation: his Petersburg is consequently transformed to Petropolis.

But in other poems, especially those written at the beginning of the twenties but published later in his volume of collected poems from 1928, he tries to face reality as it is. Two of the key words of these poems are *vremja* and *vek*, our time, our age. When they appear they are often accompanied by comparisons stressing his agony. It is not any more the histrionic fear of a grotesque fairytale from his earlier poems in *Stone* in which "toy wolves" with fearsome eyes leer through a forest of Christmas trees. This is something real, something he cannot escape. His age is a *vek-volkodav* (197), a wolf-trap, and he by mistake is the one to be trapped, it is a *vek-vlastelin* (140, 141), it is a wild beast (135):

> My age, my beast, who will be able
> To look into the pupils of your eyes
> And stick together the vertebrae of two centuries
> With his blood?

Under the pressure of this new reality the uncertain balance of the first collection is upset, the harmony broken. We see it clearly demonstrated in a poem like *Concert at the Railroad Station* (*Koncert na vokzale*), from 1921. This is the poet's return to his childhood, to the railroad station in Pavlovsk where, as we are told in the opening chapter of *Noise of Time* (*Šum vremeni*) symphony concerts were held, where Čajkovskij and Rubinštejn reigned and the air was full of the most variegated smells and noises (some details of the poem are in fact transferred to the prose book). Again, as in all Mandel'štam's important poems, the technique of contrast is skilfully used: he sets off "the glass forest of the station" (*stekl'annyj les vokzala*) against "the world of iron" (*žheleznyj mir*). And as always his words have a quite concrete meaning—the glass building of the station and the trains, rattling and roaring in and out. But there is also a symbolic meaning behind.

In the poem, memories of childhood are blended with the actual situation, dream with reality. Music, art was a means to bind, to enchant this world of iron and steel. But now the noise of time is too strong. It is too late. The harmony of old cannot be restored any more:

> At the funeral feast of a dear shade
> For the last time music plays for us. (125)

It is clear from the poems of *Tristia* that in this period of apocalyptic upheaval his main concern is with art, poetry, the word. The question he puts himself is: will poetry survive? In the night, black as velvet, he goes out into the streets praying for the word. To be sure, this is a time full of words, of proclamations and speeches. But the word he is praying for is the word without meaning, the word of poetry:

> For the blessed word without sense
> I shall pray through the Soviet night. (118)

Will poetry survive? Yes, he believes it will—in different forms than he dreamed of, it is true, but it will survive. This we learn from one of the most beautiful poems in *Tristia:*

> Take from my palms for your joy
> A little sun and a little honey
> As Persephone's bees would order you.
>
> One can't untie the boat not fastened,
> One can't hear the shadow shod in fur,
> One can't overcome fear in this dense life.
>
> And only kisses are left to us,
> As fuzzy as the little bees
> That die when they leave their hive.
>
> They rustle in the limpid groves of night.
> Their homeland is the dense forest of Taygetos;
> Their food is lungwort, mint, and time.

So joyfully take my wild gift:
A simple dried out necklace
Of dead bees that turned honey into sun. (116)

The poem begins in a quiet, restrained tone of joy. The poet offers his poetry as honey and sun—a modest gift, in his own opinion, as we see by the double use of *nemnogo*.

Then follows in the second stanza a tone of resignation underscored by the thrice repeated *ne: ne otvjazat', ne uslyxat', ne prevozmoč*. No one can make loose a boat that is not moored—this seems almost like an allusion to the poem on the Admiralty Building in which the poet proclaimed the power of art in liberating Man. Now he realizes that in a world in flux, where everything is adrift, poetry cannot give this freedom. No one can hear the shadow shod in fur—meaning that no one can foresee or escape his own death, he will only know that death is always following him like a silent shadow. One cannot track down fear in the dense forest of life—here is a hint of the dreamlike frightening vision of life from the first poems of *Stone:* fear is lurking behind the trees. But this is no longer a matter of fairytale wolves. This is fear proper.

And yet his resignation is not complete. Art is still there to help us, although no more the art of daring Gothic cathedrals of stone. This time Mandel'štam has chosen a quite different symbol, a very simple one: tiny fuzzy bees. Their homeland is, he says, the forests of Taygetos, that is Greece but not, as might be expected, the forests of Hymettos. This is Taygetos, the high mountain overlooking Sparta, the domain of Artemis, a wild, impenetrable forest, rarely met with in Greek or Roman poetry.[3]

What Mandel'štam wants to say here is apparently that the honey produced by the bees is not the sweet honey of Hymettos but a honey with a different, darker, wilder taste. This is further stressed in the following line telling us that their nourishment is lungwort, mint and Time. These are words which Mandel'štam has used in his earlier poems (107, 110). He seems to like placing them together—they are, after all, connected by alliteration and the oxymoron of their bitter and sweet smells. But their nourishment is also Time. By this Mandel'štam apparently wishes to emphasize that poetry lives in historical perspective—we hear again an echo of the words "time," "ages" so important in the poems from this period.

But these bees are compared to kisses, are actually transformed kisses—this is one of the really daring metaphors of the poem.[4] I think Mandel'štam wants to say by this that poetry is created by love, not love in a narrow but in a more general sense such as the word passion (*strast'*) has in Pasternak's poetry.[5] It is a creation which springs from the senses. And the bees are to be interpreted as symbols of the words. Like the bees, words in a sense die, vanish when they are spoken. But before they die they have transformed their honey, the secret beauty of the words, of the language, into sunshine, into poetry. So what the poet is able to offer his reader is, as he says, a necklace of dead bees, a string of simple, common words which put together by the poet form a thing of beauty.

Generally speaking, Mandel'štam in *Tristia* develops and continues the principles of style of his first collection. The new painful themes do not shatter the verse form. His impressions of a time of chaos, his songs of sadness and loneliness are moulded into a verse with the same firmness as in *Stone*. He tries to keep a poetic distance to these new intrusive elements of reality. Even if his view of a world conquered with such difficulty in *Stone* is toppled he nevertheless endeavours to maintain the balance in his poetic form.

It is, however, easy to notice that the contrasts he is trying to balance have now grown in intensity and strength. The tension is much stronger, in fact approaching the limits of the possible: tension between words and groups of words, between sentences, between images (we notice, for instance, how he now quite commonly makes use of oxymorons and synasthesias: ("black ice"; "burning snows"). The imagery plays a more important part than before: daring images cross the poems like sudden flashes of lightning, many of them returning in other poems, reappearing in different contexts. His choice of elements of reality is more fastidious and elliptic, often leaving us with enigmatic gaps.

As an example of these features of style let us consider one of his poems describing *Siena:*

> In a clear pool what a steepness!
> The Siena mountains intercede for us,
> On the mad rocks the stinging cathedrals
> Hover in the air, where there is wool and silence.
>
> From the hanging staircase of prophets and kings
> The organ, the fortress of the Holy Spirit,
> Descends, and the sheepdog's cheerful bark and friendly fierceness
> The shepherds' coats and the judges' crooks. (106)

It begins with an exclamation, possible to understand only in connection with the following lines. "In a clear pool" is a kind of oxymoron, trying to give at the same time an impression of something clear and transparent and something dimmed and hazy. In reference to the poem as a whole we may understand it as an allusion to the hazy atmosphere of Tuscany. The following "what a steepness" refers, then, to the town itself, built on steep hills. Thus in this line the poet is giving a kind of first impression of Siena from afar, an abstract, general view although made up of concrete elements.

It is the next line that first sets the poem in concrete place, telling us that it is Siena the poet is speaking about. The religious significance of this town is expressed as if the steep hills form our contact with heaven and God—again a transformation of a concrete image, the town still seen at distance. Next, as the poet gradually zooms in on the town, comes the sight of the cathedrals which seem to "hang in the air." We observe the tension between the syntagmas: "mad rocks," "stinging cathedrals," a juxtaposition of wool and silence. In this juxtaposition a concrete and an abstract noun, taken from different spheres, are placed side by side. They remain separate entities by virtue of their different meanings and yet hold together by a euphonic device (the repeated Š; cf. in *Stone*, nr. 21: *gde tuman i tišina*). Of the two nouns the second is easy to understand. The first, however, seems enigmatic to us in this context and finds its explanation first in the following stanza. It refers, as we shall see, to the sheep grazing on the meadows, but here, in this context, we can also understand it as an allusion to the clouds.

Now the poet approaches the town still closer, developing a new series of images. The town is presented as a huge hanging staircase once descended by prophets and emperors. Now the cathedrals are descending, being compared to an organ and a fortress at one and the same time. Besides the cathedrals he sees other things descending too: shepherds in sheepskin coats with their sheepdogs. Still we are given the impression that the poet is observing everything at a certain distance: he does not see the dogs themselves running down the staircase of the town but their "cheerful bark," their "friendly fierceness" (again this tension between noun and adjective). Nor does he notice the shepherds themselves descending but their coats (*ovčiny*) and their crooks, giving a historical biblical allusion (*posoxi sudej*).

In this picture there seems to be, as so often in Mandel'štam's poetry, a certain contrast: the cathedrals representing a higher reality, Man's metaphysical longing, and the shepherds, their sheep and their dogs, representing this world, our everyday life. But still there is a perfect balance between these contrasting planes. The expression "the crooks of the judges" evokes a biblical atmosphere and thus the two contrasting planes merge into one: we see a biblical landscape, and a timeless idyll.

Although in *Tristia* Mandel'štam continues the firm verse of *Stone* we can observe certain new features. There are, as Kirill Taranovskij recently pointed out in an interesting paper on Mandel'štam's verse, certain poems from 1922 which are written in a new kind of *dol'niki:* if his earlier *dol'niki* (from 1910-12) are characterized by isosyllabism then the syllabic scheme of the poems is now completely destroyed.[6] Further, the poem beginning with the line *Voz'mi na radost* ("Take for your joy") (116) has iambic rhythm but no rhymes. And as a third group of experiments there are also a few poems written in free verse; among them *He Who Found a Horseshoe* (*Nashedshij podkovu*) written in 1923 (136) which is one of Mandel'štam's most beautiful; space will not allow me to discuss it here.

With the tension of the words and images becoming increasingly stronger, with the balance shaken, development pointed in the direction of a free verse, a verse close to the general development of European poetry at this time. This seemed a natural line of development for Mandel'štam's poetry but he does not take this step. There are certainly many explanations. One of them is that "time" had a new blow ready for him. Mandel'štam became, as we know, a victim of the literary politics of the thirties.[7] His poems preserved from this period are to be looked upon more as personal documents than as a real continuation of his earlier poetry. If many poems in *Tristia* deal with the vital problem at that time of whether poetry would survive the turmoil and the new demands put to it, the poems of the thirties reflect the more personal question of the poet's own survival. As we know now, he died in a transit camp in Vladivostok. The official date is given as December 27, 1938.

W. GARETH JONES

A Look Around: The Poetry of
Andrey Voznesensky

Andrey Voznesensky has come to be acknowledged as one of the most exciting and talented of contemporary Russian poets. The brilliant sound of his verse, the breathtaking rhythms and rhymes, the sophistication of his visual imagery, in a word, the virtuoso technique of the poet is admitted. Yet praise is given grudgingly. Critics seem to suspect the glitter on the surface of the verse, and its captivating but occasionally strident sound. Can it be that the reader is being hoodwinked by a manipulative technician, and that there is little substance beneath the brilliant surface? An example of the reservations felt by readers of Voznesensky is a review by Peter Levi in which he states:[1]

> However powerful the poem may be, I will not much want to read a poem in which the artist is a kind of suffering or exulting god, or one in which other characters are dressed in language of however dazzling a quality to play mere cartoon rôles in life. There seems to be a lack of grasp of real life, a lack (which seems inseparable from the sensation of being shouted at) of something I not only value but apparently need in poetry; one expects better of a Socialist poet.[2]

My aim here is to show that Voznesensky has a grasp of life and has something to say about it. To find out what he has to say, the motifs making up his poetic universe must be examined closely, and in particular those recurring images and themes which re-echo throughout his work and are productive of others. Voznesensky's poems should not be read in isolation: the significance of a poem such as *Parabolic Ballad* (*Parabolicheskaya ballada*) may be distorted, as I shall seek to

From *Slavonic and East European Review*, XLVI, No. 106 (1968), pp. 75-89. Reprinted by permission of the *Slavonic and East European Review* and the author.

show, by being treated as an isolated poem. In his collection *Antiworlds* (*Antimiry*[3]) the prelude of three poems, *A Fisherman's Monolog* (*Monolog rybaka*), *Marilyn Monroe's Monolog* (*Monolog Merlin Monro*), *The Rublyov Highway* (*Rublyovskoye shosse*), which are later repeated, suggests to the reader that this is not a collection of separate lyrics, but a book of poetry to be read as a book. And this work is held together by motifs which appear again and again. The mere statistical recurrence in poetry of certain themes, of course, is not in itself significant. What is important is their weight, their complex of significance, their organising power within a poem and their power to produce new themes. Themes may recur with the regularity of signposts, but it is with those signposts which lead us on to new areas of experience that we should be mainly concerned.

> It is unbearable when undressed
> in all the posters, in all the papers
> having forgotten
> That there is a heart in the centre
> They wrap herrings in you
> Eyes crumpled
> Face torn
> (how terrible to recall in
> "France-Observer"
> one's own photo with its mug
> Self-confident
> On the other side of the dead Marilyn).[4]

Here in *Marilyn Monroe's Monolog* is the mainspring of Voznesensky's poetry; the anguished sense of self, abandoned in an indifferent or hostile world, subjected to looks which make one an object. This terrible sense of being looked at, of being an object in a world of contingency is at the centre of the monologue. The poet finds himself in an existentialist predicament of the Sartrian sort, and Sartre (not merely a decorative figure, perhaps, for Vosnesensky who portrays him in *Paris without Rhymes* [*Parizh bez rifm*] and to whom he dedicated the poem *Avtodigressiya*) examines a similar image of a tattered newspaper photograph when discussing the problem of the *other person* who is able to make an object of *myself*: "Je pourrais ressentir de l'agacement, de la colère en face d'elle [i.e. this image in the other's mind] comme devant un mauvais portrait de moi, qui me prête une laideur ou une bassesse d'expression que je n'ai pas."[5]

Conscious of himself as a hideous object side by side with dead herrings, the poet identifies himself with Marilyn Monroe and chooses her—a thing observed by others—as the symbol of the human condition. As a cinema star, controlled and objectivised by director and producer, she is the extreme case of the human-object stared at by others. On the 100-metre screen in a drive-in cinema she is looked at not by people even, but by motor cars:

> I remember Marilyn.
> Cars watched her.
> On a 100-metre screen
> in a biblical sky,
> between abundant stars,
> over the prairie with its tiny billboards
> Marilyn breathed,
> they loved her . . .
> The cars succumb and desire.
> It is unbearable.[6]

What drives Marilyn Monroe to suicide is this sense of being watched and contemplated on advertisements in underground, trolleybus and shop, on prairie billboards, a draining of her personality by others presaged at the beginning of the poem by the heavy tread of "For whom? With whom? Who?"

Again the same horror at being watched is expressed in the poem (America, Smelling of Gloom) . . . with a grim and almost hysterical humour where Voznesensky describes his pursuit by 17 FBI cameras which again capture him in a series of absurd photographic stills. The same agony before the crimson eye, "the staring eyes of Freedom," is felt again and a hint given of the Passion story:

> What torment to be crucified,
> through every birth-mark,
> When into you from head to toe,
> eyes are lodged like bullets![7]

Not always is the feeling of being observed expressed with such bitterness. There is wry humour in *Marshe O Pyus* where the poet is aware of himself as just another obsolescent object viewed by a Picasso figure with a ball-bearing eye, and in *N'yu-yorkskaya ptitsa* where he is under the gaze of a mysterious robot-bird. The gaze may be lyrical in feeling as in *Lezhat velosipedy* . . . where the look emanates from the wheels of a pair of bicycles which are a symbol of lovers' bodies. Often this self-consciousness at being watched is linked with an awareness of nakedness. This is an example of the way in which a key theme becomes dominant in its expansion: the sense of

being observed is heightened by the expansion of the motif to take in
nakedness and is given a strong sense of eroticism. Marilyn Monroe is
undressed in her advertisements, and in *America, Smelling of Gloom*
. . .

> And the pissoir looks at you,
> like the eye of a plaster goddess.[8]

Despite the horror of being watched, Voznesensky is acutely aware
that only in others' eyes does our self have a mould and that we cannot escape this, as we learn in

> What are you? What?!—You look with longing
> Into books, through windows—but where are you there?
> You press as against a telescope,
> against men's immobile eyes![9]

II

In this awareness of the other's gaze, there is also an awareness of the
distance between you and him, a sense of space. Sartre explains, "Le
regard d'autrui me confère la spatialité. Se saisir comme regardé, c'est
se saisir comme spatialisant-spatialisé."[10] In Voznesensky a key motif
expressing this spatiality is that of movement in a restricted line by
vehicle—train, motor cycle[11] or car where the passenger, despite the
movement, is separated from the natural world and isolated from his
fellows. Yet paradoxically in this isolation he is not an individual but
part of the mass of an automobile civilisation. This motif interweaves
with that of being-looked-at in the drive-in cinema of *Monolog Merlin
Monro* where the actress is eyed by cars. Merely cutting a way through
space without organising it in any way, the apparent determined motion of vehicles, is, in fact, aimless: in this sense suiciders are motor
cycle riders. The objectifying question *Kto ty?* (Who are you?) again
carries the poet away on the restricted line of a bicycle track. The motif is always associated with a draining away of personality, an objectifying of the self: in *Italian Garage* (*Ital'yanskiy garazh*) Chevrolets
have replaced Paolo and Juliet, tomorrow a red motor cycle will smash
and kill; we are born not to live life but to squeeze speedometers; the
degradation of female virtue in *Otzovis'* begins with motor cycles and
continues with limousines; in the poem about the two Ol'gas, a girl
who is half Russian, half French, Russian country scenes and the Orthodox ritual are contrasted with sterile dreams at the wheel of a Re-
nault car. This indifference of the vehicle to life and art is stressed

when we see buses and cars rolling over a bridge in Paris where Mayakovsky's face is impressed into the highway like a face at Hiroshima.
An attempt is made to break out of the bonds of this restricted motion
in *Cycles on a Vertical Wall* (*Motogonki po vertikaľnoy stene*) where
again the motifs of motion and being an object of looks are interwoven. The girl on the wall-of-death is the object of the stares of the
circus crowd, but she seems to try "like the daughter of Icarus" to
break free from gravity and the absurd restriction of a motor cycle's
single track movement. For a moment the poet seems to believe that
she has succeeded:

> The horizontal essence of woman
> comes to me in a dream and flies![12]

But this is merely an illusion of unrestricted horizontal movement and
the girl has merely changed her vertical anguish to horizontal anguish:

> And she is still rocked by the track
> And her eyes are full of such—
> horizontal
> longing![13]

What is this world of space in which the poet is aware of himself as
an object? On the one hand it is a world heavy with absurd objects, a
"zoo of things" as we are told in *Marshe O Pyus*. On the other hand,
it is paradoxically a fluid world, drifting away in all directions, a world
in which man has no stability. It is the physicist struggling to order a
chaos of infinitesimal parts with his cyclotron who is the hero of our
time as he grapples with the world's fluidity in *A Fisherman's Monolog*:

> The flight of stifling falling stars,
> the computation of towns and woods
> trembles like a watch movement
> in his robust hand—[14]

Tumannaya ulitsa, perhaps, manages to state the paradox of this
world: here the subject is disorientated since his universe is at the
same time opaque and dense, as well as being fragmentary and fluid.

In his poetry Voznesensky seeks to break free from the shackles of
being an object in the world, in order to refashion the world: to vola-
tilise the density of his universe, to lighten its opacity, to regroup the
scattered things, and curb its viscosity. And through this apparent paradoxical movement Voznesensky achieves a dynamic equilibrium in
his verse.

III

He faces the world with a hard look. In Voznesensky's poetry neither beauty nor reality lies passively in the eye of the beholder. If he himself is made a victim of another's eyes, then he will turn his own look against the world. It is an intense visual awareness of the universe which is at the base of his work, and it is not surprising that Voznesensky is a graduate of the Moscow Institute of Architecture, does a lot of painting and feels that Andrey Rublyov, Joan Miró and the later Le Corbusier have given him more than Byron.[15] Other artists figure in his poetry: Picasso, Rubens, Raphael, Modigliani. The fascination of the theme of the sequence *Mastera* for Voznesensky, perhaps, is that the architects had their artistic life extinguished by having their eyes put out.

We have seen how the poet is observed as an object, and how this motif is interwoven with an awareness of his own body and may be given a specific sexual characteristic. Voznesensky retains the same complex motif when he puts himself into the role of voyeur. In *Siberian Baths* (*Sibirskiye bani*) he plays the faun, observing women leaping naked into the snow from a steaming bath-house (although it is worth noticing how the motif is kept in equilibrium here when one of the women at the close of the poem turns, and by throwing a snowball demonstrates her own ability to objectify another person). In *Tayga* the sexual relationship of the watcher and the watched is conveyed by showing a girl caught upside down like a Thomasina Thumb in thousands of dewdrops: she is taken in a look multiplied over and over again in the reflection of the drops. The attack of the watcher is not always playful. It may be cruel as in *Striptease* (*Striptiz*) with its insistent rock'n'roll rhythm and the watching eyes swelling like leeches, although again the motif is kept in equilibrium as the watcher at the end of the poem falls back into the embarrassment and shame of the watched, as the stripteaser faces him, mocks his accent and uses him to order a drink.

Interwoven with the motif of the look and nakedness is the image of clothing which is an obstacle linking the aggressive look and nakedness. Voznesensky, to use a perceptive cliché, undresses with his eyes. He anticipates the stripteaser's nakedness in *Striptiz*, "Takes off her scarf and her shawl and all the tinsel" (and her scarf recalls the poet's own scarf and his extreme self consciousness of his own body in *My Scarf, My Paris* . . .). In *Wedding* (*Svad'ba*) he eyes the bride in her transparent skirt; the plashing of the clothes of the girl pillion rider in *The Rublyov Highway* draws attention to her body as do the wall-of-death rider's high boots in *Cycles on a Vertical Wall*. In a gentler way we are made aware of the defenceless nakedness of a girl observed in a telephone booth through the observed details of her coat, lipstick and earrings.

The poet within the same motif through which he communicates his own metaphysical doubt, affirms his place by being not merely the watched object, but by becoming an aggressive voyeur who can "undress with his eyes." Or, in other words, by becoming an artist. Is he also able to rearrange the world of his metaphysical doubt, a world oppressive in its opaqueness and density, and alarming in its fragmentation and fluidity?

He is able to attack the dense world of solid objects with his eyes as in *Paris without Rhymes* a poem prompted by the *ravalement*, the spring-cleaning of Paris. Before his eyes, the sandblasters rip away the solid grimy skin of the city, a sight which prompts the poet to go further:

> And I said: "How necessary it is—
> to tear away the outer layer from objects,
> to see the world without its wrappings,
> vicious schemes and bargee walls! . . .[16]

He metamorphoses the solidity of the city's objects into a naked transparency so that even Notre Dame dissolves leaving behind merely the luminous rose of the cathedral. The superfluity of objects in the world is attacked in *Roman Holidays* (*Rimskiye prazdniki*) in which Romans throw out old possessions from their homes to the rhythm of the peal of New Year bells. Again the poet delights in the disappearance of objects which seems to lighten the density of an oppressive world. This attack on a too solid world is linked within both these poems with the image of the undressed other person. In *Paris without Rhymes*, a nun is embarrassed by naked men and the president of a men's club is shamed by being discovered in a secret liaison with his wife. In *Roman Holidays* an obsolescent man is hurled from his bedroom, a naked carouser is caught in a restaurant and at the close of the poem:

> And through their skirts until morning
> like lamps
> through lampshades
> women's bodies shine.[17]

Nakedness is an ambiguous quality in Voznesensky. Just as a look can turn him into a mere object, but also enable him to see the world without its false trappings, so nakedness suggesting shame, embarrassment and the selfconsciousness of self may also paradoxically suggest innocence and delight in a dense world made light and fluid. This ambiguity gives rise to much of the essential dynamism of Voznesensky's vision and it is hinted at in *Lessons in Polish* (*Uroki polskogo*):

> "Uroda"—means beauty.
> How simple! . . .[18]

It is through this ambiguity that Voznesensky's motifs are kept in equilibrium.

Undressing an object with an aggressive look is not sufficient in itself to desolidify a dense world. An object remains an object and the voyeur remains impotent. But it is interesting to note that a naked object (or an object in which the body is indicated by fetishist details) often merges with, and drifts into, a sensual image of water. Thus the "plashing" of the girl's clothes in *Rublyov Highway* dissolves a solid picture. In *Tayga* the lover who is content to observe the girl at a distance in the dewdrops, is aware of the precious instability of the myriad drops of water. Women in these poems are often metamorphosed into water as in *Mountain Spring* (*Gorny rodnichok*) where a girl runs to a mountain spring with her skirt seen as a spraying watering can, so that Voznesensky is able to see two miraculous streams in which it is impossible to say which is the girl and which the spring, so triumphantly are the solid objects of his world dissolved. In this water, of course, one is able to immerse oneself while maintaining one's innocence and integrity: there is a sense of baptism in these water images, the sense that one can fall into the world, and yet save oneself. Thus the beatniks in *A Beatnik's Monolog* (*Monolog bitnika*) to save themselves from the "rapacious things of the age" dive naked into water. The same innocence and cleansing baptism of fire and water is experienced in *Siberian Baths:*

> The purity of fire and snow
> with the purity of nakedness.[19]

If the solid world can be made to run away in cleansing water, then it is also possible for its opaqueness to be dispelled in fire and light. The innocence of the Siberian bathers is reached through a baptism not only of water but of fire. There is innocence too in the fir tree, ablaze with light (like the girl in *Yolka*) which breaks through the solidity of its place:

> Fir trees
>   jet
>   wings
>   burst through ceilings![20]

Fire and water merge again in *A Fisherman's Monolog* in which the churning up by motor boats of the solidity of water is imagined as the disintegration of coal as it burns:

> Motor boats ply,
>   like coal,
>   the water burns.[21]

Salutes blazing like searchlights across the dark Moscow sky are recalled in *Georgian Birches* (*Gruzinskiye beryozy*) where it is the transparency of the birches that inspires the poet. And again they dispel the solid opacity of the world and achieve a kind of innocence:

> I love their weightlessness
> their most high form
> I check my conscience
> against their white purity.[22]

The blaze of light, which we experience again in *Report on the Opening of GES* (*Reportazh s otkrytiya GES*) is rare in Voznesensky. More usual is the soft transparency or steady translucency which suffuses many of his poems. It is what remains when the poet's aggressive look has stripped away the heaviness of the world. All that remains of Notre Dame in *Paris without Rhyme,* is the crimson translucency of the rose window. Cowsheds in rococo and wedding-cake stations are demolished to give way to the transparency of a modern airport building as in *New York Airport at Night* (*Nochnoy aeroport v Nyu-yorke*) where the airport is a "retort of neon," "heaven in an aquarium glass," "a glass of blue sky without the glass." Translucency is sought by the poet, conscious of his own unclothed body in *Return to Sigulda* (*Vozvrashchenie v Siguldu*). He consciously sees his cottage through the hills, as its fertile stone can be seen through the flesh of a plum:

> And our cottage with its three windows
> through the hill among the blocks of forest
> shows, as a stone
> shows through a plum.[23]

Here the idea of translucency expands the cottage into a fertile image. We ourselves are seeds in the greenery drawing thoughts like

juices from the earth. The solid oppressiveness of the world dissolves
as the cottage windows open their shutters and suck in lilac, a flower
which is light, fragmented, yet whose fragmentation is contained
within a definite form: this is a recurring image in Voznesensky's
poetry:

> Clearings dissolve into us,
> as night dissolves day,
> as the windows dissolve into the garden
> and suck in the lilac.[24]

In *Roman Holidays* women's bodies shine transparent through their
skirts like lamps through lampshades. In *A Fisherman's Monolog* people are seen as gods when they work translucent to their hair. In *Autumn in Sigulda (Osen v Sigulde)* a mother is as transparent as a co-
coon. At the sawmill of *Lonzhyumo* men's bodies shine transparent
through their pitch-dark overalls. Lilac, green, the blue of the sky, the
silver of birch, the red of plum and cherry: these are Voznesensky's
key colours creating the translucency and luminosity which breaks
down the oppressive solidity of his world of doubt.

When Voznesensky indicated Andrey Rublyov as an artist with
whom he was in sympathy, no doubt he had in mind the characteristic
luminosity and exceptional transparency of the great icon painter's
palette whose colour range too is similar to Voznesensky's. Rublyov
used colour to create an illusion of lightness and airiness within a solid
design: in this way he sought to show grace, innocence and spirituality through the material. It is this tradition that Voznesensky follows
in breaking down the density of his world by the luminosity and translucency of his images, and we see an acknowledgement of his debt to
Rublyov in the third poem of his introduction to the collection *Antiworlds, The Rublyov Highway* in which the solid image of the motor
scooters:

> Past the sanatorium
> the scooters soar[25]

is made light and airy by a recollection of the resonance of Rublyov's
colours:

> The lovers at the handlebars are
> like Rublyov angels.
> Like a fresco of the Annunciation
> with its brilliant white
> behind them women shine,
> like wings on their backs.[26]

Andrey Rublyov painted within the bounds of an architectural tradition which demanded a certain simplification of line and form in its icons. Voznesensky's architectural training has helped perhaps to create the deep sympathy he has for Rublyov, and developed in him his acute visual awareness and his appreciation of the significance of clean, uncluttered lines which we have already noted in his poetry.

If colour is one remarkable aspect of Rublyov's art, then another is his sense of composition and line. We may recall his complex use of dynamic curves within a simple circle theme in his masterpiece *Trinity*. The curve has a fascination too for Voznesensky, the dynamic curves of Modigliani as well as Rublyov's as in *Tvardovsky Sang in Florence at Night* (*Pel Tvardovsky v nochnoy Florentsii*):

> And the porters below in wonder
> recognised in this tune
> swan-like Modigliani
> and the Rublyov curve of Madonnas.[27]

It is a complex construction of curves that make up one of Voznesensky's best known poems *Parabolic Ballad*. The basic theme of this poem is not, perhaps, the superficial social theme of the artist versus philistinism, but as we are told in the title, the curve of the parabola itself. The poem is a construction of parabolas: a rocket's path, a rainbow, Gauguin's round journey, a beer mug, a wormhole, the curve of a girl's shoulders. It has been shown how Voznesensky fragments and illuminates the dark density of his world of metaphysical doubt, but how does he curb the superfluity of things? The curve and the parabola give shape to the teeming things of a world which is seeping away. The physicist engages this fugitive world of a myriad particles with his cyclotron: Voznesensky with the curves of his verse. The parabola of *Parabolic Ballad* takes the poet through a universe of uncountable stars, heavy yet with their brittle, fragmentary nature wonderfully expressed through the music of the line:

> And the devil bore me
> between the heavy, ambiguous stars of Tbilisi![28]

The parabola here embraces and gives form to a shapeless, ambiguous universe and the image is again matched by its human side, the human parabola of the curve of a girl's shoulders in a dark, formless doorway. In *There You Sit, Pregnant, Pale* (*Sidish' beremennaya, blednaya*) . . . with its barren straight lines of the railway, crossing gates, coaches and upright windows, it is the curve of a pregnant woman's belly that suggests fertility and an affirmation of life found in the curve of our planet:

> How the planet understands them
> with its huge belly.[29]

The same creative force of the curve is demonstrated in *Ballad of the Full Stop* (*Ballada tochki*) where Voznesensky refuses to see the bullet that killed Puskhin as a full stop: the trajectory of the bullet is a curve which has a second projection beyond death. There is no full stop in nature and the curve stands as a guarantee of immortality, as do other curves in this poetry such as those of Mayakovsky's bridge and of the rose window of Notre Dame.

IV

We have traced then the main outlines of Voznesensky's verse. He is acutely aware of himself, of his own body and embarrassed by the sense of being yet another object in a world of valueless objects, a world at times oppressive in its heaviness and density and at times frightening in its fugitive fragmentariness. This is his sense of fallenness, his metaphysical doubt. But Voznesensky does not rest there. As an artist, he is able to attack the world and affirm himself. The seen becomes the seer. The object becomes the triumphant subject. He volatilises the density of the world and lightens its darkness so that in the luminosity of what has been made transparent true existence becomes apparent. And he gives shape and life to a drifting fragmentary universe by his dynamic curves and parabolas.

Voznesensky is also a civic poet who has written a number of poems on the theme of Lenin. What is interesting in these poems is to see how Lenin is placed firmly within the general topography of Voznesensky's poetry (and it is, therefore, difficult to agree with Sir Maurice Bowra that *Lonzhyumo* is a poem "which, despite considerable eloquence and ingenuity, is profoundly conformist at heart").[30] Lenin appears in these poems not in any social or historical situation, but within that condition of metaphysical doubt felt by the objectified person. This condition is conveyed in the introduction to *Lonzhyumo*, *Aviastuplenije* where the person is again viewed as an object of love or hate:

> [And we understand] . . .
> that we are sent on our way
> and are waved at cunningly

> by some with a mother's scarf, and by others
> with their fists[31]

or objectified by life itself:

> Earth
> you accompany us with your April look,
> lie on your back, silent as the night.[32]

The sense of defenceless nakedness is conveyed by the empty trousers
we leave behind, or the sheriff who reports with his fly undone in
Lenin's Sequoia (*Sekvoya Lenina*). Two motifs merge when the catch
of this zip fastener is seen as a railway engine moving along darkening rails. This barrenness of the direct motion of transport (an image,
of course, in which the individual is lost in an unconscious mass) is
repeated in the image of people receding from life leaving nothing behind but the tail-lights of their cars:

> But people depart, cutting into the nocturnal spurs
> of their roads
> tail-light autographs![33]

and the setting of *Lenin's Sequoia* is "automobile California."

But as the poet and artist is able to use his eyes to refashion his universe, so is Lenin:

> Direct and with a large forehead like a lens
> he gathered into an angry focus
> what the hall thought.[34]

Even in death, Lenin looks through people like an X-ray in his mauso-
leum. In the Russian game of gorodki (where the aim is to hit wooden
chocks piled in certain patterns out of an area with a wooden stave)
we see Lenin screwing up his eyes in order to attack with them:

> Right!—his shirt is opened
> right!—his eye screwed up,
> right!—and the chocks go flying.[35]

Just as the poet's eye attacks the solidity of his world, so the Leninist
eye aims to shatter the geometrical solidity of the chock patterns
within the contingency of the game. For the player the disarray of
the chocks, the destruction of the careful pattern signifies something
positive. The scattered blocks of wood in their random positions signify paradoxically that the player is "scoring in the game." It is in this
way that Leninism scatters the conventional geometrical shapes of im-

perialism, clericalism, and fascism. Out of these conventional shapes comes a creative randomness. Lenin, like the artist, dissipates and dissolves things but the destruction is kept in equilibrium and we become the witnesses of creative metamorphoses. In *Lonzhyumo* men are at work in a sawmill which smells, among other things, of "a dialectic of perception." Men are at work sawing wood, but this particular destruction releases a flood of energy and creativity and a series of new destructions held in brilliant equilibrium by the poet. Solid logs are broken under the saw, releasing sweetness, music and light dissipated in a shower of wood-shavings. Solid planks give way to new forms: ships and violins. The scream of the saw and wood gives way to the new creative sounds of violin music and the comforting creaking of a ship at sea which tells the builder that the ship is sound:

> Let the pine be dense in its bark,
> its innermost part is light
> you tear it and torment it,
> to make music!
> So that it becomes the singing strength
> of shipbuilders and violinists . . .[36]

Although the solid trunks are volatilised by the poet, yet the sound finally fading into the air has far greater power than the original object. Also the poet brings his destruction of raw material towards a human conclusion in the shipbuilders and violinists. Into these motifs, which are those of Voznesensky's poetry as a whole, Lenin is placed:

> Lenin was
>   from the breed
>   of those who saw away
>   and uncover the essence of things.[37]

The motif of the curve is used to characterise Lenin's thought:

> From here
> he thought
> rocket-wise.
> His thought made an arc,
> and shattered
> the parapets
> by the Winter Palace in the snow![38]

Fragmented profusion may be given a curved pattern by Lenin as in *Lenin's Sequoia* where the profusion of foliage is shaped by the living crown of the tree, and humanised by its comparison with the curved patterning of fleeting profusion in a display of fireworks over Moscow. Voznesensky's delight in the image of lilac with its profusion of flowers held in a pattern on the bough has already been mentioned. In *Lilac Moscow-Warsaw (Siren' Moskva-Varshava)* lilac is given a curving movement and light as is Lenin's sequoia:

> Around the planet like a green chandelier
> through constellations and villages
> whistles
> a travelling lilac![39]

This ability of Lenin to shape the universe is the ability of an artist: the crowns of the sequoia recall the same image of the crown of trees in *Crowns and Roots (Krony i korni)*, a poem associated with Pasternak and dedicated to Leo Tolstoy. In *Ballad of the Full Stop* the curving trajectory of a bullet leads to a second life for poets, and for Voznesensky it is significant that the Lenin of *Lonzhyumo* was also a victim of a bullet:

> It is poetical to tame the Universe!
> And for being a poet
> as once at Pushkin
> at Lenin
> was fired a poisoned pistol![40]

Brittleness, brashness, technical brilliance are not merely qualities of Voznesensky's verse but an integral part of what he has to say about his existence. Face to face with a world in which existence may appear gratuitous and obscene, Voznesensky on the one hand gives acute expression to this human predicament while simultaneously wrestling with it and attempting to bring his world to a tense, dynamic equilibrium. In this he evokes the aid of artists, and, more boldly, Lenin, who is less of an historical than an existential Lenin set firmly within the topography of Voznesensky's poetical universe.

A Note on Soviet Prose

The relatively liberal policy toward literature which prevailed during
the years from 1921 to 1932 made possible the production in the prose
genres of a number of works which are quite congenial to the taste
of Western intellectuals. The history of Soviet prose begins with the
formation in Petrograd in 1920 of a group which called itself the
"Serapion Brotherhood," whose basic tenet was that literature should
develop independently of political and social ideologies. The "Brotherhood" was named for a character in one of E. T. A. Hoffmann's
Tales who believed in the reality of his own poetic vision. They came
together in a troubled period, and they received support from Maxim
Gorky (1868-1936) who had already established himself as an enemy
of Bolshevik excesses, both political and literary. Perhaps the most
prominent among the older members of the group was Evgeny Zamyatin (1884-1937) whose lectures on the craft of literary prose at the
Petrograd "House of Arts" were a landmark in the history of Soviet literature. Viktor Shklovsky, one of the leading formalist critics, was also
an influence at their meetings. Most of the young men who met under
the aegis of "Serapion" were quite young, and many of them achieved
eminence in Soviet prose. Lev Lunts (1901-1924) was a brilliant
young playwright and the author of many statements which set forth
the ideas of the "Brotherhood." The author of four well-made plays,
he emphasized in his theoretical statements the importance of literary
structure. His early death put an end to one of the most promising talents in Soviet literature. Both Boris Pilnyak (1894-1937) and Vsevolod
Ivanov (1895-1963), who were associated with the Serapion Brothers, are dealt with in one of the essays included here. Venyamin Kaverin (1902-   ) was a member of the group who produced skillfully written prose throughout the Soviet period, and who was active
in the liberalizing movement during the sixties. His best known novel

is *Artist Unknown* (*Khudozhnik neizvesten,* 1930) which attempts to state the claims of art against the expedient pressures of the new age. Mikhail Zoshchenko (1895-1958) specialized in short sketches describing trivial events of everyday life with a humor based both on situation and on language. Konstantin Fedin (1892-   ) is a prolific writer both of short stories and of novels that demonstrate considerable stylistic power. Probably his best work was done in the twenties, when he produced many excellent short stories, and the experimental novel *Cities and Years* (*Goroda i gody,* 1924), which attempts to depict the Revolution and the men who took part in it on many levels and on a broad canvas. Both Leonid Leonov (1899-   ) and Valentin Kataev (1897-   ), while not members of the Serapion Brotherhood, made original contributions to the revival of prose and of the novel during the middle 1920's. Critical essays in this collection are devoted to the most important and enduring figures in that revival, Yury Olesha (1899-1960) and Isaac Babel (1894-1941).

The writers we have mentioned had no clear Party affiliations, though they accepted the basic premises of the Revolution. In addition to these so-called "fellow-travelers"—a term coined for them by Leon Trotsky—there was a numerous contingent of prose writers who called themselves "proletarian," and whose writing was oriented to the needs in literature of the party and state. Their work was intended for mass circulation, and they avoided on the whole experimentation with the medium in the modern manner. Some of them made a respectable contribution to Soviet prose: we should mention Alexander Serafimovich (1863-1949) whose novel *The Iron Flood* (*Zhelezny potok,* 1924) deals with the retreat of a Soviet army during the civil war, Dmitry Furmanov (1891-1926) whose famous novel *Chapayev* (1923) depicts the character and activity of a charismatic peasant military leader, and Alexander Fadeev (1901-1956), author of *The Rout* (*Razgrom,* 1926), a novel which examines in the manner of Leo Tolstoy the individual human beings in a partisan detachment operating behind the lines of the white armies. There were many others whose names might be mentioned, and of course the best product of the "proletarian" movement was the work of Mikhail Sholokhov (1905-   ).

During the earliest period the accent of modernism could be heard in Soviet prose. Writers experimented with various levels and varieties of language (Pilnyak, Ivanov, Zamyatin), and they tended to concentrate on the medium of expression rather than on content. A literary manner known as "ornamentalism," which involved a style intricately mannered in syntax and vocabulary, was distinctive of the twenties in

Soviet literature. At first the traditional novel form was neglected and until the middle of the decade of the twenties the shorter forms—sketches, stories, and novellas—predominated. The shorter forms were preferred by most writers (Babel, Zoshchenko, Zamyatin) because they lent themselves to observing, successively, fragmented bits of a terrible existence, to revealing pieces of reality without attempting large structure or philosophical synthesis. As time went on and the Party ideology exerted greater pressure on literature, writers felt increasingly the demand to produce substantial novels and to make broad generalizing statements about contemporary reality. The novel then became the dominant Soviet literary form, and such it has remained. Fyodor Gladkov's long novels of postwar reconstruction, *Cement* (1925) and *Energy* (1939), served as prototypes of a numerous genre, the "construction" novel, which came to be dominant in the thirties and, with occasional periods of backsliding, remained so until the present day. The meaningless authoritarian term "socialist realism" has been used since the early thirties to characterize Soviet literature as a whole, and while this term means anything the authorities say it means, its general import is that literature must be used to inculcate correct and healthful attitudes toward life. Much of the writing produced under that rubric is worthless as literature, but Professor Mathewson's article ("Four Novels") examines for literary quality certain superior representatives of the genre.

In the late 1950's and 60's a period known as "the Thaw" set in, and there were many new departures in Soviet prose, some of the most important of which are treated here in special articles. Boris Pasternak's (1890-1960) *Doctor Zhivago* is a poetic and symbolic novel which calls in question the basic assumptions of the Marxist approach to literature as well as to life. Alexander Solzhenitsyn's (1918-   ) novels and stories are more than an exposé of the brutal oppression of Stalin; they are also a rich literary investigation of the contemporary Russian language. Yury Kazakov (1927-   ) specializes in short stories that explore individual emotional experience, and a number of young writers have followed his example. While the official emphasis is still on prose that deals with social themes, there occurred in the late 1960's and early 1970's a "broadening" of socialist realist precepts.

Andrey Sinyavsky, in the essay "On Socialist Realism" which he published abroad under the pseudonym "Abram Tertz," made the point that for over a generation "Purpose" has dominated Soviet literature. The "Purpose" in this case was imposed on literary men; it did not grow organically and naturally out of literary and intellectual life; in fact the "Purpose" inhibited literary growth, or forced it underground, sometimes stopped it altogether. The remarkable and wonderful thing is that in spite of the superimposed "Purpose," Soviet literature has offered us some of the finest examples of twentieth-century prose. Indeed literature in the Soviet Union, both poetry and prose, has demonstrated astounding vitality. However unfavorable the environment, it continues to live.

THE EDITOR

GLEB STRUVE

Gorky in the Soviet Period

The name Maxim Gorky (pseudonym of Alexey Maximovich Pesh-kov) is closely linked with Soviet literature and its fortunes. But his attitude toward the Revolution was by no means uniform, and the theme "Gorky and the Revolution" falls into several distinct periods. It also implies much that is still obscure, and it must be left to the future impartial historian of the Revolution, provided he has access to all its archives, to shed light on all these blind spots.

Despite his long personal association with Lenin and with the Bolshevik party in general, and his uncompromising pacifism during World War I, which made him sympathize with the Bolshevik attitude on the question of the war and its further conduct, Gorky was hostile toward the Bolsheviks between the two revolutions in 1917 and in the early days of the new regime. Later he exchanged this attitude for one of benevolent neutrality (a Soviet critic described it as "benevolent incomprehension"),[1] and from 1918 to 1921 he devoted himself to the task of saving the remnants of Russian culture and of helping its representatives. It was to him that such institutions as the House of Arts and the House of Scholars (Dom Uchonykh) owed their existence. He was also instrumental in organizing a vast publishing undertaking known as Vsemirnaya literatura (World Literature), which enabled Russian writers and scholars to earn their livelihood by translations during the abnormal years of War Communism. Gorky's personal friendship with Lenin and his great fame and prestige outside Russia made it possible for him to take at times an independent attitude toward the new government's policy, and especially to exer-

From *Russian Literature under Lenin and Stalin, 1917-1953* by Gleb Struve (University of Oklahoma Press, 1971), pp. 59-64. Reprinted by permission of University of Oklahoma Press.

cise his influence on behalf of some victims of the Red Terror in its initial stages. For instance, if we are to believe Zamyatin, Gorky did all that he could to save Gumilyov from execution and was terribly upset when his efforts in Moscow on behalf of Gumilyov were forestalled by the authorities in Petrograd.[2]

Gorky was also responsible for helping and encouraging young writers, in whom he had always taken a great interest. Many of the now-famous Soviet authors remember with deep gratitude the encouragement they received from Gorky. It was he who "discovered" Vsevolod Ivanov and helped Fedin to his feet, and in general, the Serapion Brothers as a group owed much to Gorky's sympathetic interest and help.

In 1921, Gorky left Russia for reasons of health (the hardships of War Communism and the heavy load of work he took upon himself in those years had intensified his earlier tuberculosis) and went to live near Berlin, where he started *Beseda*—"a review of literature and science"—while continuing to contribute to *Krasnaya Nov*. In 1924 he retired to his villa in Sorrento, where he had lived before the Revolution, and there he remained until 1928, in a kind of self-imposed exile. His attitude toward the new regime during this period was ambivalent. He kept in touch with the Soviet Union, and his works were printed there; he never relented in his hostility to its open enemies, both Russian and foreign; but on several occasions he spoke out in frank criticism of it, as for instance in connection with the trial of the Socialist Revolutionaries. In his book published in 1929, Gorbachov wrote of Gorky: "Gorky in his article about Vladimir Ilyich Lenin [*Russky Sovremennik,* 1924] mentioned somewhat coquettishly . . . the fact that he did not quite believe in the good sense of the masses. Gorky hardly ever believed in it in earnest and was always a bad Marxist."

To Gorbachov, Gorky's "romantic Socialism" had little to do with the militant tasks of the proletariat. He saw Gorky as "a revolutionary democrat," a kind of Menshevik, interested above all in fighting for the "Europeanization" of Russia, against the age-old backwardness of her masses.[3]

However, in 1928, Gorky made a short triumphant re-entry into the Soviet Union and was feted there on the occasion of his sixtieth birthday. A year later he went to Russia again, this time to remain there until his death. His role as the *doyen* of Soviet letters and as an influential force in all matters of literary policy, facilitated by his new-found friendship with Stalin, was particularly great during the last four years of his life. Certain aspects of Gorky's activities during this last period will be touched upon in later chapters.

As far as his own contribution to Russian literature since the Revolution is concerned, three points are to be noted: (1) quantitatively speaking, it was not very great and cannot compare with Gorky's pre-Revolutionary output; (2) it was almost entirely retrospective; and (3) its quality was on the whole very high—some of his post-Revolutionary writings will undoubtedly rank among his best. This is true primarily of his nonfiction (I do not mean, however, his political journalism of the last years). His *Vospominaniya o Tolstom* (*Reminiscences of Tolstoy,* 1919) is justly regarded as one of his masterpieces and as one of the most interesting and penetrating pieces ever written about the great Russian writer. It is not, as D. S. Mirsky rightly pointed out, that Gorky is anything like Tolstoy's intellectual equal, or that he understands Tolstoy better than did some others. It is rather the vividness of his vision of Tolstoy the man, and the brilliant manner in which he conveys certain aspects of Tolstoy to the reader, that matters. Very interesting also, even if not so brilliant and revealing, are his reminiscences of Andreyev and Chekhov, and his portraits of some other of his contemporaries, some of which are to be found in his *Zapiski iz dnevnika* (*Notes From a Diary,* 1924). *Moi Universitety* (*My Universities,* 1923) forms a worthy sequel to *Detstvo* (*Childhood,* 1913) and *V lyudyakh* (*In the World,* 1915); the whole of this autobiographical trilogy, with its wonderful character drawing and its earthy realism, will remain for posterity as Gorky's most memorable creation.

After leaving Russia, Gorky published several stories in *Beseda* from 1923 to 1925. They are also retrospective, but two of them reflect his preoccupation with the problems and inner workings of the Revolution. One is a very interesting study, in the form of a confession, of the mind of a schizophrenic, a revolutionary who betrays his comrades and turns secret-police agent. This is "Karamora" ("Daddylonglegs"). Another, "Rasskaz o geroe" ("The Story About a Hero"), is of a counterrevolutionary brought up on Carlyle's hero worship, who might just as well have been a revolutionary and who ends by becoming a bandit and a hangman. Both stories show Gorky's predilection for unusual characters, for people with a quirk, and both reflect strongly the influence of Dostoyevsky, for whom Gorky professed an intense dislike. There are also echoes of Dostoyevsky, especially of the latter's *Notes from Underground,* in "Rasskaz o bezotvetnoy lyubvi" ("The Story of an Unrequited Love"), one of Gorky's most effective stories.

Delo Artamonovykh (*The Artamonov Business,* 1925) was Gorky's first regular novel since *Matvey Kozhemyakin* (1911). It was better than any of his middle-period work and showed that, as a novelist, he was by no means a spent force. Its theme and atmosphere recalled *Foma Gordeyev,* but its structure was more firm and more compact. It is the story of three generations of a self-made bourgeois family. All the characters—the old Artamonov, the founder of the family's prosperity, a strong, self-willed man, one of those to whom Gorky, for all his hatred of the bourgeoisie, felt instinctively attracted; his sons and grandsons, in whom there are already signs of imminent degeneration; their wives; and other episodic characters—are portrayed with Gorky's uncommonly keen gift of observation. As is usual with Gorky, the element of healthy robustness and vitality is combined with an insight into the dark, somber side of life, not only in its outward manifestations but also in the inner workings of human nature. In spite of the lifelikeness and variety of its characters, of whom Gorky shows not only their darker sides, there hangs about the whole novel that atmosphere of gloom which makes him in his mature period, despite all his propensity to romanticism, a true representative of critical realism. The same is true of *Zhizn' Klima Samgina* (*The Life of Klim Samgin,* 1927-36). But this long epic of forty years of Russian life (it was to be continued) is one of Gorky's failures. With its multitude of characters and its extremely uninteresting hero, it is diffuse and dull, and it reveals glaringly Gorky's lack of constructive ability.

Gorky's two post-Revolutionary plays, *Egor Bulychov i drugie* (*Egor Bulychov and Others,* 1931) and *Dostigayev i drugie* (*Dostigayev and Others,* 1932), which are among his best realistic plays, are also retrospective in nature.

From the above it should be clear that, as an artist, the post-Revolutionary Gorky was looking back and seeking inspiration in the past. His few stories dealing with contemporary Soviet life are of little importance and interest.

The significant role which Gorky played in Soviet letters in the first years of the Revolution does not mean that as a writer he had any real influence on early post-Revolutionary literature, no matter what some of its representatives may say now. Mirsky was on the whole right when he wrote in 1926 that Gorky's work "is profoundly unlike all the work of the younger generation—first of all, for his complete lack of interest in style, and, secondly, for his very unmodern interest in human psychology."[4] The position, however, was reversed soon after Gorky's return to Russia, not because Gorky himself had changed in the meantime but because post-Revolutionary Russian literature had moved much closer to Gorky—to his realism tinged with revolutionary romanticism. This *rapprochement* will become evident in the further account of developments in Soviet literature.

When Gorky died on June 18, 1936, his death was lamented throughout the Soviet Union as an irreparable loss to Soviet letters. It was later ascribed to the evil machinations of the enemies of the Soviet Union, the "Trotskyites" and the "Fascists." In a volume of biobibliographical information about Gorky we read under the year 1936:

> Winter and spring Livon in Crimea, at Tesseli. On the instructions of the worst enemy of the people, the superbandit and international spy, Judas Trotsky, an anti-Soviet, "Right-Trotskyite" gang of traitors, spies and assassins sets about preparing the murder of Gorky. . . . *May 30.* As a result of the conceived plan of murder and the creation of harmful conditions for Gorky's health he fell ill with influenza at Gorki (near Moscow). . . . *June 8.* The illness took a turn for the worse in consequence of the saboteur methods of treatment applied by the murderers.[5]

This version of Gorky's death was generally accepted in the Soviet Union, and in a report surveying Soviet literature during a quarter of a century Alexey N. Tolstoy spoke of "the murder of Gorky, dictated by the Fascists to their direct agents."[6] This legend about Gorky's death is but part of the general mythmaking which played such an important part in Stalin's Russia. The true facts are still unknown and may not become known for many years to come.[7]

Victor Shklovsky once wrote: "Gorky's Bolshevism is ironic Bolshevism which does not believe in man. By Bolshevism I do not mean belonging to a political party: Gorky never belonged to the Party"; and further: "Gorky does not at all believe in mankind. He does not like all men, but only those who write well or work well." These "paradoxes" of Shklovsky's are much nearer the truth than the official "icon" of Gorky the humanist which has been painted all too often. Gorky is still waiting for someone to strip his true face of artificial hagiographic varnish—to do for him what he did for Tolstoy.[8]

RICHARD A. GREGG

Two Adams and Eve in the Crystal Palace: Dostoevsky, the Bible, and We

"Prophetic" is a quality which few thoughtful readers would deny Zamiatin's *We*. For if its moral argument (the irreconcilability of "pure" communism and individual freedom) has, to a disturbing degree, been confirmed by the course of twentieth-century history, so have some of its boldest technological predictions (for example, state-enforced restrictions on human fertility, Communist-inaugurated space travel). Even its genre (an original blend of political satire and science fiction) has proven to be a prophecy of sorts, anticipating, as it does, the more celebrated satirical fantasies of Huxley and Orwell.[1]

That these oracles have impressed the readers of *We* is as it should be. That they have distracted them from less obvious aspects of the work is not. For, objectively considered, *We* is a Janus-faced novel. It looks backward as well as forward. The philosophical problem it explores had engaged one of the greatest Russian minds of the previous century; its closest literary ancestor is a classic of Russian literature; and, as we shall see, underlying much of its plot is a famous myth of Judeo-Christian religion. Only when the traditional aspects of *We* have been properly assessed can the edge of its satire be fully felt.

The philosophical debt which the novel owes to Dostoevsky's thought in general, and to *Notes from the Underground* and *The Brothers Karamazov* in particular, will not detain us long, for it has received its due elsewhere. The ethical dilemma confronting Zamiatin's hero, D-503, namely, that freedom and earthly happiness are incompatible and that benevolent totalitarianism destroys the former as it ensures the latter, evidently derives—as Professor Peter Rudy has already

From *Slavic Review*, XXIV, No. 4 (December 1965), pp. 680-87. Reprinted by permission of the *Slavic Review* and the author.

noted[2]—from Ivan Karamazov's legendary Grand Inquisitor, who rebukes Christ for refusing to trade man's freedom for the miracles, mystery, and authority offered by Satan and praises the Church for having rectified the error. Another scholar, Mr. D. J. Richards, has called attention to a more far-reaching parallel when he noted that D-503 in "confiding to his diary his anti-social sentiments and his tortured speculations on the irrational nature of man becomes a literary descendant of Dostoevsky's hero in the *Notes from the Underground.*"[3]

As far as he goes Mr. Richards is surely right, but one wishes he had gone a little further. For the evidence suggests that Zamiatin drew artistic as well as ideological inspiration from the *Notes*—and not, perhaps, from the *Notes* alone. That the "underground caves"[4] which once housed the insurgent enemies of *We* derives from the spiritual "underground" which housed Dostoevsky's enemy of society, or that the huge glass dome which encloses the United State is Zamiatin's hypostasis of Dostoevsky's hated Crystal Palace[5]—such debts cannot, of course, be proven. Similarly, one cannot be sure that the mathematically regulated existence of D-503 "invested in the sacred cyphers of the Table"[6] derives from Dostoevsky's vision of an arithmetical utopia where "all human actions will be tabulated by those laws, mathematically";[7] or that the regulated sex life of the citizens of the United State (pink slips, assigned hours) was inspired by Dostoevsky's forecast of a race of robots who "desire nothing except by the calendar."[8] But, taken collectively, and in the light of Dostoevsky's known philosophical influence on *We*, such correspondences raise suspicions. When Zamiatin's "square root of minus numbers"[9] (symbol to D-503 of the irrational in life) is compared with Dostoevsky's "extraction of square roots"[10] (symbol for the purely rational in life), these suspicions are bound to grow; and when the Dostoevskian leitmotif $2 \times 2 = 4$ (another symbol of rationality and finitude) is heard to reverberate in Zamiatin's satirical hymn to rationalism: "Two times two, forever in love/ Forever joined in passionate four/ Most ardent lovers in the world/ Eternally welded two times two,"[11] they approach something like certitude.

Whatever ideas the *Notes* may have suggested to Zamiatin, the central metaphor or myth of his novel was drawn from a much older source, though it is possible that this debt, too, may have been suggested by Dostoevsky. The source in question is the Biblical story of Adam and Eve, which Zamiatin incorporated into his tale of a communist paradise, and the satirical uses of which Dostoevsky had—albeit in rudimentary form—anticipated in *The Possessed*. For when in the chapter entitled "Among Us" the revolutionary theoretician Shigalov[12] predicts that mankind in search of a socialist utopia will "through boundless submission by a series of regenerations attain a primeval innocence something like primeval paradise" (a moment later it is called "an earthly paradise"),[13] he is not only summarizing the prehistory of *We* but naming its central metaphor. And shortly thereafter, when Pëtr Stepanovich Verkhovensky, describing his own (perverted) concept of the future totalitarian society, exclaims to Stavrogin, "We shall consider how to build up an edifice of stone. For the first time! *We* will build, we and only we!"[14] he may have supplied Zamiatin with his title as well.

But to gauge the possible extent of Zamiatin's indebtedness to Dostoevsky is more difficult (and less important) than to see how the myth actually works itself out in the novel. The action of *We* has barely begun when Zamiatin drops his first small hint of the mythical shape of things to come. As D-503, still a joyful cog in the machine of the United State, passes proudly in review (Entry 2), he reflects that "not past generations, but I myself have won a victory over the old god and the old life, I myself have created all this"—a piece of pompous self-deception which the heroine (I-330) is quick to perceive. Addressing her future lover for the first time, she mockingly remarks: "I beg your pardon . . . but you gazed about like an inspired mythological god on the seventh day of creation."[15] Although there is, in truth, nothing very godlike in the shuffling and neurotic D-503, his delusion is not without significance. For just as Adam, the servant and mortal replica of Jehovah, once labored for his Maker in the fields of Eden, so D-503, the dedicated architect, labors to improve the "glass paradise" (the phrase is his)[16] of the Well-Doer. And it is precisely because the United State has restored that perfect community of interests between master and man which had once reigned in Eden ("The Ancient God and we [were] side by side at the same table,"[17] the poet R-13 later explains to the hero) that "Adam's" momentary confusion is possible.

To do the Well-Doer's will on earth is, of course, the vocation of our hero—a vocation which the crafty, beautiful I-330 seeks to subvert by inducing him to taste the delights of freedom and knowledge, that is, of Evil. In essence this is, of course, an imitation of Genesis. And just as the Biblical authors and their successors used certain traditional images to describe the fateful event—a forbidden food, a bite, a figurative fall, and sinful intercourse—so Zamiatin in relating D-503's loss of innocence uses his considerable ingenuity to ring the changes on these symbols. The seductive charms of Eve and her first fatal bite are thus telescoped into the recurrent images of I-330's sharp teeth and "bite-smile," which have such a fatal fascination for D-503; the moral fall of Adam becomes literal in *We*: "Down, down, down, as from a steep mountain,"[18] descends the hero into the site of his transgression (the Ancient House); it is there that a green and forbidden liqueur offered by I-330 replaces the forbidden fruit of Genesis, the consumption of which—here Zamiatin follows Milton rather than Genesis—on the hero's next visit leads to sinful and guilty intercourse with "Eve." When it is all over, the latter pointedly remarks: "Well, my fallen angel, you perished just now, did you know that?"[19] There was, in truth, no need to labor the point; for D-503 feels a guilt quite worthy of his ancestor departing through the Gates of Eden: "I, a corrupted man, a criminal," he reflects in anguish, "have no place here. No, I shall never be able to fuse myself into the mechanical rhythm . . . I am to burn eternally from now on, running from place to place, seeking a nook where I may hide my eyes."[20]

Zamiatin exploits his myth in a manner that is neither mechanical nor, on the whole, obtrusive. Indeed, he drops his symbols so gently that their presence seems to have gone unnoticed. Perhaps it was to forestall such an event that on one occasion he expounds his Biblical design explicitly and in detail. His mouthpiece is the poet R-13, who in Entry 11 describes to D-503 the plight of the modern state in these unambiguous terms:

> You understand . . . the ancient legend of paradise . . . That legend refers to us today, does it not? Think about it. There were two in paradise and the choice was offered to them: happiness without freedom, or freedom without happiness . . . They, blockheads that they were, chose freedom.

And a moment later:

> It was he [the Devil] who led people to break the interdiction, to taste pernicious freedom—he, the cunning serpent. And we planted a boot on his head, and squash! Everything's fixed. Paradise again! We returned to the simplemindedness and innocence of Adam and Eve. No more meddling with good and evil and all that.[21]

Of course the poet cannot know what the reader knows—that his interlocutor is at that very moment "meddling with good and evil" for all he is worth. And it is this very ignorance which allows him to deliver the *coup de grâce*, when he playfully adds: "Oh you . . . Adam! By the way—about Eve . . ."[22]

The reader who accepts Zamiatin's gambit and starts looking for further Biblical parallels will not be disappointed. He will note, for instance, that the Well-Doer becomes the Lord God of Genesis: "It was he, descending to us from the sky. He—the new Jehovah in an aero";[23] that his guardians (official custodians of virtue, that is, conformity) are angels: "He, my Guardian Angel," writes D-503 of one of their number, "decided matters";[24] and that the world lying beyond the Green Wall of the United State and visited by the New Adam and Eve after the Fall (Entry 27) is clearly that wilderness "east of Eden" where the first sinful couple had taken refuge.

But if *We* is to some significant degree Zamiatin's ironic retelling of Genesis chapters 1-4, where, one may ask, is the Archfiend without whose odious designs and serpent's shape no account of the story would be complete or even meaningful? The answer is provided by that enigmatic friend of Eve, S-4711, whose letter stands for Satan, serpent, and snake alike,[25] and whose collusion with Eve, "double-curved" body, manner of locomotion ("gliding over the . . . glass . . . the running body . . . like a noose"),[26] and deceitful disguise (". . . if he should discard the deception of clothes and appear in public in his true form . . . Oh!")[27] make his diabolical vocation clear. And if the frivolous reader would inquire how such a deformed creature could have ever enjoyed the favors of the beauteous I-330, Zamiatin has a no less frivolous answer ready. For who could be more ingratiating, more insinuatingly seductive than he who wears the world's most famous perfume for a name—4711? Subtlety, thy name is Eau de Cologne!

Zamiatin does not allow such occasional playfulness to blunt the edge of his satire, which cuts deepest when it diverges most widely from its model.[28] For if the Biblical argument is that in order to be worthy of God, Adam should have resisted Eve's blandishments, the moral of *We* is that to be worthy of man the new Adam ought to succumb to them. Hence, if Genesis is tragic because Paradise was lost, and man's happiness forfeited, its modern analogue is tragic because, in the end Adam is saved, and his "glass paradise"—putatively at least—preserved.

The use of ingenious mythical parallels can, as the record of contemporary fiction attests, become a habit-forming authorial indulgence. It should not, therefore, surprise us that midway through the novel Zamiatin is tempted to introduce a second Biblical pattern, though it is doubtful whether its artistic integration into the novel as a whole is entirely successful. The earliest trace of this can be found in Entry 20, when Zamiatin makes his penitent hero (he has illegally gotten O-90 with child) ponder the equity of the death sentence awaiting him: "This [then] is that divine justice of which those stone-housed ancients dreamed, lit by the naive pink rays of the dawn of history. Their 'God' punished sacrilege as a capital crime."[29] This rather shadowy equation of Christianity and communism evidently pleased the author (who was a friend of neither ideology), for two chapters later D-503, relishing the sensation of selfless solidarity with the community (he is going through one of his conformist phases), puts the case more clearly:

> In the ancient days the Christians understood this feeling; they are our only, though very imperfect, direct forerunners. They knew that resignation is a virtue, and pride a vice; that "We" is from God, "I" from the devil.[30]

Several chapters later the same conceit crops up again; this time, however, it is presented from the insurgents' standpoint: "Our—or, more exactly, your—ancestors, the Christians, worshiped entropy like a god," explains I-330 to her lover. "But we are not Christians."[31]

That a disciple of Dostoevskian ethics could depart from his master's metaphysics so far as to see Christianity as the father of communism was an irony which Zamiatin evidently understood and even exploited through parody. For as *We* draws to its tumultuous close, the hero finds himself in a situation (Entry 36) which bears a bizarre but unmistakable resemblance to that of Christ in the Legend of the Grand Inquisitor, the philosophical importance of which has already been noted. Like Ivan's Christ, though in a very different way, D-503 has tried to liberate mankind.[32] Like Him, too, he has failed in his endeavor and has returned to earth, where he is taken prisoner and summoned into the presence of the austere and loving leader of the terrestrial forces for an accounting. Silent (like Jesus), he listens to the stern arraignment by his superior as the latter rejects the concept of freedom ("[Man] longed for that day when someone would tell him what happiness is, and then would chain him to it"),[33] and defends the enemies of Christ:

> Remember—a blue hill, a crowd, a cross? Some up on the hill, sprinkled with blood, are busy nailing a body to the cross; others below, sprinkled with tears, are gazing upward. Does it not seem to you that the part which those above must play is

the more difficult, the more important part? If it were not for them, how could that magnificent tragedy have been staged? True, they were hissed by the dark crowd, but for that the author of the tragedy, God, should have remunerated them the more liberally, should he not?[34]

Like the Grand Inquisitor, the Well-Doer knows that the forced benefactions of the good society outweigh the freedom which Christ—and now D-503—would offer. And the hero, whose forty days of temptation in the wilderness of doubt (there are forty entries in his journal)[35] and thirty-two years of age at his "death" are obvious allusions to his Christlike role, feels a solitude akin to that of Jesus before His crucifixion:

> If only I had a mother, as the ancients had—my mother, mine. For whom I should not be the Builder of the "Integral," and not D-503, not a molecule of the United State, but merely a living human piece, a piece of herself . . . And though I were driving the nails in the corpse or being nailed to it (perhaps it is the same), she would hear what no one else could hear.[36]

Perhaps, indeed, his solitude is greater; for Jesus' apostrophe on the Cross was, after all, addressed to Somebody. The New Saviour has no one.

D-503's ultimate decision is, of course, the opposite of Christ's. Instead of dying so that men may be free, he lives so that they will remain slaves. Yet, paradoxically, even as he submits himself to the machine which makes soulless robots of its victims, he is—if we accept his own identification of communism and Christianity—behaving like a Christian. And in the words written on the eve of his self-sacrifice— "Perhaps then [that is, after the operation] I shall be reborn. For only what is killed can be reborn"[37]—one can hear ironical overtones of the Christian promise that only he who loses himself shall find himself, or that to live in the spirit is to die in the flesh.

To describe some of the more important symbolic patterns in We is not to affirm their artistic success. In particular, the compounded ironies occasioned by D-503's appearance as both the First and the Second Adam seem to blur and blunt more than they intensify. And other symbolic allusions (I have not tried to discuss them all) raise similar doubts.[38] But if We is read today, it is less for its artistic merits (which are uneven) than for the boldness and ingenuity of its satirical concept (which are very great). In this concept the Biblical patterns described here play a role of the first importance.

CHRISTOPHER COLLINS

Islanders

The years 1916 and 1917 found Zamyatin living abroad for the first time. He had been sent to England to supervise the construction of Russian icebreakers. His stay there resulted in three works set in England, *Islanders* (*Ostrovityane*), *Fisher of men* (*Lovets chelovekov*), and (a play based on *Islanders*), *The Society of Honorary Bell Ringers* (*Obshchestvo pochetnyx zvonarey*). England must not be regarded as the target of these works so much as the artistically appropriate setting for the phenomena being satirized.[1]

Islanders will be read here as a study of alienation in modern society. The term has been used by so many modern critics, philosophers, and writers in such a variety of contexts that a working definition must be made before proceeding. One view expressed in Western letters today is that the modern writer must be alienated if he is to be a good writer.[2] Alienation in this context means alienation from the society surrounding the writer, disagreement with the values and standards accepted by society at large. A writer in complete agreement with his society, with commonly held standards and values would have very little to say, and very little impetus to say it. This concept of the writer as heretic is not new and was heartily affirmed by Zamyatin in his critical essays.

It is, of course, psychically unhealthy to be alienated from society at large, and we should partially sympathize with pleas for recognition of the modern writer's martyrdom in the name of art and truth; but there are other, more destructive forms of alienation which only the heretic may escape. If adherence to the values of modern bour-

From the author's dissertation, *Eugene Zamyatin: An Interpretive Study*, Indiana University 1967. Reprinted with the author's permission.

geois society leads to alienation from Self, nature, or God, then the
individual, the writer-heretic, or the writer's protagonist-heretic may
find a more meaningful, unalienated life in rejecting society. He
necessarily suffers some alienation from society as a result, but he
avoids alienation in more important respects and benefits from his
healthy relationship and integration with the other elements of his
existence.[3]

In *Islanders* traditional British reserve, conformity, and propriety
are seen joined with the modern industrial age to alienate the protagonist, Campbell, and most of his fellow citizens, from Self and from
nature.

One might suppose that a work set in twentieth-century urban
England and dealing with alienation might include comments (or
diatribes) found so frequently in other contemporary literary or
philosophical works on the city—the anonymity, the loneliness, the
slums, the garish advertising, the atmosphere of the fast buck, the
all-pervasive noise and filth, the violence, the absence of wildlife,
trees, and grass. Such is not the case here. Zamyatin's fictional English city is an exciting place to live in for people like the Irish lawyer
and Don Juan, O'Kelly, and for the striptease dancer, Didi. Away
from the city they would certainly sink into the provincial muck of
Zamyatin's early stories. The city does not alienate them from Self
or from nature. Far from discouraging their free sexual expression,
the city, in its anonymity, gives them privacy. Nor, as will be seen
below, does the city stop them from responding to nature.

The three most important forces in the story—traditional propriety,
modern industrialism, and freedom and integration with Self and
nature—are represented in three key images that appear throughout
the narrative. These images are, respectively, the portrait of Campbell's late father, Sir Harold Campbell, the electric iron (which
Campbell must purchase before he can consider marriage or sexual
relations with Didi), and Didi's porcelain pug, Johnny. Each of these
objects occupies an honored position on the mantel above the fireplace in the apartments of their respective owners. (Fire in Zamyatin's usual image for Energy and passion, and as such, is nearly holy.
There is always a fire in the fireplace in Didi's apartment, but there
are no fires in Campbell's or in Lady Campbell's apartments.)

In position and importance these objects can be considered as holy
images, a kind of icon. Lady Campbell, Campbell, and Didi each
have their revered icons. Campbell's rejection of Didi's icon and the
placing of his icon on the mantel next to it is symbolically an indica-

tion of the attempted replacement of one religion by another in the
life of Didi.

When Lady Campbell's apartment is first described, the portrait
on the mantel of her late husband, Sir Harold, is one of the few objects mentioned (38).[4] Her first words in the story are: "My late husband, Sir Harold, always used to speak out against . . ." (21). Aside
from appeals to the authority of her late husband, she has very little
else to say. When others discuss her son's "disgraceful" participation
in a boxing match and the resulting injuries, her only comment is:
"All I can think is: what would my late husband, Sir Harold, say . . ."
(55). When the Vicar Dewley and his flock, the Society of Honorary
Bell Ringers, discuss Campbell's plans to marry a striptease dancer
having an affair with another man, Lady Campbell again is capable
only of: "My God, what would your deceased father, Sir Harold,
say . . ." (79-80). Her last words in the story, like most of her other
words, include a reference to her late husband as an absolute moral
authority. The icon of Sir Harold is the holy image of British propriety. The deadness of the saint in the icon is emphasized in many
ways. The portrait is of a person physically dead, belonging to a dead
past. His title and the fact that he is dead are emphasized in each
of Lady Campbell's utterances. The absence of the slightest conjugal
or filial affection for the departed husband and father is an indication
of the deadness of even his actual life with them in the past. Although dead, he exercises great power over Lady Campbell, as indicated by her reverent invocations, and by her head being frequently
jerked back, as if by unseen reins (40, 55, and elsewhere). Lady
Campbell is a death figure herself, with her "mummy" shoulders and
décolleté (21, 42, and elsewhere), her gray dress, gray hair, and
especially her lips "wriggling like worms" (21, 40, and elsewhere).

The resemblance between Campbell and his late father is mentioned several times; each has the same square, solid chin. Campbell
has a high opinion of his mother and does not wish to offend her. In
response to an "indecent" question by Didi he echoes his mother's
allegiance to the dead authority of propriety: "What if my mother
could . . ." (31).

Sir Harold, the law, and propriety are related to each other and
with death. When Campbell is commanded by his mother to sit down
and listen to the instructions of the Corporation of Honorary Bell
Ringers—a sort of kangaroo court sitting in moral judgment—the
portrait of the late Sir Harold is invoked first. Only at this point is it

noted that the portrait shows Sir Harold in his wig and robe, the first reference to his profession. He was literally a judge, and he is here metaphorically a judge presiding over the trial of his own son in this moral court, and the judgment leads to the eventual execution of his son as prescribed by an actual court. In *Islanders* the law does not exist to protect man from criminals, big business, or big government, or even to serve as the arm of the powerful and the privileged. The law as shown here is concerned solely with propriety. The references to points of law in the work are: the insistence that, as a matter of form, Didi's ex-husband ought to pay her alimony, even though she was unfaithful to him; O'Kelly's remark that he had invented a portable, inflatable suitcase to circumvent the law requiring a couple registering in a hotel to possess at least one suitcase; and the execution of Campbell, considered by the "decent" people more a matter of propriety than one of moral or social justice. O'Kelly sums it up: "In the final analysis, the role of the law is nothing more than the role of your dresses, ladies?" (25). That is, the purpose of each is to restrain the natural, cover it up, and impose a mask of propriety on it. That O'Kelly is a lawyer does not indicate that he has any interest in joining the late jurist Sir Harold in the support of the rule of law, but rather his wish and talent for circumventing the law in his own interests and in the interests of his clients.

The second icon is the electric iron Campbell purchases as the first important step in setting up a household for himself and his future bride, Didi. There are to be no sexual relations and no wedding until he has enough money to rent a house and furnish it properly.

The chapter dealing with the arrival of spring, with flowers and trees in bloom, is entitled "The Electric Iron" (59). For Campbell, the iron is far more important than the stirring of external nature, or the stirring of Didi's sexual desire. Didi complains of the heat, unbuttons her blouse, and puts Campbell's hand on her breast. He is tempted, but "Campbell, thank God, grips the steering wheel again and steers steadily toward the little house with the electric iron. Campbell withdrew his hand" (61). Campbell's first sentence to Didi when she visits him after secretly spending the night with O'Kelly is "Iron" (71). They then go shopping. Campbell has been full of doubts inspired by the anonymous letter he received, but he is completely reassured by the shopping trip; this is what a happy marriage is to be about. The iron is bought first, then other things, including night clothes for Didi. "With each purchased thing Didi became more and more his wife" (72). By mocking contrast, Didi had already become (sexually) the wife of O'Kelly the night before, without benefit of clothes or electric iron. In fact, the same King Street which provides Campbell the electric iron also provides O'Kelly flowers to grace the room where he makes love to Didi.

Campbell and Didi return from shopping to Didi's apartment. When O'Kelly arrives he finds the iron on the mantel next to Didi's icon, the porcelain pug. " 'Next to Johnny?' he looked reproachfully at Didi" (73). Didi is now quite unhappy. The iron has been purchased and placed on a level with her icon, her beloved porcelain pug. Campbell's open dislike for the pug bodes ill for the future.

Didi then spends the afternoon aimlessly tearing up lined paper. O'Kelly explains that these lines are considered of the utmost importance in the city of Jesmond, that they are the rails along which the proper life ought to move. As a symbol, the electric iron is related to, and perhaps sums up, the metaphors of the rails used here and frequently by the Vicar Dewley, as well as the entire concept of enforced, mathematically, mechanically perfect happiness preached by the Vicar. Whereas the portrait of Sir Harold represents the dead hand of tradition, the iron represents what Edward J. Brown calls "a symbol of conventional propriety, as well as of a life neatly pressed and patterned."[5] It also refers to the dehumanization of man in the age of the assembly line and the age of mass consumption, for, like the ubiquitous, nameless Sunday Gentlemen, with their equally nameless and indistinguishable wives, children, and houses, and like "buttons, Fords, and The Times" (43), the iron is produced by the thousands. Industry depends not only on mathematics and mechanics, and on the interchangeable parts of the assembly line, but on reliability, efficiency, and strict scheduling. Industry depends on, and therefore encourages, a consumer goods mentality in the society as a whole. As contemporary writers and philosophers argue frequently, what is good for industry and trade may not necessarily be good for people, since people tend to become dehumanized and alienated when they function as cogs in a great economic machine. The Vicar's concept of enforced mathematical happiness and strict adherence to schedule owes something both to the Grand Inquisitor and to the efficiency expert of the twentieth century.

Another obvious metaphor relating to the iron, and to the age of the machine and mechanical happiness, is that of Campbell as a truck. Campbell's initial appearance is as a truck (9). He proceeds slowly, deliberately, "like a heavily loaded truck . . ." (15). Early references to him include: ". . . the truck traveled only on pavement" (24); ". . . you could hear how the heavy truck puffs, unable to move from the spot" (27); "Paper—that's something defined. The fog in Campbell's head cleared, the truck pulled its cargo swiftly and surely along the well-traveled highway" (29); and ". . . now the truck will start moving . . ." (31). When Campbell departs the world of propriety and mechanical happiness, as he does briefly in the boxing match, in his partly suppressed desire for Didi, and in his flight from discovering Didi in bed with his rival, his thoughts and emotions are described in terms of a car or truck plunging ahead without steering (44, 57, 81).

Didi's icon is her porcelain pug Johnny. Unlike the other icons, Johnny makes no demands, he just smiles incessantly at Didi and her love life, just as the moon smiles on lovers in the park: "The bushes were intensively alive all night, they stirred, whispered, and all night the moon walked about over the park with a monocle in his eye and looked down with the beneficent irony of the porcelain pug" (60). The pug is further identified with the moon, when "the moon plunged into the light batiste clouds" (61), while Johnny plunges into the white batiste and rosy waves of Didi's breasts (60 and 62). Johnny is more physically alive than the other icons. He comes down from the mantel frequently, to be caressed and talked to by Didi. He is wet by her tears and kisses and warmed by her touch. In his smile, friendliness, and ugliness, he is said to bear a remarkable resemblance to the human being O'Kelly—"two drops of water" (33). Not only more alive than the other icons, he is more alive than Campbell. After Campbell evades sexual relations with Didi, she presses Johnny to her breast and he kisses her (61). Didi speaks *na ty* with Johnny, but *na vy* with Campbell. As the icon of the all-wise, all-understanding, all-loving life, Johnny is even able (although reluctantly) to kiss the Vicar Dewley (58).

It is Johnny to whom Didi turns shortly after her divorce from her first husband to beg him not to be angry if again she gets "a little bit" (*nemnozhko*) married (57). Johnny, never one to make a moral judgment, does not object. The same Johnny seems to approve when, in the following chapter, Didi asks him if she may go to O'Kelly.

Campbell instantly senses Johnny's values and the threat to his world of propriety and electric irons: ". . . there were immediately established, without any visible reason, poor relations between Campbell and Johnny" (32). As Campbell lies in Didi's bed (alone) recovering from the boxing match, "the whole night the porcelain pug guarded Campbell with a grin and disturbed his thinking" (50). Didi's sexual desire and the identical smiles of Johnny on the mantel and the monocled moon in the window annoy Campbell to the point where he leaps up angrily and turns Johnny's face to the wall (61). Didi will not permit her icon to be so treated and puts it to her breast. Campbell then sullenly juts out his square chin at the moon.

Thus, the portrait of the deceased Sir Harold is an image of dead propriety, and the equally lifeless electric iron is a symbol of the age of the machine; and both are symbols of the pursuit of status and serve for their owners and worshipers as images, models, and moral authorities for alienation from the spontaneous, the natural, the free, especially free sexual expression, and, in short, from the Self. But Johnny the porcelain pug comes down from the mantel, and even though it is an inanimate object, it enters into a complex web of relationships and identities with nature, animals, and people. For Didi and for O'Kelly the porcelain pug serves as a symbol of, and a moral authority for, their spontaneous, natural, free life, in which propriety and social or economic status are not factors, a life in which the Self is neither crushed nor covered over.

A symbolism of clothes is also of importance as regards alienation. First, clothes cover the natural body. Bourgeois society regards the natural, naked body as indecent. Campbell won't remove his jacket for the doctor in the presence of a lady, even though he is seriously, or even, for all he knows, mortally injured as the result of an accident. And he never removes his square shoes. To do so would be to expose his bare feet. (The foot is often considered in dream or myth a phallic symbol. For a discussion of the preference Englishmen in the story *Islanders* have for waterproof shoes, see below.) Didi, the incarnation of the natural life, is appropriately a striptease dancer by profession. The bare body, the natural, is capable of exerting a powerful influence on even those as well-clothed and well-indoctrinated as Campbell. It is the sight of her body on stage that leads to his otherwise unthinkable infatuation and his appearance in a boxing match. The second and last sight he has of her body, in bed with his rival, leads to murder and to Campbell's consequent execution. Related is the obvious symbolism of Mrs. Dewley's pince-nez—with it on she is cool and reserved. When it is off or lost, as it is when Campbell becomes a patient in her home, and when he is executed, Mrs. Dewley becomes human, emotional, and loving.

Second, the wearing of conservative, neat clothes, properly selected for the social occasion, displays one's respect for tradition and one's conformity in taste and morals with one's fellow citizens. The Sunday Gentlemen all wear identical suits and top hats. Their wives are all dressed in pink and blue. By contrast O'Kelly's jacket is a mess, and often unbuttoned (24). On the occasion of Lady Campbell's dinner party, O'Kelly "spoils" everything by appearing in a morning coat instead of the proper attire (40). And in his enthusiastic, spontaneous gesturing and talking he grossly spills sauce on his clothes (40).

Lastly, one notes the white flannel nightcap of the Vicar and his fellow citizens, an image of comfortable complacency, apathy, and isolation. The nightcap certainly discourages marital sexual relations. It is pulled over the ears to keep out the birds' singing. And the night before Campbell's execution, when human beings ought to be taking action, or, at the least, unable to sleep because of human concern, the Vicar, in flannel nightcap, "with arms folded on his chest, as prescribed in 'The Doctrine,' snored peacefully . . . the whole world slept peacefully, snoring, in its flannel nightcap . . ." (88).

As in the case of Turgenev's *Fathers and Sons* the degree of alienation from Self is partly demonstrated by the relation with external nature.[6] Zamyatin's story, unlike most of Turgenev's works, is set in the city, and hence the possibilities for relationship with external nature would appear to be limited. There are no gardens, no fields, no forests, not even grass underfoot. One might expect all the characters, whether alienated from Self or not, to suffer from the artificial environment of the city, and seek to escape it. But through the extensive use of a symbolism involving sun, weather, and water, Zamyatin is able to indicate the characters' alienation from, or relatedness to, nature, and therefore to imply the degree of alienation from Self.

When outdoors, the Vicar Dewley frowns from "the too bright sun, and the impermissible racket of the sparrows" (8). Indoors, he is much happier with sunlight diffused and softened by window panes (66). Lady Campbell objects to bright sun and pulls down her blinds so that the sunlight becomes "more moderate and decent" (38). Her son, reflecting the self-alienation of his mother and of bourgeois society at large, also objects to bright sun. In his apartment he pulls down the blinds to shut out the sun. Up to this point the lustful Didi has managed to remain faithful to her fiancé, Campbell, despite his repeated refusal to have sexual relations with her and despite his

steady talk of buying furniture and the iron. But the closing of the
blinds to shut out the sun is the crucial action that leads immediately
to Didi's resolution to offer herself to O'Kelly:

> "But I want sun," Didi jumped up.
> "But dear, you know very well I'm working so that we can
> begin buying the furniture as soon as possible, and after
> that. . . ."
> Didi suddenly broke out laughing, did not hear the rest, and
> went to her own room. She put the pug on the mantel, looked
> into his charmingly ugly mug.
> "What do you think, Johnny?"
> Johnny obviously thought the same thing. Didi began to pin
> on her hat in a hurry . . . (67).

Didi then goes with O'Kelly to the beach at Sunday-By, where the
sun "made the blood boil" (68). She soon agrees to spend the night
with him.

References to the weather, the clouds, rain, the seasons of the
year occur frequently. The Vicar includes "the taking of fresh air"
in his weekly schedule (7). (We can well suppose he would enthusiastically endorse H. G. Wells's hopes, satirized in My, for weather
control.) But for the most part the Vicar and his fellow Jesmondians
simply prefer to isolate themselves from the weather and from the
seasons: "At night came a flood of bird singing, not taking any account of the fact that at 10 o'clock decent people went to bed. Decent
people angrily slammed their windows shut and thrust themselves
into their white nightcaps" (60). A similar isolation from the rain
and from the night air is one of the key symptoms of alienation of the
protagonist in Ivan Bunin's Gentleman from San Francisco.[7]

The Sunday Gentlemen's standard greeting to each other is "Fine
weather, isn't it?" They go home and discuss the weather and little
else with their families (19). The weather remains only a subject
of polite conversation with them; they are never involved with it.
They do not sweat or shiver from temperature extremes, and the
weather and the seasons do not have the slightest effect on their
work, leisure, or emotions. The Vicar Dewley's great social presence
of mind is indicated by the remark that even while dozing he is always prepared to open his eyes and say "Fine weather, isn't it?" (66).

In her longing for Campbell, Mrs. Dewley comes to a partial realization of her alienation: "Mrs. Dewley went somewhere, with the pink
and blue ladies, spoke of the weather, and meanwhile the clouds
kept rushing along and swelling" (20). Before Campbell's arrival,

she is bored by the Vicar's puerile enthusiasm for efficiency and schedules and sits glumly by the window watching the "swift, swelling clouds" (8).[8] After Campbell is injured in an accident, brought to her house, and nursed back to health, she becomes human and longs for him. Now she sits at the breakfast table, looks past the Vicar "perhaps at the clouds" and smiles (18). Campbell is never able or willing to perceive her love, and his recovery results in his leaving the house. She feels she should act, but is unable to act: ". . . she looked out the window, the swift, swelling clouds rushed on, and one ought to run after them, one ought to do just that . . ." (20). The implications of the cloud images will be discussed at greater length below in the discussion of water symbolism.

While the Sunday Gentlemen in top hats remain unaffected by the heat, and Campbell flushes only from embarrassing social situations, O'Kelly is the only one present who pants and sweats freely from the heat at Lady Campbell's dinner party. While "decent" people slam their windows on the spring, others spend the night in the park, and keep the bushes alive; Didi commits adultery in her first marriage, she confesses, simply because the weather was nice (34); and the June weather is directly related to Didi's increasing lust. She complains of the heat and unbuttons her blouse in Campbell's presence. The heat of the sun mentioned above is involved in her increasing sexual desire for O'Kelly at the beach.

The bourgeoisie are very much antiwater. It is noted at almost every one of her appearances that Lady Campbell's ribs stick out like a broken umbrella (21, 55, and elsewhere). Mr. MacIntosh, as his name suggests, is interested in keeping out the water. (In the play adaptation of *Islanders* he is a raincoat dealer.) O'Kelly notes that Englishmen are fond of waterproof shoes (62). A connection between the passion for waterproof shoes, Campbell's refusal to remove his shoes when injured, and the ultimate meaning of the desire for isolation from water is suggested in Mr. MacIntosh's enthusiastic proposal (approved by the Honorary Bell Ringers) that the church journal increase its advertising revenue by accepting advertisements for rubber prophylactics—whose purpose, of course, is to isolate and render ineffective the life-giving moisture.

Didi and O'Kelly do not isolate themselves from the water. After they have sunned themselves well at the beach, they plunge eagerly into the surf. Leaping into the water is the necessary action when overheated by the sun. Buffeted by waves, and by her desire, Didi is unable to resist and agrees to sleep with O'Kelly.

The association of water and sexual expression is made more explicit in other images. Didi's breasts are termed "white and pink waves" (62), and the breasts-clouds parallel was noted above. Didi's short, wet, curly hair is mentioned twice with strong sexual associations (43, 51). Full of unsated desire, Didi smells sweet and pungent, like the *levkoy* flower "dry from lack of rain" (62). There is no direct description of Didi and O'Kelly's love-making, but the night they spend together is described metaphorically: "Heat slept. There stood a milky, wet fog" (70).

In conclusion, the unhappy protagonist, Campbell, the Vicar and Mrs. Dewley, Lady Campbell, and other Honorary Bell Ringers are thoroughly alienated from Self and from the natural world. Their alienation is seen in their everyday life and is symbolically emphasized in their choice of holy images, their clothes, their rejection of nature, and particularly their isolation from water.

Like D-503 in *My*, Campbell makes an unsuccessful attempt to break out of his prison. He enters a boxing match, becomes infatuated with a striptease dancer, but is unable to escape the alienation-imposing values of his bourgeois society, loses his fiancé, murders his rival, and is executed.

The other Honorary Bell Ringers do not even attempt to escape their prison. They avoid the boredom of alienation by becoming spectators. Just as they were spectators of the weather and seasons rather than participating in them, they are spectators of life. The mob of spectators, metaphorically an enormous serpent, appears both at the boxing match to witness real human conflict and to yell for blood, and at the prison gate to be present at real human death and to yell for an execution. (They are the *Honorary* Bell Ringers—the real bell ringer tolls the bell as the signal for the hangman to spring the trapdoor and hang Campbell.)

The Honorary Bell Ringers, and especially MacIntosh, the specialist in moral problems, are always ready to forego their sterile talk of the weather and to smack their disapproving lips over the scandal of the boxing match and over Didi's affair, and even to intervene enthusiastically in such a way that murder is not a totally unexpected result. The murder and the execution are further grist for the spectators' mill.

Didi and O'Kelly, although they may be somewhat socially alienated in being more or less ostracized by the "decent" people, do not suffer the slightest loneliness thereby, and, more important, are not alienated in the slightest from Self or nature. They never talk about weather or the private lives of others; they are too busy leading their own spontaneous, free, private lives. But modern bourgeois society, argues Zamyatin, finds such lack of alienation from Self and nature both an intolerable insult and rich fare for gossip. Ostracism and meddling are the natural consequences and, in this case, lead inevitably to the unhappy end of Campbell and O'Kelly.

ROBERT A. MAGUIRE

The Pioneers: Pil'nyak and Ivanov

Boris Pil'nyak is one of those writers who miss greatness but who alter
the literary history of their country in a decisive way. He lacked a real
gift for fiction—an incandescent vision capable of fusing good intentions, prodigious reading, and keen powers of observation into compelling art. He was instead a borrower, an eclectic, the diligent pupil
of Belyi, Remizov, and Bunin. Yet his lack of originality determined
his importance, for he adapted the techniques and strategies of his
teachers to the new themes of Revolution and Civil War. Through him,
they took on a respectability that they could no longer command by
themselves; and because he was extremely popular and widely imitated during the early twenties, they left a deep and lasting impression
on the new literature.

He began around 1915 as an allegorist in the "primitive" vein,
which writers had been mining since the turn of the century in rebellion against reason, humanism, and esthetics. The cult of violence and
death (Andreev), of sex and instinctual will (Artsybashev), of children, savages, and outlaws (Sologub, Gumilyov, Gor'kii), the attempt
to destroy beauty with nonsense, dissonance, ugliness, formlessness,
or artlessness—these had been but a few of the ways in which the
theme displayed itself. Pil'nyak's palette in the early stories was subdued by comparison, his vision on the whole lyrical and benevolent,
and his technical resources ruthlessly conventional. All these stories
proceeded from the idea that nature knows best. "An Entire Life"
(Tselaya zhizn'), for example, tells of two birds who mate, release
their young into the world without regrets, and finally separate when

From *Red Virgin Soil*, by Robert A. Maguire (Princeton University Press,
1968), pp. 101-47. Reprinted by permission of Princeton University Press and
the author.

the male can no longer provide. Sentiment, loyalty, even habit—the bases of human marriage—have no place in this superior realm of sheer instinct. "A Year of Their Life" (God ikh zhizni) unites the whole world in one vast procreative urge: the hunter Demid mates with Marina in the spring and fills her with child; a year later Makar, the bear who is Demid's constant companion, comes to maturity and goes off in search of a mate of his own. What is embarrassing in paraphrase does not come off at all badly in context. Pil'nyak works here in a quiet, subdued way with his animals and nature-men and does not overstate the simple and obvious moral of his tales—virtues that he unfortunately let atrophy as he went on.

But these excursions into exoticism were merely exercises; his ambitions reached higher. "The Snows" (Snega), another story from the same period, foreshadowed the direction they would take. Here the hero is an intellectual who has wearied of civilization and the deceptive importunings of the mind, and has finally unlocked the secret of life through a liaison with a simple peasant woman. "Yes," he muses, "a year closer to death, a year further away from birth"—that is all there is to it. His former mistress comes to understand this, even though she cannot accept it. "There have been hundreds of religions, hundreds of systems of ethics, esthetics, science, philosophy; and everything has changed and is still changing, and there is only one thing that does not change: everything living—man, rye, a mouse—is born, breeds and dies. . . ."[1]

The conflict which is merely implied in most of the other early stories is here stated outright: instinct versus intellect, nature versus civilization, chaos versus logic. It remained Pil'nyak's characteristic theme, no matter how intricately he embroidered it. Usually, however, he grants his heroes no such blissful repose in the arms of their discovery. He prefers to catch them at the moment when they have become aware of the conflict within them, and he then watches it tear them apart. For man is both agent and victim, pulled by the competing claims of intellect, which wills toward consciousness and seeks it in a self-definition through system and order, and instinct, which is formless and timeless, and constitutes the ground of all being. Hence the paradox, which Pil'nyak contains in the recurring image of the caged wolf, that man builds higher and higher barriers to shut out what he yearns after. Nearly always, man tries to escape his self-made prison, but the serene and ordered life behind them has sapped his vitality. Once outside, he can never return; he has left all illusion behind. This is the truth that those impassioned seekers, the men of science, discover in the story Zavoloch'e. Their journey to the Arctic is a journey back into time in quest of man's primeval state. But they find there only a dimensionless universe of cold and ice. Their minds shout out across the empty spaces that planlessness must have a plan; but only the gelid wind replies. This is the answer to their quest. They cannot accept it, but they know it is true.[2]

For his longer stories, Pil'nyak works this conflict into a whole cosmology. The aboriginal idyll now lodges in a vast and mysterious realm called "Asia," or "East," or "Mongol." Ranged against it is the world that man has created in order and symmetry, with urban machine civilization standing at the pinnacle: this is called "Europe." There is nothing in the universe which does not serve one or the other. Each realm has agents carrying on ceaseless sabotage. Each has an army that wages tireless warfare with the other. Each also has its internal emigrés, men who look longingly at the other world, yet who do not really wish to leave their own; and it is on these divided and guilt-ridden souls that Pil'nyak focuses his gaze, watching the emotional balance tip now one way, now the other. It was when he began to set the history of Russia, particularly the recent history, into this cosmology that he found his true voice and won his fame. The Revolution of 1917 became, in his works, the decisive and final encounter in this vast cosmic struggle. It is the subject of his first novel, *Bare Year* (*Golyi god*, 1922).

For Pil'nyak, the Revolution is not the conflict of proletariat and bourgeoisie, but of East, represented by the peasantry, and West, represented by urban Russia. And what of the Bolsheviks? The peasants cannot even pronounce the word "revolution" correctly; but they understand that it bears no resemblance to what the Bolsheviks claim to be doing. "Beat the Communists," they shout. "We're for the re-lo-voo-shun (*revolyukhu*)!"[3] For the Bolsheviks, as the servants of a "scientific" ideology, are merely defending, under another name, that whole structure of civilization which true revolution has risen up to topple. Some of Pil'nyak's choicest sarcasm is reserved for them:

> In the Ordynin house, in the Executive Committee (there were no geraniums gracing these windows), people in leather jackets, Bolsheviks, would assemble upstairs. Here they were, in leather jackets, every one of them erect, a lusty leather lad, every one of them sturdy, curls spilling down the back of his neck from under his cap, skin pulled taut over cheekbones, folds at the corners of the mouth, sharp-creased movements. The pick of Russia's soft-boned and misshapen folk. In leather jackets—there's no getting at them. Here's what we know, here's what we want, here's where we're put—and that's that.[4]

They are actually counter-revolutionaries. But their prideful intellects must pay: Asia triumphs, sweeping everything away, even the peasantry; and the final vision opens up an austere and eternal Paradise, which is undefiled by man's presumptuous sin of mind:

> The forest stands austere, pillar-like, and against it the snowstorm hurls itself in fury. Night. . . . New, ever new snow-furies hurl themselves against the forest pillars, wailing, screeching, shouting, howling a female howl of frenzied rage, falling dead, and behind them more, ever more furies rush on, never relenting, ever increasing, like the head of a snake—two for every one cut off—but the forest stands like Il'ya Muromets.[5]

Pil'nyak's universe was constructed from ready-made materials. To see the Revolution as a spontaneous upwelling of the peasantry was to express a commonplace of the time. As Blok said: "Bolshevism and the Revolution exist neither in Moscow nor in Petersburg. Bolshevism —the real, Russian, devout kind—is somewhere in the depths of Russia, perhaps in the village. Yes, most likely there. . . ."[6] "Asia" called up a thousand years of history, first recorded as the chroniclers turned their eyes eastward on the hostile nomads of the far-reaching steppe; then battened into myth by the ingress of the Mongols; constantly renewed by the eastward-running expansion of Russian trade and military power; ornamented by the discovery, toward the end of the nineteenth century, of the philosophies of China and India and the literatures of Persia and Turkey; animated more recently by new religious enthusiasms that sprang from the rediscovery of Orthodoxy, the fascination with anthroposophy, and the authority of Vladimir Solov'yov. One of its offshoots, the two-Russias theme—"Asia" or "Europe," village or city, soil or salon—had absorbed intellectuals for a century or more. Pil'nyak's version owed most to the so-called Eurasians: in the contempt for the Russian intelligentsia as products of Western civilization; the rejection of Europe not so much for itself as for its irrelevance to Russian problems; the denial that capitalism (a European invention) could contribute to Russia's development; the interpretation of the Revolution as a cleansing, renewing event; and the assertion that Russians are neither Europeans nor Asians, but a mixture of both, or Eurasians.[7]

Pil'nyak pulled these familiar ideas together into a single view of the world and set them in a new literary context. He rooted the themes of Easternism and primitivism specifically in the peasantry and recast the two-Russias theme in terms of the social conflicts of his time. The result was a version of the revolutionary experience that struck an immediate response in the twenties and has haunted Russian writers ever since. It has taken on the firm flesh of myth. Against it pulls the Bolshevik version, the official myth which casts the proletariat as hero. But this myth has failed to penetrate the literary mind; one cannot think of a single distinguished work of Russian fiction that is built upon it. It has been imposed from above, and during periods of relative relaxation, it is all but ignored by the writers. The literature of the recent "thaw," for example, has revived all the old questions of the relationship of the intellectual to the world of the senses, the realm of nature, the soil, and the peasantry. The presence of these two competing myths, and the vain attempts that have been made to mate them, ensure that Soviet culture is in no danger of becoming monolithic within the foreseeable future.

. . .

Pil'nyak's views of the Revolution placed him in the extreme right wing of the so-called "Fellow Travelers." This was the name given by Leon Trotskii to writers who supported the aims of the Revolution in a general way, but were themselves neither proletarians nor Communists, and took no active part in political life.[8] They comprised the majority of the best new literary talents in Russia, and it mattered a great deal to the Bolsheviks which way their loyalties turned. As one observer put it: "At a time when we see the flourishing of petty-bourgeois, philistine literature, which is hostile to us, we must rally the writers who are on our side because this is the only way we will be able to wage the war of ideas in the book market."[9]

The plan, in short, was to form a "center" which would attract writers who were sympathetic, or at least not openly hostile to the new regime; to bring them together under Communist Party auspices, without any hint of coercion; and gradually, through example and patient persuasion, to win them over completely. At the same time, such a "center" would presumably hasten the "decomposition" of bourgeois literature by cutting off transfusions of new blood, and also work against groups like the Proletkult and the futurists, whose radical proposals for a new literature were unpalatable to many Bolshevik leaders. Finally, the lie would be given to those Russian émigrés who were charging that the Communists ruled a cultural desert.

The center for this ambitious program was to be the literary and political journal *Red Virgin Soil*. It was established in 1921, under Communist Party patronage. Its editor was Aleksandr Voronskii, a faithful Bolshevik of many years' standing and an experienced journalist. His passionate interest in creating a new Russian literature, his sensitivity to esthetic values, his insistence that art must be first of all artistic and only then ideologically pure, and his tact and skill in handling writers made him the ideal man for implementing the delicate cultural mission of the Party.

Pil'nyak's views of the Revolution posed a strong challenge to this new policy. They could not be dismissed or ignored, for his popularity ran high among readers and among many young writers as well. It is significant that the first substantial article on a prose writer to appear in *Red Virgin Soil* dealt with Pil'nyak. And Voronskii himself did the honors.[10]

Voronskii began like a skilled boxer by softening up his opponent. He praised Pil'nyak's stories and novels as brilliantly accurate portraits of the Russian provinces during the Civil War. He was even willing to grant that in certain isolated cases the Revolution might indeed represent a peasant revolt against the city and against the Communists. But—and here the "but" meant everything—he could not accept this representation as a valid commentary on the Revolution as a whole. Pil'nyak's regurgitated Slavophilism had bespattered his natural talent. Even more distressing to Voronskii was Pil'nyak's primitivism, his suggestion that the Revolution merely reenacted the sex drive on a grand scale. Voronskii worked up a righteous indignation over the one sentence that was to dog Pil'nyak forever after: "I feel," says one of the characters in the story "John and Mary" (Ivan-da-Maria), which was not published in *Red Virgin Soil* "that the entire Revolution—the entire Revolution—smells of sexual organs." "To whom and for what purpose," huffed Voronskii, "is all this pathology necessary? The result resembles a . . . Rozanovish mysticism of sex, or the conversion of the world into a brothel."[11] Pil'nyak must jettison this rotting cargo, make his convictions worthy of his impressive gifts of observation, and turn his outward acceptance of the Revolution into a true commitment. Only then could he begin to develop into a Soviet writer. "We have entered a period," Voronskii intoned, "of a real and genuine reworking and inner rethinking of everything we have experienced over the past five years. The artist who fails to understand that will quickly find himself behind the 'spirit of the time.'"[12]

So far Voronskii was saying no more than one might expect from a man who, as a Bolshevik, defended the proletarian myth: the casti-gation of Pil'nyak repeated the terms used by dozens of other like-minded critics at the time. But Voronskii made one important qualifi-cation: he assumed that Pil'nyak meant well, was a sincere artist, and could change. That being the case, the young writer's lapses into ex-ecrable taste and political obtuseness were obviously the result of ig-norance. Once he had become aware of the reactionary nature of his ideas, he would recoil in horror and mend his ways. That was where the critic came in: he worked as a kind of ideological witch doctor who, by exposing the roots of evil, helped the writer to exorcise it. Pil'nyak's primitivism was a symptom of the age, Voronskii insisted, not some rare illness. It even had its good side, for it represented a commitment to reality and fresh air in reaction against the "decadent" literature of the pre-war period, and documented the deep disappoint-ment that young writers felt in the "values of contemporary bour-geois culture." Yet basically it was unhealthy; as writers like Zamyatin had shown, it suggested "tiredness after the stormy days of Revolu-tion," and had the power to titillate latent impulses toward escapism into a world of the exotic and fantastic.[13] Now that Pil'nyak under-stood that, he was bound to reform.

Voronskii spoke like a dispassionate physician perhaps to make it easier for Pil'nyak to work this transformation and save face: a sick man, after all, need blame only the virus, not himself. In the final analysis, however, Pil'nyak was expected to give clear indication that he had taken his medicine and restored his talent to health. The alternative was worsening illness: "sorrow, mysticism, despondency, slush, spineless romanticism" would lead to artistic death and burial among third-rate decadents like Artsybashev.[14] As if to reinforce his point, Voronskii never published in Red Virgin Soil any of Pil'nyak's blatantly "Slavophile" works, such as "Sankt-Piter-Burkh," and he ex-cerpted Bare Year to exclude all the ruminations on history, the Rev-olution, and sex.

Voronskü's statement had special importance because it reached beyond Pil'nyak to all the young writers of the time, not just to those who had succumbed to "primitivism." It gave notice that an unfortu-nate class origin did not necessarily exclude a writer from a career in the field of Soviet letters. Past sins could be forgiven; and sincere evidence of a desire to change would bring sympathetic understand-ing and support. Voronskii bent over backward with Pil'nyak—and, by implication, with all the new writers—to avoid seeing any evidence of malice. He even chose to ignore the obvious sarcasm of Pil'nyak's portrayal of Bolshevik activists in *Bare Year*, taking them instead as models of the new man. (It is possible that as a very literal reader in this stage of his development as a critic, Voronskii may have missed the sarcasm completely, though it is difficult to see how.) . . .

"Much has been given to Pil'nyak," Voronskii observed, "and the demands on him ought to be increased."[15] And so they were. It was apparently expected that Pil'nyak would examine his heart, sharpen his quill at a new angle, and start producing works that answered to Voronskii's careful documentation of strengths and weaknesses. And it may well be that Pil'nyak tried to do just that, or at least tried to create the impression that he was doing so. *Materials for a Novel* (*Materialy k romanu*), written in 1923 and published in two installments in *Red Virgin Soil* in 1924, looks like a deliberate attempt to court Voronskii's favor.[16]

Materials for a Novel tells of the rise of industry in Russia. Like many other twentieth-century works with industrial themes—Gorkii's *The Artamonov Business*, for instance, or Leonov's *Road to Ocean*—it covers a large expanse of time, beginning with the first tentative efforts to tame nature and ending with a glimpse of a future ruled by the machine. Somewhat in the manner of Upton Sinclair, Pil'nyak treats his setting (Kolomna and environs) in such detail as to create a sense of documentary reality. He focuses on two periods of violent social upheaval in Russia—1905 and 1921—and, in his usual manner, explores their impact on a variety of people and institutions. As in *Bare Year*, we are taken to the decaying country manor, the petit-bourgeois house, and the primitive socialist collective. But this time the fulcrum is different. Pil'nyak moves his story mainly on the inner life of a factory, which unfolds over a period of some sixty years. This much certainly seems to represent an advance toward acknowledging modern times. Pil'nyak goes even further, by making a distinction between the oppressive machine civilization of capitalism, and the liberating machine civilization of Communism which he wraps in a luxuriant lyricism reminiscent of the so-called Smithy poets. The distinction is one that the Communists themselves make, of course. As Voronskii had reminded Pil'nyak:

> The progressive movement of the human spirit is measured by man's power over nature, and if this movement has at present been brought to a halt by "complete mechanization," the reason is to be found in social inequality, in the decay and disintegration of the [social] order based on man's sway over

man, and not in the fact that technology as such has destroyed
everything spiritual.[17]

This very argument turns up in *Materials*, where it is put into the
mouth of the Bolshevik hero, Andrei Kozhukhov.[18] The sweeping condemnation of all technology in favor of a life of pristine simplicity is
assigned to a most unattractive specimen of the old intelligentsia, the
engineer Erliksov. Although pre-Petrine Russia remains the ideal,
scarcely a trace remains of the "historiosophy" and "Asiaticism" that
Voronskii had found so offensive in *Bare Year*. There is a new attitude
toward the Bolsheviks as well. The portrait of Kozhukhov panders to
the Bolshevik self-image, without the slightest tinge of irony: Pil'nyak
makes him the only character to appear in both parts, fits him out
with an Old Revolutionary past that was shopworn even in 1924, and
endows him with the storybook qualities of resoluteness, vision, and
humanity. Finally, Pil'nyak seems to play up those quirks of his style
that Voronskii had singled out for special praise: the lyricism is lusher,
the treatment of the various regional human "types" fuller and more
detailed, the landscapes more colorful and precise. And he makes several authorial intrusions to assure the reader that the fragmentary nature of his work, which so many critics had complained about, is
deliberate.

It is tempting to interpret these changes as calculated responses to
the remarks that Voronskii had made in his silhouette. We cannot be
sure whether they were or not; but the fact that *Materials for a Novel*
was the first substantial piece of prose fiction by Pil'nyak ever published in *Red Virgin Soil* suggests at least the possibility that Voronskii saw them that way. If so, he was badly mistaken. Pil'nyak made
no break with his earlier work but merely redeployed its components.
The basic myth remained intact, only now we see it in the process of
enaction: its unfolding defines history and creates the rhythm and
movement of the story. Everything begins with "some men who
yearned to walk along the swamp paths, who took it into their heads
to raise Rus' up on her hind legs, traverse the swamps, lay out roads
with a ruler, fetter themselves with granite, iron and steel, cursing
tranced Rus' of the wooden huts—and they set out . . ." [I, 4]. And
so the towns, cities, factories grew and slowly subdued raw nature.
But what seems like progress is really a prideful flexing of the intellect
and the will which in turn teach man to fear and then to abandon the
very thing that makes him whole. It is the Eden myth. In fact, Pil'-
nyak locates it in a kind of garden:

If you turn off the main road, drive through the field, ford Black Creek, make your way first through a dark aspen wood, then through a red pine wood, skirt some ravines, cut through a village, drag up and down dry valleys, jolt through another forest over the snags, then cross the Oka in a ferry, just as people did three hundred years ago, pass through meadows and willow groves, then where the path is lost, effaced, obliterated in the tall green grass—you will come to Kadanok, to the Kadanok swamps. Here there are no roads. Here the wild ducks cry. Here it smells of ooze, peat, swamp gas. Here live the thirteen Sisters Ague and Fever. Here on sandy islets the pines grow rank, here by the bog the alder thickets stand close together, the heather carpets the earth—and at night, when the thirteen Sisters Ague and Fever roam, green swampfires, fearsome fires, skim silent and cold over the waters of the swamps, and then the air smells of sulphur, and the frenzied ducks cry in terror. Here there are neither paths nor roads—here roam wolves, hunters and tramps. Here you can wander into a quagmire and get stuck. . . . [I, 8]

It is a self-contained and harmonious universe (the language that evokes it is invariably rhetorical); yet because it holds the mystery of life and death, it is also sinister and terrifying. It asserts itself, again and again, through "rebellion, the rising of the masses" aimed at "shattering the iron horses and the roads"; it "smashes against the concrete and iron, against the steel of the cities" and once more "vanishes in the byways" (I, 4). This savage dialectic ends just as the Marxists have predicted, with the triumph of technology. Man has won; happiness ensues.

But there is a catch. Just as the Utopias envisaged by Kirillov, in Dostoevskii's *Possessed,* or by Pozdnyshev, in Tolstoi's *Kreutzer Sonata,* depend upon the extinction of the human race—in the first case through mass suicide, in the second through sexual continence—so the Utopia envisaged by the Bolshevik hero of *Materials for a Novel* depends upon the sacrifice of man to the machine which he has created for the purpose of freeing himself from all dependence. The final scene of the story foreshadows the paradox:

Behind the glass the turbines and the steam dynamo ran noiselessly in the glaring light. No people were to be seen. They peered in, they saw: leaning against the grille below the turbine, his head resting on his chest, slept a fitter, with a rag in his hand. A greaser entered, carrying a tea pot and a piece of bread, went over to the stairway leading to the boiler room, and walked down it.

"Look," Forst said to Kozhukhov. "It's night. There's a long time to go yet before the change of shift. . . . The machine is consolidated human genius. The fitter is asleep, the greaser has gone to drink tea with the girls who haul the coal. . . . The machine is running by itself, without man. . . . Look closely, see how it's running . . . it's running all by itself, without man! . . . Remarkable. . . ." [II, 96]

Man has outsmarted himself. In the end he must face the annihilation he has tried to escape. History has come full circle. The Eden he builds is a mocking copy of the Eden he has tried to flee: smokestacks for trees, lamps for stars, generators for suns, railroad tracks for rustic paths, machine oil for primeval muck. And he settles for it with a sigh of relief, though it is infinitely more terrible than what he has pulled against. But, debrained, he can no longer appreciate the irony. In Pil'nyak's work he carries on the tradition of anti-industrial fiction that Kuprin's *Moloch*, Upton Sinclair's *The Jungle*, and Gor'kii's *Mother* had helped create for Russian literature.

All Pil'nyak's works are allegories, none more obviously so than *Materials for a Novel*. The events, settings, characters, even the imagery are structured on opposing parallels that recapitulate the root myth: country/city; field/factory; soul/mind; past/present; peasant/worker, and so on, with the second element representing a corruption or parody of the first. The characters serve as vehicles of the allegory. One polarity is represented by the peasant girl Dasha (the Eve of Pil'nyak's paradise): "from all her being wafted all the stupefying odors of her forest habitation . . . and all of her seemed to be hewn out of a cobblestone—a huge bosom, a huge stomach, a huge behind, huge hands" [I, 18]. The other is represented by the Bolshevik Andrei Kozhukhov, the pragmatic dreamer, who is dedicated to making the peacful mindless existence of people like Dasha purposeful and useful by harnessing it to the factory. Dasha is so far unspoiled; but her announcement that she plans to go to work in the factory as a cleaning woman indicates that the process of decay has already set in. What awaits her is painted in the typically lurid colors of anti-industrial fiction:

the machine would consume her simple morality and ethics, consume her healthy flush, force her to push coal carts up to the furnaces, to inhale soot and the wisecracks of the foreman.

Then the foreman would have her come to his apartment or, on a holiday, to the Lurov woods on the other side of the Oka, and there she would make the rounds, just as all factory girls do; and in those lice-infested barracks, where people live stacked one on top of the other, where there is no joy and can be none, where the human rabble has gathered, she would consider it happiness that a foreman had taken her, because *that* and a bottle of vodka would be happiness. . . . [I, 22]

Between Dasha and Andrei moves Erliksov. He is an engineer who designs and builds machines, yet understands their terrible power, a man who yearns after the untrammelled state of the natural man, yet distrusts and fears its anonymity. He is the human version of the caged wolf he has seen at a bazaar. Through a love affair with Dasha and through friendship with Andrei, he hopes to resolve the conflict of reason and intuition and emerge a whole man. But no resolution is possible; and finally he is literally torn apart when, in expiation of the sin of intellect, he throws himself into a huge flywheel on one of those machines he has helped to create. The god that has been brought into existence to serve man ends by subduing him.

The Russian reader, who for generations had treated the personages of fiction as flesh-and-blood individuals, found himself balked and frustrated by Pil'nyak's people. They have no individuality. They never change or develop; they lack depth, mind, motivation; they scarcely even possess a physical existence, so meager an allotment does the author give them of his not inconsiderable powers of description. As Viktor Gofman has aptly observed, they do their acting behind the scenes, and present us with the results in the form of letters, diaries, and speeches.[19] As mere emblems, mere vehicles of moods and ideas, they can, at most, open windows onto events. Pil'nyak is essentially a writer of situations and settings. He is at his best in mass portraits: the proletariat, the peasantry, families, villages, towns, periods in history.

History, for Pil'nyak, is neither a story nor a random succession of incidents, but a myth that is central to all of life. Assuming different forms but remaining essentially the same, it is immune to time and to man's efforts to direct it. What looks like historical change is only an intensification of forces that have been present all along. Thus *Materials for a Novel* really ends the moment it begins back in what is conventionally called the sixteenth century, with an act of self-enslavement performed in the name of self-liberation. This concept of history is also a concept of time. The attempt to blur the reader's sense of past and present through sudden leaps in narration suggests the workings of a "subjective" time such as we expect in literature. But at bottom, a strict law operates even here. The order in which events unfold is really always the same, regardless of what men think or how the author may rearrange their components; the outcome is foreordained. Time, like history, is a constant state of being, a unity which makes all events and experiences simultaneous. We can neither allot it with our calendars and clocks, nor manipulate it with our fancies.

Pil'nyak virtually defines that change in the concept of time which went along with the decline of the novel toward the end of the nineteenth century. It is intimated in Chekhov's sense of the repetitiousness of life and in his predilection for circular structures (as in "The Cart"); it is occasionally seen in Bunin (*Brethren* is one of the best examples); but it is peculiarly a theme of the Symbolists, from whom Pil'nyak probably took it. In the service of this concept, the usual strategies of narrative prose are sacrificed. Pil'nyak works, as he described it, through "associations of parallels and antitheses" [II, 64], and not by unrolling a story line in time and space. We must therefore read him as we read so much modern poetry—vertically, as it were, piecing together a picture from scattered clues. He deliberately destroys scenes or episodes that threaten to develop even a rudimentary story interest. . . . In this respect, he stands apart from the writers of the so-called Serapion Brotherhood, like Kaverin, Grin, and Vsevolod Ivanov, who considered "plotlessness" one of the more unfortunate characteristics of older Russian fiction and tried to remedy it in their own writing. We are reminded instead of Belyi's technique of evoking chaos through sudden shifts of setting and perspective. But Belyi, at least in *Petersburg* and *The Silver Dove*, uses a gridwork of traditional plot to sustain his work. Pil'nyak does nothing of the kind in *Materials*. Nor does he pay the slightest respect to the conventions of genre; in fact it is here that the breakdown of those conventions, which had begun in the late nineteenth century, reaches its extreme. "Materials" is an apt description of the process: although "for a novel," the work is an assemblage of diary-entries, letters, historical tracts, ethnographical sketches, anecdotes, dramatic monologues, political slogans, high rhetoric and obscene expletive, exquisitely crafted "literature" and unstructured babble. We have before us a compendium of virtually all the styles of prose language that were being produced at the time. They are juxtaposed in seemingly random fashion to support Pil'nyak's notion that all of human experience—not just what we traditionally reserve to the province of literature—serves a great timeless myth. It is his way of suggesting universality.

It was this appearance of unstructured artlessness verging on chaos that enhanced Pil'nyak's reputation at the time as a "realist," an observant chronicler of his age. Actually, art lurked beneath every utterance. *Materials for a Novel*, like all Pil'nyak's work, has a unity which is created not merely by the pervasive central myth, but also by a carefully crafted repertoire of formal devices.

Perhaps the most common of them is repetition. Here we find virtually a catalogue of the rhetorician's art: anaphora ("Gody shli: / Devyat'sot devat'nadtsatyi. / Devyat'sot dvadtsatyi. / Devyat'sot dvadtsat' pervyi. . . ." [II, 77]); paramoion (*"prishol, poshol po shasham.* . . ." [I, 4]); parachesis (*"davno narodam vosslavlennyi.* . . ." [I, 4]); paragmenon ("Muzhiku nashemu kak dikar'—sla-vya-ni-nu,—reshat'sya, reshit'sya, reshat'." [I, 6]); homoioptoton ("zhili vmes*te*, v tesno*te*, smra*de*, p'yans*tve*, verili bog*u*, chort*u*, nachal'stv*u*, sglaz*u*. . . ." [I, 10]); and many others.

Even more strikingly, Pil'nyak has at his command a basic fund of incidents, themes, and images which travel from one work to another, not as leitmotifs (for their meaning varies from context to context) but simply as bricks and mortar. Much of *Bare Year*, for instance, was assembled from an earlier collection of stories entitled *Grass* (*Byl'yo*). Within a single work, whole phrases, lines, paragraphs, and even scenes may be repeated at various points. Sometimes the repetition is subtle, as, for instance, where the basic structure of a scene is retained, but the contents strung upon it are varied—a kind of exergasia. Usually, however, we have to do with word-for-word recurrences, so much so that *Materials* looks like a pastiche of self-plagiarisms. This technique serves several purposes. For one thing, the repetitions act as stimuli, which condition the reader to react . . . with pity, boredom, or anger: we soon learn what is expected of us, even if we refuse to satisfy the expectation. For another thing, they provide loci (in a kind of tautotes) around which individual scenes can be structured—as, for example, the word "stove-couch" (*lezhanka*) which organizes the otherwise chaotic interior of a certain house: "in the house there is a stove-couch—by the stove-couch . . . on the stove-couch . . . by the stove-couch . . . beside the stove-couch," and, at the end, "in front of the stove-couch" [II, 63-64].

Finally, the repetitions reinforce Pil'nyak's theme that all life is fundamentally the same because it exists in a timeless present and merely recapitulates, in different contexts, all that has ever happened. In effect, Pil'nyak was writing one great work throughout his career. It was never completed, but we see parts of it in the novels and stories he did produce.

Andrei Belyi uses repetitions as well; like Pil'nyak, he has a repertoire of images that travel from work to work. But there is an important
difference: Belyi is a symbolist; Pil'nyak is not. Each work of Belyi's
represents an organic structure in which the image has a plurality of
meanings that depends upon its position in the work as a whole and
its interrelationships with other images, meanings that reveal themselves gradually, as the work unfolds, in a series of epiphanies. Pil'-
nyak's images are nonsymbolic. They carry no hidden meanings; they
are signs which refer directly to concepts, and their function never
changes within one work, and very often not from work to work.
They are an apt illustration of a point that one of the characters in
Petersburg makes: "Don't confuse allegory with the symbol: allegory
is a symbol that has become common currency. . . ."[20] Wolf, peasant,
wind, snowstorm, factory, Revolution are the emblems, the tags of
Pil'nyak's world—a static world, in which appearance and reality are
one, and things are shown after they have happened, not while they
are in process. By naming something he fixes it forever. The "idea" of
a Pil'nyak work becomes obvious fairly early, sometimes on the very
first page, as in *Materials;* what follows merely elaborates or
embroiders.

Closely related to repetition is the literary echo, which Pil'nyak, like
Belyi, Remizov, and Bunin, uses lavishly. One of the most striking
illustrations can be found in the description of the factory in *Materials*. Here Pil'nyak cannibalizes a stock nineteenth-century Russian
literary landscape. "These places," we are told, "had everything in
order not to be that poetry which for centuries was considered genuine." The landscape, in other words, does not lack anything; it contains all that the faithful reader of Turgenev or Goncharov might expect. But it is different. Surveying the environs, like the sensitive
narrator of Karamzin's "Poor Liza," the author observes the "ancient
Moscow river," now "choked with piles of wood, boxes of peat, barges
on the water, a whistling steamer, and the water can't be seen. . . ."
The verdant hills along the river bank? Now "hills of slag." The wind-
ing rutted rural road? Now "two tracks of iron rails for carts." The
endearing diminutives for nature beloved of Karamzin and Turgenev
are here too—only now we find not "dear little birds" (*ptichki*) or
"pretty little bushes" (*kustochki*), but a "dear little locomotive" (*paro-
vichek*) and "pretty little carts" (*vagonchiki*). The rustle of leaves has
become the hiss of the factory, which is "very boring"; the inevitable
monastery on the distant hill is "unnecessary"; the sky is something
one now "does not feel like looking at"; the old estate set in the linden
trees or acacias has undergone a transformation too: "before you, three

chance linden trees, a poplar—and beyond the poplar, in the acacias, a 'guest house,' a 'house for bachelors,' cement houses with tile roofs in the style of Swedish cottages, houses for engineers—peaceful and solid." And the placid rural village, complete with idyllic mother and child, has turned into "little huts like bird houses, with front gardens rank with poppies and burdocks, with little boys covered in dust and with a woman by the gate and a suckling pig in a mud puddle. . . ." [II, 65] The literary echo, besides serving the theme of corruption and decay, adds the dimension of memory and pathos to the story. And as an ironic statement, it hurls an accusation as well—an accusation that the writers of the nineteenth century were either too heavy-handed to pick out the thread of reality, or else deliberately lied about what they saw, using "fiction" to distort or conceal the truth. In this respect too, Pil'nyak carried on yet another theme of the literary generation before him.

Many of these devices, to be sure, are purely ornamental. That is to say, they do not serve the basic myth and fulfill no essential thematic or structural role: they can be moved from place to place, expanded or shortened, even done away with entirely. Such, for example, are the imitations of peasant sayings that stud *Materials for a Novel*: "Two poods of bread is a horse, half a village of houses is a pood" [I, 6]. At one point, Pil'nyak weaves a whole long passage of such sayings, real and invented [I, 8-9]. Or he may employ literary references in the same way:

> A thief, a plain fool and an Ivanushka the fool, a boor, a toady,
> a Smerdyakovian, Gogolian, Shchedrinian or Ostrovskiian, type
> —and with them the fools in Christ's name, the Alyosha Kara-
> mazovs, the Juliana Lazarevas, the Serafim Sarovskiis lived to-
> gether. . . . [I, 10]

Yet such devices—often mere catalogues—do make an essential contribution to the work as a whole; for they help create and sustain that rhetorical, highly artificial tone which permeates every part and confers a unity. Even the most careless and seemingly artless effects may be elaborate rhetorical constructs. Pil'nyak's sentence structure, for instance, which creates an impression of extraordinary randomness, is actually built upon the principle of parataxis, with the word "and" serving (much as in Old Russian literature) both to link the paratactical units and to set them off, as relative pronouns do. The same point can be made about many of Pil'nyak's "realistic," even "naturalistic" descriptions. Consider the factory in *Materials*:

> smoke, soot, fire—noise, clang, shriek and iron's squeak—semi-
> darkness, electricity instead of sun—machinery, tolerances,
> gauges, cupola furnaces, open-hearth furnaces, smiths, hy-
> draulic presses and presses weighing tons. . . . [II, 66]

Certainly, this is an effective piece of impressionism; but it is also
highly artificial, with the rhythmic grouping (smoke, soot, fire—noise,
clang, shriek), the careful contrasts of visual, audial, and light-dark
effects, and the paratactical syntax. Even the machines are not so
much functional pieces of equipment as brand names chosen for their
exotic sounds.

This atmosphere of artificiality is deliberate. It asserts a principle
of literariness which openly and defiantly manipulates the "material."
Its motivation, in *Materials*, is provided by an author-persona who
introduces and ends the story, makes the links between scenes and
events, fades into the background when other narrators or "eyes" come
forward, affects a helpless attitude in the face of experiences he pretends merely to be recording, and participates in the story himself,
with his own distinctive manner of speaking. In these respects, he
resembles the typical narrator of the *skaz*. But he is not that; he is too
sophisticated, too conscious, too calculating a literary intelligence.
Every move he makes is carefully planned. Even those passages that
resemble free association are highly organized interior monologues. The
author-narrator leaves us in no doubt about his function in the work,
for he frequently resorts to what the Russian Formalists called "baring
the device." "I came out of Belyi and Bunin," we are told, "many people do many things better than I, and I consider myself entitled to
appropriate this 'better' or such things as I can do better (Oh Peregu-
dov and Dal', I conceal from nobody what I have taken from you for
this story!)" [I, 3]. The fourth "fragment" is introduced in the following way: *"from the chapter entitled 'Rubbish,' which does not fit
into the plan of the tale, but which nevertheless is essential before
proceeding to the development of the action"* [I, 15].

It is this willful, often playful self-assertiveness that gives warrant
to the great variety of styles and genres in the work. No attempt is
made to conceal art. On the contrary, art is thrust in the reader's face,
with all its underpinnings exposed. Through arbitrariness, through
artificiality, through the exploitation of a range of material seemingly
snatched at random, the literary mind proclaims its right to do as it
pleases. In many ways, the capricious literariness of this and other
works by Pil'nyak calls to mind the verbal prestidigitation of many
Old Russian writers, such as Daniel the Exile and Ilarion, who worked

in a period when literary talent was measured by the number of sources one could bring to hand and weave together into new tapestries. From the more recent past, it carried into the twenties that cult of artificiality which the Symbolists, in particular, had practiced ("Oh, books are more beautiful than roses!"[21]), in their belief that the created world is superior to the world of nature, the inanimate higher than the animate.

Pil'nyak exerted a powerful influence on the young writers of the time. His view of life, his stylistic mannerisms, his imagery were all widely imitated by fellow travelers like Nikolai Ognyov and proletarians like Artyom Vesyolyi. People spoke of the "Pil'nyak school" in literature, or, disparagingly, of "Pil'nyakovitis" (*pil'nyakovshchina*). Through him the new writers encountered Bunin—in the keen, almost painful sense of a lyrical nature that stands apart from man; Remizov —in the rhetoric, the love of source-snatching, the cult of ancient Russia's songs and sayings, the highly "literary" view of the world; and especially Belyi—in the word play and the sense of irony that verges on the grotesque. But none of these beginners approached their elders in quality or in range. Though both generations shared a similar view of the world, the indebtedness of youth to age was to a large extent superficial. The newer writers took over the tricks, devices, and mannerisms but ignored the literary systems on which they were based. . . . Belyi was well aware that people regarded Pil'nyak as his pupil, and it plainly annoyed him. He complained, according to Viktor Shklovskji, that "Pil'nyak's things produce on him the impression of a picture that you don't know from what distance to look at"—in other words, that Pil'nyak merely borrowed materials and assembled them mechanically, without regard for the context from which they came.[22] But Pil'nyak showed one way in which it could be done; and it was a lesson that his followers, in turn, learned well.

After *Materials for a Novel*, Voronskii never again published a large-scale work by Pil'nyak, nor a critical study of him comparable in scope and seriousness to the silhouette of 1922. The consensus among the critics in *Red Virgin Soil*, from the mid-twenties on, was that Pil'nyak had failed to grow, was repeating himself, and would occupy only a modest place in the history of Russian literature as a writer of period pieces.[23]

One motive for this change of heart may have been political. In the fifth issue of the journal *New World* for 1926, Pil'nyak published *The*

Tale of the Unextinguished Moon (Povest' o nepogashennoi lune). Despite his denials, everyone interpreted this story of the politically motivated murder of a prominent Communist on the operating table as a commentary on the recent death of Mikhail Frunze in similar circumstances. It raised a storm. Critics belonging to the so-called left wing of the proletarian literary movement seemed pleased. They had long disapproved of the Party's policy toward the fellow travelers, and had been subjecting Voronskii, as the chief instrument of that policy, to an increasingly vitriolic campaign for greater "militancy" in literary matters. Pil'nyak's story was dedicated to Voronskii; and in the eyes of many proletarian critics it provided eloquent testimony to the consequence of "coddling" the fellow travelers. Voronskii reacted immediately with a letter to *New World*. It read in part:

> Such a portrayal of a profoundly sad and tragic event is not only an extremely crude distortion and highly insulting to the memory of Comrade Frunze, but is also a malicious slander on our Communist Party.
>
> The tale is dedicated to me. In view of the fact that such a dedication is in the highest degree offensive to me as a Communist, and might cast a shadow on my Party name, I declare that I reject this dedication with disgust.[24]

There is some evidence that this letter was insincere: that Voronskii had not only approved of the story . . . but also believed the insinuation it contained was true. "I am being accused of inspiring Pil'nyak," he wrote in a letter to Gor'kii. "To be sure, he did find out something from me, but I am not to blame for the main thing."[25] The "something" is suggestively cryptic. Whatever it may mean, the incident embroiled Voronskii in deep trouble with "highly-placed people"[26] at a time when his own position in *Red Virgin Soil* as the editor of *Red Virgin Soil* was becoming precarious, as the result largely of new political developments within the Party and the government. If we are to believe Fyodor Gladkov, he saved himself only on condition that he make a public disclaimer of just the kind he did.[27]

But the political situation could have been only a secondary motive. Voronskii, after all, never made a final break with Pil'nyak—which he surely would have done if it had been merely a question of discarding a political liability. Right up to the end of his tenure as editor, he even published an occasional story or sketch by Pil'nyak, and, in his surveys of literature, consistently treated him with respect, if not enthusiasm. More to the point, perhaps, was that Pil'nyak's influence on the other writers of his generation had begun to decline sharply around 1925. At work here, no doubt, was a shift in literary fashion. Simplicity, straightforwardness, psychological analysis, strong characters, coherent structure—the very antitheses of the things for which Pil'nyak had been admired—defined the terms of this shift. Pil'nyak was simply left behind—an anachronism at the age of thirty-one. Also left behind was the kind of criticism that had made Pil'nyak acceptable in the first place to Red Virgin Soil and probably to most Marxist readers. If—as is quite possible—Voronskii had published Materials because he thought the work represented a fundamental change in direction by Pil'nyak, then he did so while operating according to a canon that made works of fiction literal transcriptions of "life" and therefore easily mistook ripples on the surface for great upheavals in the depths, a canon that wished to discover such changes because it set up the critic as arbiter and assumed that the writer hung gratefully on his every word. But greater sophistication brought with it new ways of reading that exposed underlying patterns of the kind that Voronskii probably had missed; and experience undoubtedly brought an awareness that the critic and the writer are natural enemies.

But Pil'nyak had begun to change too. After 1925, he all but abandoned the "ornamental" style, the Eurasian themes, and the allegories, in favor of a kind of lyrical reportage. "Speranza" (Red Virgin Soil, No. 6, 1923) represents one of his earliest attempts to find a new voice. Supposedly it is a mood study of man's endless and pointless quests, symbolized by his tireless tracking of the seas. But here the theme (one of Pil'nyak's favorites) has been stripped of its ornamental splendor and exposed as the rather tedious allegory it really is. "A Story About Springs and Clay" (Rasskaz o klyuchakh i gline, in Red Virgin Soil, No. 1, 1926), tells of the return of exiles to the Palestinian homeland and could well have been written by a foreign correspondent. "Roots of the Japanese Sun" (Korni yaponskogo solntsa, in Red Virgin Soil, No. 3, 1927), an account of the author's visit to Japan in 1926, is a specimen of the literary travel diary. Pil'nyak's scattered flings at ornamentalism in the later 1920's, as in the tale Ivan Moscow (Ivan Moskva, in Red Virgin Soil, No. 6, 1927), merely recapitulate the mannerisms of yore and confirm the impression that his talent, by and large, displays itself to best advantage in a kind of lyrical journalism that focuses on event and situation at the expense of character and moral problems.

The irony was that neither Voronskii nor most of the reading public noticed, or cared to appreciate, the change, which this time was fundamental. More is the pity, because some of Pil'nyak's best work followed. The lyrical reportage stands up well even today. The novel *Mahogany (Krasnoe derevo)*, perhaps his finest piece of longer prose fiction, was published in 1929 but never reached the Soviet reader, for it was printed in Berlin and immediately banned in Russia as a political obscenity. Until the end of his career, some ten years later—he was arrested in 1937 and died apparently in 1941—Pil'nyak remained an experimenter. But so decisively had his earlier writing imprinted itself on the public mind that he could not escape it; and it was his fate to be judged by lesser works (*Bare Year* excepted) at a time when something resembling a genuine literary judgment, relatively untainted by politics, could have been made.[28]

II

Pil'nyak's closest rival for popularity in the early twenties was Vsevolod Ivanov. *The Guerrillas*, which was published in the very first issue of *Red Virgin Soil* (June, 1921), announced the appearance of a new writer who had to be reckoned with. *Armored Train 14-69 (Bronepoezd 14-69)* and *Azure Sands (Golubye peski)*, which followed in quick succession in the same journal, established him as practically a classic in his own time. Both writers were the first to attempt to make literature out of the experience of the Civil War. Comparison was therefore inevitable. In practically every important way, they were set poles apart, with Ivanov much the worthier specimen of what people expected of a "new" writer.

There was, first of all, the matter of style. No one could deny that Ivanov's work showed some streaks from the same brush of "ornamentalism" that had bedaubed Pil'nyak: the variety of language-levels within a single work, with special affection for dialect and regionalisms; an ear for word play and the devices of rhetoric; a tendency to lyricize nature at the expense of character. But these traits worked toward different ends in Ivanov's stories; for he focused on plot, as we would expect from a member of the Serapion Brothers. We find no great displacements in time and space; rather, we are carried along by an onflowing narrative where events seem to follow one another chronologically. Because Ivanov rarely interprets for the reader (one of Pil'nyak's worst habits), he forces us to engage the narrative directly. Working without a visible "philosophy," let alone an elaborate cosmology like Pil'nyak's, he creates the impression that he is merely interested in spinning a tale. By comparison with Pil'nyak, his colors are bland; he understates, applies the ornamentalist effects sparingly, and does not caress himself publicly.

The Siberian setting of nearly all Ivanov's early works helped make his reputation. Not that it was anything new: it had been used by Dostoevskii in *Notes from the House of the Dead,* by Leskov and Shishkov in their ethnographical sketches, by Mel'nikov-Pecherskii in his novels, by Chekhov in the account of his trip to Sakhalin Island, by Goncharov in *The Frigate Pallas.* But the edge had not been dulled either for readers or writers: Siberia had never engaged the literary imagination to the extent that, say, the Caucasus had. And in the early 1920's that area took on a far greater importance than ever before: there brother had fought brother in some of the bloodiest encounters of the Civil War; there foreign interventionists had staked out their claims and long continued to defend them. It seemed that in those vast expanses the very fate of the new Russia was being decided. Ivanov, himself a Siberian (not a European Russian on a holiday, like most of his predecessors), wrote about this land in a way that seemed photographically accurate at the time, and therefore quite alien to the vague, metaphysical "East" of Pil'nyak's work.

Like Pil'nyak, Ivanov attempts, in the personages of his fiction, to create a sociology of literary types. But again, his focus is different. Pil'nyak, as we have seen, is interested in the extremes of the social scale: the nobility and the intelligentsia on the one hand, and the unspoiled peasantry on the other. Ivanov has his noblemen, his intellectuals, and his peasants too; but they are mere backdrops. Instead, his vision angles toward the lower strata of society and comes to rest upon those people who have only the vaguest class ties (like artisans), or who have become *déclassés* altogether (like sailors, circus entertainers, or wanderers). Such people have the greatest mobility; and it is mobility that interests Ivanov. He introduced a new type into Soviet literature: the man who is pulled out of the faceless masses by war, steps over the shards of the old society, and harnesses his energies to the surge of events—a man like Seleznev (*The Guerrillas*), the rich peasant become guerrilla leader; or Zapus, the sailor turned revolutionary (*Azure Sands*); or Vershinin, the fisherman converted into Red commander (*Armored Train 14-69*). These were the first heroes of the new literature, the earliest figures in that mythology of Revolution which Soviet writers, in the absence of living models, have been called upon to create.

But it was a certain mood, a certain atmosphere in Ivanov's work that impressed readers more than anything else. Voronskii seems to have been the first to devise a tag for this mood, in an article he wrote on Ivanov in 1922. He called it "joyousness" (*radostnost'*), by which he meant the evocation of a world "where everything is suffused with powerful, primitive vitality, with beauty, with virginal immaculacy and purity, where people, like the nature surrounding them, are pristinely whole and healthy."[29] This view of the world, Voronskii thought, was rooted in Ivanov's background. His father epitomized the upward struggle of the proletariat: from mine worker to schoolteacher through relentless self-education. Ivanov himself, much like the young Gor'kii, had tramped about Russia in a variety of odd jobs. Talent, ambition, and circumstances had snatched him from anonymity: his career impressed Voronskii as a "graphic argument for the Revolution," a "graphic index of what a great step forward [the new intelligentsia of humble background] has taken, of how much fresh, creative energy it carries within itself."[30]

More than anything else, this "joyousness" measured Ivanov's distance not only from Pil'nyak—a celebrant of disharmony, decay, gloom, and despair—but from the pre-war generation that had cultivated "egocentrism, psychologism, Andreevism, Dostoevskianism and . . . inner desolation"—in other words, the writers from whom Pil'nyak derived.[31] Readers could find in Ivanov none of those tortured examinations of conscience that some of the older writers, like Blok, had been conducting in public; none of the self-pity that characterized the protagonists of Zamyatin's stories of urban life during the Civil War; none of the tragic sense of history that drenched the recently published first volume of Aleksei Tolstoi's *Road to Calvary;* none of the cool detachment from current events that Akhmatova, Pasternak, and Bunin exemplified; none of the pathology of sex and insanity in which Fyodor Sologub was supposed to revel. Ivanov seemed to break clean from all that and to be writing in an honest, straightforward, and unambiguous manner about the simple, yet fundamental things that touched all Russians in those times: violence, death, heroism, honor, shame, victory, defeat. He made much the same impression on readers as had Gor'kii with his first stories, which were regarded as reaffirmations of life against a prevailing climate of despondency in literature. . . . But the younger writer was considered healthier: . . . for he seemed innocent of that sense of frustration that dogs so many of Gor'kii's characters. Intervening events had made all the difference. A rule-of-thumb formula could well have been: Gor'kii plus Revolution equals Ivanov.

These qualities of joyousness, health, energy, freshness, and newness defined the image that Voronskii wished to create for his journal as well—the title, *Red Virgin Soil,* implied as much. The inauguration of the literature section of the first issue with *The Guerrillas* had a deep symbolic importance for Voronskii: he said that the work "marked out the artistic physiognomy of the journal . . . ,"[32] and he put it forward as an illustration of what he meant when he talked about "new" writing. It is therefore not surprising that Ivanov became virtually the official belletrist of *Red Virgin Soil,* at least until mid-decade. Voronskii published more by him than by any other prose writer: thirteen short stories, three long tales (*The Guerrillas, Armored Train,* and *Khabu*), one novel (*Azure Sands*), and excerpts from another (*Severostal'*).

But, like almost all the other critics of the time, Voronskii misconstrued Ivanov. The things they found in him are there, to be sure; and the contrast with Pil'nyak and with the preceding literary generation is valid up to a point. But what everyone failed to see was Ivanov's fundamentally cynical, nihilistic, and despairing view of the world.

Ivanov was proclaimed a master of character drawing. As Voronskii put it: "standing above everything is the 'joyous and intoxicating earth,' and its master—man."[33] True enough, "man," when considered by himself in these stories, *is* life-affirming, healthful, and positive. But he cannot be wrenched out of his surroundings. This has always been a strong temptation for Russian critics, in their obsession with "types" and "heroes" in literature. It is generally unsound practice; when applied to Ivanov, it is disastrous. For the fact is that Ivanov builds his work not on character, but on plot and situation. The three early long tales—*The Guerrillas, Armored Train,* and *Azure Sands*—are not vehicles for "heroes" but adventure fictions, constructed from individual scenes strung upon a rudimentary plot line and arranged according to the classic adventure formula of goal—frustration—resolution.

Consider *The Guerrillas,* which tells of four happy-go-lucky carpenters who commit a crime against the established authority, take to the hills, are pursued by the law, turn into guerrillas, die heroic deaths, and become Red heroes. The tale is built on a series of set pieces. There is a campfire scene, a barn-building scene, a hunting scene, a peasant-holiday scene, and so on. Each of these scenes has its own set of characters who disappear when the action moves on. A few, like the carpenters, do turn up in a number of places, but they are the typical "wandering" characters of the adventure story who function merely to link one scene to another. They have no fixed or consistent personalities, but instead take on the coloration of whatever situation they participate in. Note what happens to the detachment of Polish Uhlans that sets out from the town in pursuit of the guerrillas:

> But the further they moved away from the town and into the depths of the fields and forests, the more their character changed. . . . the Uhlans, and with them Ensign Visnevskii, felt the way a tired sweating man feels on a hot day as he undresses and slips into the water. Remaining back there, by the little squat houses of the district town, were those things which the town had imprinted on them for almost half their lifetimes —respect, restraint, and a great deal else that keeps the heart always on guard. All that was at once rubbed into dust and scattered to the winds by the endless ancient fields, the forests, the narrow ruts of the roads, overgrown with grass, and by the possibility of disposing of human life at will.[34]

The schoolteacher Kobelev-Malishevskii—Ivanov's contribution to that stock fictional character of the early twenties, the neurotic intellectual—plays informer to the Uhlans, betraying the whereabouts of the guerrillas. But when we next see him, he has himself joined the guerrilla band, with nobody apparently the wiser about his earlier treachery. We are spared any hint of how this change might have come about, of how his character, weak and pathetic at the outset, turns strong and resolute. Here again it is situation that rules. An informer is necessary to motivate the pursuit of the carpenters, in order that they may become guerrillas. The teacher is the likeliest candidate, presumably because he is the only intellectual in the story, and intellectuals are not to be trusted, at least not in Ivanov's world. Later, the situation requires someone who can make posters and draft proclamations for the guerrillas; and the teacher, as the only person in sight who possesses the necessary skills, is again trotted out. There is not the slightest suggestion that he is merely an opportunist. Actually, he is not a character at all, but a servant of the situation.

What of the carpenters, who turn up in practically every scene and appear to be the real "heroes"? They do change from dim-witted artisans to class-conscious partisans; but we are shown only the results of change, in successive stages, not the process. Furthermore, their experience is not cumulative; they themselves have no awareness of their transformation, for it depends not on inner growth, but entirely on situation. Ivanov carefully establishes them from the outset as moral, intellectual, and emotional neutrals who would not even be carpenters if physical necessity did not require it. They happen to wander into a village to celebrate a holiday. The homebrew is flowing; the law

swoops down to seize the still and make arrests. In the ensuing commotion one of the carpenters kills a policeman and all four flee to the
hills to escape retribution. With them goes the owner of the still, the
rich peasant Seleznev. A punitive expedition sets out from town,
forcing the fugitives to resort to active resistance in order to survive. Beyond some vague talk about fomenting an uprising in the
town and establishing a peasant government independent of the Reds
(something the Reds themselves seem to forget when they later decide
to canonize these men), they have no ideas, no plans, no visions. Even
their martyrdom is a result of stupidity: they stumble into a trap and
are killed.

Armored Train 14-69 offers a more conventional-looking hero in
Vershinin, the commander of a band of Red guerrillas whose mission, deep in the wastes of Siberia, is to blockade a White armored
train. The task rests heavy on him, for he can see no way of stopping
tons of onrushing steel with small weapons and bare hands. The fact
that he has a decision to make gives him a certain depth. Ivanov even
decks him out with something resembling a revolutionary consciousness: he senses a "disorder" in the world which he wishes to put right.
"My heart's squealing," he says, "like a cat that's been tossed out into
the cold. . . ."[35] But all this is mere window-dressing. Vershinin does
not suffer from any sense of failure to measure up to his ideals, for he
has no ideals. His entire career has merely followed the swath of the
fitful wind of circumstance. A fisherman in an obscure Siberian village,
he has been conscripted to fight the Japanese and the atamans. Later
he finds himself chairman of a revolutionary staff (*revshtab*) because
the job is open and he is handy. Finally, he becomes a guerrilla commander precisely because he lacks resoluteness, will, and mind. He is
a servant of the collective will of his men, whose ideology is superior:
the private-property instinct, we are told, still simmers within him, but
his men have already developed an "international" or "proletarian"
outlook on life. The solution to the problem of stopping the train
emerges not from him but from the unconscious will of his subordinates. Because this tale shows a unity of time and situation, we are
easily persuaded to take Vershinin as a personality in his own right.
Actually, he is a perfect example of the de-heroized hero, the slave of
circumstance, who graced many a work of fiction in the early twenties.

Significantly, Ivanov fails in his one conscious attempt, during this
early period, to create a major character who stands independent of
his milieu: Vas'ka Zapus, the hero of *Azure Sands,* a novel about the
fortunes of war in a remote Siberian town which is forever changing

hands. Zapus is supposed to represent a kind of universal man who combines vision, common sense, and activism, owes allegiance to no person and no geography, and moves from situation to situation with the ease of the folk hero, redressing wrongs and spreading inspiration. Though a demi-god (legend has already worked his name over), he possesses those earthy qualities—a crude sense of humor and a passion for women—deemed essential for a leader of men. Yet Ivanov fails to bring him to life. He merely recapitulates the current clichés about Red military heroes. The real hero of *Azure Sands* is the chaos of war in Siberia; Zapus is merely its servant, and ultimately its victim.[36]

Each of Ivanov's three major early works, then, is an adventure tale that experiments with a different kind of hero: *The Guerrillas* with a mass hero, *Armored Train* with an individual hero who tries to match instinct and event, *Azure Sands* with a hero who seeks to dominate circumstance. In each case, however, situation rules. And in each of these tales the story resolves itself and ends when the heroes have fulfilled the function that situation demands of them: when the carpenters finally are martyred, when Vershinin finally heeds the collective will and has the train stopped, when Zapus has accumulated enough deeds to ensure his status as a folk hero. Even the details that attach to them serve the requirements of structure and pace. At the beginning of *The Guerrillas*, for example, we see Ivanov hovering over the trivial daily round of four carpenters who are extraordinarily ordinary. His purpose, however, is not to establish their "characters," but to delay the unfolding of the action. Gradually he shaves the detail, quickens the pace, moves from specific to general statements, from individuals to masses, and abandons the hour-by-hour time scale for a concept of time where whole months are covered in a single sentence.

Ivanov's treatment of character reminds us somewhat of early Kievan literature, where personality attaches not to individuals but to the situations or institutions that individuals represent—to princedom, not to princes; to monkhood, not to monks. Each situation carries with it a new set of requirements and attributes; and from an accumulation of situations, the reader may piece together something like a picture of a person. Erich Auerbach has called this a paratactical technique of characterization.[37] In Ivanov's work, however, such pictures rarely take shape, because he uses the paratactical technique not to create personality, but rather to destroy any possibility that personality can exist. For him, men are hopelessly fragmented creatures, lacking memory, incapable of learning from experiences, and unable to exercise any control over events; they therefore act illogically, irrationally, and inconsistently. If sheer accident appears to play a decisive role in their lives, that is because each new situation presents them with a totally unexpected set of requirements, to which they must hastily adjust or perish. War makes the point brutally clear; perhaps that is why it is Ivanov's most effective setting. Men's only sense of reality, even of existence, hangs on their fidelity to circumstances moment by moment. They are at the beck of necessity.

It is a cruel necessity at that, because it is senseless and arbitrary. Ivanov's landscapes serve it well. They are flat, colorless, devoid of warmth, contour, or proportion; they form an endless, trackless present through which his men wander without purpose or goal. Ivanov's refusal to intervene with commentary (as Pil'nyak could not have resisted doing) makes this world even more remote, more awesome, more terrifying. The marvel is that he was read as a regionalist in those days.

It is a world in which death is the only certainty. Yet even death is not a very important happening for Ivanov's shadowy men; it is merely the sudden termination of a pointless existence that they have never understood. Still, it is the key to Ivanov's ironic vision of life. Consider the short story "How Burial Mounds Are Made" (Kak sozdayutsya kurgany) which was published in the fourth issue of Red Virgin Soil for 1924. Here the setting is one of those dots on the vast map of Siberia, where the fruits of battle—some 8,000 corpses—lie stacked awaiting burial. To get them underground is both a problem in engineering and a race against time: the ground is frozen solid, making excavation impossible; the corpses are frozen too, yet spring is approaching and, with it, the prospect of rapid decomposition and plague. Finally, a grave is scooped out of the earth, the corpses dumped in, and the dirt heaped up in the shape of a Scythian burial mound.

These corpses are not reminders of guilt that must hastily be shoveled out of sight; they are simply objects that, at worst, take up space and endanger health, and at best, provide temporary employment for the natives. They are regarded with the casual boredom of the observer who has seen too much of death. Though the atrocities of more recent wars have somewhat jaded our sensibilities, the tone is still effective, and we readily recognize its kinship with the shock effects that Garshin, Andreev, and Babel' cultivate so skillfully in their treatment of war. Ivanov wishes not merely to shock, but to insist on the parallel, and thereby the irony, with the Scythian burial mounds that stud the area in which he sets his story. These belong to a heroic past which comes over in a highly lyrical style that jars with the predominant laconicism:

> The burial mound we had climbed still held the smells of the last autumn, over which someone is sure to shed tears, and the earth lay in joyous spring emptiness.
> My companion began to speak, much more slowly than he had that morning, about the Scythians who had inhabited these parts, about the heavy bronze bits and stirrups of thoir saddles, about the primitive art of the burial mounds; and 'he went on to recall how in the sea at Kerch on a clear day you could see the columns of a Greek city that had been swallowed up, and how the sea still casts up amphoras filled with rotted black grain.[38]

Ivanov's point here is man's tendency to romanticize the ordinary, and to gloss the horrible. But the Scythian burial mounds stand after all as a testimonial to death; and death lacks any romance or heroism, as Ivanov shows in his account of how modern burial mounds are made. Indeed, death, being commonplace in wars, is banal. Yet the deception will go on: "And a thousand winters from now some young archaeologist and poet will dig open the [twentieth-century] burial mound and will understand nothing."[39]

The famous climax scene in *Armored Train 14-69* develops the irony of death much further. The White train is approaching; the line must be blocked. But how? The guerrillas have no artillery; the terrain provides no material for a physical barrier; and time has run out anyway, as the rumble of the onrushing engine grows louder and louder. Suddenly it is clear: only a body across the tracks can do the job. None of the Russian peasants in the band can bring himself to make the sacrifice; but the Chinese, Sin-Bin-U, lies on the rails, is duly mangled, and brings the train to a stop. This scene is lodged in Soviet literature as a tribute to proletarian self-sacrifice on an international scale, and Sin-Bin-U has taken his place in the exclusive club of non-Russian martyrs to the cause of the working class. But there is something strange about it. Why should one body suffice to stop a whole train? Why should none of the Russians in the group be willing to offer his own body? Obviously the presence of a single body cannot arrest the forward motion of a train. What does, then? It is the very banality of the gesture. Gunfire, explosions, and barricades are all part of the accepted genre of death, and give meaning to the heroics of resistance and counter-resistance. But a body on the tracks belongs to pulp-fiction and melodrama. The Russian peasants cannot be persuaded to lend themselves to such an enterprise, not because they fear death, but because they fear the touch of something so patently ridiculous. Possibly this kind of death, because it is histrionic, impresses the Whites (who are comic-opera types) not as the mangling of an enemy, but as the sacrifice of one of their own. More likely, however, the very banality of the act creates such an absurdity that further resistance is unthinkable. Another minute and all are likely to burst into laughter.

This notion of death and sacrifice casts a pall upon the traditional modes of heroism. Ivanov tends to ridicule conscious heroics; yet his sense of the ridiculous is too refined to do no more than destroy them. Heroism constitutes an unsettling element in any community, particularly in the military. In acting itself out, as a kind of blood sacrifice, it helps restore a balance. But at the same time, it seems to reaffirm all the values of the ordinary, unheroic life that have been threatened.

Let us consider the little story "The God Matvei" (Bog Matvei). Matvei is a peasant who turns up in Denisyuk's front-line regiment, which has been pinned down for three weeks by the Whites. Asserting that he is God, he orders an end to the fighting. To strengthen his claim to divinity, he performs a kind of miracle, by prancing around in full view of the Whites, whose bullets have no effect on him whatever. Denisyuk's peasant soldiers are appropriately awed. Then Denisyuk himself puts Matvei's divinity to the test by sending him—on a white horse, of course—in front of his soldiers' guns. It is a joke, for the ammunition is blank; yet the soldiers do not quite believe that the bullets are not live. Denisyuk then loads a rifle with real ammunition, fires at Matvei, brings him and his horse down, and administers the *coup de grâce*. And his soldiers, "inaudibly, and what is more, unaware of it themselves, laughed."[40] Matvei is buried, the regiment then sweeps on to overrun the White positions, and Denisyuk himself dies the heroic death he has always wanted. Matvei has played the role of sacrificial, propitiatory victim. The peasant soldiers know perfectly well that death is natural, ordinary, and unheroic. Matvei threatens their natural world with miracles. But men do not want miracles, because they *are* out of the ordinary; they prefer assurances that their own world is real. Matvei, like all heroes, defies and in that sense ridicules the real world; his death serves to punish his presumption and to reaffirm that man, for all his frailty, still reigns supreme and may kill his gods if he so desires.

Because heroism in *The Guerrillas* and in *Azure Sands* is set on a grander scale and deflated even more abruptly than in "The God Matvei," the irony turns savage. The action of *Azure Sands* is built upon the attempts by various combatants to capture Ust'-Mongol'sk, a sleepy and remote town which has acquired momentary importance as a military objective, although nobody knows why. At the end, all the heroes die—White, Red, and Green alike—and the town again sinks into its age-old, unchanging round. In *The Guerrillas,* the contractor Emolin starts the four carpenters out on the adventures that eventually make them Red heroes. And it is he who has the last word: as the guerrillas are being solemnly interred, to the strains of the "International," Emolin, who has been untouched by any of the events he has set in motion (or contracted, in the literal sense), stands over the grave and observes, with irreverent levity: "Say, they was re-e-eal good lads."[41] So much for sacrifice!

For many Russian writers of the nineteenth and early twentieth centuries, military fiction provided an effective means of commenting upon human ideals and social values. The reason, perhaps, lay in the special position that the military life occupied in society. Young men of all classes of society were expected to perform service as a duty; but for the well-born it was more than a duty—it was an essential part of personal polishing and social education. In this respect, Russia differed markedly from the United States and even England, where soldiers have always been isolated from the mainstream. Military experience, then, provided a test of virility and of ideals, not just of the individual soldier, but also—because of the close linkage of civilian and military life—of society as a whole. That is perhaps why Russia's defeats on the battlefield, which were relatively insignificant as purely military events, had such a devastating effect on society. The Crimean War of 1853-6, the clash with Japan in 1904—such events generated profound social crises; for the military virtues of honor, valor, and sacrifice had been the highest values of society itself. The failure of those values in a military context could not help but reflect directly upon society as a whole.

It did not take the writers long to discover and probe these connections. Turgenev's *Rudin,* for example, which was written toward the end of the Crimean War, is set in a civilian society. And it is a society that asks, as does the novel, whether or not vital ideals any longer exist, and if so, where they can now be probed: are not idealists truly "superfluous" men, like the hero himself? Rudin finally puts his ideals (which are the ideals of the intelligentsia of his time) to the test in a quasi-military situation—on the barricades of Paris during the events of 1848—and perishes. Leo Tolstoi was of course highly skilled at exploring the implications of military life as a testing ground for social values, in works like "The Raid," *Sevastopol Tales,* and especially (even in the title) *War and Peace,* which began as an attempt to explain the Crimean defeat. The military fiction of the last quarter of the century—Garshin's "Four Days" (1877), Andreev's *The Red Laugh* (1904), Kuprin's *The Duel* (1905)—is an eloquent chronicle of the disintegration of society that culminated in the Revolution of 1917. That event put forth new values, although they did not for many years begin to rule society as a whole; and the Civil War was their testing place. The final military victory of the Bolsheviks in 1921 was taken as implicit proof of the vitality and essential rightness of those ideals, as victory in total war usually is.

The military experience, then, had a symbolic value as profoundly significant in 1921 as throughout much of the nineteenth century. That fact, when set within the tradition of military fiction, made the works of Ivanov far more than mere adventure tales. Most of his heroes are associated in one way or another with the Bolsheviks, and thus partake, if only indirectly, of the repertoire of Bolshevik slogans and ideals. But it is all for nothing. Ideals do not help Vas'ka Zapus shape events. They neither save the guerrillas from their doom, nor dignify their death: the old world, in the person of the contractor Emolin, has the last word over their grave. . . . And in the most "ideological" of the early works, *Armored Train,* such ideals find their highest expression in the almost absurd sacrifice of Sin-Bin-U to a collective will which is otherwise paralyzed.

Ivanov, however, is only remaining faithful to his central vision of the world. If necessity rules all, then values of mind and spirit cease to matter. Man's business becomes sheer survival, and even that depends not on him, but on a capricious and unpredictable fate. As Seleznev, in *The Guerrillas,* observes: "A man—what is he—you can always make a new one. A man is dust."[42] Ivanov does not scorn biological man (for that is all that counts), but rather humanistic sentimentalism—the disease of ideologues and intellectuals for him as well as for Pil'nyak. Such men invariably perish. And there is no grandeur in their defeat. But Ivanov's vision is far gloomier than Pil'nyak's, for he proposes no idyll, no harmonious and balanced center: his universe is fragmented, meaningless, and without pity. Man can only bow to it.

This vision brings Ivanov far closer to the writers of the previous generation than anyone suspected at the time. The wonder is that the critics, almost without exception, misinterpreted it. One could reasonably have expected that the Marxists, in particular, would have been sensitive to situation and setting, wherein lay the center of Ivanov's world. As it was, they did not seem even mildly disturbed by the inconsistencies and downright absurdities in his characters, though these are at times so obvious that one suspects Ivanov of waving them as red flags. Wish projection undoubtedly encouraged much misreading. Good writers sympathetic to Communism were needed; and Ivanov, to all outward appearances, filled the bill—with heroes from the lower classes, a style that seemed relatively accessible, and an absence of philosophizing about the "accursed questions." In short, he exhibited a relative freedom from those mannerisms that people associated with the old "bourgeois" literature and found typified in Pil'nyak. With their tendency to read works of fiction as sociological "documents," the critics did not scratch the surface until the middle of the decade.

By then Ivanov had begun to simplify his plots and his situations, move away from military settings, and make an attempt at character drawing. His theme remained the same; but now, in starker surroundings, it began to reveal itself to even the hardiest misreaders. The critics grew suspicious; enthusiasm gave way to wary uneasiness; even Voronskii's ardor cooled.[43] But Ivanov had a keener sense of the conditions for literary survival than did Pil'nyak; he made the appropriate adjustments. The beginnings of yet a new style came in 1927, with the stage version of *Armored Train*. Here Ivanov removed the sting of irony, cast out ambiguity, and produced an unmistakably "proletarian" work, in which Vershinin appears not as the passive and ideologically defective agent of the collective mind, but as a resolute, positive hero with unimpeachable credentials.

By then, Ivanov's major work was over. Nothing he did in the last four decades of his life matched, in quality or in influence, what he had written in those six years. Through his early writings, Soviet literature made contact with two of the vital themes of the previous generation: the themes of necessity and death.[44] Ivanov's contribution was to reclothe them in the images of the time and, in so doing, to show how the right trappings could make an unacceptable view of life acceptable. Possibly he did not think of his work in those terms; but the technique was convincing and has, no doubt, been consciously exploited by many a Soviet writer since then who has struggled with the problem of making sudden adjustments to new political situations. Voronskii's contribution was to set, in his article of 1922, the terms for the misinterpretation which made Ivanov's eminence and influence possible, and to provide, in *Red Virgin Soil*, a prestigious forum for his work.

NILS ÅKE NILSSON

Through the Wrong End of Binoculars: An Introduction to Jurij Oleša

1. Jurij Oleša's novel *Envy* opens with an amusing picture of one of the main characters, creator of the salami trust "The Quarter." We are present when he gets out of bed in the morning; we hear him singing in the lavatory; we see him doing his gymnastics. For the last operation he is stripped except for jersey drawers, done up in the middle of his stomach by a single button. This turns out to be not just an ordinary button; it has another function too: "The pale blue and pink world of the room is spinning around in the mother-of-pearl objective of the button."[1]

This magic button introduces at the very beginning a highly characteristic device Oleša uses throughout the whole novel when describing people, objects, settings. He seldom gives us a direct and straightforward description, a simple full-face view of an object or a person. Instead we usually see his world of objects and people reflected in buttons, mirrors and metallic surfaces; we catch distorted glimpses of them through glass windows and bars; they appear enlarged or diminished through binoculars, telescopes or microscopes. Light and shadow may suddenly change their proportions and inter-relationships and make us see things we had never suspected before. Rain and wind may make them depart from their everyday course and reveal them from a new and unexpected side. And, if we only know the trick, if we are only shown how, our eye is ever eager to accept the most unexpected optical illusions, of which our world is full.

The morning sun is rising. We learn to know it from Andrej Babičev's suspenders: "In the metal clips of his suspenders there are two

From *Scando-Slavica*, XI (1965), pp. 40-68. Reprinted by permission of *Scando-Slavica* and the author.

burning clusters of the sun's rays."[2] The sun is setting, and, merely to tell us, Oleša introduces a gipsy with a brass bowl: "The day was closing shop. A gipsy in a blue waistcoat was carrying a clean brass bowl on his shoulders. The day was moving off, riding on the gipsy's shoulder. The disc of the bowl was bright and blind. The gipsy walked slowly, the bowl swayed gently, and the day wheeled inside the disc."[3]

These are just two examples chosen at random. Let us now take a closer look at the many devices Oleša uses in *Envy* and in his short stories. Let us see how they function in the context and try to find a background to and a common explanation for them.

We can start with the window. It may seem difficult for an author to have achieved any special effects by presenting an object or a person through an ordinary window. But Oleša knows how to do it: a glass pane is not always reliable from a strictly realistic point of view. When Andrej Babičev drives off to his work "his laughing face swayed through the window of his limousine like a pinkish disc."[4] Looking at the clouds reflected in a window something strange can happen: "Clouds were moving across the sky and the windowpanes, and in the windows their paths were getting entangled."[5] At the end of *Envy* Ivan Babičev and Kavalerov enter a glass gallery, where several panes have been broken; and it is here that they obtain a peculiar picture of the heavens: "The sky was broken up into sections of varying blueness and varying remoteness from the observer."[6] Later, Andrej Babičev passes through the same gallery but now the author regards him from the outside; a cubist effect is created: "Somebody was walking along the porch, and the windows were dismembering him as he went. Different parts of his body moved independently. It was an optical illusion. The head ran off ahead of the rest of the body."[7]

Turning from windows to the mirror, we might well expect this to be one of Oleša's favorite devices. To be sure, the looking-glass is our most common means of reflecting things, of giving us an indirect picture both of ourselves and of the reality around us. On the other hand, it has already been used so frequently in fiction to give, for instance, a description of an interior; by this means, authors could dispense with a long enumeration of furniture and objects, bound to impede the flow of narration, and just give rapid glimpses of a few accessories necessary to the context. Further, the well-known trope of holding up a mirror to nature, the idea of the novel as "a mirror carried along a roadway," has given this image definite connotations: it has become a symbol of literary realism. Thus the mirror could hardly interest Oleša very much; his sparing use of this device shows, however, that he knows that even an ordinary mirror is sometimes able to disclose unusual things. When Kavalerov wakes up the morning after he had come home drunk "he saw an uncommon sight in the mirror—the soles of his feet in close-up."[8] When Anna Prokopovič and her husband won the magnificent bed in a lottery, they drove it away on a cart: "The blue sky appeared and disappeared, reflected in the swaying mirror-arcs, as if lids of a pair of beautiful eyes were opening and then slowly drooping again."[9]

But there is a variety of mirrors that Oleša actually does like. When Kavalerov and Ivan Babičev meet for the first time it is in front of a street-mirror. Here the author makes a pause to tell us how fond he is of such mirrors. They possess a quality quite lacking in ordinary mirrors. When a pedestrian spots a street-mirror, he says, the world around him suddenly changes: "The rules of optics, of geometry have been shattered. The very motive force behind you is shattered, that which made you move and go precisely where you did go. . . . The streetcar that just disappeared from your sight is again rambling past you, cutting off the edge of the avenue like a knife chopping off a slice of cake. A straw hat hanging on a blue ribbon over somebody's wrist (you saw it; it attracted your attention but you did not have time to turn toward it) is back, sailing across your field of vision. There is an open space in front of you. You are certain that it is a house, a wall. But thanks to your gift you know that it is not a house. You have broken a mystery. It is not a wall; there is a mysterious world here where everything you have just seen is repeated with the stereoscopic clarity and neatness of outline that one gets from looking through the wrong end of binoculars."[10]

Here Oleša mentions another of his favourite means of obtaining a different view of reality. One passage in *Envy* does express his fondness of this instrument in a way similar to his praise of the street-mirror. But it is, as we notice, not the common use of binoculars that Oleša is interested in, just as he does not care for ordinary mirrors: "I find," he says, "that a landscape viewed through the wrong end of binoculars gains in brightness, clarity and stereoscopy. The colors and contours seem somehow more precise. An object is still familiar but becomes at the same time suddenly small and strange."[11]

The next step from the binoculars would be the microscope. In fact, we meet this transformation in one of Oleša's short stories, *Our World* (*V mire*). One day, as he is sitting on a bench somewhere on the coast in the south, his eye fastens on a little flower on the edge of a cliff. It stands out clearly against the blue skies: "I concentrate my vision, then suddenly something happens in my brain: somebody turns the screw of an imaginary pair of binoculars, trying to bring the picture into focus. And now the focus is sharp: the flower stands before me translucent as a section under the microscope. It has become gigantic. My sight has been given microscopic strength. I am become a Gulliver in the land of the giants. The tiny little flower, not bigger than a straw, frightens me. It is terrible. It looms before me: a construction of some unknown grandiose technique. I see giant bowls, pipes, joints, levers. And the reflexion of the sun on the stalk of the vanished flower I see as a blinding metallic glare."[12]

After the microscope, the next step will be to look for the telescope. Although the word is mentioned a few times in *Envy*, Oleša has in fact devoted a special little sketch to it, entitled *In Summer* (*Letom*). When one night he happens to look at the stars through a telescope, he experiences a surprise similar to those given him by the street-mirror, the binoculars and the microscope. The telescope transforms his earlier idea of the sky: "Now you know that this is Sagittarius, this is Cassiopeia, this is Perseus, these are the Pleiades, and this is Andromeda. The sky is no longer just a display of fireworks. It has, so it seems, stopped before your eyes. You experience a stunning feeling which cannot be compared with anything else."[13]

But there are still other things, not necessarily instruments, which can produce similar effects. One is the play of light and shadow which Oleša uses in *Envy* with the skill of a stage director. One evening Andrej Babičev is talking to his brother from a balcony: "Babičev turned abruptly and came back into the room. His shadow leapt diagonally across the street and almost caused a storm in the foliage of the garden opposite."[14] And a moment later, when he rushes out on to the balcony once more: "Now there is indeed a storm in the trees. His shadow, like a Buddha, falls over the city."[15] Another time a huge cloud "with the outline of South America" is moving towards the town. "The cloud gleamed in the sun, but its shadow looked threatening. The shadow, with astronomical slowness, was creeping over Babičev's street. All those who had already entered the mouth of the street and were moving against the current saw the approach of the shadow and felt things darkening before their eyes. The shadow was sweeping the soil from under their feet. They were walking as if on the top of a revolving sphere."[16]

One Sunday morning Ivan Babičev and Kavalerov are walking through the holiday-deserted city. There is a fascinating display of light and shadow: "The light, broken by traffic, remained all in one piece, as though the sun had only just risen. They were walking across geometrical patterns of shadow and light, or rather through a three-dimensional field, since the light and shadow intersected each other not only on the flat but also in the air. Before they reached the Moscow City Soviet they found themselves completely immersed in shadow. However, in the gap between two buildings there was a large block of light. It was very thick and dense, and it was no longer possible to doubt that light was made of matter: the dust tearing around inside it could easily pass for waves in the ether."[17]

In *The Tale of the Meeting of Two Brothers* we get the opposite picture, the play of light and shadow at night: "The evening was black. The lanterns were white and circular, the tarpaulins glowed redly, and the abysses below the wooden gangways were deathly black. The lanterns swung back and forth on their humming wires. It was as though the darkness was raising and lowering its eyebrows. Around the lanterns, insects were fluttering and dying. As they swung upward, the lanterns made the windows on their way blink, and then, as they descended again, tore out the outline of some far-off house and hurled it at the construction site. And then (until the swinging lantern came to rest) the scaffolding came to life, everything was in motion and the building set sail straight at the crowd like a high-decked galleon."[18]

In this passage the wind, as we notice, plays an important part. In fact, the wind is also able to disorder things, to play tricks on our eyes and reveal objects from a new angle. Gusts of wind fan a flamingo vase into a flame, setting the curtains alight.[19] A draught gives Kavalerov "a wing" and anesthetizes half his face.[20] When he sits down to drink a beer in an open-air restaurant he watches "the wind trace delicate shapes out of the corners of the tablecloth."[21] In the soccer game at the end of *Envy* we find a particularly good example of the wind at work: "Then the wind butted in. A striped awning collapsed. All the treetops swung far to the right. The ring of idlers dissolved. The whole picture disintegrated. People were running to find shelter from the dust. Valia took the full force of the blast. The light dress, pink as a shell, flew up and Kavalerov saw how transparent it was. The wind blew the dress over Valia's face and Kavalerov saw it outlined in the pink, fanned-out material."[22]

There is a similar episode in the story *Love;* here the wind is part of the transformation of the world through the love besetting Šuvalov: "They took leave of each other standing in the draught, which in this world seemed to be very active and many-voiced. It opened the doors downstairs. It sang like a charwoman. It ruffled Lola's hair, picked up Lola's hat, released the wasp and blew it into the salad. It was whistling. It picked up Lola's nightdress and stood it on end."[23]

Rain too has the same faculty of letting us suddenly see a landscape or a well-known object in a new, fresh light: "After rain the city acquires brilliance and stereoscopic relief. Anyone can see it: the streetcar is carmine; the paving stones are far from being all the same color, some of them are even green; a housepainter who was sheltering from the rain like a pigeon has come out of his niche and is now moving against the background of his brick canvas in a window."[24] In another passage Oleša tells us how after a shower "the city sparkled as if hewn out of Cardiff coal."[25]

But there are still other means of getting something new out of the world around us. We do not always need some kind of instrument. We can simply use our eyes. The world is full of wonders if we only have time to discover them. At the beginning of *Envy* Kavalerov says that he spends his time in Andrej Babičev's apartment observing things, astonished by all the mysteries of our everyday life: "Have you ever noticed that salt falls off the edge of a knife without leaving a trace —the knife shines as though nothing had been on it; that a pince-nez sits on the bridge of a nose like a bicycle; that a human being is surrounded by tiny letters like a scattered army of ants: on forks, spoons, plates, on a pince-nez frame, on buttons, on pencils?"[26]

We can also choose a special angle; if, for instance, you look at something from above you will get an often surprising impression. Kavalerov stands on a bridge and looks down on a boat: "From my bird's-eye view, a tugboat slid swiftly by. From this height, I saw, instead of a tugboat, something looking like a huge almond cut in half lengthwise. The almond vanished under the bridge."[27] Later in the novel, Kavalerov looks down on the town from the roof window of a huge building: "From this vantage point, it seemed to him that the little yard was groping for breathing space. All the surrounding stone hulks were pressing in on the little yard. The yard lay like a doormat in an overfurnished room. Strange roofs revealed their secrets to Kavalerov. He saw weather vanes full size and skylights whose existence nobody down below suspected; he caught a glimpse of a child's ball irretrievably lost when it had rolled into the gutter. Among the antenna-spiked buildings beyond the yard, the cupola of a church, freshly painted with red lead, filled an empty spot in the sky, and it seemed as if it had been wafted along on the breeze until Kavalerov's eye had caught it. He saw a trolley in the terribly remote street, looking like Siamese-twin question marks facing each other, and also another observer, leaning out of a faraway window and either eating something or sniffing at it, who in his obedience to perspective was almost leaning on the trolley."[28]

Kavalerov has similar experiences when he is looking at something from below. When Andrej Babičev finds him in the gutter, he is driven away in a car: "Coming to my senses, I saw a pale sky, growing lighter and rushing like water from the soles of my feet to somewhere behind my head."[29] Later, at a construction site, he is searching for Andrej Babičev, but gets only a sudden glimpse of him as he passes above him on an iron girder: "He flew by above me. Yes, he literally rushed past through the air. In an absurd foreshortening, I saw his rigid flying figure—not his face, only his nostrils. I saw two holes, as if I were looking at a statue from underneath."[30]

Still another thing able to cause interesting optical illusions is distance. Things look different at different ranges. If an observer lets his imagination run away with him, the most exciting transformations can take place. At the airfield Kavalerov watches a plane take off and notices "how with the changing distance, the plane kept changing into various objects. Now it was a gunlack, now a pocketknife, now a trodden lilac blossom."[31] The same thing happens when he stands on a street corner for a good hour, watching the inside of a bell tower where the ringer is working with his twenty bells. Because of the distance he cannot see him or his bells very clearly, and so he lets his imagination work along a metaphorical line.[32]

There exists, however, yet another way of observing and describing things. One can put oneself—deliberately or not—into a special emotional state, where things present themselves in a new light. One can, for instance, imagine that one is still a child among grown-up people, a lilliput in the world of giants. And this is just what Kavalerov does when he wants to tell us about Anička Prokopovič's fantastic bed, made of expensive wood, varnished with dark-cherry lacquer and with inset mirror-arcs on the inside of its ends. The strange architecture of this bed could, as it seems to him, be described best of all from the perspective of a lilliput or a child. If he were, for instance, Anička's own little son, "then neither distance nor scale nor time nor weight nor gravity had to be taken into consideration, and I could have crawled inside the narrow passages between the frame of the bedspring and the edge of the bed; I could have hidden behind the columns which today seem to me no thicker than a broomstick; I could have set up imaginary catapults on its barricades and opened fire on the enemy who would beat a hasty retreat over the soft boggy ground of the quilt, leaving behind the dead and the wounded; I could have held receptions for foreign envoys under the mirror-arcs, exactly like the king in the novel I had just read; I could have gone off on fantastic journeys along the fretwork—higher and higher, up the legs and buttocks of the cupids, climbing over them like climbing on a gigantic statue of Buddha, seeing only one bit of the huge details at a time; and then, from the last arch, from a dizzying height, I would have slithered down the terrifying precipice, into the icy abyss of the pillows."[33]

There is another state, also connected with childhood, which Oleša is particularly fond of. This is how Kavalerov describes it: "On this sofa, I fly back into my childhood. It's blissful. Like a child, I have at my disposal the tiny time interval between the first heaviness felt in the eyelids, the first melting away of things, and the beginning of real sleep. Once again, I know how to prolong this interval, enjoy it, fill it with the thoughts I want and, before sinking into sleep, still in control of my conscious mind, observe how my thoughts acquire a body of dream substance, how the ringing bubbles from the submerged depths become rolling grapes, how a heavy bunch of grapes is formed, a whole vineyard thick with bunches, and then there is a sunny road beside the vineyard, and the warmth. . . ."[34]

It is not a dream—although dreams also play a certain role in *Envy* —but the particular state between dream and wakefulness, a state in which everything is real and unreal at the same time, in which all objects by the power of his imagination are interchangeable, and can be transformed into something else: a world of fairytale and wonderful metamorphosis, the world of a poet.

To a poet or a child such fantastic transformations seem quite natural. But such a state is characteristic not only of a child but also of a man in love: he too lives in a world of unexpected analogies and metaphors. We find an illuminating example of this in *Love*. Before Šuvalov falls asleep he follows the pattern on the wallpaper: "He realized that that part of the pattern on the wallpaper, that section of the wall under which he was falling asleep, had a double existence—the usual one, the daytime one, ordinary coronets with nothing remarkable about them, and another existence, a nighttime one which only opened itself up to him five minutes before he dived into sleep. Suddenly, a part of the pattern came close enough to touch his eyeballs, was magnified, revealed previously unseen details, changed its appearance. On the threshold of sleep, close to childhood's sensations, he did not resist the transformation of familiar and lawful forms, especially as the transformation was touching: instead of the rings and spirals he discerned a she-goat and a chef in his white cap . . .

—And that is a violin key, Lola said, understanding him.

—And the chameleon . . . he said, already asleep."[35]

Thus we get a peculiar triumvirate in Oleša's works: the child, the lover, the poet. They are all related to each other; they share the same source of happiness. They all have that special sight which unfolds to them an "invisible world," a world unseen by other people. To those so gifted all things in the universe are wonderfully connected with each other. This makes it so easy for their imaginations to work along metaphorical lines. Oleša's world is not only a world of unusual perspectives and optical illusions but also—and for the most part just because of them—a world of startling metaphors. An object loses its firm contours, becomes material pliable to the will of the imagination, which starts to form new things out of it. But this is not all; there is a further stage. As sometimes happens with the imaginations of children, the metaphor itself comes true, is materialized. It is not just a simple comparison, made in passing. We witness a fantastic metamorphosis.

When Kavalerov stands on a bridge looking down on the tugboat gliding under him he compares it to an almond. But in the next second the metaphor is materialized. What passes under the bridge is not any more a tugboat which looks like an almond. It *is* an almond. When the narrator in the story *The Cherry-Stone* stands at a streetcar stop waiting for Nataša, people for some reason start asking him which car they should take. Soon he feels like a policeman who must have a ready answer to all questioners. After a while it is no longer a comparison. The metamorphosis takes place: he is already a policeman, with a truncheon and everything.

A good example of how the imagination works is to be found in the scene just mentioned, where Kavalerov is listening to the church bells. A bell ringer is working with his twenty bells of various sizes. Kavalerov watches him at a certain distance, and the distance starts to distort the proportions and evoke fantastic associations. It is, as it seems, not the ringer who pulls the ropes, but the contrary: "twenty bells were tearing him apart."[36] The ropes are transformed into cobwebs; the ringer becomes a mysterious musician—black, ugly, a Quasimodo. And then, by a sudden shift of associations, the ringer is now a laborer manhandling different-sized pieces of hardware.

And the sound itself also starts a play of imagination. First he hears the noises in a restaurant or a railway station. But after a while the sounds arrange themselves into a little tune: "Tom-vee-ree-lee." These words carry the associations further. They remind him of a name, and suddenly "there was some Tom Vereley floating around in the air." Kavalerov sees him now clearly before him, a handsome young man with a rucksack, on his way to the town, to Andrej Babičev's house, where he already hears him walking up the stairs, knocking on the door. Dream and reality now cross each other (as in the first act of Ibsen's *The Master Builder*). In fact, somebody knocks on the door, waking Kavalerov up from his metaphorical play, and a real Tom Vereley appears: it is Volodja Makarov, Andrej Babičev's protégé, a swarthy young man holding a bag.

The most amusing examples are to be found in *Love*. Right at the very beginning, where Šuvalov is waiting for Lola in the park, he notices how his thoughts all the time take an unpredictable, metaphorical course, and how he, against his own will, makes strange observations about the trees and flowers, observations which he would never have made before. And when he wakes up the next day after a night spent together with his beloved "the transformation of the world that had started the day they met had been completed." He has achieved the power to materialize his thoughts. The old metaphor of a lover, for instance, comes true. It does not surprise anybody. " 'Flying on the wings of love,' somebody said behind a window as he passed."[37]

What we learn from Oleša's stories is that there exist two worlds—the world we ordinarily live and act in, and an "invisible world." This "invisible world" is part of our common, everyday reality, only we do not usually notice it. One has to know the trick. Window-panes, street-mirrors, binoculars, rain, wind, unusual angles, optical illusions —all these things are keys with the magic power of opening the closed door to this fantastic world, a world which to Oleša is as real and important as the "visible" one. Some know how to manipulate them without instruction: the poet, the child, the lover. But nobody is locked out from the enchanted garden of poetry. Oleša extends a generous invitation to everybody. He is always willing to give the necessary instruction and encouragement. Anyone can see it, he says about the town renewed and refreshed, gleaming in bright colors after a sudden shower.[38] Everyone who pays attention can do likewise, are his encouraging words about the optical illusions with the flower on the cliff.[39]

2. The existence of an "invisible world" will provide us with an answer to the natural questions arising after we have acquainted ourselves with the list of Oleša's devices: why is he so fond of them? why does he, wherever possible, avoid any direct presentation of characters, objects or landscapes? So as not to leave us in any doubt, he has, moreover, given a simple and clear answer in his story *Our World*. Having recounted his experience with the eye as a microscope, he concludes: "You have to look on the world from a new point of view" . . . adding: "It is extremely useful for an author to occupy himself with such fantastic photography. And furthermore—this is no distortion of reality, no expressionism. On the contrary: this is pure, sound realism."[40]

Such a statement seems to imply an indirect address to the RAPP critics: when it was written, the word "fantastic" was not in high esteem, and Oleša's way of linking it with "realism" must certainly have smacked of "formalism" to those critics. But there is also another meaning behind this statement, and a very important one. The use of the word "fantastic" could be understood to mean that Oleša was interested in mystic or metaphysical speculation. Apparently he wants to defend himself against such an interpretation. His "invisible world" has no metaphysical or mystical connotations; it is, as I just mentioned, quite simply part of our reality. In fact, it is our world, only seen from a different angle. By his term "fantastic photography" he has in mind, above all, a wider-angled view of the field of realism, a discovery of new things around us, things which are always there, although we do not usually notice them. It is true that he recommends his readers and fellow writers to look at the world through the wrong end of a pair of binoculars, but the reason for this is not any desire to obtain a distorted picture ("no expressionism"). On the contrary: as he points out, in this way you will in fact get a clearer, sharper, more distinct picture of reality.

If we now should try to outline the background to Oleša's favorite devices and his concept of fantastic photography, we have to start with a writer to whom Oleša, in fact, makes a direct allusion in *Envy*, without, however, mentioning his name. When Ivan Babičev takes Kavalerov to show him his "Ophelia," they cross an empty lot. Ivan points out various discarded objects just to convince Kavalerov that this is not a dream. Suddenly he spots a bottle: "There is a bottle. Wait, it is still whole, but tomorrow the wheel of a cart will smash it, and if, soon after us, some dreamer follows our path, he will have the pleasure of contemplating the famous bottleglass, celebrated by writers for its ability to reflect light, to glint amidst garbage in a waste land and create mirages for lonely travellers."[41]

This "famous bottle" is, of course, that mentioned by Čexov in a letter from 1886, when he tells his brother Aleksandr how to achieve the effect of a moonlight night "by simply writing that the glow is like a light from a star flashed from a broken bottle on the milldam."[42] As we know, Čexov himself used this image in the story *The Wolf* written the same year; later, in *The Seagull*, he lets Trigorin repeat the same recommendation. This bottle has become a kind of symbol for Čexov's impressionism: opposing a too painstaking realism, Čexov gave a call for more economy and concreteness in all kinds of description.

It is easy to feel this sense of economy in everything Čexov wrote. However, he can hardly be said to have developed the special kind of indirect description that we find in this well-known example. It is true that a sunrise or sunset is often presented by the sun reflected on the cross of a church, in some window-panes, or in a river. As Bicilli has pointed out, this device is to be found throughout Čexov's stories.[43] In *The House with a Mezzanine,* to give but one typical example, he describes "a village with a tall, narrow belfry on which a cross glowed with the reflection of the setting sun."[44] But we can hardly consider such an image as very new or daring at that time.

It is true that the following prose generation did learn a great deal from Čexov; his call for economy, especially, was taken up by many writers.[45] Oleša was certainly one of them; further Čexov had something more to give him: the device of indirect description. Now, as we have already seen, Oleša makes much more out of it than Čexov ever tried to do. In Čexov it is mostly a means of avoiding the long, tedious descriptions of earlier realism; by mentioning the church and the sunset at one and the same time he could save at least one sentence in the indispensable presentation of the setting. To Oleša the indirect description is, as we have seen, an important part not only of his poetics but also of his view of the world.

Although Čexov may provide us with one clue to this favorite device of Oleša's, he does not really explain the special use Oleša makes of it. Here we must look for other writers. When Oleša brings together words like "realism" and "fantastic," we are, of course, reminded of Dostoevskij; in fact, he does the same thing in some of his letters, pointing out that most critics consider fantastic and exceptional is to him the very essence of reality. Now Oleša and Dostoevskij are certainly very different as writers, and a closer comparison will not lead us far. Nevertheless, Oleša's "fantastic photography" points, without any doubt, in the direction of Dostoevskij, Dostoevskij the writer, struggling with the concept of realism, asking himself if "the fantastic has or has not the right to exist in art."[46] Here Oleša felt a certain kinship with Dostoevskij; he was, as Dostoevskij, ready to answer the question in the affirmative, and even, as also Dostoevskij did, to state that this was in fact "pure, sound realism."

For the same reason Oleša interested himself in another writer, a writer who also explored the fantastic element in our everyday life, namely Edgar Allan Poe. When discussing his "fantastic photography" he is, in fact, making direct reference to Poe. What he has in mind is *The Sphinx*. It is characteristic for Oleša that this is a story in which the fantastic element is given a very natural explanation at the end. Poe relates here how one day, while sitting at an open window overlooking some river bank and a distant hill, he suddenly catches sight of "a living monster of hideous conformation, which very rapidly made its way from the summit to the bottom, disappearing finally in the dense forest below."[47] As it later turns out, the monster is simply an insect, wriggling its way up a thread, which some spider had wrought along the window sash; the hill in the background and the author's position in the window had caused an optical illusion.

There is also another master of fantastic photography who is brought to mind in this connection: Nikolaj Gogol'. A rather interesting parallel to Oleša is to be found in the story about Ivan Ivanovič and Ivan Nikiforovič. At the beginning of the story Ivan Ivanovič is sitting outside his house watching various things that Ivan Nikiforovič's maid is carrying out to air: a uniform, dress coats, white cashmere trousers and other kinds of clothes, including also a sword—"All this taken together made up a very interesting spectacle for Ivan Ivanovič, while the sunbeams, catching here and there a blue or a green sleeve, a red facing or a bit of a gold brocade, or playing on the sword-point, turned it into something extraordinary."[48] . . .

The ever-shifting spotlight of the sun on the clothes creates such a peculiar effect that Gogol' has to explain it by a long comparison. It is, he says, "like the show played in the villages by strolling vagrants when a crowd of people closely packed looks at King Herod in his golden crown or at Anton leading the goat; behind the scenes the fiddle squeaks; a gipsy claps his hands on his hips by way of a drum, while the sun is setting and the fresh coolness of the southern night imperceptibly creeps closer to the fresh shoulders and bosoms of the plump village woman."

The common denominator in both scenes is, besides the fancy clothes, the sunlight; in the former instance the morning sun, in the latter the sun of evening. In the morning scene the sun is apparently acting as a "device of detachment"; it makes everything theatrical, uncommon, strange. We get a sudden new view of familiar objects; this is quite in line with what we find in Oleša's writing. It is also interesting to note that in the same story there is an example of the optical illusions which Oleša is so fond of: "The room into which Ivan Ivanovič stepped was quite dark because the shutter was closed, and the sunbeam that penetrated through a hole in the shutter was broken into rainbow hues and painted upon the opposite wall a garish landscape of thatched roofs, trees and clothes hanging in the yard, but all the other way round."[49]

However, we do not have to go so far back in time, for there is a contemporary writer who, I think, has been the most inspiring model for Oleša in the field of fantastic photography. This is Evgenij Zamjatin. In fact, the now very familiar passage from *Our World,* the one about the flower, comes very close to a passage in a lecture by Evgenij Zamjatin on contemporary Russian literature. If we look at our own skin through a microscope, he says, we will doubtless be frightened at first. "Instead of your pink, smooth, soft skin you will see kinds of clefts, enormous hillocks, pits; from a pit rises something of the same girth as a young lime-tree—it is a hair; beside it there is a big clod of earth—this a speck of dust. What you see will have very little in common with the usual kind of skin: it seems to you improbable, nightmarish. Now ask yourself this question: which is the truer, which is the more real—the pink, smooth skin, or this one with the clefts and hillocks? Having given it a thought we have to answer: it is this improbable skin, which we see through the microscope, that is true and real."[50]

It may not come as a surprise to us that Zamjatin in the same context makes an allusion to Dostoevskij and his fantastic realism. At this time Zamjatin believed he had found a concept which could explain the new trend in Russian prose after 1910. He called it, as we know, "Neorealism." This was a synthesis of realism and symbolism, an opposition to and yet a continuation of the sweeping trends which had dominated Russian literature in the 19th and the beginning of the 20th century. This meant a realism of a new kind, a realism unafraid of symbolic planes and fantastic implications. The writers had to try new devices and uncommon angles to get something new out of the old theme of "byt." And, as the example with the skin under the microscope tells us, Zamjatin saw a truth more real than that of ordinary realism in such fantastic close-ups of reality.

We do not know very much about Oleša's connections with Zamjatin. We can hardly presume that he had any possibility of listening to Zamjatin's lecture on contemporary Russian literature; for it was held as early as in September 1918, and at the Folk University in Lebedjansk. But Zamjatin repeated his example in his article *On Synthesism* (*O sintetizme*), which was printed in Petersburg in 1922.[51] It became, as it seems, a kind of slogan for the trend of "Neorealism"; we can, for instance, hear an echo of it in an article by Aleksandr Voronskij, published in 1923.[52] It is hard to believe that Oleša did not become acquainted with Zamjatin's articles and reviews when he came to Moscow from Odessa at the beginning of the 1920's to start his career as a writer. Apart from his interest in the burning issue of science and art, of man versus the modern world of machines, which should have directed him to Zamjatin's writings, nobody who cared for the technique of prose (and Oleša was certainly one who did care) could fail to overlook or disregard Zamjatin's views.

3. Thus we have many masters of indirect descriptions and fantastic photography before Oleša enters the picture. He is, to be sure, fully aware of this fact and does not hesitate, as we have seen, to pay, directly or indirectly, his tribute to them. He was bound to feel a certain kinship with these writers in their attempts to broaden the concept of realism, however different they might be from him in other respects. What now still remains to discuss is the main principle behind his use of fantastic photography: that the task of literature is to give a fresh view of the everyday world around us. This is not exactly a new idea, to be sure. It has been expressed now and then by various poets and prose writers, especially since the days of Romanticism. To Edgar Allan Poe "novelty and unexpectedness," "novel arrangements of old forms" are basic concepts. Coleridge speaks of the "sense of novelty and freshness with old and familiar objects."[53] In one of his poems Browning lets a painter say

> We're made so that we love
> First when we see them painted, things we have passed
> Perhaps a hundred times nor cared to see. . . .[54]

It may be interesting to compare how close this comes to one of Dostoevskij's statements, that "one can know a fact, one can see it a hundred times oneself and still fail to get the same impression as when someone else, a man with special gifts, stands behind you and points out that fact to you, explains it to you in his own words and makes you look at it through his eyes."[55]

However, it is only after the Symbolists that this idea becomes an essential part of the general view on literature and appears on the programmes of various poets and groups. Several reasons can be found for this; it is a problem which should actually be brought up in a somewhat wider context. I will here simply restrict myself to some points that are, perhaps, of special relevance to Oleša.

In part, this view appears as a natural answer to the claims of declining Symbolism. The poet's concern was no longer with the "absolute"; now he was back on earth again, he had to content himself with what he could approach and understand with his senses. If poetry was to restrain itself from presenting philosophical or religious truth, all that remained for the poet to investigate was the world around him. Poetry should not discuss or explain any more, it should "render" (as the English Imagists put it).

Still, this was no return to simple realism, but to a reality full of hidden wonders. ("Wonders should be the primary concern of the novelist" said Apollinaire).[56] The feeling of discovering anew a lost world, of seeing everything as if for the first time, is emphasized, for instance, by Gumilev's first proposal to name the new post-symbolist trend "Adamism." Poetry became an adventure, the poet a seafarer with still many unknown continents before him, to use one of Gumilev's favorite images. Like the little "rubber boy" in Oleša's story *Liompa*, the poet is wandering through a reality where everything is new and still has no name, a world of fantastic discoveries and transformations. Of the senses, the important one to the poet was sight. Visual and concrete metaphors dominate the verse of this period. One catch-word of the era is "to make it new," as Ezra Pound formulated it.

An important aspect of this trend was a belief that the poet is a man who breaks the spell of automatization, a spell which permanently threatens our perception of the world. This was usually based on the philosophy of Henri Bergson, so popular at that time. Again and again in his works Bergson presents the same image of the poet: "Il y a, en effet, depuis des siècles, des hommes dont la fonction est justement de nous faire voir ce que nous n'apercevons pas naturellement. Ce sont les artistes. . . . Nous regardons à peine l'object, il nous suffit de savoir à quelle categorie il appartient. Mais, de loin en loin, par une accident heureux, des hommes surgissent dont les sens ou la conscience sont moins adherents à la vie. La nature a oublié d'attacher leur faculté de percevoir à leur faculté d'agir. Quand ils regardent une chose, ils la voient pour elle, et non plus pour eux. Ils ne perçoivent plus simplement en vue d'agir; ils perçoivent pour percevoir. . . ."[57]

These ideas were taken up in England by T. S. Hulme;[58] and indeed they fitted in very well with the programme of "rendering," so important to the Imagists. Very similar ideas were expressed in a Russian booklet, *The Resurrection of the Word* (*Voskresenie slova*), published in 1914 by Viktor Šklovskij. In it he stresses that "we do not experience the usual things; we do not see them, we merely recognize them. We do not see the walls of our room. It is so difficult for us to notice a mistake in a proof, because we cannot make ourselves see and read the common words: instead we merely 'recognize' them. An epithet may at first sound fresh and give new lease of life to its noun, but if it is repeated sufficiently often we will not experience its freshness any more: it will have already become commonplace. And not only single words or expressions can be fossilized in this way but sentences and even whole books as well."[59]

There is a particular passage in one of Oleša's stories which seems to be a perfect illustration of such ideas. In *The Cherry-Stone* the hero is walking along a familiar road to see his Nataša. He has taken the same route many times before without noticing what he is passing. Suddenly he understands that there is an "invisible country" everywhere waiting for you to discover it. This realization begins to come to him when he feels like throwing a stone at a wall. He bends down after a stone, and in so doing his eye falls on an unexpected and remarkable thing: an anthill. He realizes that this is the first time for twenty years that he has really seen an anthill. "Oh, I have surely stepped over anthills more than once during these 20 years—surely more than once? I did see them, of course, but when I saw them the thought 'Now I am stepping over an anthill' never entered my mind; my mind merely registered the word 'anthill,' that was all. The living image was instantaneously replaced by a term coming up helpfully at the right moment."[60]

The same thing now happened with the stone. He threw it from him. But at the next moment he heard, as it were, a cry from the stone: "Wait! Look at me!" And then I actually remembered. I should have taken a close look at it. Why, really that stone was a remarkable thing. And now it's disappeared there in the bushes. And though I held it in my hand I don't even know what color it was. Perhaps it was lilac-colored; perhaps it wasn't homogeneous but consisted of several separate parts: perhaps something petrified was locked into it, the remains of a beetle, or a cherry-stone; perhaps the stone was porous, and perhaps what I picked up wasn't a stone at all but a weather-worn bone."[61]

We meet a variation of such ideas in books and articles by Aleksandr Voronskij, one of the most influential critics of the 1920's. He has, it is true, never admitted any influence from Bergson and does not refer to him in his works. Certainly, his aesthetic ideas have in part a different background and, above all, a different aim; he was anxious to give them a Marxist touch, or, in other words, to apply them to the special conditions prevailing in Russian literature after 1917. But often they come very close to Bergson, and we can hardly presume that he was ignorant at least of the general European discussion which circled round certain of Bergson's concepts in those days.[62]

It is easy to quote from almost any of his articles to prove this. To limit ourselves to just one example, let me choose a passage from an article, published in *Krasnaja Nov'* in 1923, entitled *Art as a Means of Knowing Life* (*Iskusstvo kak poznanie žizni*). Here it is easy to recognize his attempts to bring his ideas of art as discovery and revelation into harmony with the new literary situation. Still more interesting is it to note his use of the "microscope image," giving it the same sense as Zamjatin and Oleša did: by enlarging objects the artist gives us a new view of them, a view which is truer than "the most real reality" (cf. Oleša's defence of the microscope and fantastic photography):

A true work of art is always astonishing in its novelty, always deeply moving, and it always seems a discovery. The life around us moves from day to day in its well-known familiar course. And even when that life is disturbed, even when its most solid supports have been undermined, still our consciousness and our feelings are inevitably slow and backward in their development; our minds don't keep pace with what's actually happening in life; we remain in thrall to the past; our eye is incapable of perceiving, of making out that which is coming to birth in the midst of violent change, and flood, and catastrophe. But a genuine artist possesses an eye, an ear, and an "inward sense" capable of grasping, in the midst of the dizzying storms of life, things that we pass by without noticing, things that still make no impression on us. Out of tiny details he creates in his imagination something great and significant. People and objects he can magnify in his artistic microscope, and he ignores what is already established and known. He raises life to the level of a "pearl of creation." He gathers up and brings together details and features that are scattered around us, and he isolates and focuses upon what is typical. In this way he creates in his imagination a life that is condensed and purified, a life better than reality, and closer to truth. And we ourselves begin to see, with the artist's help, things we had not noticed before but which are present around us, or which are coming into being in a prophetic anticipation of the future.[63]

There are many other passages in Voronskij's criticism which could be quoted as parallels to Oleša. When Voronskij says in one of his other articles that right from our childhood years prejudices, the pressure of the environment and society, illness and overwork will result in the fact that "the most important and the most beautiful things in life and the Universe become invisible to us,"[64] he comes close to Oleša's idea of the "invisible country." And when he says that the special ability of "seeing the world as it is in itself" is something we may attain "only in childhood, in our early years and at exceptional moments of our life,"[65] we are reminded of the special triumvirate of the child, the poet and the lover in Oleša's world. Voronskij too makes a division, similar to that of Bergson, between artists and "ordinary people," and the title of one of his books, The Art of Seeing the World (Iskusstvo videt' mir), could, in fact, fit very well as a general characterization of Oleša's works.

The rather puzzling fact in spite of all such parallels is, however, that Voronskij never showed any special interest in Oleša. He devoted articles to writers like Gor'kij and Aleksej Tolstoj, Marcel Proust and Knut Hamsun, but he left, as far as I know, Oleša's Envy unnoticed. At first glance it appears as if he here could discover a writer after his own taste, a writer who could have served as an almost perfect illustration to the thesis of literature as "the art of seeing the world" or of "removing the veils" from reality. A closer examination will, however, easily show that there still were considerable divergences between the two as to the means and aims of such slogans. Further, when Oleša's first work appeared, Voronskij was under attack from the RAPP critics, and after 1927-28 his activity as a critic declined rapidly. On the other hand the book Iskusstvo videt' mir appeared in 1927, i.e. the same year that Envy was published, and the title and the book itself could not for that simple reason have had any influence on Oleša (although, it is true, some of its articles had been published earlier). But otherwise is it difficult to see how Oleša could not know Voronskij's earlier articles and the discussion they gave rise to; evidently they do after all constitute part of the background to his outlook on art and life, as was also suggested by some critics.

To give one more variation of the idea of "novelty and freshness with old and familiar objects" in contemporary literature I should like to mention James Joyce's well-known "epiphany." In *Stephen Hero,* Stephen Dedalus tells Cranby about the clock of the Ballast office in Dublin:

"I will pass it time after time, allude to it, refer to it, catch a glimpse of it. It is only an item in the catalogue of Dublin's street furniture. Then all at once I see it and I know at once what it is: epiphany.

—What?

—Imagine my glimpse at that clock as the gropings of a spiritual eye which seeks to adjust its vision to an exact focus. The moment the focus is reached the object is epiphanized."[66]

To Dedalus "it was for the men of letters to record these epiphanies with extreme care seeing that they themselves are the most delicate and evanescent of moments." The problem of seizing and rendering such moments of sudden revelations also preoccupied prose writers such as Marcel Proust and Virginia Woolf. As we know, the "moment" also plays an important role in the aesthetics of Dostoevskij (cf., for instance, his view on Puškin's *Egyptian Nights*).[67]

A further discussion would carry us too far. Nevertheless, we cannot fail to notice how close Joyce's passage about the spiritual eye which seeks to adjust its vision to an exact focus comes to Oleša's already often-mentioned passage about the eye as a binocular or a microscope, seeking its focus. Joyce's epiphanies are, to use Oleša's language, anything but sudden glimpses of the "invisible country" (although Joyce, of course, is much more interested in psychology than Oleša is). This should not, however, lead us to any hasty conclusion about Oleša and Joyce. It only stresses once more that general background I have tried here to point out. There was a certain general idea about the aims and methods of poetry, topical in Europe at this time. It is reflected in various ways in different writers and different countries, but we can easily recognize the common traits, sometimes even find very similar expressions for the same experience. The above discussion has, I think, clearly demonstrated how well Oleša fits into this trend.

4. At first glance it appears as if Kavalerov and Andrej Babičev were perfect illustrations of the two types Bergson suggests in his aesthetic works: the man of action and the artist, the people who perceive for

the purpose of action, who think in standardized categories, and, on the other hand, the people who perceive for the pure pleasure of perceiving, who "see *the* table where others see just *a* table." Such a division seems to suggest a solution to the old conflict of the artist contra society. The artist has his special tasks in society, which are as important as those of the bureaucrat or the scientist. It is his job to discover aspects of reality that we are too busy to notice, aspects which are beyond the reach of the special tools and methods of science. This should, it would seem, give him a certain satisfaction of performing a useful mission in modern society, and balance the inferiority complex which has become one of the artist's obsessions since the rapid advance of science and technology during the past hundred years.

But it is not quite that simple. Those of Oleša's heroes who have been given the faculty of apprehending the invisible country soon find that this is a double-edged gift. There are very definitely moments when Kavalerov feels it a burden and a torment. "I do not want to speak in images. I want to express myself simply,"[68] he exclaims in despair. And in his letter to Andrej Babičev he is anxious to explain that he is able not only to describe Valja in metaphorical language—which Andrej cannot understand—but "in ordinary terms" as well.[69]

More manifest still is the dilemma of poor Šuvalov in *Love*. Here the situation is almost the opposite. Although Kavalerov is a man with a natural talent for "thinking in images," he nevertheless sometimes desperately wishes he were just an ordinary man, deprived of this fatal gift. Now Šuvalov is that ordinary man. We may imagine that he has never before in his life come upon a metaphor or caught a glimpse of the "invisible country." But love has changed everything for him. He is now tortured by his mysterious, newly acquired power of seeing things he never saw before, of transforming reality around him. He bursts out against his beloved: "I hate you. Once I used to know that that was a ladybug and nothing but. Well, I could perhaps have made a few guesses as to its origin and name, whether it had any religious or other significance. But now, since I have met you, something has happened to my eyes. I see blue pears, and I see the resemblance between a toadstone and a ladybug."[70]

Šuvalov's situation might well bring to mind a similar one in a novel by Jean Giroudoux, a writer to whom the contemporaneous critics liked to compare Oleša. In *Bella* from 1926, Fontranges after Bella's death suddenly becomes aware of the power of poetry; in the midst of his grief he involuntarily makes comparisons, creates poetic metaphors—a thing he had never done before: "C'était la première métaphore qui jamais eût traversé le front d'un Fontrages. C'était le mouvement le plus facile de l'imagination, mais Fontranges en frémit comme d'un changement de nature. Que se passait-il? Allait-il devenir poète maintenant? . . . Bella le soulevait au-dessus de ce monde où il avait passé cinquante-sept ans sans faire une comparaison. Gilbert retirant de son trou des cailloux plats. Fontranges pensa que Bella, dans ce sol pierreux de Paris, faisait une retraite avant d'entrer dans la terre profonde. Il n'y avait pas de doute, c'était encore là une comparaison.—Qu'est-ce que je peux bien avoir? se demandait-it. Tout le jour, il eût ainsi de petits accès d'imagination. Il s'arretait chaque fois, comme un écardiaque pendant l'arrêt de son pouls. Un dieu inconnu illustrait la vie de Fontranges . . . Que ne peut-on comparer dans la vie? De chacun de ses meubles, de chacun de ses gestes, de chacun des jeux de lumière du jour ou des lampes, il sentait maintenant qu'il lui eût suffi d'un peu d'intelligence et d'un peu d'invention pour dégager de délivrer un génie scintillant. Qu'il allait être consolant de vivre, si le monde réel se cousait ainsi à un monde imaginaire."[71]

This dilemma is, in fact, the main theme of *Envy* and of most of Oleša's short stories. It is not the usual romantic conflict between dream and reality. Kavalerov is not the successor of, let us say, Piskarev in Gogol's *Nevskij Prospekt*. Our world is not simply a detestable world to be avoided at any price. In many respects it is a most exciting place. Kavalerov may take his refuge in bed, in dreams or in his favorite state between sleep and wakefulness, just as Piskarev desperately reaches for his opium in order to escape from reality and revive his dreams of pure beauty. Nevertheless, this world attracts him again and again. It is, among other things, an excellent field for visual revelations and sudden discoveries. But this is still not enough for Kavalerov. There is in him at the same time an explicit desire to experience reality in the same simple, self-evident way that most people do. This is one important explanation of the envy the title tells us about: envy of Andrej Babičev, of Volodja and Valja, of people for whom life is simple and straightforward, for whom the adjustment to a new society does not involve any problems.

Kavalerov may despise and even hate Andrej, his way of eating, his whole appearance, his materialistic approach to life. But he cannot also help feeling certain envy of him. Andrej moves around freely in the new world; he is accepted everywhere; in his way he is a famous man. If Kavalerov had been a man like Piskarev he could have parted from Andrej with a smile of contempt and contented himself with a "he has his world, I have mine." Instead he is now repulsed and attracted at the same time. In the presence of Andrej he feels a permanent need to assert himself. He has to convince himself that he is no more inferior a representative of his age than this "sausage-maker." His letter to Andrej expresses it very clearly: "But does that make me an unworthy son of our century, and you a good one? Does that make me nothing and you something great?"[72] Characteristic is the scene in which Kavalerov tries to get in to the airfield but is stopped by a soldier at the gate. He has to produce some kind of invitation card and he does not have one. " 'Comrade, I am no ordinary citizen,' I began excitedly, unable to find anything better to say. 'What do you think I am? Just a bystander? Kindly let me through. I belong over there.' "[73]

It is a symbolic scene. It is true that Kavalerov has just noticed that aviation has changed since the days of Lilienthal, when an aircraft with its light, transparent wings resembled most of all a beautiful bird. Now it looks more like a ponderous fish. "How quickly aviation has succumbed to commerce." It is the same thing that frightens him in Andrej Babičev—the development of modern man into something materialistic and commercial. Nevertheless he claims that "I belong over there." He is also "a son of his age." What he is most of all afraid of is to be taken for a nonentity, for a petty bourgeois. In fact, he feels superior to Andrej, because he stands above the reduction of life to a materialistic, petty-bourgeois happiness which is symbolized in Andrej's sausage (the end of the story thus involves his second and decisive capitulation to Andrej because here he surrenders to the same limited materialistic "happiness" he has fought against in the person of Andrej). What makes him say "I belong over there" is a feeling that there is no way back and that people like Andrej after all are only temporary phenomena. His hope for the future is embodied in Valja. Before her his envy is changed into a painful, nostalgic yearning for this other world, to which, as it seems, he does not have the right invitation card:

"Sunlight slipped down her shoulder, and her collar-bones gleamed like two daggers. They remained like that for five seconds, and Kavalerov grew cold as he realized what an incurable nostalgia would remain in him forever. He knew he was watching a creature from a different world, alien and puzzling, while at the same time he felt how hopelessly charming she looked, how oppressively unattainable she was—because she was a little girl and because she loved Volodja. He felt how unslakable was the temptation."

When he approaches her with the words: "I have waited for you all my life. Take pity on me," his words do not reach her, she does not hear him and she passes him without an answer. "She ran, leaning against the wind."[74]

It is obvious that the conflict between Kavalerov and Andrej as well as Kavalerov's inner conflict, his attraction to the new world and his repulsion by it, has its specific Russian explanation, that they are closely connected with the political and social situation in the Soviet Union after 1917. I do not need to take up this question here, especially since this is the very aspect of the novel which has been most widely discussed since its appearance. It is instead, I think, more important to stress another part of the background, one which has attracted less attention.

On one occasion Kavalerov tries in vain to convince Andrej that he too belongs to the new world. He does it with words he thinks should be sufficient as an introduction card: "My youth coincides with the youth of the century."[75] But Andrej is too busy to listen. In one of Oleša's short stories, in which he looks back on his childhood, he says almost the same thing about himself as a highschool-boy: "You were of the same age as the century."[76] This is not the only parallel which could be drawn between *Envy* and the short stories. As a matter of fact, they offer good explanations for many things in the novel. The hero of these stories could often be taken for Kavalerov as a young boy.

The highschool-boy has an open mind to the modern development of science and technology. In his family he stands out, in his own words, as "a European, a journalist, a technician"[77] against the general stuffy petty-bourgeois atmosphere. He knows all the heroes of the new century by name: Latham, Farman, Wilbur and Orville Wright, Lilienthal and the Voisin brothers. He tries to acquaint his parents with the sensational news that "Blériot has flown across the Channel";[78] he tries to convince them of the beauty of a word like Issy-les-Molineaux, the Paris airport. But they do not understand the magic of words like these, nor does Orlov, his sister's student boy-friend. Thus he meets with the same fate as poor Kavalerov when he tries to convince Andrej about his solidarity with the new century: nobody pays any attention to him.

The boy is, as it turns out, interested not only in aeroplanes but in other modern technical wonders like cars and bicycles as well.[79] Orlov, the student, is the object of his envy because he is the owner of a bike, and the boy would do almost anything for the happiness of borrowing it for just a moment. And what a triumph when he meets the famous Utočkin, the racing motorist and aviator, and is given a ride in his car. But there is something that mars his happiness. His love of these symbols of the young century is, as it turns out, a love without response. As Kavalerov puts it: "Things don't like me."[80] *The Chain* is a story about that unrequited love. His ride on the borrowed bike comes to a painful end, as does his triumphal return with Utočkin.

This particular story gives a picture of an alert young boy, interested in technical things, showing him to be just as boys usually are. Other stories, however, reveal a different side: a boy who retires into his shell, who lives in his imagination, who soon learns the lot of the lonely: "loneliness—for ever, a lonely fate, man's destiny to remain lonely everywhere and in everything."[81] The contrast between these two attitudes reflects a well-known conflict of childhood: the sensitive boy who is anxious to be a member of the gang, to play with the tougher ones, but who will never grasp how to really handle a bat, a bike or a car. There will be no gang introduction card for him; he will always stand there outside their circle and its enticing symbols with his longing for community participation, and with his envy. Oleša's heroes carry this psychological conflict of childhood with them into adult life, and there it takes on fresh complications because of the special conditions of the society they have to live in as adults.

The conflict of Oleša's hero thus has its psychological as well as its specific sociological and political background. But it is at the same time a conflict well known to writers outside Soviet Russia as well, it is a conflict of our century. Such non-Soviet examples may have other implications, but a parallel to Oleša will sometimes be interesting enough in itself. Let us take Guillaume Apollinaire's *Le Poète Assassiné* from 1916. With this, Apollinaire wanted to demonstrate the dilemma of poetry at the beginning of our century. The hero is no longer set against the philistine, the bourgeois, as was usually the case in the preceding century, but against the scientist—the scientist who considers poetry an unnecessary luxury in modern society and states that in our days "true glory has forsaken poetry for science, philosophy, acrobatics, philanthropy, sociology, etc."[82] (cf. Kavalerov's yearning for glory and his complaint that there is no more glory for people like him in the Soviet Union). And this scientist demands that the poet shall no longer be afforded a place in society, a verdict which results in a general persecution all over the world. Further, the hero is killed, although he claims to be the greatest living poet. Later, however, Apollinaire tried to resolve this pessimistic note by seeking "conciliation between the work of the scientist and the modern artist."[83]

We meet many variations of the same fear in Russian and European literature at this time, a fear of what modern technology may mean for the poet and poetry as well as for mankind and the human heritage in general. That this fear is part of the literary background to Oleša's *Envy* is obvious; in the same category are Zamjatin's *We* (in spite of the fact that the book was not published in the Soviet Union)[84] as well as Chaplin's *Modern Times* (which was released after the appearance of *Envy;* cf. Oleša's interest in Chaplin and his hero).[85] Oleša's place in this marked trend will, I think, stand out more clearly only when studies will be made not only of the utopian theme in Russian literature of the 1920's but also of the topical discussion on the art and science of the same period.

Now, compared to *Le Poète Assassiné* Kavalerov is not exactly a poet (or, rather, he is not introduced as a poet); neither is Andrej Babičev a scientist. Yet Andrej is an inventor of sorts, for he has actually contrived to manufacture a sausage. This may sound ironical, but in his way he could pass as a representative of the modern hero; the turn of the century brought, as Anna Balakian has put it, "the advent of the supremacy of the scientist in the history of human progress, not the *pure scientist* who dealt with the abstract, but the man who applied the principles of science and *produced.*"[86] And Babičev is, as Oleša stresses again and again, just such a "producer," a "proizvoditel." But as a producer he looks to Kavalerov very much like the old enemy of poetry, the unimaginative bourgeois who now appears with the pretention of belonging to the new technocratic nobility.

It was Apollinaire's idea that poetry had something to learn from the modern scientist, above all from his imagination and inventiveness. However, what Babičev lacks is just imagination, all his imagination is capable of is a sausage.[87] In Kavalerov's opinion he has brought something of the old Russian "meščanstvo" into the new society; thus he has smeared the pure dream of the new beauty bound up in the modern technical society of the turn of the century, the dream of "le merveilleux moderne." That is why we here get a reverse situation to that in *Le Poète Assassiné;* Kavalerov and Ivan Babičev are evolving plans to murder the inventor and producer, Andrej Babičev.

I think we could stop here. What I have tried to do in this brief introduction to Oleša's works (his later period is not treated here) is to outline some important features and suggest their background. In his view on art and life Oleša is, as we have seen, connected with some well-known Russian masters of "fantastic photography," but he also stands out as an interesting representative for a general trend in Western literature as well.

WILLIAM E. HARKINS

The Theme of Sterility in Olesha's *Envy*

Iurii Olesha's short novel *Envy* (Zavist', 1927) has been greatly admired and even has some claim to be considered the "great Soviet novel."[1] Yet comparatively little has been written about *Envy* since the first flood of reviews and articles, many uncritical, appeared in the Soviet press between 1927 and 1933.[2]

Envy is a complex novel, sometimes described as expressionistic, written in a variety of styles and with many planes of meaning.[3] Elements of realist, romanticist, and symbolist styles are present. Dreams, fantasies, and lies are introduced, often as reality.[4] It is a work in which the author's ideological intentions are far from clear or unambiguous, a work deeply hedged with irony. And it is a work that can yield much to discerning analysis.

The present article does not have as its object a general study of the novel, but rather attempts to concentrate on a single psychic trait which dominates the work and touches deeply almost all its characters. The approach is "Freudian," though the author dislikes the word; except for a few specific concepts and the terms which designate them, the method is based on an analysis of symbols and images which tend to be universal in meaning and which, though partly obscured by contemporary rationalistic modes of thought, have been familiar to men through the ages.[5] No effort has been made here to impose on the novel the views of any particular analytic school, and the author would contend that his method proceeds from an analysis of the work itself and its symbols as much as from the writings of Freud and his followers.

From *Slavic Review*, XXV, No. 3 (1966), pp. 443-57. Reprinted by permission of the *Slavic Review* and the author.

Envy is dominated by the theme of castration and sterility, a sterility extending to all areas of life, including those of career and creativity.

The novel opens with a description, from the point of view of the young hero, Nikolai Kavalerov, of Andrei Babichev's matutinal functions: "Mornings he sings in the toilet."[6] Thus we are introduced to a scene of sheer physicality (largely without sensuality) unparalleled in Soviet literature. Andrei Babichev is sleek, a giant. His virility and masculinity are at first emphasized; as the author tells us, he is "a model male being," who has "a splendid groin," "the groin of a producer" (*proizvoditelia*). This last is clearly a pun which combines the implication of sexual potency with that of business efficiency (Babichev is director of the Soviet food trust).

But is Babichev really so virile? Olesha's short, cryptic statements have a certain obvious irony (the sentence "He is a model male being" is set off in its own paragraph, a device which suggests either very great emphasis or irony), and, as the portrait of Babichev continues, traits appear which contradict this picture of healthy virility. Babichev's masculinity is not that of a young athlete but of an older man of great height and bulk; it is a masculinity in which certain features, if not precisely feminine, tend to an indefinite sexual character which might be described as "neuter." Andrei Babichev suggests a eunuch. Olesha tells us that he resembles a "great big fat child" and that, when he descends the stairs, "his breasts shake in cadence to his steps." Feminine or effeminate characteristics, even, are intimated. His name, Babichev, suggests *baba,* an "old woman." He makes liberal use of eau de cologne, perhaps a strange practice for a Soviet commissar of the 1920s. He takes in young men to live with him, and one of these, Volodia Makarov, he has virtually adopted; though there is no more specific hint of homosexuality, this could scarcely be expected in a Soviet novel (we are, of course, told by Kavalerov, who catches sight of a birthmark on the small of Andrei's back, that Andrei must be an aristocrat and hence that he must be guilty of "aristocratic inclinations," a phrase possibly calculated to carry implications of homosexuality).

Other effeminate or sexless characteristics are mentioned. Andrei is described as a "glutton," another trait which suggests the eunuch. Both his present and his past (about which very little is said) are seemingly devoid of sexual companionship; he does not have (and apparently never had) a wife, mistress, or children. And in spite of his physicality, so strongly emphasized in the opening scene of the novel, he would seem to lack sexual desire or interest. He is director of the Soviet food trust; thus he fulfills the symbolic role of a nourisher and provider, a role which gives him an almost embarrassingly feminine part to play. His relation to his adopted lodgers is as much that of a protecting, nourishing mother as of a father, and his lodgers react to him in these terms. In the letter he leaves for Andrei when he quits his apartment, Kavalerov writes, "You have warmed me. You have let me stay at your side. I have slept on your marvelous sofa." And Volodia Makarov, Andrei's chief protégé, writes to Andrei that "I gaze at you, and suddenly you return my glance, and at once I close my eyes, as with my mother."

True, we see Andrei Babichev chiefly through the eyes of Kavalerov, who is envious. Is this not unjust to Andrei? Is he, as a Communist and organizer of progress, not intended to play a heroic role? Is his relation to Volodia not an idealistic one, which the foul-minded Kavalerov seeks to defame?

Yet Olesha never intercedes to rehabilitate Andrei in the reader's eyes after Kavalerov has "defamed" him. In the second half of the novel, which is narrated not by Kavalerov but by the author, Andrei appears in an only slightly more favorable light, and he is now obscured by the more intriguing character of his brother Ivan. Nor could we expect Andrei to play a heroic role once he has been introduced as a partly comic figure. Moreover, Babichev is quite conscious of his own limitations, or at least certain of them, and says of himself, "I still stand up to my belly in the old order and will never quite crawl out of it." The reference here to the belly, though proverbial, is possibly not accidental.

This confused array of traits, some masculine, others which suggest an effeminate man or eunuch, puzzle us until we grasp the essential principle which Andrei represents: he is a hermaphroditic figure. As hermaphrodite he combines masculinity with femininity, but a masculinity and femininity which tend to neutralize one another: for masculine sexuality Andrei substitutes an intense career drive, while his feminine sexual tendency satisfies itself as latent homosexuality through the adoption of young men. He combines in himself the roles of provider (father) and nourisher (mother), and this is the inner reason why he is characterized as hermaphroditic. For he seeks to win for the utopian state which he represents the same fusion of both parental roles, and he identifies himself with that state.

In a fantasy scene in which the two brothers compete for the attention of the crowd, Ivan Babichev accuses Andrei of attempting to destroy the family. Andrei's pet project, the Chetvertak, a restaurant where nourishing food will be served so cheaply that kitchens will become obsolete, threatens the stability of the family as an institution. Ivan says in accusation:

> Comrades! They seek to take away your chief possession: your family hearth. The steeds of the Revolution, thundering on the back stairs, trampling our children and our cats underfoot, breaking up our beloved hot plates and cakes of pressed tea leaves, will tear into your kitchens. Women, your pride and your glory is threatened—the hearth! With the elephants of the Revolution they are trying to wreck your kitchens, mothers and wives!
>
> What has he told you? He has sneered at your pots and pans, at your sanctum, at your right to place a pacifier in the mouths of your babes. What does he teach you to forget? What does he seek to crowd out of your heart? Your home— your beloved home! He wants to make you vagabonds on the wastelands of history. Wives, he spits in your soup. Mothers, he dreams of wiping from the faces of your infants all resemblance to you—that sacred, beautiful family resemblance.

Though the argument is comical, there is of course more than a grain of truth in Ivan's charge. For if the members of a family are no longer to eat at home but in a restaurant, the sacred unity of the family will indeed be threatened.

Does Andrei seek to destroy the family because he himself has no family? In his youth he became a radical and went abroad, leaving the home of his mother and father, a priggish and conservative high-school principal. His radicalism may well have originated as a revolt against family ties. And now we grasp the underlying principle behind his career and his goal: by assuming for himself the role of mother as well as father, he seeks to eliminate these functions and relationships in private life. The state itself shall become mother and father. Hence Andrei, as director of the food trust, becomes nourisher and provider, not only for Volodia Makarov and Kavalerov but for all Soviet citizens. His negation of the family is illustrated not only in his fantasy debate with his brother Ivan but also in a memorable monologue which occurs near the novel's end: "I have no need of a son; I am not a father, and he is not a son. We are not a family. . . . We are not a family; we are humanity."

That Andrei seeks to deny the family is an anti-bourgeois, leftist gesture of a type quite possible in the 1920s.[7] But it is also rooted in a

personal need to disguise his own craving for the consolations of a
family life he has abjured for himself. His great hope is that Volodia
will prove to be a really "new man," the leader of a new Soviet generation. In the very monologue which contains the passage just quoted,
he declares that he will disown Volodia if the latter proves to be a
fraud, if he is not really "new"; then Andrei will drive him out. It is
at this point that he protests that the two of them "are not a family."
But in fact he and Volodia *are* a family, for they live together as
father and son, with the complication that Andrei, as nourisher, has
taken over the mother's role as well. Is not his insistence that the two
of them do not constitute a family a rationalization to hide from himself the homosexual implications of their relationship? But, even
deeper, is not Andrei concerned that he is impotent, that he can have
no real son? Hence his denial that the two of them constitute a family
and (through his activity as food commissar) his denial of the significance of the family as a social unit.

It is perfectly true, of course, that in Soviet novels of the 1920s
Communist heroes normally lacked both sex life and family life, and
were usually depicted as not pining for either.[8] But in a work as
sophisticated as *Envy* this can hardly be more than a parody. The
demon of revolution leads man to deny love and the family; this is a
cliché of revolutionary teachings and fictional portrayals of revolutionaries. Like Jesus, who denied his mother and brothers, the revolutionary heroes of Chernyshevskii and of Soviet novelists of the 1920s
and 1930s abjure both love and family ties. Andrei Babichev is of
course a parody of this ideal. He does not deny himself and his own
flesh; on the contrary, that flesh is very real, and the novel is full
of his physical characteristics: he is sleek, a giant, he has a "splendid
groin," he is a glutton. He does not deny himself or his flesh from
choice but from the prison of his own impotence. He seeks aggrandize-
ment of self, and concealment of impotence, through identifying himself and his compulsive nourishing-mother nature with the utopian
activities of the state itself.

In the same spirit, Andrei's creations are likewise a parody of true
creativity, for he cannot create. His Chetvertak is the dream of a
nourishing and protective mother figure who seeks to take over these
functions of the family for the state, with which he ambitiously identifies himself. Yet, in its goal of comfort and plenty, it is still a bourgeois dream. And Andrei's other creation, a new sausage, is even
more clearly a repulsive parody. Along with the Chetvertak it is his
"child," the creation of a mother and protective mother mentality. In

its shape a sausage suggests feces, a symbolism which Olesha's lovingly sensual description of the new sausage does little to mask. The child may confuse the act of defecation with that of giving birth; in the child's view, both excrement and babies are "born," and Andrei's sausage is in a sense the "child" of his spirit.[9] "Sausage maker" (*kolbasnik*), the epithet Kavalerov hurls in the face, is the one epithet by which we invariably remember him, and even Volodia, his protégé, accuses him of "using primitive methods" (*kustarnichat*) in his sausage works.

Andrei Babichev's protégé, Volodia Makarov, is in some ways the most enigmatic character of the book. His rudeness, his absurd desire to "turn himself into a machine," his Spartan indifference to the beautiful Valia, for whom he is content to wait an even four years—all this has led critics to see him as a figure of satire or of polemical criticism.[10] His role as an athlete also seems a bit ridiculous, and as the "soccer player" he makes a fitting match for Andrei Babichev, the "sausage maker." On the other hand, his part in the soccer match against the Germans is clearly a heroic one. Olesha seems truly to have idealized sports without irony; sports are one of his favorite sources of imagery, and he is known to have been fond of soccer as a boy.[11] Early in life a physician advised him, because of a weak constitution, to give up soccer. Did he then become a frustrated athlete, given to an excessive and a bit masochistic admiration for sports heroes? There is little doubt that he intends Volodia to be a truly "new" man, whose twentieth-century character is demonstrated by his affection for machines and his interest in sports. True, there is nothing typically Soviet in these traits: Volodia could as well be an American—or a Japanese (his smile recalls a Japanese, we are told several times)—and the critics were quite right in rejecting him as a hero of the new Soviet order. His rudeness and seeming lack of humanity are characteristic of the "new man"; they may well alarm the author, but no doubt he views them with a somewhat respectful apprehension.[12] Rather than an antihero, Volodia is a hero who does not come off; his alter ego is the equally enigmatic and even shadowier Valia. Whether it is his devotion to machines, to discipline, and to sports or his rudeness and indifference to tradition and culture which appeal more to Andrei and Valia is hard to say. His "newness" implies contempt for the old, and this is of course quite normal for Soviet youth of the 1920s. Here the motif is serious but again mixed with an element of ambiguity and parody.

Volodia and Valia are hardly intended to be seen as sterile, for to them belongs the future. Yet they are apparently sterile, whether or not the author envisioned them as such. Volodia wishes to turn himself into a machine, to subject himself to an inhuman discipline, to wait an even four loveless years for Valia, to kiss her only on the day of dedication of the Chetvertak. All this seems inhuman; Volodia is a machine, and not a human being. True, Olesha is fascinated by the machine's power to imitate life; in *Envy* he compares the first airplanes to birds, and in a later story, "Aldebaran," he sends two lovers to visit the planetarium, which serves them as an effective substitute for a starlit night. Yet the machine cannot love; it can only destroy.

Valia, Volodia's fiancée and Ivan Babichev's daughter, is so shadowy as to be little more than a dream figure; she hardly appears in the novel, and we see her primarily as described by others, particularly as the object of Kavalerov's romantic imagination (toward the end of the book he dreams of her as carried through the air, wafted by the sound of band instruments). She flies through the air—this, a favorite image of Olesha's, represents freedom and, perhaps, the liberation of sexual orgasm.

The hero of *Envy* is Kavalerov, and, indeed, the first half of the novel is seen through his eyes and recounted by him. Critics have long viewed him as a character influenced by Dostoevski's Man from the Underground.[13] There is much truth in this comparison, but one must also note a link, however slender, between Kavalerov and the author himself. Kavalerov's observations on sleep as a means of return to childhood suggest Olesha's own musings and childhood reminiscences, while Kavalerov's recollections of man's first attempts at flight, which so fascinated him as a child, are also clearly autobiographical.[14] It is true that Kavalerov turns out essentially unsympathetic; this may be the reason why Olesha dropped him as a narrator halfway through the novel and took over the narrative role himself. Thus the reader might finally see Kavalerov as he is and judge him accordingly.[15]

The name Kavalerov is obviously derived from the noun *kavaler*. The word in Russian originally meant "cavalier," "escort," but has come with time to have more vulgar connotations and is roughly equivalent to English "boy friend." The name thus suggests Kavalerov's romantic nature and his quest for idealized love, but it also ironically hints at his failure, rooted in his own personal inadequacy, to achieve the quest of his dreams. Kavalerov is a romantic trapped in a nonromantic age. As a romantic, he dreams not only of love but also of personal glory. But since he has nothing to contribute to his world, he is willing to settle for gratuitous, even infamous, notoriety; he would cross Niagara on a tightrope or commit some heinous crime for which posterity would remember him. As a traditionally Russian type of "superfluous man," Kavalerov proves unable to achieve even this kind of notoriety. In his frustrated ambition he is opposed to Volodia Makarov, who wins fame as a member of a soccer team. Volodia's role as a goalkeeper for the Soviet team is also contrasted to the individualistic playing of the German star, Hetzke, who strives only for his own personal reputation. Through Kavalerov, Olesha presumably wishes to expose the futility of the romantic dream of personal glory, as opposed to the successful cooperation of the collective. The ultimate comparison, of course, is one between capitalist and socialist orders.

Kavalerov's frustrated desire for fame turns to envy, and he becomes a concentrated focus of that feeling. But even envy cannot bring him to action, and his plan to kill Andrei Babichev, whom he despises as a "confectioner" and a "sausage maker," comes to nothing.

The drive for fame is basically a seeking for recognition from others, first and foremost from the father, and it serves as a compensation for attentions never obtained from a real father. In fact, Nikolai Kavalerov is engaged in a search for a father surrogate. He first looks, almost pathetically, to Andrei Babichev for some sort of attention or recognition, and it is at least in part Babichev's failure to give him these which arouses his feelings of hatred and envy. In Ivan Babichev he finds a seemingly more satisfactory father substitute, and at one point in the novel he speaks of Ivan as his "teacher."

But Kavalerov, as an embodiment of frustrated romanticism in a "realistic" age, is also engaged in a second quest, a search for love. It is possible that these two quests—the search for a father and for a love object—are contradictory; in a romantic literature, in which emotion tends to be an absolute, either quest is frequently viewed as total and exclusive, and the combination of the two may appear slightly comic. Yet it is possible that in real life an individual may engage in both quests at once; indeed, the satisfaction of the search for the father or a father substitute might provide the individual with a sense of security essential to carry on a search for a love object. We need not, of course, judge Kavalerov's makeup only from the point of view of realistic psychology; he can better be considered as a romantic figure who embodies, expressionistically, two of the eternal romantic quests.[16]

For Kavalerov both quests are destined to be frustrated and the desired goals replaced by parody substitutes. Whatever our opinion of Andrei, he is a commissar and hence a person of some importance; there can be little doubt that Kavalerov does seek recognition and affection from him. Whether he could accept this recognition and affection from Andrei, from any representative of the new order, or, indeed, from anyone, is of course questionable. He can scarcely find satisfaction from Ivan Babichev either, a buffoon and fraud who, like himself, seeks to substitute gratuitous fame for real accomplishment. Ivan is too like Kavalerov (and Kavalerov hates himself) to serve as a satisfactory father surrogate.

Similarly, not the ethereal Valia but the fat, lecherous widow Anechka Prokopovich constitutes the end of Kavalerov's search for love. He despises the widow, but in the end is compelled to take refuge in her huge and terrible bed. And in nightmare fashion he is asked to share this woman (who symbolizes all the repulsive aspects of a mother figure) with his own would-be father surrogate, Ivan! This is expressionism, of course, not realism; the question of whether Kavalerov could in actuality accept such a triangular relation, with its aspects of incest and unending Oedipal conflict, is left unanswered as the novel ends. Presumably he could not, but the ending is clearly not a realistic one but an expressionistic representation of his own symbolic castration. His apparent resubmission to the role of child with its concomitant Oedipal conflict points to passive acceptance of his own castration. Indeed, such acceptance is implied by Ivan Babichev's final speech, in which he preaches not feeling but indifference.

For Kavalerov, bed and sleep serve as symbols of another, more nostalgic, return to childhood. Sleep leads to dreams, which are timeless and fresh as those of a child, and hence each act of falling asleep is a leap back into the peaceful world of childhood dreams. The comfortable sofa on which he sleeps at Andrei Babichev's invokes this magic return in him. For Olesha such a childhood is, in spite of Freud, innocent and presexual; it seeks neither recognition from others nor conscious sexuality. But sleep and dreams are ambiguous symbols for the adult: dreams may be sexual, while bed and sleep also suggest sexuality. Indeed, the description of Kavalerov's lapse into sleep on Andrei Babichev's sofa carries more than one hint of masturbatory activity:

> By deliberately moving I call forth the twang of its new, tight, virginal springs. My movement results in separate drops of sound which come from the depths. The motion of bubbles of air, crowding to the surface of the water, is suggested. I fall asleep like a child. On the sofa I execute a flight back to childhood.

And the widow's enormous and terrible bed is likewise sexual in its symbolic implications: it is at once the goal of Kavalerov's yearnings and the symbol of his fear of and disgust at sexuality, his fear of his own impotence. The bed itself is a vaginal symbol in its implicit connection with its owner and its function in the sexual act. It is even said to "resemble an organ" (the pun is as possible in Russian as in English). But it provides no pleasure, only torture; it is a rack rather than a bed. Thus Olesha writes of it that it is "a terrifying bed . . . with its sides as steep as a barrel. In it bones crack."

As an ogre-like mother figure, the widow Anechka implies castration. The figure of the castrating mother is well known in psychoanalytic literature. Freud speaks of the male's revulsion at his first sight of the vagina, often the mother's vagina which he has glimpsed while very young. The absence of a penis in woman seems to threaten his own penis.[17] The fantasy of a castrating vagina, of a *vagina dentata*, is also well known, and this is the type of vagina which Anechka's terrible bed seems to suggest. In the first scene in which she appears, Anechka is described as wielding a knife which she flashes in her hand. She has just cut up the organs of some animal to feed to her many cats. These organs suggest, by association as well as appearance, the male genitalia.

That Anechka represents castration may seem a paradox, for she is the only really sexual figure in the novel. It may seem even more paradoxical to observe that sexual intercourse itself may imply a fear of castration and so arouse the male's anxieties. But this is a truism, embodied in the traditional mythic figures of the timid youth paralyzed by his first sexual experience or of the mature man whose vitality is sapped by a siren or a succubus.

As a mother figure, Anechka and her bed also symbolize for Kavalerov retreat from active sexual competition, retreat to a childhood world of presexual innocence. True, indifference is not the same thing as the child's paradise of innocence, but only the adult's self-conscious counterfeit of innocence. Both Anechka's bed and the sofa at Andrei Babichev's have the same end of returning Kavalerov to the state of childhood; in the latter case Olesha celebrates that return as a "flight back to childhood" through dreams. Kavalerov cannot consciously persist in competing either for fame or for a sexual object, for he has so little chance for success; only by withdrawal and a counterfeit return to childhood can he preserve his sanity. But Olesha is aware that such a flight back to childhood, however nostalgic, is a hopeless one, and so Kavalerov's return is to a "childhood" in which the conflicts of adulthood are still vividly alive—he is doomed to eternal castration by the mother and to eternal conflict with the father.

Kavalerov's sexual failure is developed in a dream of his which comes near the novel's end. In the dream he lies, concealed behind the socle of a pediment, at the foot of a flight of stairs which he does not climb. At the top of the staircase stand Andrei Babichev and Volodia. Up to them floats Valia, wafted by the music of a band. Kavalerov shrinks back to take cover under his blanket (transplanted, apparently, into his dream from the real world of his bed). The dream is obviously sexual, but Kavalerov's failure to climb the stairs suggests his failure to achieve a sexual object.

As the novel progresses, Ivan Babichev tends more and more to replace Kavalerov as the novel's hero and the focus of Olesha's interest. Kept off the stage deliberately to increase suspense, he appears as a complete figure only in the second part of the novel. He is introduced partly to fill the gap created by Kavalerov's inadequacy. He is the ideologist of a *Weltanschauung* toward which Kavalerov has been drifting, as it were, intuitively. He is also introduced as a foil to his brother, and the kinship of the two brothers is of course deliberate on the part of the author.

In several characteristics Ivan Babichev suggests Charlie Chaplin, and Olesha's interest in Chaplin is well known.[18] Both wear a derby hat, both are buffoons, both mock vested authority. There are also significant differences: Ivan Babichev is short, like Chaplin, but he is also stout. His stoutness marks his kinship to his brother Andrei and suggests that, like his brother, he too is fundamentally impotent. Psychoanalytic theory holds that the clown exhibits himself to compensate for a sense of sexual inadequacy; such exhibition even tends frequently to be transvestite or bisexual in character.[19]

Ivan is a burgher (Chaplin usually plays a proletarian), a burgher turned Bohemian. To be sure, we are asked to believe that he was once married, that he has a daughter, Valia. But it is difficult to imagine Ivan, the buffoon and tramp, the "king of vulgarians" (*korol' poshliakov*), as ever married. His relation to Valia is symbolic: she has been taken from him by Andrei and Volodia Makarov, and he now seeks to lure her to return. His claim to be her father is his claim to be a true apostle of the romantic dream, but in fact he is a false prophet, and Valia was never his. She, the princess of the fairy tale, has no real father, and falls share, ironically, to the unromantic masters of the future, Volodia and Andrei. Ivan's real child is the fantastic machine, Ophelia, who turns on her creator to destroy him.

There is something in Ivan of the buffoons of Dostoevski. Like them he is a frustrated member of the middle class, like them a compulsive liar and dreamer and masochistic seeker for attention from others. But, even though all his threats turn out empty lies, there is something a bit terrifying about Ivan. He is introduced very gradually and rather late in the novel, like a figure of suspense (a procedure illustrated in the novels of Dostoevski by Svidrigailov and Stavrogin). He is a leader of the multitudes of the frustrated and the disaffected, and he well understands that even utopia cannot satisfy their real desires or salve the wounds of their injured and disaffected spirits. A recent study suggests that Olesha conceived Ivan as both an "anti-Lenin," that is, a spirit of resistance to the Leninist social order, and an Antichrist.[20]

Ivan Babichev is the ideologist of Kavalerov's frustrated romanticism. Unlike Kavalerov, he has a sense of perspective where he himself is concerned and is well aware that he belongs to a dying order which cannot survive. Hence he argues that the main thing for a dreamer is "to make a scandal," "to go out with a bang, so that a scar will be left on the ugly mug of history." Ivan preaches revolt, though he realizes that thus he is jeopardizing his own freedom; indeed, he is arrested, interrogated by the GPU, and released with a warning to desist from his activities.

Ivan Babichev preaches his gospel of protest to actresses dreaming of fame, to unhappy lovers, old maids, bookkeepers,[21] persons consumed with ambition, fools, knights, cowards—to everyone considered a "decadent." He fears that the new socialist order will progress at the price of eliminating all human feelings. Hence he develops his celebrated "conspiracy of feelings." Among those feelings he fears threatened are love, tenderness, and pity. But it is apparent that Ivan does not really believe in such feelings; though he professes to believe in love, he preaches to a pair of newlyweds that they "need not love one another" and warns the groom that the child of his loins will devour him. The feelings which Ivan actually values are those which serve to estrange the individual from his fellow men: pride, envy, jealousy, foolish heroism. Thus Ivan's "conspiracy of feelings," preached in the name of life, is against life. But Ivan is not entirely wrong, either, and the author leaves the conflict unresolved. For utopia alone will not bring husband and wife to love each other, nor will it eliminate old maids or unrequited lovers. For such Ivan provides at least the balm of words and dreams.

The most terrifying aspects of Ivan's revolt are bound up in the

conception of a machine, Ophelia, which can do anything, and which
is created to kill Andrei and destroy the Chetvertak. Of course, such
a machine does not actually exist. Still, the machine Ophelia does
appear in several imaginary scenes, and in the expressionistic plane
of the novel it apparently functions as if it were real. Ophelia is a
nightmare fantasy, a machine created by feelings of envy and hatred
as the weapon of a "conspiracy of feelings," to destroy machines and
the whole technological order. True, Ophelia is said to be human,
to sing songs, pick flowers, to love, weep, be jealous, behold dreams.
As human, Ophelia is an expressionistic embodiment of Ivan's protest
against a machine civilization. Ivan gives his fantastic machine the
name of Ophelia because that name is for him "the most human, the
most touching"; Ophelia, who went mad from unrequited love, is
the representative of the whole crowd of solitary eccentrics to whom
Ivan preaches. Their estrangement may lead to madness, and the
name Ophelia does in fact suggest madness. And Andrei accuses
Ivan of being mad, for madness is the final culmination of those feelings of estrangement which Ivan cherishes.

The word for machine in Russian (*mashina*) is feminine in gender.
Indeed, the tendency to conceive of machines as feminine may well
be deeper than the casual association of grammatical gender, as in
the case of English, where a machine when personalized is often referred to as "she." Thus the myth of Ophelia seems to be rooted in
an unconscious pattern which regards the machine as animate. Moreover, the machine has an ambiguous symbolic meaning with a long
literary tradition. The machine is dead—technology is contrasted to
the organic world—but also, paradoxically, it is alive, or at least provides an imitation of life or a parody of it. The machine is opposed
to life as a counterfeit of it. This is the inner sense of the expressionistic myth of the machine which turns on its human master and destroys him.[22] This myth is found in *Envy*, where, in a fantasy scene,
Ophelia impales her master on a long, needle-like proboscis.

Ivan realizes and fears that Ophelia may turn against him. His fear
is justified by his final realization that woman and life are not with
him in his conspiracy of feelings, but against him. Hence Ophelia, as
irrational feminine principle, must kill her own creator. She is feminine by virtue of the ironic fact that woman, who represents life, is
not with Ivan in his revolt, for it is directed against life.

Though Ophelia is clearly feminine, she has a phallus, the needle
on which Ivan is impaled. What is the purpose of this apparent contradiction? Castration of the male is not the natural role of the female; it

is itself a contradiction. The sexual castration of one male by another might be a natural expression of sexual competition, but the castration of a male by a female frustrates the biological role of both sexes. Ophelia's phallus is an expressionistic symbol of this contradiction.[23] And the symbol is needed to illustrate Ivan's impotence: he and his conspiracy of self-destructive feelings can create only a monster which destroys him. Lifeless, Ophelia is a monstrous parody of that sterile technological order which she has been created to destroy.

In these observations I have ignored the question of the extent to which Olesha was conscious of the motifs of castration and sterility he employed in *Envy*. The question is perhaps not quite so relevant as might appear at first sight. Relatively little is known of Olesha's life, but even if more biographical information were available, it might not help us. Such psychic attitudes as fear of sterility or of castration are not necessarily manifested externally, for they are normally not conscious fears. Only a very close, and presumably a long, acquaintance with the author would give us reliable information. But such conflicts are often manifested in symbolic projections, among which imaginative literature falls; it is just to Olesha's writings, then, that we can look for the proper evidence. This is not because we are seeking more information about his life, which is in a sense irrelevant for us, a private fact, but because we are seeking to connect and illuminate the various aspects and planes of the work of fiction we are studying.

Still, two anecdotes from Olesha's memoirs may be of some interest and relevance. Olesha was extremely fond of the circus. Once as a young man he witnessed a performance by three acrobats, two men and a girl. He tells us that he fell in love with the girl, with the way her hair flew in the breeze. Several days later he saw the same two men on the street. With them, however, was no girl, but a young, unattractive boy of bad complexion who spat, and whom Olesha at first took for an assistant. Suddenly he realized that this was the "girl" with whom he had fallen in love. And, Olesha adds, he remained in love with her all his life.[24]

In the second anecdote Olesha tells of how, late in life, he handled a woman's mask, how the hollows of the nose and cheeks reminded him of a smile, the smile of a young and beautiful face. And he writes:

> When you threw it down, it fell on the table with an almost inaudible sound. It was all lightness, all charm, all love.
> Few objects, perhaps, were so charming as that mask. It was woman.[25]

These reminiscences illustrate an obvious sexual ambivalence, a turning away from real flesh-and-blood woman to an ethereal creature, a woman who is pure Platonic ideal, light, airy, unreal, symbolized metonymically by hair flying in the breeze or a mask, whose contours are only the obverse of the facial lines of a real woman. We can now better comprehend the ethereal character of Valia.[26] For both Kavalerov and Olesha love is etherealized escape from the horror of oppressive reality, symbolized in the novel by the ogre woman, Anechka.

It is not my purpose to overturn existing interpretations of *Envy*, most of which emphasize ideological attitudes toward socialism and the conflict of "old" and "new" orders. Indeed, the present study only seems to confirm the ambivalence which earlier critics have detected in Olesha's attitude concerning the old and the new: both orders are for him sterile and opposed to life as organic force. The right way is a third way, which would be a synthesis of the organic and the technological.[27]

The male characters in *Envy* are all sterile. The female figures (Anechka, Ophelia) are castrators. Only Valia is an exception, for she scarcely exists, and even in the domain of the author's fantasy she is a shadowy figure, a creature of dreams. She is hardly a sexual figure, or her sexuality is repressed, a sacrifice, presumably, to a value conflict between sexual and idealized romantic traits in the author himself.

Both brothers are impostors. Both pretend to stand for life itself, though both have enough insight to realize, and at times even to admit, their imposture. Kavalerov looks to each of them in turn to find the secret of life but is disillusioned with both. Both fail to comprehend life and are forced to admit their failure. Andrei concerns himself only with the tasks of nourishing and providing, abandoning both sexuality and creativity. The utopian state can only nourish; it cannot love or create. It is a sterile hermaphroditic parent. But the individual's rebellious response is also sterile, and leads to his spiritual castration by the new technological social order. Ivan with his strange gospel consoles the frustrated who themselves have failed to find life or to win the objects of their ambition or sexual desire. Both brothers admit their sterility, but both seek also to conceal it by attracting followers, by adopting spiritual sons. Thus *Envy* presents us with a choice of two worlds in conflict, both of which are sterile: the old order, with its romantic escapism, and the new, with its cult of technology and contempt for human values.

VIKTOR SHKLOVSKY

Isaac Babel: A Critical Romance

I find myself somehow reluctant to take a close look at Babel. An author's success must be respected, and the reader should be given the opportunity to learn to like a writer before trying to figure out the reasons for his success.

I'm ashamed to take a close look at Babel. His story *The Rabbi's Son* (*Syn rabbi*) contains this passage: "The girls, planting their unpretentious bandy doe legs on the floor, stared coldly at his sexual organs, that stunted, tender, curly-haired masculinity of a wasted Semite."

So for my article on Babel I have chosen the method of lyrical distancing. Once there was old Russia, enormous, like a mountain spread wide with furrowed slopes.

Some people wrote upon her with pencils, "This mountain will be saved."

That was before the Revolution.

Some of those who had written on the mountain in pencil worked on Gorky's *Chronicle*. Gorky had just arrived. He was stooped, discontented, sick, and he wrote the article "Two Souls." A highly erroneous article.

A story by Babel appeared in one issue. It concerned two young girls who tried unsuccessfully to perform an abortion. Their father held the post of prosecutor in Kamchatka. Everyone noticed that story and remembered it. Then I met Babel himself. Average height, high forehead, huge head, a face unlike a writer's, quiet dress, entertaining conversation.

Came the Revolution, and the mountain was cleared away. There were some who still ran after it with pencils in their hands. There was nothing left for them to write on.

Just then Sukhanov[1] started to write. Seven volumes of reminis-

From *Lef, zhurnal levogo fronta iskusstva*, No. 6 (1924), pp. 152-62.

cences. They say he wrote them before the events happened, since he foresaw everything.

I arrived from the front. It was autumn. Gorky's *Novaya Zhizn* was still being published.

In it Babel wrote some comments under the heading "The New Day." He was the only one who maintained his stylistic sangfroid throughout the Revolution.

Babel's sketches dealt with such things as how plowing is done today. It was then that I became better acquainted with him. He turned out to be an imperturbable man with a concerned voice, and a lover of fine feeling.

For him fine feeling was as necessary as a country house (*dacha*).

I met Babel for the third time in Petersburg in 1919. Petersburg was covered with snow in winter, as if the city itself stood snowbound in the middle of a road, only it was something like a latticed snow fence along a railroad track. In summer Petersburg was covered by a deep blue sky. There was no smoke from the chimneys, and the sun hung over the horizon; no one interfered with it. Petersburg was empty—its inhabitants were at the front. Among the cobblestones on the streets the grass in little shoots of green flame struggled up towards the sun.

Side streets were already grassed over.

In front of the Hermitage, on the wooden pavement which was resonant right at that place, children played at skittles with torn up blocks. The city was beginning to be grown over, like an abandoned military camp.

Babel lived on 25th of October Street, No. 86.

He lived alone in his furnished apartment; his visitors came and went. Maidservants saw to his needs, cleaned the rooms, emptied the buckets with bits of unfinished food floating in them.

Babel lived, contemplating at leisure the city's hungry lechery. His room was clean. He would tell me that "nowadays" women could be had only before six since the streetcars stopped running after that.

He had no feeling of alienation from life. But I had the impression that when he went to bed, Babel would sign his name to each completed day as though it were a story. The tools of the man's trade had left their mark on him.

A samovar inevitably graced Babel's table, and even sometimes bread. And that was a rarity in those days.

He was always a warm and willing host. A certain retired chemist used to visit him, a Tolstoyan and also a teller of incredible anecdotes.

He was the man who, having publicly insulted the duke of Baden, appeared at his own trial in Petersburg to testify against himself. (However he was pronounced insane and punished only by having his laboratory confiscated.) He was a bad poet and an indifferent critic, that most unlikely man, Peter Storytsin. And Babel valued Storytsin.

Kondrat Yakovlev visited him, a few others, I myself, and some veterans from Odessa who were always ready to tell a tale, along with other assorted Odessites, who told all the stories that were written in them.

Babel wrote little, but steadily. It was always the same story—about two Chinamen in a brothel.

He loved that story as he loved Storytsin. The Chinamen and the women kept changing. They grew young, aged, broke windows, beat up a woman, organized this or that.

A good many stories resulted from all this, and not just one. Though he had not really finished with his Chinamen, Babel went away one sunny autumn day, leaving me his grey sweater and leather satchel. . . . There was no word at all from Babel; it was as though he'd gone to Kamchatka to talk to the prosecutor about his daughters.

Once a visiting Odessite, after having spent all night losing at cards in a well-known house, and having borrowed enough the next morning to cover his loss, offered me as a sign of gratitude the information that Babel was either translating from the French or putting together a book of stories from a book of anecdotes. Later, when I was wounded and was passing through Kharkov, I heard that Babel had been killed while with the Red Cavalry.

Fate, in its own time, worked a hundred changes in each of us.

In 1924 I again met Babel. I learned from him that he had not been killed, though he'd been beaten at great length.

He hadn't changed. He could tell even more interesting stories. From Odessa and the front he had brought with him two books. The Chinamen had been forgotten, stowed away in one particular story.

The new pieces were beautifully written. I don't think there's anyone else nowadays who writes as well as he does. He has been compared to Maupassant, because readers sense a French influence, and they are quick to name a sufficiently worthy object of comparison. But I prefer another name—Flaubert. The Flaubert of Salammbô. The Flaubert of that marvelous operatic libretto.

The shiniest jackboots, handsome as young girls, the whitest riding breeches, bright as a standard against the sky; even a fire blazing as bright as Sunday, cannot be compared with Babel's style.

A stranger from Paris—from Paris alone with no touch of London—Babel saw Russia as a French writer a century earlier, conscripted into Napoleon's Grande Armée, might have seen it.

The Chinamen were no longer needed; their place had been taken by Cossacks from French illustrations.

Connoisseurs of flattery say that its very effective if your "sweet talk" is couched in abusive language. "The peculiar force that results from the use of words whose lexical coloration [sense—ed.] is the opposite of their intonational effect arises from the fact that one feels the incongruity." (Yury Tynyanov, *The Problem of Poetic Language*)

Babel's principal device is to speak in the same tone of voice of the stars above and of gonorrhea.

Babel's lyrical passages are not successful. [. . .]

In his descriptions Babel adopts an elevated tone and enumerates many beautiful things. He writes:

> Here we are, you and I, walking about in this magic garden, this Finnish forest that almost baffles description. All our lives we shall never see anything more beautiful. And you can't see the pink edges of the frozen waterfall, over there by the stream! You are blind to the Japanese chiseling of the weeping willow leaning over the waterfall. The red trunks of the pines are covered by snow in which a thousand sparks are gleaming. The snow, shapeless when it fell, has draped itself along the branches, lying on their surfaces that undulate like a line drawn by Leonardo. In the snow flaming clouds are reflected. And think what you'd have to say about *Fröken* Kirsti's silk stockings; about the line of her leg, that lovely line!"

True, this passage ends with: "Get yourself some eyeglasses, Aleksandr Fyodorovich, I beseech you" (*Line and Color—Liniya i tsvet*).

Babel is gifted, and he is able, by the device of an irony communicated just in time, to render acceptable the highly colored objects he describes.

Without the irony it would be painful to read such things.

He even anticipates our objections and provides a designation for his tableaux: "opera":

> The scorched town—broken columns and, dug into the earth, the hooks of the little malevolent fingers of old women—seemed to me raised aloft in the air, as snug and chimerical as a dream. The crude brightness of the moon flowed down on it with inexhaustible force. The damp mold of the ruins flowered

like the marble of opera seats. And I waited, disturbed in spirit, for Romeo to appear from the clouds, a satin-clad Romeo singing of love, while a dismal electrician in the wings keeps a finger on the moon-extinguisher.

I used to compare *Red Cavalry* (*Konarmiya*) with Gogol's *Taras Bulba*. There are decided similarities in certain techniques. That "letter" telling of the murder of a father by his son is a Gogolian plot turned inside out. Babel also uses the Gogolian trick of enumerating family names, a device that may have its roots in the classical tradition. But with Babel the enumeration is suddenly broken off. The Cossack Melnikov writes:

> For thirteen days I've been fighting with the rear guard, protecting the invincible First Cavalry, and am finding myself under hot rifle, artillery, and air fire from the enemy. Tardy has been killed, Lukhmannikov has been killed, Lykoshenko has been killed, Gulevoy has been killed, Trunov has been killed, and the white stallion is no longer under me, so, in line with the changing fortunes of war, don't count on seeing your beloved divisional commander Timoshenko, Comrade Melnikov, but we'll meet again, in—to be blunt about it—the kingdom of heaven, though rumor has it the old man in heaven hasn't a kingdom, but a regular whorehouse, and there's plenty of clap on earth already, so maybe we won't see each other after all. So long then, Comrade Melnikov.

Babel's Cossacks are all insufferably and ineffably handsome. "Ineffable" is a favorite word of Babel's. Babel makes use of two contradictions, which in his work take the place of plot: 1) His style is in contrast to the life he describes, and 2) that life is in contrast to the author himself.

He is a stranger in the army, a foreigner who has a right to be surprised. When he describes the military way of life he accentuates the "weakness and despair" of the observer.

In addition to *Red Cavalry*, Babel has written *Odessa Tales* (*Odesskie rasskazy*). These are full of descriptions of various bandits. The atmosphere of banditry and the bandits' motley chattels Babel requires as a justification of his own style.

We recall that the divisional commander had "jackboots that looked like girls"; but consider the aristocrats of the Moldavanka district, who "were girded in crimson vests. Russet jackets covered their steely shoulders, and azure leather burst its seams around their fleshy feet" (*The King—Korol*).

Babel is a stranger in both worlds. He is a stranger even in Odessa. There he's told: "Forget for a time that you've spectacles on your nose, but autumn in your heart. Stop raising hell at your writing desk and stammering in public. Imagine for a moment that you raise hell on the streets and stammer on paper." Of course those remarks don't describe Babel. He isn't like that at all; he doesn't stammer. He's a brave man. I even think that "he could spend the night with a Russian woman and the Russian woman would be satisfied."

Because the Russian female loves eloquence. Babel plays the part of a foreigner because that device, like irony, facilitates his writing. And even Babel would not dare attempt high emotion without irony.

When Babel writes, he keeps the music to himself while describing the motions of the dance, yet at the same time he renders the whole piece in a high register. No doubt it was from the epic that he borrowed the device of giving answers which repeat the questions:

Benya Krik in the *Odessa Tales* talks that way:

> Grach asked him:
> "Who are you, where do you come from and what do you fill your lungs with?"
> "Try me out, Froim," answered Benya, "and let's stop playing around."
> "Let's stop playing around," said Grach. "I'll try you out."

And the Cossacks in *The Letter* (*Pismo*) speak in the same way:

> And Senka asked Timofey Rodionych:
> "Are you doing all right, Dad, in my hands?"
> "No," Dad said . . . "doing badly."
> Then Senka asked:
> "And Fedya, when you cut him up, was he doing all right?"
> "No," said Dad, "Fedya did badly."

Babel's books are excellent books. Russian literature is as grey as a siskin; it needs crimson riding breeches and boots of sky-blue leather.

It also needs the thing that Babel understood when he left his Chinamen to fend for themselves and set off with the "Red Cavalry."

Literary heroes, girls, old people and young people in all their possible situations are long since played out. Literature needs concreteness, and it must interbreed with our new way of life in order to create a new form.

TRANSLATED BY JOHN PEARSON

ANDREY SINYAVSKY

Isaac Babel

The literary heritage left by Babel is not very voluminous. This leading Russian writer willingly accepted the title "craftsman of silence"; he took a long time maturing and finishing his works and was never in a hurry to turn them over to the public. His care for the perfection of each phrase, for purity of language, seem more the work of a poet than of a prose writer. No one more than he has justified the famous formula of Jules Renard: "Prose ought to be a poem which is not divided into lines."

The most important work of Babel is *Red Cavalry*, in which his method and his style found their most complete expression. The tales that compose it, published in various periodicals from 1921 to 1924, then collected as a book in 1926, raised him at once to the first rank of Soviet writers.

What strikes one first of all in Babel is the variety of characters, of situations, and of styles. A sublime pathos appears alongside images of the most brutal reality, painted with the precision of a naturalist. Light and shadow, the beautiful and the hideous, are juxtaposed in combinations that are unexpected and often bizarre. The law of contrasts directs the development of subjects, the selection of details, the juxtaposition of words. The choice of heroes in Babel's narratives, of the characters that people *Red Cavalry*, is very significant in this regard. In their psychology good and evil rub elbows and interpenetrate, and in one and the same character, traits cohabit that at first sight seem irreconcilable: cruelty and magnanimity, brutality and tenderness, infamy and innocence. Even the appearance of Babel's heroes is often paradoxical: " 'Warsaw is ours' howled the Cossack in bast shoes and a derby hat. . . ." Such also is the language of the illiterate mass who

From *Oeuvres et opinions*, No. 8 (August 1964).

rise above their ignorance, the common but salty language of disheveled revolutionaries. Political slogans mingle with a frequently obscene argot, journalistic clichés with coarse oaths: "Let's die for pickled cucumbers and the world revolution!"—here is an example of language that is as expressive and as contradictory as the character of the men who use it.

Babel has taken for the material of his tales impressions gathered in 1920 during the Polish campaign of the First Cavalry Army. But this has nothing to do with a chronicle of military history. He is careful to avoid copying events "in their raw grandeur." Deliberately, he condenses colors, alters proportions, creates confrontations between extremes in the life and the consciousness of his heroes. His whole effort is centered on the rough-hewn man of the masses, loaded with defects and vices, but compelling admiration by his courage, even his heroism. Far from idealizing his characters, Babel carries the play of black-and-white to grotesque lengths, accentuating and exaggerating at will, and makes us see in his Red Cavalry the moral and esthetic greatness of these men, even though they are stained with blood and mire.

Several tales, developing an argument which is essential for anyone who wants to grasp the main idea of Red Cavalry, present two different points of view: the dream of a good-natured and harmless revolution, without bloodshed, to which is opposed the author's conviction: "It's impossible not to shoot, because it's revolution."

The ideal of virile humanism is embodied in the soldiers and the officers of Red Cavalry, who chide the narrator for his softness, his poor adjustment to the rigors of military life. One of the basic points of Babel's style is that the narrator is not necessarily the spokesman of the author and cannot be identified with the real "I" of the writer, which is hidden, camouflaged under the twists and turns of the action. Constantly ironic in regard to his autobiographical hero, Babel takes pleasure in uncrowning, even humiliating him. Their contrast with this pleasantly scatterbrained intellectual makes even more striking the heroic traits of the combatants of the Red Cavalry.

The depiction of characters and the artistic weaving of plot in Red Cavalry reveal to us the two sides of the work of Babel. The lucidity of the realist does not chill the impetuous temperament of the romantic. His heroes of flesh and blood bathe "in torrents of luxury and power," in a climate of the marvelous and the extraordinary. Handsome, gaudily clothed, camped in a rich setting, they often seem to us like figures in an epic, whose very appearance compels wonder.

"Savitsky, the commander of the 6th division, rose at my approach and I was struck by the beauty of his giant's body. He rose, and the purple of his breeches, his raspberry-red cap pushed a little to one side, the decorations pinned to his chest, cut the hut in two as a banner cuts the sky."

Babel is prodigal of bright colors, of resplendent, glistening garments. We find "the pearly mist of birches," "clouds sailing like swans," blood flowing "like a brook with coral foam," in short, all the battle gear of romantic literature. The tone rises readily to the emphatic and the sublime. The author can't resist uttering sentiments which suffuse his book with waves of emotion that sometimes seems affected. But this sentimentality is only the canvas for scenes and personages conceived in a quite different register, rigorous and stripped-down to the point of asceticism.

Babel—like his heroes—does what one least expects at any given moment. At points of extreme dramatic tension, these characters manifest a remarkable calm. On the other hand, they sob, tear their garments, pass from despair to jubilation, for reasons which may seem to us very trifling. One of these heroes, Afonka Bida, weeps hot tears on learning of the discharge of his commanding officer, but remains unmoved when it is a question of carrying out the last wish of a mortally wounded comrade. "You must waste a cartridge on me. . . . Those Polish bastards will be coming, they'll make sport of me." In Babel, emotional reaction is in inverse proportion to the event that excited it.

Babel's restraint is extreme. As soon as a heroic exploit or a tragic event comes up, he affects impassivity, letting the action speak for him. His characters die and kill with simplicity, without self-serving poses, without impressive eloquence. All the more moving are those scenes whose very bareness creates their horror and their majesty. This is how squadron chief Trunov goes to certain death by engaging in unequal combat with an enemy airplane:

> He scaled the envelope, sat down on the ground, and, grunting with the effort, pulled off his boots.
> "Here," said he, handing the boots and the envelope to the machine gunners. "They can still be used, they're brand new."
> "Good luck, chief," mumbled the machine gunners in reply, shuffling around, unable to make up their minds to leave.
> "Good luck to you too," said Trunov. "Well, anyway, boys—"
> And he headed toward the machine gun installed on a mound, behind the sentry box. Andrey Vosmiletov, the tradesman, was waiting for him there.

"Well, OK," Trunov said to him, setting up the machine
gun. "You're staying with me, right?"

"Jesus Christ!" answered Andrey, terrified. He gave a short
sob, blanched, and burst out laughing: "Christ and damn!"

And he aimed the second machine gun at the plane.

In episodes of this kind, the essence of the action is concealed.
Babel does not explain to us what is happening. He pretends not to
know about motives, and contents himself with relating the action,
the bare external facts of the case. It is up to the reader to draw conclusions from them, to confront the facts and see, under the calm recital of events, their deeper significance. Certain phrases spoken incidentally inform us that Trunov is sacrificing his life in order to divert
the enemy plane from the wood where the squadron has taken refuge.
These phrases are proffered in a tone which gives the impression that
it is a question of an unimportant incident.

> The major and his three gunners performed beautifully in
> this battle. They went down to an altitude of three hundred
> meters and aimed their machine gun at Andrey first, then at
> Trunov. All the bullets fired by our men had not done the
> slightest harm to the Americans; the planes left without notic-
> ing the squadron hidden in the wood. So after waiting a half
> hour we could go and pick up the bodies.

The author sees fit to dilute the heroism of this scene and to send
us off on a false scent. Hence the know-how of the American gunners
and the ineffectiveness of our machine gunners which might lead one
to believe that the death of Trunov and Andrey was useless. And finally that little tag-end of a phrase with such a detached sound:
"After waiting half an hour," whose unbearable inner tension is concealed under a bland exterior.

The lack of agreement between the form and the content of a remark, between the meaning of a sentence and its intonation or its
vocabulary, is customary in Babel. The terrifying is told gently, the
sublime, coarsely. Tragic events are related to us with the vulgar
awkwardness of an illiterate, bordering on burlesque. The purpose of
this is to deflate solemn bombast, to bring the story down to earth.

The same is true in the brutally physiological descriptions he uses
to tell about the habits and the characters of the heroes of *Red Cavalry*. Taboo topics, ultrarealistic images, fill Babel's tales, contrasting
violently with the most exalted romanticism. They serve as dissonances
in this verbal symphony with its many expressive elements and insert
themselves in the romantic context like deep shadow next to brilliant
light.

The presence and the interaction in Babel of such different elements (the fantastic and the documentary, the sparkling metaphor and the trivial statement, the lyric flight and the unemotional recital) give to his images and his language an unequaled power of expression. Neutral and colorless phrases are almost totally absent from his texts. The language is laden with sensibility and creates images that are almost physically perceptible, almost dazzling: "The barn was crammed with new-mown hay, as exciting as perfume"; "an odor of lilies pure and strong as alcohol." Supersaturating his style, Babel pushes to the extreme the materiality of the world and the clarity of the image of it that he offers.

The laconic style in which our author excels goes along with this intensity of verbal expression. It is not just a question of the art of brevity in writing. Revealing to us in one of his tales his most cherished thoughts about style, Babel credits his brevity with enormous expressive power:

". . . I am speaking of style, of the army of words, of an army in which all the arms are in movement. No metal can pierce the human heart with such paralyzing violence as a period placed at just the right spot."

It is the quest for the greatest possible expressiveness that motivates Babel's laconic style. The more confined the verbal space, the weightier the significance of each word that penetrates our consciousness like the point of a lance, provoking an explosive reaction. The prose of *Red Cavalry* would be unsuitable for a novel of large dimension: it is made to deliver quick blows, and the violent effects the author is fond of would be weakened if used over too long a space. The style of our epoch, said Babel, consists "in courage, in restraint, and it is full of fire, of passion, of power, and of gaiety."

The maturity and extraordinary originality of Babel's talent are fully manifested in *Red Cavalry*. This said, one may observe how the most unexpected artistic traditions meet and intermingle in his work.

Maxim Gorky played an exceptionally important role in Babel's literary career. Like many other Soviet writers, Babel passed through the school of Gorky. To him he owed his literary debut. It was Gorky who in 1916 published in his review *Chronicle* the first stories of Babel. In them the author of *Red Cavalry* can be only dimly discerned. The tone of the narration is dull, lacking in expression and poetry. This was chiefly the result of the paltry inner experience of the young writer, freshly arrived in Petrograd after a period in a commercial school. In the time that followed, Babel temporarily abandoned literature. He took off on long travels, took part in grain requisitioning campaigns, fought with the Army of the North and in the First Cavalry Army. After these experiences he undertook again the craft of writing. Having plunged, on the advice of Gorky, into the whirlwinds of revolutionary reality, he had not only stored up experiences and impressions, but he had also found his place in the struggles of his times and had taken a position on both the artistic and the ideological level. Such was the road that led him to *Red Cavalry*, which introduced a new stage in his life and his work. Very significantly, the gestation of this book was likewise linked with the name of Gorky. Babel sent him his new stories and Gorky replied that "he might begin now." Understandably Babel considered Gorky "his first and principal teacher."

But along with this his style indicated predilections that were quite foreign to Gorky. One must cite to this effect Babel's piece *Odessa* (1916), his first attempt at an esthetic program. Russian literature, Babel affirms, developed till now under the sign of Petersburg, grey, morose, and crepuscular, to which must be opposed another symbol of faith—Odessa, city of the sea and of the sun, blossoming in a perpetual climate of festival and of light.

This sunlit esthetic, proclaimed from the writer's earliest youth, is masterfully embodied in the *Tales of Odessa*, published at the same time as *Red Cavalry*, in 1923 and 1924. The Odessa cycle is distinguished not only by a heady "local color," but also by esthetic principles that are clearly new. The talent of Babel appears in a novel light.

It is a gush of gaiety, of joy, of light. The humor of Babel, purposely suppressed in the accounts of the war, where it served mainly to accentuate the atrocious and the tragic, gives itself free rein here and becomes the preponderant element. The mischievous smile of the author of the *Tales of Odessa* is a sign of exuberance, of energy, of joie de vivre. This laughter is born of youth and health, of the fullness of physical and moral vigor, of a happy springtime acceptance of life. "The boys dragged the girls behind hedges, and the sound of kisses rose over the tombstones."

Descriptions of customs (weddings, burials, marriage proposals, and so forth) occupy the first level of *Tales of Odessa*. But these are fantastic pictures which seduce precisely by their unusual character, the brilliance of their exotic colors. Babel's Odessa is a fairyland where local images and national traits are surrounded by a halo of legend. At Odessa the power of His Imperial Majesty ends, and there begins the realm of Benya Krik, the gentleman-burglar, king of the bandits of Odessa. Here ragged Jews perform prodigies of valor, defy the police, and terrorize the rich. The women have Titanic strength, unheard-of height, and stentorian voices. The beggars drink Jamaica rum and smoke cigars which have come straight from the plantations of John Pierpont Morgan.

Here everything is excessive. "Odessa had never seen and the whole world never will see such a funeral." And so on—up to the drunken workman who sprawls "right in the middle of the universe" and not just in the gutter. Odessa is promoted to the rank of center of the world, it comes to be administered by marvelous laws and traditions. The image of the real city is enriched by the dream of the famished barefoot beggar. And precisely because most of these pictures exist only in the imagination of Odessans, the exaggeration, the bragging became an unending source of comedy. Just the opposite of *Red Cavalry*, the romanticism of *Tales of Odessa* is subordinated to the humor, and performs the function of a conventional device, purposely exaggerated by the author. What in *Red Cavalry* borders on the sublime here provokes hilarity. In *Tales of Odessa* the most prosaic things take on the air of an epic. At a wedding celebration the wine brings forth "belches as loud as a battle trumpet." The account teems with amusing incongruities, absurd comparisons, exaggeration, and droll fakery.

Babel worked very strenuously on the cycles which compose *Red Cavalry* and *Tales of Odessa*. In each of these collections the tales are linked by subject, by material, by theme, and by style.

From 1925 on Babel's pace slows; he spreads himself over a multiplicity of genres and types of writing, tries his hand in the theater and in the cinema (*Sunset*, produced in 1928, the scenario *Benya Krik*, and so forth). His short stories and tales of the second half of the twenties and of the thirties are marked by extremely unorthodox content. His style undergoes noticeable changes. He evolves toward a less expressive prose, toward broader, more circumstantial forms.

In May 1939, Babel was arrested and soon after perished. But his projects and his writings of the last period permit us to say that this was for him a time not only of preparation but also of work in progress on books of great interest.

Publishing only the works about which he felt completely confident, Babel wrote much more than he published and didn't like to divulge his literary projects, his conceptions of art. We can, however, judge of his esthetic ideas, of his searches and his meditations, as indicated in several stories dealing with the theme of art, and chiefly in his autobiographical writings of the years 1925-30. These evocations of the years of childhood came, in order of importance, immediately after *Red Cavalry* and *Tales of Odessa*. A direct line of descent links them to the autobiographical accounts of Gorky. Moreover, the first of these pieces, *The Story of My Dovecote (Istoriya moei golubyatnei)*, was dedicated to Gorky. Babel here in his way replies to the famous question of Gorky: Why did you begin to write, and what childhood impressions inclined you to your vocation? The emphasis is placed on problems that are of capital importance for Babel: the romantic and the realistic vision of the world, dream and reality, the truth of fact and the truth of fiction. Thus, while recounting his childhood, he analyzes his evolution as a writer and defines his conception of literary creation.

In this connection one must examine the story *My First Honorarium (Pervy gonorar)*. In order to understand it correctly, one must consider the particular characteristics of Babel's style: the nonconformity of content and form, the tendency to "debasement" through contrast, and to mystification which creates the illusion of the documentary exactness of an autobiographical account when it's really a matter of pure fiction. Whether they were founded on fiction or on authentic fact, the works of Babel should always be viewed in the perspective of art and analyzed according to the logic of art and not of life.

In the story in question, *My First Honorarium*, the artist's noble role is degraded to the contrivance of a hoax calculated to shock the conventional taste. His first honorarium, the author says, was the money which, when he was young, a prostitute refused, touched by a story— which was itself shocking enough—that he had reeled off to her. In this pseudoautobiographical form, in this crude representation of the most sordid venal love, Babel offers moral and esthetic ideas rich in exalted poetry and philosophic profundity. The young hero of *My First Honorarium*, devoured by the passion to write, and by love for the one who sees in him only a client among many others, tells her a fanciful story of his unhappy childhood. This story, a real work of art, moves the girl to the point where she repays him with a sincere and honest love, really his "first honorarium," and the only thing capable of repaying the torment and the illumination of artistic creation.

The narrative of the hero, presented as a worthy model of the literary craft, is at the same time so unconventional and so simple that the most audacious fiction takes on the force of complete authenticity.

In a general way, the problem of truth and fiction has always obsessed Babel, especially in that new, transitory period of his career as a writer, when his style was changing and when the realistic vision of the world was taking the upper hand. But for Babel, fiction was not the opposite of reality. The truth of fiction helped to penetrate the truth of life and to recreate it much more compellingly than a vulgar copy could. "To invent" is not "to deceive," but neither is it to copy facts just as they were or "are ordinarily." Art is the quest for the unexpected, the unaccustomed, the unique, themselves the source of veracity, for real experience always contains new elements and assumes discovery, creation, and not the repetition of what is already known.

In his speech at the First Congress of Soviet Writers, in 1934, Babel said: "Without elevated thought, without philosophy, there is no literature." His work corroborates this profession of faith. It bears the imprint of noble thought and perfect form. During his lifetime, criticism did not always pay homage to this philosophical aspect of the narratives of Babel. Fascinated by his skilled craftsmanship, it hardly looked beyond the beauties of his style. All the more because the author purposely disguised his thought, refused to impose it, or to present it circumstantially in grandiloquent and ostentatious declarations. In Babel, thought always fosters concrete images which speak by themselves, which form the inner content of a work intended for an attentive and thoughtful reader.

TRANSLATED BY CATHERINE BROWN

HUGH MCLEAN

Zoshchenko's Unfinished Novel: *Before Sunrise*

By one means or another, by subterfuge and camouflage, books were written and published in the Soviet Union, even during the Stalin era, which show the spark of true creativity, which, however fumblingly, attempted to find new forms for conveying new reflections on various aspects of human experience. One such book was Mikhail Zoshchenko's *Before Sunrise* (*Pered voskhodom solntsa*), two instalments of which appeared in the magazine *Oktiabr* in the autumn of 1943. Unfortunately, both Russian and Western literary scholars have failed to take adequate account of this remarkable work. The Russians, of course, were prohibited from doing so. After two instalments of *Before Sunrise* had appeared, its publication was stopped and the author subjected to a series of abusive political attacks, obviously inspired by the highest authorities; and since that time, thaw or not, there has been no sign of reversing the decision. *Before Sunrise* is still under a ban in Soviet Russia and seems likely to remain so. On the other hand, Western students of Soviet literature have largely contented themselves with re-hearsing the unpleasant facts connected with its suppression, retrospectively interpreting this display of ideological whip-cracking even during the relatively liberal war period as a premonition of the still harsher fate which awaited Zoshchenko and others in the Zhdanov era after the war. But the book has not been treated *in extenso;* the present article is an attempt to initiate such a discussion.[1]

Zoshchenko calls *Before Sunrise* a *povest* (novella), a term which usually signifies a work of narrative fiction of a length somewhere between the short story and the novel. But as we read the text, we may

From *Survey*, No. 36 (April-June 1961), pp. 99-105. Reprinted by permission of *Survey*.

doubt the appropriateness of this classification, both with respect to its character as fiction in general and its genre in particular.

The first question, is it fiction, is a thorny one for all literature, and particularly so for this work, in which the relation between *Dichtung* and *Wahrheit* is more than usually intimate. If this is fiction, it is fiction on the borderline of autobiography. Not only is the narrative presented in the first person, but the "I" is explicitly identified with the author himself. For instance, in the prologue, "I" announces, "Ten years ago I wrote a story called *Youth Restored*"; and it is a fact that in 1933 Mikhail Zoshchenko did indeed publish a book with this title. Innumerable other details coincide with known facts of Zoshchenko's own biography. Therefore, if the narrator is a fictional character, he is in many verifiable respects a fictional shadow of the historical Zoshchenko. The further question of whether the narrator's *private* experiences are also Zoshchenko's cannot be answered at this point; for this we would need extra-literary documentation not now available. But for our present purpose the problem of historical truth may be disregarded and the autobiographical element in *Before Sunrise* considered only from the point of view of its literary function.

It would appear that for artistic purposes of his own Zoshchenko is deliberately underlining the literature-life relationship, in fact attempting to erase the borderline between the two. Although this is a work of literature, he wants it taken seriously as a human document, a statement about life, and he therefore presents what he says as confession rather than invention. This device of apparently equating a lyric hero with a real author is of course an ancient stratagem in the literary world; it was a trademark of the Romantics, though they did not invent it.

As a matter of fact, throughout his literary career Zoshchenko had been fond of toying with the ambiguous relationship between the two planes, manipulating and often deliberately confusing them to achieve various effects. One of the devices is the use of a character labelled "the author," who may belong to either plane. Many of Zoshchenko's satirical pieces, especially from the 1920s, contain stray musings about life and the world which are presented as informal colloquies between the author and his readers; but the naïve substance and unliterary language of these digressions often seem to imply that the true author is hiding behind a mask of irony. In a collection of *povesti* called *Sentimental Tales* (1929) Zoshchenko lays bare this device, directing ironic attention to the literary trick itself. The book contains three prefaces, supposedly to three successive editions. The first two are signed by the putative author, one I. V. Kolenkorov, who expresses his gratitude to "the well-known writer Mikhail Zoshchenko" for his assistance in putting the tales into final form. In the third preface the assistant comes out from behind the scenes and announces:

> In view of previous misunderstandings the author informs his critics that the person who tells these stories is, so to speak, an imaginary figure. He represents that middling type of intellectual who happened to live on the borderline between two epochs. We were forced to endow this upstart of ours, Mr. I. V. Kolenkorov, with such things as neurasthenia, ideological waverings, gross contradictions, and melancholy. The author himself, the writer M. M. Zoshchenko, is, it is true, the son and the brother of such unhealthy people, but he has long since surmounted all that. And at the present time he has no contradictions. And if occasionally he may lack complete peace of mind, it is for entirely different reasons, which the author will tell about sometime later. In this instance it is a literary device. And the author implores his respected critics to recall this important circumstance before they open fire on a defenceless writer.

Of course even here the device is not truly bare, since the irony still undercuts any statements about M. M. Zoshchenko. He may have dropped the mask of Kolenkorov, but we may well wonder whether the new face that confronts us, though labelled Zoshchenko, is really that of the author of the book.

In *Before Sunrise*, however, quite the opposite effect is sought. Here there is no mask of irony, no wisecracks, nothing to break the illusion of the identity of the author and the narrator. In fact every effort is made to intensify it. In one instance this involves a very different use of exactly the same structural device which in *Sentimental Tales* was used to break the illusion—a preface in which the author discusses the genesis and structure of the work itself with the reader. In *Sentimental Tales* the ambiguous, bantering tone of the prefaces had only increased the uncertainty about the author's true identity; but here, in *Before Sunrise*, the tone is straightforward and sincere, the language standard literary Russian. This author tells us that after being evacuated from Leningrad to Alma Ata in 1941, he had decided after much soul-searching to continue this work, conceived and begun long before the outbreak of war, even though it seemed superficially to contribute nothing to the national struggle for survival. He had concluded that his work ultimately represented an affirmation of the forces of civilisation against the barbarism of fascism, and he therefore decided to write and publish it anyway.

After this somewhat apologetic Preface, which may have been partly designed to anticipate the charges of "raking about in one's own soul in the midst of a national holocaust" (which were actually levelled against *Before Sunrise*), Zoshchenko continues his description of the nature of the work in a Prologue which follows the Preface. The book is to be an account of the author's explorations in the realm of psychological theory, and in particular an exposition of the procedure by means of which he had "freed himself from many unnecessary discontents and become happy." In this remark we may suspect an element of the familiar Zoshchenko irony: the claim seems too optimistic to be taken at face value. But if it is ironic, the irony is not developed in the rest of the work, at least in so far as it was published.

Another function of both Preface and Prologue is to provide the basis for the logical organisation of the work. This logical, rather than narrative, structure is another reason why *povest* seems hardly the appropriate designation. For this work has the shape, not of the narrative at all, but of a treatise. It is an exposition of a theory with (narrated) illustrative data. As in any scientific treatise, a theory is stated, logically derived, and demonstrated by reference to case material. To be sure, the theory is presented in the form of a historical account of how it arose from the data, rather than reorganised according to the logical structure of the theory itself. But the form is still essentially expository, though with a narrative bias.

In his intermingling of truth and fiction, of narrative method and scientific exposition, Zoshchenko was actually trying to solve what was for him a serious artistic problem. He was searching for a new literary form more appropriate to twentieth-century needs than the narrative modes perfected in the nineteenth. One of the first products of this quest had been the work to which he refers as the predecessor and analogue of *Before Sunrise*, namely, *Youth Restored*. Here, too, Zoshchenko had expounded a scientific subject, senescence and the possibilities of preventing it. Here, too, the structure had been expository rather than narrative: a preface in which the problem is introduced and pondered at considerable length, then a narrative (not in this case in the first person) allegedly illustrating the experience of rejuvenation, and finally an elaborate apparatus of commentaries containing further illustrative and analytical material on the general subject of old age, its causes and cure.

In the Prologue to *Before Sunrise*, Zoshchenko refers back to this earlier work, calling it "an ordinary novella." But it was one to which "commentaries were attached—studies of a physiological character," and consequently *Youth Restored* had been taken as a serious treatise by "men of science," who

> treated my work with special attention. There were many debates. Arguments took place. I heard many sharp words. But there were also words of approbation . . . I even began to receive invitations to the sessions of the "Institute of the Brain." And Ivan Petrovich invited me to his "Wednesdays."

But, Zoshchenko insists, "I had not written my work for science. It was a literary work, and the scientific material was only a component part of it."

Before Sunrise is to be similar in conception, with the substitution of psychology for physiology. Scientific notions are utilised as component parts of a new literary form which the author, perhaps for lack of a better word, had called by an old name, the *povest*. But when in the Prologue the author's interlocutor (a remarkable physiologist) asks him whether *Before Sunrise* is to be a treatise or a novel, he replies, somewhat less specifically, that it is a "literary work."

> Science will enter into it as history sometimes enters into a novel.
> Will there again be commentaries?
> No. It will be a single whole. Just as a gun and a shell can be one whole.

Though similar to some extent in formal conception, *Before Sunrise* differs markedly from *Youth Restored* in one respect: the absence of irony, plus the personally poignant character of much of the material, seem to imply that this is one work by Zoshchenko which can be taken "straight." One is not inclined to suspect, as one so often is in *Youth Restored*, that the whole thing may be an elaborate spoof.

The transition from an explanation of how and why the work happened to be written, to the work itself, takes place imperceptibly in the course of the following section, entitled "I Am Unhappy and Don't Know Why." The author tells us that all his life he had been a victim of depression. At first, in his adolescence, he had considered this a sign of natural superiority: all sensitive, artistic natures were melancholy. But later experiences in the war, the revolution, and as a writer in post-revolutionary Russia, had taught him the error of this view. First of all, he found that not all depressed people are interesting: the gloomiest man he ever met—one who attempted suicide at least twice a year—was a banal and empty-headed bore who never thought of anything but food, money, and women. And he likewise discovered that by no means all talented and interesting people are depressed. Like an earlier anatomist of melancholy, he turned to his library, wondering what others had thought about his problem. While he found—and cites for our benefit—many kindred spirits among the writers of the past ("Twenty times a day the pistol comes to my mind. And then with that thought I feel better," Nekrasov wrote to Turgenev in 1857), still, many great men had not experienced anything of the kind. There was no generic explanation for this melancholy; it must be private and personal. The author was a humorist whose stories made people laugh, but the laughter "was in my books . . . not in my heart." He decided to seek its cause, especially after a particularly devastating depressive attack which occurred in the autumn of 1926.

> Suddenly I understood clearly that the cause of my unhappiness was concealed in my life. There was no doubt: something had happened, something had taken place that had had an oppressive effect on me.
> But what? What had happened? And how could I search for this unhappy event? How could I find the cause of my anguish?
> Then I thought: I must recollect my life.

This point may be taken as the completion of the introductory frame which provides the structural underpinning—logical or expository—of the work. The author is now going to recollect the most emotionally charged experiences of his life, with the aim of finding a historical explanation for his depression and even a means for curing it.

The third section, "Fallen Leaves"—a title borrowed from V. V. Rozanov, the most eloquent earlier exponent of psycho-sexual theories in Russian literature—begins the artistic core of the work, the presentation of recollections in the form of ultra-short stories, often only a paragraph or two in length, yet each constituting a single narrative whole. He decides to begin at the age of sixteen, ostensibly from the belief that nothing of great psychological significance could happen to anyone before then. The stories are arranged in chronological groups: eleven from 1912 to 1915, sixteen from 1915 to 1917, seventeen from 1917 to 1920, and eighteen from 1920 to 1926.

These stories represent a *tour de force* of narrative art. Perhaps the most striking thing about them, other than their extraordinary compression, is their dryness of tone. Once again we are confronted with a kind of paradox. If these stories are indeed taken from the author's most intense emotional recollections, he has performed a miracle of self-detachment in relating them as he does, conveying a vivid *picture* of emotion without quite communicating it, or, as Tolstoy would put it, "infecting" the reader with it.

Here, for instance, is a "memory" called "Torture," translated in its entirety:

> I am lying on the operating table. Under me there is a white, cold oilcloth. In front an enormous window. Beyond the window a bright blue sky.
>
> I have swallowed a crystal of mercuric chloride. I had this crystal for photography. Now they are going to pump out my stomach.
>
> A doctor in a white coat is standing motionless by the table.
>
> The nurse hands him a long rubber tube. Then, taking a glass pitcher, she fills it with water. I watch this procedure with disgust. So they are going to torture me. They should have let me die. At least all my grievances and vexations would end.
>
> I got an "I" [the lowest mark] in Russian composition. Besides the "I" there was an inscription in red ink on the paper: "Rubbish." True, it was a composition on a theme from Turgenev, "Liza Kalitina" [heroine of *A Nest of Gentlefolk*]. What had I to do with her? But all the same it was impossible to endure.
>
> The doctor inserted the rubber hose in my gullet. The disgusting brown tube goes deeper and deeper.
>
> The nurse lifts the pitcher of water. The water pours into me. I gasp for breath. I squirm in the doctor's arms. I wave my arms with a groan, begging them to stop the torture.
>
> "Gently, gently, young man," says the doctor. "Aren't you ashamed? Such lack of nerve, and over such a trifle."
>
> The water pours out of me like a fountain.

The prose here seems exceptionally bare—unliterary without being especially colloquial or conversational; it is more like the language of thought, of inner reflection, where no literary or rhetorical effects are needed: short sentences, exceedingly simple syntax, almost no dependent clauses. The first three paragraphs are focused—metonymically—on physical objects, not lavishly enumerated, but defined just enough to establish the reality of the operating room. The patient ("I"), the doctor, and the nurse at first appear almost as component parts of the physical setting, stationary and objective. Then the history of the suicide attempt is told, in exactly the same tone as the physical description. Emotion appears only in the fourth paragraph: "disgust," "torture," "Why don't they let me die?" But even these statements, expressed in the same short, bare sentences, seem to assimilate the same intonation of calm, restrained dryness. The fifth paragraph reverts again to history—the motive for the suicide, a low mark on a literary paper accompanied by an insulting comment. The climax of the "memory" is now prepared for: the actual pumping of the stomach—the physical setting activated, set in motion like a film. And the crowning moment, the eruption of water from the narrator's stomach, is presented without emotional overtone.

Not all the "memories" are as intense and personal as this one. Some are only witnessed rather than experienced by the narrator. But all of them, like this one, are actually whole short stories with a coherent narrative structure, a graphic setting, and revealing characterisation, and not only of the narrator himself.

The second group of "memories" covers the war period, when the author served at the front as a junior officer. Despite the horror, the wounds, and even a gas attack from which he suffered permanent heart damage, he describes this period as relatively free from the spiritual anguish which had made his earlier life so wretched. To be sure, in the beginning he had worried about being a coward in battle, and he had some difficulty in maintaining his dignity and authority with enlisted men—like the historical Zoshchenko, he was not only very young at this time, but very short. But in most of the episodes the trouble is external—the misery is in the world, not in the self. Why this should be so is not explored at this point.

In both the third and fourth groups of "memories" the centre of artistic attention also shifts to some extent from the inner to the outer world. There is material here which might be of genuine value to an historian of the period: vivid images of a dislocated and disintegrating society, seen from the vantage point of an incredible variety of places and jobs. "In three years [1917-20] I changed cities twelve times and professions ten. I was a policeman, a bookkeeper, a cobbler, an instructor in aviculture, a telephone operator for the border patrol, a detective, a court secretary, and a government chief clerk." After 1920 the "memories" take on considerable literary-historical value as well, with interesting vignettes of the leading literary personalities of those days—Remizov, Zamyatin, Shklovski, Blok, Esenin, Gorki, Kuzmin, and Mayakovski.

There is also, of course, much material of purely personal significance, some of it highly charged with psychological meaning, sometimes with philosophical overtones as well. A particularly ferocious scene the author witnessed in a zoo evokes one of these rare comments. A bear cub has managed to stick its paw into the next cage, where there are two grown bears, a male and a female. One of them has seized the little bear's paw in its mouth and is worrying it furiously. Screaming in agony, the little bear thrusts another paw through the bars; this is in turn seized by the other adult bear. People run up, shouting and throwing things at the bears. This only excites them more. One of the little bear's paws has now been completely gnawed off and lies on the floor of the cage. At last the keepers succeed in driving off the adult bears, and the little one is led off to be shot. Roaring with excitement, the adult bears copulate. "And I began to understand," the author concludes, "what animals are. And what makes them different from people." But the implication appears to be that they are not different, that people do, or would like to do, the same kind of thing as these bears—a misanthropic note that also lurks in a good deal of Zoshchenko's humorous work.

At the end of the third section the author looks back over the sixty-three memories he has resurrected and finds nothing sufficiently exceptional to explain his extreme deviation from the normal human state. He therefore decides to carry the search further back in time. The fourth section, "A Terrible World," deals with the period between the ages of five and fifteen. Here we are given thirty-eight memories, not further divided into sections or dated. Though many of them are unpleasant, and some even tragic—for example, the sudden death of his father, preceded by marital difficulties between his parents—still, nothing extraordinary appears, no experience sufficiently appalling to warp a personality for life. Even in childhood the trouble seems to be already present. As his mother says, he is a child with a "closed heart," incapable of loving. But why this should be so remains a mystery. He decides to explore still further back into the past.

The fifth part bears the same title as the work as a whole, "Before Sunrise." First the author actually manages to resurrect twelve scenes from the ages between two and five—scenes even briefer and more compact than the preceding ones. From a literary point of view these infantile memories seem to lead him to a further refinement and compression of his genre, the ultrashort story. Now only a few lines are left, yet somehow they still make up a valid "story," and effectively recreate the infantile experience. Here is a specimen.

Myself

A plate of kasha. A spoon is moving towards my mouth. Someone's hand is holding the spoon.

I take the spoon away. I am going to feed myself.

I swallow the kasha. It is hot. I roar. In my anger I bang the spoon around the plate. Spatterings of kasha fly into my face and my eyes.

An unbelievable scream. It is me screaming.

The mode of presentation is here pared down still further: details are few, and there is no elaboration. But what is given is sufficient to create a strong visual image which metonymically conveys the emotions of frustration and rage. One also notes the ascription to the infant narrator of an unusual degree of artistic detachment: he separates himself from his own scream, just as the mature author distances himself from the experiences he relates.

But even the two-to-five memories do not provide the ultimate clue to the mystery of the author's unhappiness. Attempts to resurrect still earlier memories fail. He is therefore logically driven back to the point where he started. Unaided, he cannot "remember" the cause of his misfortune. He must therefore seek some other basis for proceeding. From narrative he reverts to exposition. He begins to "study" psychology, and in the same ostensibly naïve manner rehearses the results of his readings and reflections with readers who are assumed to be ignorant of the subject, though with apologies to the "enlightened" ones among them who may know it already. First he outlines the Pavlovian theory of conditioned reflexes. Then he tries to apply this theory to his own psychological disorder: somehow a mistaken connection had been established in him. Some fear experienced in infancy had been "misunderstood" and a reflex association established which caused him to re-experience the fear whenever he received a certain stimulus. The fear was not causally connected with the stimulus originally, but was now irrevocably linked with it in his mind; he was like Pavlov's famous dogs salivating at the ringing of a bell, even when no food appeared afterwards.

He now tries to recover earlier memories by seeking for associative stimuli—for instance, revisiting places where he had lived as a child. These visits did actually evoke some very strong, though obscure, emotions in him, and among other things gave rise to a series of exceedingly vivid and disturbing dreams. The effort to understand these dreams leads him to an investigation of dream theory, and thus, inevitably, he arrives at the name of Freud. He consults some doctors—

apparently non-professionally—and among these doctors there were two "orthodox Freudians." They offered him ingenious interpretations of his dreams, to which he has the classical "naïve" reaction (one often feels in this work that it is a kind of "ontological recapitulation" on Zoshchenko's part of the history of psychological theory in the past half-century): he finds them too obsessed with sex and rejects them with indignation.

He therefore returns to the Burtonian method: a library investigation of the whole subject of dreams and their meaning, extending from ancient philosophy to modern science. His conviction is confirmed that Freud was mistaken in his exclusive concentration on the sexual aspect of things.

"Black Water," the final section of *Before Sunrise* as we possess it, presents the results of the author's further researches into his infantile life through dream and place associations. He finds a recurrent theme of "water" associated with various strong feelings and concludes that the apparent attraction to water he had felt during most of his life actually concealed some powerful fears. These, he feels, must have emanated from some other source, through a mistaken connection, a "bad" conditioned reflex. In the Burtonesque manner he now once again explored his library on the subject of water, searching for the—

> conditioned neural connections which led from water to something unknown, to something, perhaps, still more frightening. Without this, water would not have been a cause of horror. And so, assured of my powers, I set off further in search of this unhappy event.

At this point the publication of *Before Sunrise* was broken off, and we have no clue as to what would have followed. The autobiographical narrative material seems exhausted: there are no more memories to relate, or rather the author has passed the point on his structural framework where he could include any more. It is hard to see how the search for a "trauma" could be carried much further. Perhaps eventually he would discover, as seems likely from the material, that there was no single trauma, and perhaps he would learn to see through some of the rationalisations apparent in the existing material. It is hard to say. On the other hand, at the beginning of the work he had said that only half of the book would be concerned with his "own person"; perhaps the rest would be altogether different. For the time being, at least, its nature lies hidden behind that promise, "To be continued," a promise unfulfilled by decree of the autocratic state.

GEORGE GIBIAN

Yurii Kazakov

Despite the slimness of his works, Yurii Kazakov has already become
an author watched by those Russians who are most keenly interested
in contemporary fiction. He has not yet won such a mass following as
that of Konstantin Simonov: his works do not compare in breadth
(and, one might add, poundage) with Mikhail Sholokhov's, nor has
Kazakov established himself as a widely known public figure. But he
is being read with intense interest, especially in literary and intellectual circles, and his followers regard him as an unusual, perhaps
unique, writer on the Soviet literary scene today. Working slowly
but steadily, he has composed stories of rare excellence, a quality in
short supply in the literature of any age and country.

Yurii Kazakov was born in 1927, and since 1953, when his sketches
first appeared in the pages of Russian monthly magazines, he has published a little more than twenty stories and several journalistic accounts of his travels along the shores of the White Sea, the region
in which several of his works of fiction are set. He lives in Moscow,
but has spent periods of time with the fishermen of the North. He is
also familiar with the centuries-old provincial towns along the Oka, in
Central Russia, and with the wooded areas around them.

His first volume, *Man'ka*, containing eleven stories, was published
in Arkhangel'sk in 1958, and the second soon afterwards, early in
1959, in Moscow, under the title *At the Station* (*Na polustanke*). The
latter contains twelve stories, eight of which had already been published in *Man'ka*. His stories, sketches, and descriptions of the northern fishermen's and lumbermen's lives continue to appear in literary

From *Yurii Kazakov; Selected Stories* (New York: Pergamon Press, 1964),
pp. ix-xxv. Reprinted by permission of Pergamon Press and the author.

monthly magazines and in newspapers such as *The Literary Gazette;* a third collection of his stories, *On the Way (Po doroge)*, appeared in Moscow in 1961, and towards the end of 1961, a group of his works was published in a remarkable anthology called *Pages from Tarusa*, which was issued in Kaluga, outside the sphere of the publishing houses of the large cities, and caused excitement because of the unorthodox selection of its contents.

There are writers with an individuality so strongly marked that anything to which they have set their hand proclaims their authorship. Yurii Kazakov belongs to this category. His stories could not be mistaken for those of any other author living in Russia today. It is neither any single element of plot, character or setting, nor any one formal, artistic device, which creates the special aura of his stories, but rather a combination of several of them. As we shall see, Kazakov does favour certain kinds of character and motif, which he describes in his own manner, but his stories differ from those of other authors who in some regard resemble him, by being suffused with strong emotion. His characters' reactions to their surroundings are unusually highly charged with feeling. Kazakov is a subtle author; often he leaves his stories without a crisp conclusion. He is a master of the question unanswered, the suggestion allowed to remain equivocal. But above all, his special talent is the gift of conveying, with understatement and restraint, in musical, poetic language, the sense of an intense, private, emotional commitment.

Kazakov limits his artistic interests to a narrow range of subjects, and the literary influences which can be felt in his work are few, but pronounced (Turgenev, Chekhov, Bunin, Paustovskii, Prishvin). The stories in this volume have been divided into three groups according to their dominant themes—stories of hunting and the outdoors; of unusual characters; and of love. Forests, rivers, the White Sea—these are Kazakov's most frequent settings. Many of his lyrical paragraphs describe the impact which the sights, sounds and odours of natural surroundings make on his characters. He likes to describe outdoor activities, such as fishing and hunting, reminding us of his nineteenth-century predecessor, Turgenev in *A Hunter's Sketches (Zapiski okhotnika)* as well as of the twentieth-century author, Mikhail Prishvin.

Like Turgenev, Kazakov has the ability to create strongly delineated characters (for example, Tikhon and Kruglov in *Stariki [Old Men]*) in a few incisive paragraphs. The heroes, human or animal, whom he selects for his portraits are remarkable in several ways. First of all, they are usually presented as living alone, in isolation from a group, or at least engaging in an activity which has the effect of detaching them temporarily from the community to which they would normally belong. It is their experiences during the time when they are thus separated which arouse Kazakov's interest. His typical heroes are solitary fishermen, a father and his son hunting together in the wilderness, a boy riding along a deserted seashore. The self-sufficiency of his characters is expressed in the lonely meeting in *Autumn in the Oak Forest* (*Osen v dubovykh lesakh*), where people other than the lovers cease to matter. The sentence spoken by the narrator of the story, "No one awakened us in our house," could serve as a motto for all Kazakov's intensely private stories.

Even when Kazakov's characters are not physically alone, their inner life is withdrawn from the social life around them. In one of his stories, for instance, the action (a boy's falling in love with a girl and then losing her) takes place, exceptionally for Kazakov, in the city. There are cinemas, friends, tramcars, buses, trains, relatives, and school examinations, all the paraphernalia of urban life. The hero nevertheless lives in a universe of his own, immersed in his own perceptions and emotions.

Kazakov seems to consider human beings to be most genuine when they are by themselves. He says of Yegor in *The Renegade* (*Otshchepenets*):

> At such moments there was no one before whom he had to pretend, and his face became sad and thoughtful.

Many of Kazakov's characters, furthermore, are downtrodden creatures, somehow handicapped in life. One of his stories describes the lot of a girl who is keenly aware that she is not pretty. She is lonely and unloved; temporarily she deceives herself into believing that a young man is taking an interest in her—and then finds herself abandoned.

Compassion, a deep trait of Russian national culture, is also one of the striking attributes of Russian literature. Kazakov displays a gentle sensitivity to human suffering and a feeling of human solidarity, particularly with unfortunate beings. He seems to go out of his way to draw their portraits. He does not stop with pity, however, but shows also the triumph of his characters over their misfortunes. This is true not only of the orphan Man'ka, but still more clearly of the hunting dog in *Arcturus, the Hound* (*Arktur, gonchii pes*), one of his most moving stories.

Born blind, Arcturus is pre-eminently one of life's victims. Kazakov's account of the pummelling Arcturus suffers from a herd of cows, followed by a blow from the herder, is unbearably painful to read, particularly because Arcturus, unable to see the cows, does not know what has happened and is not only hurt physically but accepts the incident as typical of life, which to him is an enigmatic succession of injuries showered on him without reason, at random, out of the night that envelops him.

The dog's death is also rich in pathos. But like Man'ka, Arcturus is not merely to be pitied. Kazakov also glorifies him. Congenitally deprived of normal contact with life, Arcturus does learn to know the odours of the forest. He hunts; he conquers to the extent to which this is feasible for a blind dog. A victim, he is also a triumphant hero. Kazakov's admiration for him is expressed in flowing, epic language. There is no irony whatever in the dog's bearing the resounding name of a star.

Kazakov neither wallows in the sufferings of his creations, nor does he make light of them, but rather shows his characters' victories over adverse circumstances. His work is more than

> A song of human unsuccess
> In a rapture of distress . . .

It also carries out W. H. Auden's injunction to the poet:

> In the prison of his days
> Teach the free man how to praise.

In *The Renegade,* perhaps Kazakov's best story thus far, a similar attitude is expressed. By the dominant values of Soviet society (or, for that matter, by British or American middle-class standards), the hero of the story, Yegor, is in many ways a failure. He is a drunkard; he boasts; his work offers no future and little present. His life is being wasted. Something has gone wrong. He spends most of his time doing nothing, thinking about his past service in the Northern Fleet. He is, as the untranslatable title of the story terms him, someone who has "chipped" or "splintered" off. Unlike Man'ka or Arcturus, the disreputable Yegor has mainly himself, rather than circumstances, to blame for the course his life has taken. Nevertheless, Kazakov presents him as possessing one great resource—the ability to sing, and to feel the beauty of sound. His singing is not a wasted gift (as some Soviet critics of the story have concluded); it is of vital importance to him. It transforms him temporarily, lifting him into a realm of fulfilment and ecstasy. In his duets with Alenka, Yegor is transported by intense emotion. Music is to him a means of self-expression and of creation of beauty. It brings extreme happiness to him and Alenka; it saves and redeems their otherwise pitiful lives, just as hunting releases Arcturus.

Despite the aimless appearance of their everyday existence, Kazakov shows us that Yegor and Alenka possess a vision of beauty. Yegor, like many of Kazakov's other characters, is a man with a yearning. The duets are to him solemn, high occasions which seem to come from some beautiful, outside universe. Moreover, Yegor responds to the beauty of the countryside around him. He exults in the variety of life, in the villages, each of which has its own dialect, in nature—and in the Russian land. Kazakov does not hesitate to attribute this poetic sensibility to Yegor rather than to some punctual bureaucrat, neat scientist or respectable New Soviet Man in a factory.

Kazakov frequently creates characters engaged in emotional searches. They feel the mystery of nature, listening to voices apparently emanating from it; they look expectantly at the aurora borealis, or they live with their memories. Kazakov's descriptions of this attunement to some call from somewhere is very typical of him. He is the creator of characters with a nostalgia for an intense, high, somehow mysterious, experience.

Some of them, as one might expect, are children. In *Nikishkin's Secrets* (*Nikishkiny tainy*), for example, a boy responds acutely to his environment and imagines he is in the presence of strange beings. To Kazakov's children, their surroundings are fairy-tale settings endowed with a secret language. Nikishka lives both in the real world and in a dream world, which appears to him when he closes his eyes. He senses a mystery behind the everyday world and clings to a vision of a "secret world" in which everything will become understandable to him. With sympathetic lyricism Nikishka is presented as possessing to a high degree what we might call the expectancy of the extraordinary. He feels he is on the threshold of a magic state of being.

Kazakov's characters possess an unusual capacity to feel a close relationship between father and son, and between past, present and future generations. The understanding between Nikishka and his father is an example of this. Nature, a father and a son almost form a triangle, or we could think of Nature as a catalyst which brings out in the fathers and sons a feeling of communion with each other and with the eternal processes of aging. In *Hunting* (*Na oxote*) the father recalls the hunting trip during which his own father and he had lived in a hut of which only a few rotten logs remain; the son understands delicately what his father is trying to conceal—that he is looking for the place where he, in his turn, had stayed as a boy. The scene yields a sense of acceptance, slight sadness, and harmonious perception of the succession of the generations.

The awareness of the cyclical course of our life, of the maturing and decline of parents, then of their children, is a universal human experience, not the exclusive possession of any one nation. It was not a new idea even when Pushkin wrote in the second chapter of *Eugene Onegin:*

> Upon life's furrows,
> In a brief harvest, generations
> By the mysterious will of Providence
> Rise, ripen, and fall;
> Others follow after them.

Similar thoughts can be found as long ago as Homer. They form the basis of several nineteenth-century Russian novels. The succession of three generations of Rostovs, Bezukhovs and Bolkonskiis plays an important part in *War and Peace.* In Soviet literature an awareness of the future generations, and of the need to work for their benefit, is often stressed as a weapon against the fear of death and as a meaningful reason for our individual existence. Vasilii Aksyonov, for example, in his recent novel *Colleagues (Kollegi)* dwells on each generation's being a "link in the chain" which joins the ages together. To Kazakov, however, it is the personal, private sense of being located at the juncture of past and future that is important. Not an intellectual, rational assent, but an emotional grasp of it is crucial in the experience of the father and son while hunting, or of Pyotr Nikolaevich in "Hunting" when he refers to "the whirlpool of things" and says: "Life is passing."

Many of Kazakov's stories concern love. One of his best brooding studies of love, *On the Island (Na ostrove),* is the history of an accidental encounter which leads to more than the principal characters expected, yet is inevitably of the briefest duration—the fleeting approach of two human beings, followed by their parting. Kazakov does not contrive an elaborate plot. There are no complications, no striking events. Everything is subdued, inconclusive, as in the stories of Chekhov. What emerges from the story is mainly a sense that love is beyond rational understanding. Zabavin describes to Gustya the mysteriousness of love:

> Writers write about love, readers organize conferences and debate the question of whether he is worthy of her or she of

him, which of the two is better, more honest and more thoughtful, which of them is more in tune with the age of socialism.
But really not one of us in his own experience is ever able to
make out just what love is! The more I think about it the more
I become convinced that in the business of love a very slight
role is played by such characteristics as intelligence, talent,
honor and all the rest, and that the chief thing is something
quite different, something you can't talk about and can't ever
understand.

This initial statement of love's ineluctability is substantiated by the
subsequent development of Zabavin's and Gustya's feelings in the
story, as is Zabavin's other belief, which is connected with love—his
conviction of the importance of recognizing one's happiness in the
present moment. When a day later the couple discover that they are
in love, Gustya asks, "What's happened to us? Is this our happiness?
Tell me!" Sailing away, Zabavin reflects: "So this is really happiness.
This is love! How strange." It is impossible to know whether he is
happy or wretched, whether this is love or not. The man who preached
the incommensurability of love now sees that love is even stronger
than he suspected, human existence still more enigmatic.

Kazakov is not always the portraitist of frustration and unhappiness.
One of his most recent stories, *Autumn in the Oak Forest*, is important in showing that his range is wider than one might otherwise have
concluded. The depiction of complete fulfilment is also within his ca-
pabilities. In *Autumn in the Oak Forest* the vivid joy which the narrator
hopes will come with his sweetheart's visit does in fact come.

Even in this story, however, the narrator trembles superstitiously;
too many things had gone well for him that autumn, hence he fears
that his sweetheart may never arrive, or that her visit may turn out to
be less than the consummation of utmost happiness. Yet the journey
does end in the lovers' meeting, which is as exquisite as he had hoped.
It is a private, personal realization of a dream, like that of Yegor in his
enraptured duet with Alenka. In their cottage, isolated by night, forest, and snow, the two lovers are as alone and supremely happy as
Zhivago and Lara in their Varykino retreat in Pasternak's novel.

Kazakov's primary interest is in men and women of vision and
yearning. Whether they are Dickensian characters, Turgenevan men
of the people, or Russian "originals," the persons about whom he
writes tend to be questioners, brooders, not modern men snugly fitted
into a niche in industrial society. They are individuals, the centre of
whose lives lies in something deeply personal, subtle, and beyond the
grasp of practical or social reason. Launched on a personal quest for

understanding, they are lonely beings in a forest of mystery, which, nevertheless, they feel to be not meaningless, and communication with which they are hopefully and eagerly awaiting.

Kazakov likes to write of ancient towns in some ways little changed by forty years of Soviet rule, and of their inhabitants, who resemble their old-fashioned setting. Among his creations are Old Believers opposed to the Komsomol, a scoundrel of a pilgrim abusing in modern days the customs of nineteenth-century Russia, Tikhon and Kruglov in *Old Men* similar to the men in Saltykov-Shchedrin's *The Golovlyov Family*, who through some unlikely circumstance have survived until today, and other people of the past. Many of his characters sing traditional Russian songs, and some of them say prayers. His imagination is stirred by the co-existence of Old and Soviet Russia—the juxtaposition of a TU 104 jet airliner and padlocked wells, the Komsomol and the watchmen beating sticks on their rounds, collective farms and ikons.

In a few passages Kazakov seems to sympathize with the old ways, as when the prayer of the heroine of *Pomorka* leads him to imagine he sees, as though in a dream, his mother, grandmother and other ancestors, "those who have ploughed and mown," praying "not for themselves, but for the world, and for Russia, to the ancient unknown God, and to the good Nicholas the Wonder-worker." Elsewhere he refrains from taking sides and merely sets down the colourful settings and the sharp contrasts of the Russia he knows intimately. Holidays for local patron saints are still celebrated in the Soviet Russian villages he describes. Man'ka recites old-fashioned incantations of mixed Christian and pagan origin, "wild, ancient" words addressed to the boy with whom she has fallen in love. In *A House under the Hill* (*Dom pod kruchei*) young men in the House of Culture act in amateur theatricals dressed as nineteenth-century merchants, yet Old Believer families, living in old merchants' houses, in reality—not in play—still cling to the custom of keeping their coffins adorned with crosses waiting for them in their barns.

Frequently, however, Kazakov shows clear disapproval of the remnants of the Old Russia. In *A House under the Hill*, in particular, the world of the Old Believers repels the narrator, who belongs to the new Soviet life, although he fails to act against the evil world with which he comes into contact. The chief character in this story is a Saint George who shudders at the dragon's ugliness, sympathizes with the princess, and swiftly leaves the scene, abandoning her still tied to the stake.

Kazakov's sketches at times seem exceedingly slight, almost fragile.

Once we have read them, we fear to turn to them again, for fear the quality which we have sensed in them may be evanescent and disappear on a second reading. Yet it will not only be there, but it will have gained in strength. The stories have a solid grounding in the careful reporting of vivid, idiomatic language in their dialogue and in lyrical, physical descriptions. The settings, often evoked in the first paragraphs, create an atmosphere into which the characters naturally fit. The passages describing the streets and buildings in *A House under the Hill* are masterly in this way. The streets, the precipice, the houses with their closed shutters constitute a natural habitat for the people hiding within. The first paragraph of *Old Men* performs a similar function—reminiscent of the steep gorge in the opening paragraph of Turgenev's *Singers*—with its account of the village Kolotovka.

Kazakov's eye for significant detail is evident throughout his work. In *At the Station* (*Na polustanke*) the new galoshes of the stationmaster, the spot of oil on the rail at which the girl stares, and the passenger who pulls open the window and asks if there is a bazaar in the station are eloquently irrelevant details which underline the emotional charge of the story. *Arcturus, Nikishkin's Secrets, Man'ka,* and *Autumn in the Oak Forest* are particularly rich in beautiful prose poems of natural description.

Kazakov knows accurately what a small child is likely to notice during a lonely ride along the seashore; in *Nikishkin's Secrets,* he shows himself a master of the dense, yet uncluttered and poetic descriptions which impart to us a sense of towns, forests, rivers, lakes—of the physical environment of man, with its poignant sounds, movements, colours and odours.

Many of the stories, from *Renegade* to *Autumn,* are rich in examples of beautiful descriptions of nature as well as of brief images which convey the sensuous qualities of man's memory; as, for instance, in the visual symbol of the salmon, brought from the North by the narrator's sweetheart in *Autumn* which in a setting of the river Oka revives in the narrator's memory his stay by the White Sea. Kazakov's language is always fresh and idiomatic; the provincial characters speak in a lively, colloquial Russian.

In the Soviet Union, perhaps more than elsewhere, the identity and past record of a writer's public supporters and detractors go a long way towards defining his own position and the significance attributed to him by his readers. Yurii Kazakov has already been the object of several controversies in the press. He has been eulogized, among oth-

ers, by Konstantin Paustovskii, the universally respected elderly author of romantic, imaginative works of fiction, who at the time of the
Third Congress of Soviet Writers, in May 1959, published an article
in *The Literary Gazette* in which he surveyed the younger writers and
asked who among them were most likely to become the successors of
the older literary generation, composed of himself and his contemporaries.

He suggested eight promising prose writers, placing Kazakov at the
head of the list. "With their blood, they (the eight authors) belong to
the people," Paustovskii wrote,

> They have a fine knowledge of the life of the people. Espe
> cially clear and deep is . . . this popular vein in the stories of
> Kazakov and Nikitin. It is sufficient to read only two stories
> by Kazakov, "Nikishkin's Secrets" and "Arcturus" in order to
> come into contact with the sacred wellsprings of the people's
> life and poetry. The air of the immense, beloved country, the
> breath of our wonderful homeland, streams out of these stories.

On the other hand, Kazakov has found himself reproached with
decadence, aestheticism and pessimism. Prominent among his detractors was Leonid Sobolev, known for his advocacy of a strict interpretation of Communist Party directives in the field of culture. In a
speech at the Congress of Writers in 1959, he alluded to Paustovskii's
commendation of "the prose writer Yurii Kazakov as candidate Number One to replace the generation of the departing older writers," and
complained that Kazakov wrote on unworthy subjects, such as a pilgrim attempting to seduce a young girl, or, referring to the hero of *At
the Station*, "a cruel obtuse boy who leaves his bride in the country
for the sake of a sporting career in the city."

Then Sobolev revealed the history of Kazakov's participation in a
Writers' Seminar. He intended to convince his listeners that Paustovskii was grossly mistaken in suggesting Kazakov as a deserving heir of
literary leadership, but unintentionally gave a comic and self-defeating
picture of the episode. He related that "in order to bring Kazakov
close to living life" (*sic: K zhivoi zhizni*), he had been included in a
seminar of young writers of the Russian Republic, convened for the
purpose of "activization of the genre of the short story." As "a condition of participation in the seminar" each writer was supposed to write
one new story about "contemporary life." For three weeks, Kazakov
remained silent. On the last day of the course, he surprised everyone
by reading a story set in the year 1837 describing how Lermontov

watched the fatally wounded Pushkin being brought home after the duel. "Moreover, it was discovered that Kazakov had written the story long before the seminar. This is not good, not intelligent, not grateful!" Sobolev concluded indignantly.

Kazakov's undisciplined behaviour seemed outrageous to the pompous Sobolev, yet it is possible to feel sympathy for the young writer. What must someone endowed with Kazakov's ear for language and his love for idiomatic Russian think, listening to pretentious jargon such as "activization of the genre" or the tautologous cliché "close to living life"? The disagreement between Paustovskii and Sobolev over the merits of Kazakov's work typifies the division of opinion among Soviet critics and readers. Those who conceive of literature as the art of fresh individual expression admire Kazakov and eagerly await his new stories; those who conceive of literature as something to be organized in official seminars and "activized" by bureaucrats deplore Kazakov as, if not an angry, then certainly a warped young man, and exclaim over him, "This is not good, not intelligent, not grateful."

To Western Europeans who may set their standard by reference to Proust, Joyce, Camus, Salinger or Beckett, Kazakov perhaps appears quaintly old-fashioned—a mid-twentieth-century revival of Turgenev and Bunin. To many readers in Soviet Russia, however, his stories are exciting by virtue of their novelty and "differentness" from run-of-the-mill Soviet literary production. In Russia today, Kazakov appears unusual and modern because at least between the years 1928 and 1955, the Russians grew accustomed to a literature concentrating on problems of factories, difficulties of collective farm production overcome by heroic secretaries of the local Party organization, and the characters' occupational and communal involvements, while treating only sketchily their lives outside the workshop, office or laboratory. Kazakov, then, represents a break with the dominant trend of Soviet literature of the past quarter of a century, although he is not the only writer who recently has taken the path of studying the private, emotional side of human life. Vera Panova, Yurii Nagibin, and others have chosen to probe the subjective experiences of their heroes, thus reviving the traditions of the great Russian writers of the nineteenth century, when one of the glories of Russia was the psychological and moral analysis of Tolstoi, Dostoyevsky, Goncharov and others. Kazakov, then, is that strange Soviet phenomenon—a resuscitator of the past who strikes his compatriots as being *avant-garde*.

Kazakov is now solidly established as a leader of the movement

which the Russians call "young prose." Some of his Soviet critics take
the line of deploring, as if more in sorrow than in anger, what they
consider the moral defects in the works of an incontestably talented,
outstanding author. . . .

We might reply that far from indicating an inability to distinguish
good from evil, Kazakov's works demonstrate an awareness of the
complexity of life. Their objective presentation of the nuances and
contradictions in human beings is one of the characteristics which lift
his stories above the level of schematic fiction in which everything is
simply black and white, and poetic justice rewards the virtuous and
punishes the bad.

It would be wrong, of course, to impute "anti-Soviet" intentions and
convictions to Kazakov, Nagibin, and the other members of the group
which the Soviet editor and author, Vsevolod Kochetov, may have had
in mind when he attacked the writers "of the world of feelings" and
called their works "the wrong road to take towards building Communism." The error was Kochetov's; we should not imitate him. Yurii
Kazakov's stories demonstrate a deep interest in and sympathy for human beings. They are manifestations of a humanism. As such, they are
intrinsically neither pro-Soviet nor anti-Soviet. The question is beside
the point. His stories are pro-human, pro-individual, pro-life.

It would be as superficial for us to acclaim Kazakov merely because
he is a dissenter within the official set of Soviet conventions in literature (which fortunately have been relaxed in recent years) as it is of
Sobolev and Kochetov to condemn him for the same reasons. Kazakov
is worthy of note not because of any "disaffection" or "dissidence," but
because what he says about his haunting characters set against an im-
pressively captured nature is penetrating, true and beautiful.

RUFUS MATHEWSON

Four Novels

I

Four novels that appeared in completed form in the years between the overthrow of RAPP and the beginning of World War II, Mikhail Sholokhov's *The Silent Don*, Alexei Tolstoy's *Road to Calvary*, Leonid Leonov's *Road to the Ocean*, and Nikolai Ostrovsky's *The Making of a Hero*, represent a cross-section of the writing in these years, and demonstrate the full range of possibility in Soviet literature. One of the novels, Sholokhov's, quite clearly goes back to the classical Russian tradition itself. Two of the novels, Tolstoy's and Sholokhov's, resist strict classification under the heading "socialist realism" because they were conceived and their early sections were published in the twenties. Leonov's and Ostrovsky's novels are authentic products of the era of socialist realism although they differ radically in form, in approach, and in artistic worth.

These novels will be considered in a descending scale of literary value, since that has been the unmistakable direction of the historical trend. By this standard Sholokhov's novel must come first. Publication of its concluding sections in 1940 (the first chapters were published in 1928) raised a number of instructive issues because, although it was not generally admitted, Sholokhov had challenged every tenet of socialist realism in the tragic fate he devised for his hero. The most important aspects of the discussion of the novel in the USSR centered on the question: does the Soviet Union have "a right" to a tragic literature? The question is very much in point. Although they exist in attenuated and incomplete form, there are the elements of an Aristotelian design in *The Silent Don*. The novel's hero, the gifted, humane,

From *The Positive Hero in Russian Literature*, by Rufus Mathewson (New York: Columbia University Press, 1958), pp. 296-323. Reprinted by permission of Columbia University Press.

passionate Cossack, Gregor Melekhov, is a man of more than average human stature who is destroyed by superhuman forces he can neither comprehend nor control. His intellectual inability to understand history's movement cannot in itself be considered a tragic "flaw," though it does contribute to the blind sins of political affiliation with the Whites that is the external cause of his downfall.

But the basic terms of his collision with reality are moral. He prepares the way for his own destruction by a habit of impulsive decision which results in a sequence of temporary enlistments with both factions in the civil war. If this zigzag pattern of commitment were the product only of bewilderment, Gregor's destruction between implacable hostile forces would be productive only of a remote kind of pathos. But he is an assertive moral being, and beneath the inarticulated tangle of motives which produce his impulsive actions, there is a plain code of human decency and tolerance. A respect for the human person and a distaste for gratuitous acts of cruelty always underlie the other considerations—self-preservation, Cossack self-interest, love of the land—which motivate him. Acts of rape, looting, murder, or torture—committed by either side—are the determinants of his judgments.

He remains in a state of bewilderment to the end of his "strange and incoherent life,"[1] but at one moment he ventures close to an understanding of his dilemma. He had sought "one truth," he notes, which would embody his personal code and aspirations in political terms. But the world offered him "two truths," and neither fully comprehended the demands he made on life. A further step (which he cannot make) might have led him to reformulate the notion of truth's duality into the deeper division between human truth and political truth or between man in nature and man in history. Though Gregor is never permitted to know this, Sholokhov appears here to be suggesting that private moral judgment is sometimes irrelevant to the higher struggles of historical forces, and that in this fact there is genuine human tragedy.

Perhaps this is not Sholokhov's intention—and for it to be so the writer would have to betray the Communist in himself—but it is a defensible reading of the novel and it is possible to speculate about its function in Soviet society. Despite the absence of positive affirmation at the novel's end, when Gregor returns home for a brief reunion with his son, stripped of hope and aspiration, and prepared to meet his fate at the hands of the Cheka, there is a strong sense of his final reconciliation with a remote historical destiny, hence, with the new revolutionary status quo itself. It might be imagined that this effect could have a strict practical utility for the rulers of Soviet society, as a solvent of doubt, unruliness, and grievance in their own population. If this were accepted as minimum compliance with the "social command," the world might be entitled to expect the continued survival, at least, of the Russian tradition. But such "negative" effects are not officially countenanced, and we must assume that the book's publication and great success are the results of a partial accident which has been accepted because of Sholokhov's enormous popularity and his unquestioned talent.[2]

Sholokhov's novel does not deserve the designation "Tolstoyan" which is often attached to it because it lacks the human density of his predecessor's work. The very inarticulateness of Sholokhov's characters, and the unmitigated violence which engulfs all assertions of moral worth, automatically deny it such depth of insight. But its connections with the past call attention to one general question that spans the century we have been concerned with. Ever since Chernyshevsky's clumsy attack on tragedy, there has been an obvious opposition between the affirmative and the tragic vision of experience. There are not many explicit discussions of the matter in the Soviet era but the problem is never absent, and occasionally it found its way into print. Lunacharsky, himself a would-be playwright, raised the question in an article in the early twenties which discusses the tragic formula Marx and Engels sketched in the correspondence with Lassalle,[3] the situation of the premature revolutionary whose tragedy resides in his historical "inopportuneness." Trotsky, who felt that the task of the "cultural revolution" was not the building of "proletarian" art but the creative repossession of the artistic heritage, remarked in *Literature and Revolution* that he considered dramatic tragedy the highest form art had ever achieved.[4] Gorky noted in his concluding remarks at the Writers' Congress that the impending anti-Soviet war should provide writers with material for great tragic works of art[5] The problem of tragic resolutions was implicit in the approach of some writers of the declining trend in the twenties, and there had been a spate of articles in the mid-thirties on the question of "a Soviet tragedy." The matter came to a climax after the whole of Sholokhov's novel had appeared, but the final resolution of the question did not coincide with Sholokhov's formula. The full answer, as it is now formulated,[6] is to be found in two earlier articles. One of these, entitled "Prometheus Liberated" (Marxism has set him free!), declares that there can be no tragedy in the USSR because man is now master of his own fate, is no longer at odds with his society, and fulfills himself through the collective's achievements.[7] The second article, "The Dramaturgical Principles of Aristotle," reviews Hegel's and Aristotle's theories of tragedy with some sympathy and understanding, and then attempts to readjust them to fit Soviet conditions.[8] The author focuses his attention on the catharsis, as the critical moment at which new truths are apprehended, and tinkers with its mechanism so that it yields the spectator not tragic reconciliation (through pity and terror), but political inspiration (through pity and respect). The politically motivated hero thus may die (without inner defeat, of course) and the spectator will emerge from the drama determined to fuse his will with the collective's as the hero had done up to the moment of his death. This is not to be taken seriously as a tragic formula since there is no real torment, doubt, or "stretching," only physical extinction, which the hero confronts unflinchingly.[9] And it has nothing to do in the end with Sholokhov, or the Russian past, or for that matter with Hegel or Aristotle, or any one else who has thought seriously about tragedy.

II

Leonov's *Road to the Ocean* (1935) also ventures toward a tragic statement and then withdraws when it approaches the boundary between socialist realism and the larger world of art's undirected possibilities. Leonov is a gifted writer, literate in his craft, and aware of those possibilities which lie just beyond his reach. As a result of his knowledge of forbidden areas, Leonov is forced to expend a great deal of energy devising ingenious compromises between the requirements of the formula and what he might really like to say. Thus the two obligatory situations of the literature of industrialization, the exposure of the hidden wrecker-enemy and the celebration of the achievements of the Communist hero, are both in Leonov's novel, though they are disguised and set in the background. On the other hand, Leonov's pursuit of his genuine interests is clearly evident in the novel, and though he stops short of real tragic revelation, the work is permeated with a sense of the permanence, the dignity, and the value of human suffering.

His hero, Kurilov, is an old Bolshevik who holds high office in the Volga-Revizan railway, and has dedicated the whole of his life to the service of the cause. His life can be summarized, Leonov tells us, "in one infinite word: work."[10] The costs of this existence are fully acknowledged by Leonov, and more frankly than by any other latter-day Soviet writer. Moreover, they are not presented as wistful side-

lights on the character, as in Sholokhov's Davidov, but are brought
into the foreground and incorporated in the hero's image as an ingredient of his greatness. Solitude and barrenness are the consequences
of the dedicated, politicalized life, as we have come to know it. None
the less so in Kurilov's case.[11] He is denied any intimacy with his subordinates whom he encounters primarily as incompetents, liars, or
worse, and treats accordingly. His private life is equally solitary. Marriage has been a bleak, bloodless failure, and children have been denied him, first by the urgency of events, and then by the prolonged
illness of his wife. His two fumbling efforts to have affairs with
younger women after her death are failures. The friendship of an odd
crew of fellow-Bolsheviks and others, including "a poet and heretic"
and an old steelworker, is the only nourishing relationship he has with
other human beings, and it is denied him most of the time because
of their physical separation. The quality of these relationships is
conveyed in Kurilov's remarks at a birthday party that has brought
them together. He is answering an earlier speech by the poet-heretic,
Kutenko, who has proposed a toast to the younger generation which
will survive to populate the future, "which certainly neither you nor I
will see!" Kurilov replies:

> And so, Kutenko, in your opinion, socialism is for those who
> will survive. You even spoke of friendship from the point of
> view of our fate, rather than of our community of social inter-
> ests. . . . But now, as I look at your faces, those dear familiar
> old beans, I see myself multiplied in them. All of you are
> fragments of my own life; that is because we made our lives
> together, guided by the same purpose. Each of you separately
> is my friend. I did not bring you together, I did not introduce
> you to each other, and yet you are each other's friends, too.
> And if I fall out of this circle, your friendship will remain un-
> changed. It binds you by an iron and rational discipline, it
> does not spoil or disintegrate—let us not even mention those
> who betrayed it! Of this friendship you should have spoken,
> not of the dead or the unborn ones, Kostia.[12]

Inadequate as these friendships are as a source of emotional suste-
nance, they are all that matters outside the cause. But the onset of
death, which first announces itself by a sharp pain at the moment he
finishes this speech, is to cut him off from whatever comfort these
politically rationalized relations provide. Kutenko, it turns out, is right:
Kurilov's work ends, the "community of social interests" loses its value
for him, and he enters a more human plane of existence, from which

he contemplates "the common human fate" and the immensely ironic fact that he will never live to see the future he has given his life to build.

In this new state he falls back on a strange, poetic, often incoherent apprehension of the place he and his society occupy in the perspective of history. He is oddly well informed about the human past. He is, for example, an occasional student of the history of religions, for the record he finds there of human fears and aspirations. At the same time he is a dreamer and a prophet. Large sections of the novel are taken up with his explorations, in fantasy, of Ocean, the city of the socialist future. His effort to locate himself in history is the primary intellectual activity of his final months of life. Kurilov's own history is rooted, not surprisingly, in the Marxian view of progress, but there is a very un-Soviet awareness of the enormous human suffering that accompanies, and will continue to accompany, its unfolding.

Kutenko, the poet-heretic, has been right on another point, we are told, and has stated indirectly part of Leonov's design for the novel:

> He had once been attacked for maintaining that the social ma-
> turity of a class in art is acquired through tragedy, and he as-
> sumed that the tragedy of the future might consist in biological
> extinction.[13]

Kurilov reenacts this "tragedy of the future" as he dies. But his fate has the other dimension indicated by Kutenko: the awareness generated in the tension between the imperfect present, in which he will expire, and the unattained future, which has called forth all the deprivations in his private life.

This is a most sympathetic recognition of the condition of the "interim man," and a complete transposition into Soviet terms of Marx's formula for the premature revolutionary, the man whom death forces to realize that he is a discarded means, not an end, whose personal claims on life are forcibly disconnected from the continuum of society's progress, since he is not ready to die and his aspirations are not yet realized in society.[14] Several images convey the sense of Kurilov's interim position. At one point he is described thus: "Kurilov, the great hunter, the seeker after human happiness, the man mountain, from the summit of which we see the future."[15] The girl, Liza, who is closest to him at the end of his life, and is most influenced by him as a human being, sees him in similar terms. "Yes," she says after his death, "he was like a bridge, and people passed over him into the future."[16] Kurilov sees himself and the men of his time in the process of development toward the new, whole man. He is as imperfect and uncompleted as his society: "We ourselves are only rough drafts of giants, who in their own time will learn that they are only dwarfs."[17]

Kurilov is engaged in striking the balance of his life in the months before his death, but as he counts out the human cost in full detail, he never brings himself to challenge the cause of it all, his allegiance to the revolution. He is finally more concerned with justifying than with questioning the value of his life. Here Leonov has missed the opportunity to transcend the tragic *fact* of death, and, by stretching Kurilov another degree, to comment on the tragic *nature* of experience. The novel ends, rather, on a note of muffled affirmation, although it is uttered in an atmosphere heavy with grief, and Leonov has swerved back at the last moment and by the skin of his teeth into the confines of socialist realism.

The positive, life-giving word is not pronounced by Kurilov, himself, but is communicated through the effect the example of his life has had on Liza. But Liza, herself, apprehends the meaning of his life through her own suffering at his death. The fact that maturity and self-mastery come to her through sorrow brings us finally to the matter of Soviet criticism of Leonov's novel. In general the reception was chilly. The consensus of a number of critics was that the novel was "abstract," "unreal," and "weak." One article represents the lowest common denominator of these opinions, and is very helpful in bringing to light, though in reverse, as it were, a number of my own general conclusions.

I. Grinberg devoted a large part of an article, called "The Hero of the Soviet Novel," to an attack on *Road to the Ocean* as an example of the way Soviet writers should *not* handle the fusion of the social and the human in Soviet experience.[18] Grinberg's principal objection is that Leonov seems dedicated to the pointless celebration of sorrow and suffering. Liza's path to understanding is a case in point. Because of his treatment of this and other situations the novel is denounced as "false."[19] But the implication is unmistakable that it is also harmful, and in this charge there is much that is instructive.

Kurilov has the "stamp of sorrow, the shadow of an undefined grief" on him. The young people in the novel are unhappy, too. As Leonov sees it, men's interest in their leaders is in the suffering the latter undergo in the name of the common cause. Even the Utopian future he sketches is marked not only by its joyousness, but by the purity and dignity of its grief.[20] All this is wrong, Grinberg insists, and partakes of a misguided "worship of sorrow," inherited from the

diseased capitalist past. Leonov should be reminded that folklore from
the most wretched periods is "optimistic" in its effects, and that the
best of written literature from the past (he does not cite any) is distinguished by its message of hopeful joy about the human future.
Leonov's misreading of the past has betrayed him into harmful practices:

> All the harm the "soothers" and "glorifiers" of suffering bring
> is clearly seen. . . . It is necessary not to sing the sufferings,
> but to hate them, to destroy them, to struggle with them, it is
> necessary to show that the popular mass can deliver itself from
> them—and is delivering itself from them.[21]

The too frank recognition of suffering, quite apart from its celebration, might contradict the certain assurances that the removal of
all known causes of human suffering was next on the Party agenda.
Leonov had been misled, as had others, by relying too heavily on the
classical past: "Some of our writers . . . still think they can find the
key to the new man by using the old traditions of the literature of
suffering."[22] Leonov's sin is made perfectly clear, and his kinship
with the tradition, as Grinberg remarks it, does him greater honor than
his earnest but confused novel.

This is the last time we shall observe the two phases of Russian
realism in conflict with each other, and it is permissible to draw from
it certain conclusions about the political attack on literature. Experience must be viewed optimistically at all times because the Party
program offers nothing but joy, hope, and positive achievement. Suffering is irrelevant, uninteresting, and obstructive, whenever it is
brought to public attention. In this way political agitation performs
its final act of emasculation on the artist's traditional view of mankind. Let there be nothing but the solid joy of public successes. Let
man be measured and known by this alone, and let him be ashamed
of his broken heart—unless it can somehow be made to increase production. Whatever makes man suffer—his weakness, his illusions, his
miscalculations, his progress toward senility and death, his commit-
ments to unrealizable goals—is without efficacy and without general
interest for that reason. Such is the burden of Grinberg's attack on
Leonov's statement of the prevalence of human sorrow. Soviet man
is not even to have his suffering as a measure of his joy. A blank-faced
optimism, decreed by officialdom, is the only mood permitted him,
encompassing his setbacks and illuminating his next day's triumph.
Even his dreams must submit to the same kind of censorship. Kurilov's

vision of Ocean is false and harmful when it is set against Klychkov's
dream of controlling Chapaev or Davidov's dream of the happy kol-
khoz meeting its production norms with the help of electric plows.[23]

Grinberg's attack on suffering is not the same as Chernyshevsky's
repudiation of tragedy. But the same bleakly programmatic optimism
and the same simplified, politicalized view of man underlie it. Grinberg concludes his criticism of Leonov by quoting Gorky's definition
of "complexity": "Complexity is the sad and deformed result of the
. . . disintegration of the 'soul' under the living conditions of petit-
bourgeois society."[24] All else is clear, simple, unilinear, disciplined.

In the new Soviet Babbitry, suffering is simply inefficient, and
when it does make itself felt it is seen as a phenomenon that can be
reduced or assimilated by ideological ministrations.[25] For the writer
who is forced to abide by these definitions this is an irreparable loss.
The image of man he is required to work with (and accept on his
own terms) has a small, politically bound view of experience which
is proof against all shocks. He cannot be dragged forth from his political casing and exposed to the temptations or trials of the human universe. He is limited, compact, smug, and unbreakable. The writer
may acknowledge suffering but he may not show its effects. Deprived
by his political masters of the full "awareness" of suffering, he has lost
a fundamental tool of definition and illumination.

Leonov's world-view has one other important aspect: the heavy influence it shows of the humanist strain in the Marxian inheritance.
The entire novel is set against the large perspective of men's progress toward wholeness, and the central dramatic situation of the
inopportune revolutionary is translated into Soviet terms without major alteration from Marx's and Engels's correspondence with Lasalle.
The attack on *Road to the Ocean* by Grinberg and others suggests the
growing estrangement in orthodox Soviet circles of the late thirties
from those aspects of Marxism which bear most closely on imaginative
literature.

III

The publication, section by section, of Alexei Tolstoy's *The Road to
Calvary* spans the full era between the wars; the first volume appeared in 1920, the last in 1940. For this reason it is a laboratory
specimen of the important changes in Soviet writing, most notably
in the matter of the writer's control over his material. It may be that
Alexei Tolstoy simply changed his mind, but it must be pointed out,

also, that in doing so he has betrayed the vital interests of his profession and capitulated to the political invaders.

The novel has no hard center of moral purpose, nor any strong inner necessity of development. The mass of material might have been shaped to many ends; individual destinies, since they are not closely interlocked, might have been worked out in a number of ways. Only one thing is certain: the final solution Tolstoy did impose on the novel is extremely questionable, because it is introduced in the last third of the book in total disregard of what has gone before.

Despite its shortcomings, in its first two-thirds the work exhibits a number of the traditional attributes of the novel as an independent comment on experience. Tolstoy's interest in his material seems largely documentary. Thus, Part I stands as a vivid sketch of the St. Petersburg intelligentsia on the eve of the revolution; Part II is an attempt, like many others, to reflect the chaos of civil war itself. In his investigation of this not too profound level, Tolstoy has assembled a large group of sharply individualized characters, who embody, among other things, a number of contrasting attitudes toward the revolution. As an illustration of the variety of character and the honesty of presentation, consider Sapozhkov, the ex-Futurist, who fights on the Bolshevik side, but without illusions about the future: "The bourgeois world is vile, and it bores me stiff. . . . And if we win, the Communist world will be just as boring and grey, virtuous and boring."[26] In a disconnected speech he analyzes with pity and irony the dilemma of the pampered intelligentsia in the violence of civil war:

> Our tragedy, my dear fellow, is that we, the Russian intelligentsia, have been cradled in the peaceful lap of serfdom, and the Revolution has terrified us out of our wits; it has given us a kind of vomiting of the brain. It's not right to frighten delicate people like that, is it? We used to sit in a quiet country arbor, with birds singing around us, and think to ourselves: Really, it would be very nice indeed to fix things up so that everybody would be happy. . . . What silly fools we are—serve the people indeed! It's a tragicomedy. We wept so much over the sufferings of the people that our tears ran dry. And when those tears were taken away we found we had nothing to live for. . . . It all comes from our gentle nurture; we're too squeamish, we can't understand without nice little books. . . . In the nice little books the Revolution is described very attractively. . . . But our people simply deserts from the front, drowns officers, lynches the Commander-in-Chief, burns manors, hunts the merchants' wives on the railways, and digs their

diamond ear-rings from all sorts of places under their petti-
coats. No, we say, we don't want to play with this nasty people, there's nothing written in our books about such a people.
. . . What's to be done? Shed an ocean of tears at home in
our flats. . . . There's nothing left to live for. And so out of
horror and disgust, some of us stick our heads under the pillow; others slink away to foreign parts, and those who are
angriest take up arms.[27]

Sapozhkov is among the latter, though it is clear that he does so
without hope, under a crushing and well-informed sense of his own
and his country's doom. At the end of his tirade, Gymsa, the regimen-
tal security officer, enters and tells him, in a voice like the grinding
of millstones, to keep quiet: "You've started your philosophical chat-
ter again, your idiotic rigmaroles; hence I infer that you are drunk."
Gymsa has just come from an execution. Sapozhkov says to him: "All
right, I'm drunk. All right, shoot me!" To which Gymsa answers
readily: "You know quite well I'd shoot you soon enough. If I don't
it's because I take your fighting qualities into account."[28] Gymsa goes
out a moment later and Sapozhkov mocks him:

Here's the whole secret: to give a straight answer to a straight
question. . . . Does God exist?—No. May one kill a man?
Yes. What is the immediate objective?—The world revolution.
. . . Just like that, brother, without any high-falutin' emotions.[29]

If this episode reveals little else, it demonstrates that Tolstoy is still
working from an independent vantage, from which he is prepared to
consider ambiguities, to explore conflicting points of view, and to set
humane considerations against political loyalties.

It is precisely this independence of judgment that is sacrificed in
Part III. The results are striking. Characters are interrupted in the
more or less plausible drift of their careers, are hurried to improvised
destinies, are hastily converted and refurbished as moral political
beings. A highly questionable series of coincidences reunites separated
lovers and scattered families.

That the blight of socialist realism is on the book becomes evident
first when iron-jawed, clear-eyed Communists appear from nowhere
and take over the direction of events. (Up to now the Communists
have been indistinguishable as people from the other characters.
These new men are of a higher moral order.) An imperturbable, pipe-
smoking Stalin outwits Denikin at Tsaritsyn and crushes him, and the

traitorous Trotsky issues orders which are properly disobeyed and unmasked.

The disintegration of the entire fabric of the novel is clearest in the last ten pages. Two quite ordinary characters, who have been hurriedly made up on the model of positive heroes, are united with their wives in Moscow and troop off to a political meeting in the Bolshoi Theater. Before they go Roshchin, the converted White, talks intimately with his Katia:

> Katia, our task is immense. We never dreamt that we would accomplish it. Remember, we often talked about it—the whirlpool of history, the destruction of great civilizations, ideas transformed into pitiful parodies of themselves—it all seemed so meaningless to us. Under the starched dress-shirt still the same hairy chest of the *pithecanthropos!* All lies! But now the veil has been torn from our eyes. All our past life was a lie and a crime! Russia has borne a new man and this man demands the right for men to live like men. . . . A dazzling light has fallen on the half-ruined arches of the past. Everything has a meaning; everything is governed by the same laws. We have found a goal, a goal every Red Army man knows. Katia, can you understand me a little better now? I wanted to give myself to you, all of myself, my darling, my heart, my beloved, my star.[30]

With such a political resolution fastened on the novel, it is not surprising that political rhetoric permeates even the lovemaking.

At the meeting Katia asks Roshchin: "Which is Lenin?" Roshchin answers:

> Over there, in the black overcoat—he is writing quickly . . . now he is throwing the note across the table. That's Lenin. And that thin one, with the black mustache, at the end of the row, is Stalin, the man who destroyed Denikin.[31]

Against this historical tableau, the two couples listen to a speech on the industrialized future and make their declaration of solidarity with Party, state, and the official blueprint of the future. Telegin, the engineer, engages in this dialogue with his wife:

> Dashenka, I'm just wild to get to work again. If they build a network of electric power there is nothing we can't do. We have a devil of a lot of natural resources; once we get down to using them properly America can watch our smoke! . . . We'll go to the Urals together, you and I.

Dasha takes it up:

> Yes, we'll live in a log cabin with large windows, beautifully
> clean, with pearls of resin coming out of the wood. In the win-
> ter we'll have a huge fire flaming in the hearth.[32]

Roshchin addresses his Katia in the same vein ("Can you see now
how purposeful our efforts, all the blood we shed . . . have become
. . . ? And this is happening here, in my country, and this is Rus
sia!"[33]). And there the novel ends. The banality of the situation has
penetrated the emotions of the characters and the very texture of the
language.[34]

We do not know whether Alexei Tolstoy made his surrender cyni-
cally or from conviction. In any case, he has provided a perfect case-
study within the limits of a single work of the damages that result
when rough political hands are laid on an imaginative work of more
than average vitality. We may view this novel as marking one more
instance of the conclusion of the long quarrel between the writers and
the revolutionaries. The final consequences of Chernyshevsky's attempt to capture Russian realism are again made clear. Alexei Tolstoy's capitulation has this melancholy advantage.

IV

In our descent down the scale of literary value there is one more level
we must plumb to bring the journey to an end. If we address some of
the questions we have used before to one more novel, Ostrovsky's *The
Making of a Hero*, we shall find, first of all, a sameness of pattern.
But that is not all and that would not be reason enough for taking
the trouble. We shall find, in addition, a progressive deterioration in
insight and an increase in fictional disorganization that brings us
finally to the level of juvenilia which Chernyshevsky first established
as a norm in *What Is to Be Done?* We shall find final confirmation, too,
of the close kinship between the heroes of the two novels, as psychological and moral beings. Finally, this novel set the standards for much
of the writing that followed the Zhdanov blackout.

Pavel Korchagin, the hero of Ostrovsky's *The Making of a Hero*,
carries the notion of the moral monolith to the limits of plausibility
or beyond, to absurdity. To the extent that the novel is autobiographical, the author has sacrificed the essential remove from his protagonist
that enabled Sholokhov, for example, to exercise a measure of control
over his Davidov, to trace the outline, at least, of his fallibilities, and

to suggest that there are values in life not easily given up. For Korchagin the universe is completely demarcated into blacks and whites, according to his simplistic political morality. The bourgeois girl's lips twitch for cocaine; the Communist's eyes are clear and steady.

From the moment Korchagin joins the Komsomol, his only guiding principle is to serve: service is happiness; happiness, service. Since there are no other large choices, since there can be no question of moral fallibility, the only genuine tests he can undergo involve his capacity to stand physical suffering. Korchagin's body endures a severe beating in prison; in the civil war he incurs a hip wound, a head wound, a spinal wound, and a smashed knee; in addition, he contracts typhus, pneumonia, and rheumatic fever. When the cumulative effect of these afflictions result in paralysis and blindness, his "tempered" Bolshevik will responds to this ultimate challenge: he learns to become a writer and continues his life of service to the cause.

Korchagin's personal moral code is indistinguishable from the Party program. The habits of service and leadership in its name, we are led to believe, have become basic *character traits*. From this total absorption in Party work he derives whatever spiritual nourishment his intense if dehydrated nature requires. Thus powered, his actions are always successful (although it should be pointed out that the successes are never magically easy), whether he is tracking down a murderer on the frontier or discouraging kissing games among the youth. From his central fund of belief he, like Davidov and all the others, develops problem-solving virtues as required by the situation. He is endowed with technical skill, civic initiative, administrative subtlety, and military resourcefulness. As a leader he displays a range of qualities appropriate to the many roles he plays: patience, tact, indignation, courage, or, if the presence of the class enemy is sensed, intolerance and ruthlessness.

We must recall that we are always viewing Korchagin from within, as he justifies his own behavior to himself. No attention is paid to the likelihood that the people he manipulates or clashes with might regard him as a prig, a busybody, or a fanatic.[35] Since he is not seen at all from an outside vantage, we are only able to guess at the degree of the costs of his alienation from the rank-and-file members of the various communities he inhabits, or from the normal human experiences he has voluntarily foregone. We note, with a few exceptions, not the absence so much as the unimportance of friendship, love, or family ties. His personal attachments, such as they are, have an invariable political cast: they are with members of his own elite, or they are initiated, sustained, or ended on political grounds. In Korchagin's case, the question of rewards and costs must be changed to: What are the costs of nonparticipation? As it happens, they are very nearly fatal. His deepest spiritual crisis is brought on by a doctor's decision that his multiple injuries have ended his usefulness to the Party. If he cannot serve it, life is without meaning and he has no alternative but to succumb to his wounds. But by overcoming the handicaps he wins through to a new kind of service, hence to a renewal of his life.

In this extraordinarily naive and incomplete human image the myth of the monolithic, functional, political man as it was first set forth in the nineteenth century has reached some kind of apotheosis. His author would have us believe that he has made the move from life as it is with its challenges, temptations, and ambiguities, to a fabricated, self-contained universe of ideology, and anchored himself within it. Doctrine has replaced life.[30] His activist political faith "permeates" his entire being as it does with Insarov in Turgenev's *On the Eve,* and like him, if he is denied participation in his cause, he will die. In the same way, Rakhmetov's bed of nails (in Chernyshevsky's *What Is to Be Done?*) forecasts Korchagin's terrible physical battering. By accepting the total commitment of the totally political man, Korchagin has placed himself beyond the last frontier of the human habitat. He does not, like Kurilov, accept death as a release from duty, but fights against it as an inexplicable nuisance. Both men are contemporaries and members of the same Party, but beyond that a world separates them. Their respective situations measure the gap between the old Bolshevik with his memory of other standards and other worlds, and the new Stalinist man who knows nothing but what he needs to know.

V

With this novel the work of the literary investigator comes to an end. So long as Soviet writing remains on this level it is more usefully investigated by social scientists or propaganda analysts. In bequeathing the literary tradition to them, certain tentative conclusions about the angle of refraction at which reality is reflected, about the inner workings of the literary mechanism, and about literature's function in times of social crisis may be useful. The hero, it may be assumed, will be a Party member on the level of tactical command, that is, where actual day-to-day leadership is exercised. The problem he is ordered to solve will doubtless be a widespread one, and the description of the problem will be a more or less frank account of some point of friction, breakdown, or disorganization in the social or economic structure. Or, if it is a story of new construction, the peculiar problems of terrain, technology, etc., will be carefully set forth.

Beginning on this level of *is*, the hero, by a process of engineering —human, technological, or administrative—lifts the entire situation to the level of *should be* and provides in that process minute instructions for the solution of similar problems. In addition to instruction there will be inspiration and the assurance of success provided everybody does what he should. In this last transaction with the reader, there is a kind of primitive process of wish fulfillment, as in the savage's war dance in which the imagined victory of the dance strengthens him for the next day's battle. But the Soviet citizen is not given magic assurances. His active, conscious, dedicated participation is an indispensable ingredient in the success of the project. The Soviet fictional dream does not endow him with false fantasies of his strength, but a moral blueprint accompanied by detailed instructions for its use.

The above description is a rough summary of the lowest level of Soviet writing as it existed on the agitational level in the days of RAPP, and as it has dominated the postwar years. It is a literature entirely shaped by didactic needs. And it is a literature which, I should say, is characteristic of a certain kind of crisis in Soviet life—not the *crisis of event,* such as the Nazi invasion—but the induced crisis or the crisis of anticipation in which invisible future menaces—imagined or real—are evoked to drive men to work. The latter is a time of the greatest constriction, regimentation, and coercion.[37] And it is reflected in the kind of fictional design I have just described. The hero, in this context, can be read as a kind of temperature gauge measuring the degree of crisis. When the crisis is considered greatest he will tend to be most infallible, most monolithic, most parental, most mythic, and most closely identified with the Party. As and if the crisis eases we may expect to see him resume more humane dimensions, although his quotient of virtue will probably be unacceptably high and unreal for Western readers for an indefinite period.

More rewarding here than a cataloguing of the virtues and vices of the positive hero, it seems to me, is a broad characterization of him as an *alienated* man, as that concept has been communicated by the great writers of the Russian past. There is a pathos in the fact that a tradition which has since its inception called for wholehearted engagement in history should play itself out with heroes who are disengaged from life, cut off even from a recognition of their own suffering.

Soviet writers, with the few exceptions we have noted, will not, or are not permitted to, accord him that recognition.

The positive hero, unlike the estranged, "superfluous," or alienated man of the nineteenth century, is not rejected by, or denied participation in, society. The Soviet hero is promised fulfillment only through his acceptance of the institutions and values of his status quo. In the very act of conformity significant losses are registered.

He is, first of all, entirely politicized, with his needs and aspirations defined by his political allegiances. Although he is expected to respond with *inner* enthusiasm to grandiose public goals, the real locus of judgment in these matters is outside his own conscience. He makes decisions, so to speak, but no choices. He lives in a world of rationalized deprivations, subsisting on reduced rations of love, friendship, and family happiness because, he is always told, of the terrible urgencies besetting his community. Finally, he is manipulated from above and in turn manipulates those beneath him: he lives in a hierarchy of these relationships.

Is his "incompleteness" envisioned as eternal? History will give the actual answer, of course, but we should note that the framers of the old and the new versions of his moral code did expect an end to his estrangement. The children, Chernyshevsky said, were to grow up in their parents' image. Few could belong to Rakhmetov's elite which would soon disappear, but, on a lower level, the number of new men was expected to increase by arithmetic progression, through the power of example, until they composed the whole population.[38] The extension of the Leninist ethic since 1930 to all levels of the population through every channel of communication seems to contemplate the same eventual reunion of the leaders and the led. Obviously, this "solution" raises additional troubling problems: the leaders, the exemplars, it should be remembered, are interim men. The life of the interim man has been long—it is a century since he was first conceived, a third of a century since he inherited the Russian earth—but, in theory, at least, it is not expected to last forever. And if it ends, one wonders, will anyone remember how to live, as Marx hoped men would, as a "total man" in his full "human reality," "seeing, hearing, smelling, tasting, feeling, thinking, contemplating, willing, acting, loving?"[39] Or will the alienation of the incomplete, inopportune socialist man have become universalized? "Too long a sacrifice," as Yeats said in "Easter 1916," "can make a stone of the heart./ O when may it suffice?"

The pathos of the positive hero, as we have said, is that he does not know his sacrifice. Ostrovsky's novel *The Making of a Hero*, which with Chernyshevsky's *What Is to Be Done?* and Gorky's *Mother* is recognized as a major work in the tradition, provides us with a classic instance. Ostrovsky's hero, Pavel Korchagin, is often linked with Rakhmetov and Vlasov, and he stands before us today as the most celebrated example of the new Soviet man, heading the company of latter-day heroes. By the same token he presents himself to us as the apotheosis of the politicalized man and the clearest example of the official treatment of the Communist "emasculate." The writer's attitude toward his hero's wound is central in the whole aesthetic tradition we have explored. Should it be celebrated, confronted, assimilated, deprecated, concealed, or denied? If the governing type is Ostrovsky's hero, and not Sholokhov's or Leonov's, the question is closed. The fact that we know so much of the aridity of Korchagin's life suggests that Ostrovsky does not even know of his hero's deprivations. His identification with him is so thorough (in this case the novel is autobiographical) that the last pretense of fiction has evaporated. The hero's blindness coincides with the author's. It is as if we had been given a nihilist's view of Bazarov, or an atheist's view of Ivan Karamazov. The emasculated Myshkin goes mad, but the Soviet saint writes with abandoned admiration about himself.

The image of the hero as it has been cast from Belinsky to Zhdanov and the treatment of that image in literature has falsified the very values which the new man and the new literature were supposed to realize. The aesthetic of radicalism is self-defeating, if indeed it is not a contradiction in terms, when considered in the light of the tradition we have examined. It has led finally to the incomplete portraiture of incomplete men.

EDWARD J. BROWN

Solzhenitsyn's Cast of Characters

My purpose in this paper is to examine the human material Solzhenitsyn reveals to us, particularly in *The Cancer Ward* (*Rakovyi korpus*)
and *The First Circle* (*V kruge pervom*), and to examine this material
in relation to the reality that his books reflect, or refract, or in some
way shape into an artistic whole. Of course, the relationship of literary figures to reality has given rise to problems. I have never been
able to agree with Belinsky (the *early* Belinsky!) when he said that the
artist has nowhere "seen" the characters that he has known, and
that those characters are the product of a kind of "creative dream, an
artist's somnambulism."[1] There should be no question in anyone's
mind that Solzhenitsyn really saw the characters he portrays, or
imagined them on the basis of convincing evidence. He had no need
of a creative somnambulism: indeed his own life has been a kind of
nightmare.

I will not be concerned with any purely literary problem, pure in
the sense that it may be treated in abstraction from reality, but quite
frankly and unashamedly with the statement concerning certain moral
problems which Solzhenitsyn develops through his characters, their
public and private lives, and the complex interactions among them
during their sojourn on the various levels of Stalin's inferno.

The first thing that must be said about Solzhenitsyn is that, whether
or not he is a great writer, he is certainly what might be called a
serious writer. Since the word serious is not often used as a critical
term I should indicate that I am speaking of the serious writer who
consciously involves his art with human problems, both immediate,
in the sense of *zlobodnevnye*, and ultimate, in the sense of *proklyatye*

From *Slavic and East European Review*, XV, No. 2 (Summer 1971), pp.
153-67. Reprinted by permission of the *Slavic and East European Review*.

—that is to say moral and philosophical. He is necessarily involved with human problems; for him the problem is the thing, and what he has to say about it is important; he takes care of the sense, then the sounds and the symbols take care of themselves. Like Dante he is able to accommodate in his hell both the immediate political enemies whose policies he abhors, and poets and philosophers who reflect on man and the universe. In this sense Dante is both a serious writer and a great artist; and so, perhaps, is Solzhenitsyn.

Solzhenitsyn as an artist is an adept and resourceful organizer of his material. Consider *The First Circle*. The central narrative covers just three days during Christmas week, the season of joyous tidings brought to men. The main thread of interest and suspense is a kind of detective story in which the reader knows who the guilty party is but the police do not, and all our human sympathy is with the hunted criminal, a man whose crime was that he once, quite unaccountably and on Christmas eve, did a single good deed, a good deed in a dark and naughty world. He made a phone call to warn a man that he was about to be framed. But how far indeed, if I may continue my reverse paraphrase of Shakespeare, that little candle sent its beams. The recondite scientific activities in the *sharashka* are made to revolve around the police problem of running that criminal to earth, of finding the man who did the deed; out of that chase, and in a way incidental to it, grow in incredible profusion the biographies of a score of prisoners, each of whom himself has a history of pursuit and capture by the police, and most of whom—there are some notable exceptions—now devote their talents either to catching another one or to protecting the conversations of the arch-jailer, Stalin. And the outcome of this detective story is unique in the history of the genre. The voice identifier that will pin the crime on the real criminal is never perfected, and the police never know for sure that Volodin is guilty, though Rubin believes that he has narrowed the list of suspects down to two. Now the rules of the genre would seem to require that the police have been foiled, and the story has reached a dead end, since the evidence is insufficient. But the police in Stalin's Russia operated in an impenetrable world of their own. They arrest and destroy both suspects, and we learn that they needn't even have gone through the farcical police chase at all. They'd already arrested several young chaps who happened to be standing around at the phone booth where the call had been placed, and since they've been arrested they'll surely be sentenced; they were ready to arrest all the other suspects and convict them anyway. Why take chances? And what Solzhenitsyn has demonstrated quite incidentally is that in the Soviet Union even the detective story genre, to the extent that it reflects reality, must be in a state of degeneracy. How can there be suspense if you know that someone, whether innocent or guilty, possibly even an incidental character who couldn't have had anything to do with the crime—those chaps standing around the phone booth in the Arbat, for instance—will surely be caught and punished. How can interest be maintained if the police don't really have to find out who done it? Such a system not only degrades the police and dulls the edge of detection, it destroys the detective story.

Pursuit of the culprit, Volodin, is the slender thread of plot, and around this thread Solzhenitsyn skillfully weaves a rich tapestry of human characters, both inside and outside the prison. While the actual plot of the novel is bare of events, the life histories of the characters—each one a kind of sketch for a possible novel—are rich in every kind of vicissitude. Those biographies reveal in terms of firsthand experiences the overwhelming tragedy of Russian life during the Stalin period: the bloody and senseless horror of collectivization is given to us in the peasant Spiridon's wonderful narrative; the sacrifices and hopes of the First Five Year Plan in the story of the engineer who built the dam on the Dnieper River, then was imprisoned for much of his life; the destruction of the Party is summed up in the scene from the Kharkov inner prison in 1937 when thousands of imprisoned comrades sang the International and other revolutionary songs; the Second World War with its heroism and frustration, in the biographies of the prisoners Nerzhin and Rubin. The biographies reveal every level of Soviet life: student life and the shabby dormitories of the University in the story of Nadya; artists and art workers in the experience of Nadelashin, a genuine artist who tries to but can't satisfy the cheap tastes of his nouveau riche clients; the dull workdays of policemen and jailers: Shikin and Myshin at the idiotic job of reading and hearing denunciations; the plush apartments and vulgar ambience of those who have "made it" in Soviet life: the prosecutor Makarygin worshiping at his expensive "tobacco altar"; the glib vacuity of Stalin laureates in literature and their critics: the writer Galakhov—who interviews a Soviet diplomat to elicit such details of his life as may be suitable for inclusion in a new novel on the heroism of Soviet diplomats. The essence of Solzhenitsyn's art, I would suggest, is the exposure of what has heretofore been hidden from view, and in this he is a direct descendant of nineteenth-century Russian literature.

Solzhenitsyn, it is often said, is an anomaly in the eighth decade of the twentieth century. A couple of generations after Bely, Joyce, and Kafka, and in the same decade with Beckett and Butor, Russia offers us this curiously powerful writer who quite frankly derives from the realistic novel of the nineteenth century, and who takes pains to point out his affinity in both theme and manner with Tolstoy, and even with Dostoevsky, and whose whole work embodies the nineteenth-century Russian conviction that a great book must be more than "just literature" (*eto ne tolko literatura!*) but a true commentary on the shape and body of his time. It may not be perverse and it may be instructive to compare Solzhenitsyn with Kafka, and particularly with two of the latter's works that deal with trials, prisons, and punishment, *The Penal Colony*, and *The Trial*. In both of those works a man is punished through the operation of some Law that is either completely arbitrary or else inscrutable, and he is caught in a penal system which assumes his guilt. The soldier who is to be killed by the exquisite machine in *The Penal Colony* has had no defense; he doesn't know the charge against him; he doesn't know his sentence— but his guilt has never been doubted. Many passages in that story remind us insistently of *The First Circle*. "The captain came to me an hour ago," says the officer responsible for the execution. "I wrote down his deposition, then I appended the sentence to it, then I had the man put in chains. It was all very simple." The novel *The Trial* begins, as we know, with the statement, "It seems somebody had denounced Josef K. because, though he had done nothing wrong, he was arrested." Now the Law in whose name his trial proceeds—and it is not indeed a formal and defined process but rather a kind of "summary court in perpetual session"—is never accessible to clear confrontation. Josef K.'s guilt, too, is always taken for granted, and at last he confesses to it, although the full list of his venial offenses would never even have justified his arrest. The correspondences between Kafka's fictional world and that of Solzhenitsyn are numerous and striking—and some people have been tempted to apply rather loosely the overused adjective "Kafkaesque" to the latter. But the two writers are diametrically opposed in their methods, their materials, and their purposes. Kafka's *Trial*, we may say, is a kind of metaphor of the human condition, fashioned by a man whose actual life passed in relative freedom and relative prosperity, but whose ontological malaise prompted him to create fantastic, dreamlike images that reflect the state of his own soul. No one has ever suggested that the events described in *The Penal Colony* and *The Trial* could have happened. But Solzhenitsyn's stories not only could have happened but literally did happen to so many millions of people that we may be tempted to apply to *The First Circle* the old Marxist bromide about realism as "typical characters in typical situations." Solzhenitsyn is an old-fashioned realistic writer raised on the Russian classics and probably not greatly aware of modern tendencies, but the reality he depicts is itself fantastic. I'm reminded of Dostoevsky's remark about his own brand of "fantastic" realism. In one of his letters, we recall, he said: "I have my own special view of reality in art; what the majority consider to be almost fantastic and exceptional is for me the very essence of reality. . . . In every issue of a newspaper you find accounts of the most real, and yet amazing, facts. For our writers they are fantastic . . . nevertheless, such things are reality, because they are facts." Solzhenitsyn's fantastic world, like Dostoevsky's, closely imitates the real lives of actual people. And in one other respect Solzhenitsyn is radically different from Kafka. Kafka's books are laden with a sense of guilt. As modern critics have noted, he shows us a world in which modern man, burdened by his feelings of guilt and isolation, seeks vainly for salvation. Solzhenitsyn's prison characters are actually much happier: they *know* they're *innocent*; they recognize clearly the features of the Law that violates them, and they abhor it; and for them salvation is ready at hand: a prisoner can be true to himself, refuse to cooperate, *not* work on a device that will help to ensnare innocent people, preserve his own moral nature against the massive pressures of the Stalinist system—indeed the fact of incarceration itself offers evidence that the man at one time had a measure of courage and inner integrity. Solzhenitsyn's world is much brighter than Kafka's; it's far more cheerful than the world we experience in modern fiction as a whole. And the last irony of his work and his career is that, execrated though he is by the Soviet literary bureaucracy, he has beautifully embodied in his work their precept that the writer must take an optimistic view of things. We note that he writes not of Ivan Denisovich's prison life as a whole, but of *one day* in that life, and a good day at that; that his hospital scenes are laid not in any ward but in a *Cancer Ward*, where men are obliged to ask themselves the essentially moral question, "What Does One Live By?"; and that the prisoners in his greatest novel are in the *first* or *top* circle of hell. Indeed everything is for the best in the worst of all possible worlds, and in Chapter 47 of *The First Circle* we even hear a fervent prayer and have more than a flicker of hope for the "resurrection of the dead."

As a matter of fact Soviet literature could, and in fact one day may, claim Solzhenitsyn as its own, since he practices faithfully many of the precepts that ostensibly guide the Soviet writer: 1) he depicts contemporary reality; 2) he is a deeply moral writer and his moral message is clear and simply presented; 3) totally preoccupied with exposing the evil around him, he plays no literary bead games with the reader, but confronts him openly and honestly, to say what he has to say. What the typical Soviet writer only seems to do or does speciously, Solzhenitsyn does honestly and with fervor.

Thematically his major concentration is on the facts of his own life. In *Cancer Ward,* for instance, we may find rich possibilities of symbolic interpretation, but we must not lose sight of the fact that the cancer ward is primarily and principally just that: a crowded medical facility in an outlying republic, the facts of which are given in faithful detail: clinical information in the form of symptoms, diagnosis, and treatment; the outward aspect of the patients, their essential gestures of pain and despair, the problems of the nurses and doctors, and the inner lives of all these people. One of Solzhenitsyn's functions as a writer—and here another Marxist bromide comes in handy—is to provide knowledge of reality (*poznanie dejstvitelnosti*). He provides knowledge moreover of a reality concealed from general observation: this is the essence of his art; he consciously breaks down the enforced segregation of the incarcerated and the cancerous. No, Solzhenitsyn is not Franz Kafka, nor was meant to be. Only in a state of relative affluence and in freedom can a writer afford ontological malaise, and he needs much leisure if he is to learn to play the bead game well. Solzhenitsyn is concerned with problems of the real world; he can't bother to create a phantasmagoric reality that's all his own.

Solzhenitsyn's characters are realized with great precision and economy of means, but without obtrusive literary artifice. His great strength lies in his power of empathy, his insight into the experience even of human beings who are totally different, even antipathetic to himself. The Soviet police bureaucrat Rusanov, who built himself a career by writing denunciations, in order to distract his thoughts from the tumor that may kill him, meditates upon the good things in his life: his proper family, his finely furnished and conventional apartment, his orthodox children who have the expected problems, his predictable dog "Dzhulbars" lying on his little rug in the hallway. Everything would seem to be in order in his stuffy little philistine world. And the thoughts of Rusanov suddenly take the form of a kind of mental tape-recording, exactly reproducing the man's trite and dismal idiom.

But thoughts of home provide him no consolation in his misery, and when Rusanov turns his meditation to affairs of state a mind unfolds that looks like a matrix for any day's edition of the newspaper *Pravda*. A cerebral cortex is exposed that harbors only such neural activity as is proper for a Soviet man of the responsible class. Rusanov is a human mechanism seemingly devoid of ideas, morality, or honor, existing in a tightly curtained void impenetrable even to the thought of death. And I would suggest that the exposure, and perhaps ultimately the liberation of such curtained or, to use Milosz's phrase, captive minds, is the principal business of Solzhenitsyn as an artist. And indeed an artist *can* have a business.

The revelation of this mind takes place in the pages of his novel without self-conscious literariness. It's doubtful that these passages can be described accurately as internal monologue, and to suggest any connection with the stream-of-consciousness school would be an affectation. The author is explicitly present to control the material and to focus our judgment on it. The one pervasive and powerful device that Solzhenitsyn uses to expose his negative characters is irony, and it is irony of the most elementary kind: their reflections and conversations have one meaning to themselves and another to the author and to any human being whose moral sense has escaped atrophy.

Solzhenitsyn in an interview with a Yugoslav critic once described the technique of his novels as "polyphonic," perhaps suggesting thereby an affinity with Dostoevsky. The novels are polyphonic in the sense that there are frequent shifts from one dominant viewpoint to another: they are structured out of many competing centers of attention. In *Cancer Ward* attention shifts from the inward experience of one character to that of another, and as the viewpoint shifts, the style of thought and expression—the gestures of language—also change in keeping with the character. We are told that Solzhenitsyn was once ambitious to be an actor; the frustrated actor found an outlet for his talent in multiform linguistic mimicry, which ranges from Stalin's harsh and alien accent to the singsong, proverb-prone speech of Tyotya Styopa and the beautiful peasant speech of Spiridon, which is curiously interlaced with history and politics.

Linguistic mimicry is one of Solzhenitsyn's methods for setting a character before us, but his treatment of persons involves another kind of mimicry. I would suggest, one that is paradoxical and almost perverse. Solzhenitsyn is unlike any modern writer that I know of in sheer descriptive power and in the importance he gives to visible, objective details of the real world. In this respect he has been compared often enough to Tolstoy, but I think the comparison may be a little misleading. Certainly we don't find in Solzhenitsyn Tolstoy's persistent use of metonymic detail in the treatment of characters: there is no one who repeatedly presses a person's hand downward when he shakes it, as Prince Kuragin does in *War and Peace;* there is no eternally recurring down on anybody's upper lip; there is no one who looks at us *cherez ochki;* no bare female shoulders repeatedly luxuriate to recall for us the whole body and movement of a voluptuous woman; and there is no muscle twitching on anyone's "fat calf." I would suggest that Solzhenitsyn's descriptions, in their completeness of detail, ironically mimic the police record and the security questionnaire. For each character we learn in meticulous detail his age, his height, the color of his hair, even in many cases the color of his eyes. We are told of peculiar distinguishing marks: Nerzhin's deeply wrinkled face and the furrows on his forehead, Rubin's black beard, Spiridon's round face and thick reddish brows, and Sologdin's speech peculiarity. The purpose of the police record is identification, and Solzhenitsyn's detailed descriptions are such that every character is not only vividly presented before us, but is easily recognized—identified—every time he appears. And there is still another type of record—the security questionnaire—the contents of which for each character we learn in considerable detail. Answers to questions such as social origin, activity during the civil war (where applicable), party status, various occupations, war service, number and location of relatives, friends and associates, list of addresses where resided—all such questions are answered—*ischerpyvayushche*—in the biographies of Sologdin, Spiridon, Nerzhin, Rubin, Pryanchikov, Ruska Doronin, and many others. Solzhenitsyn has transformed the kind of information you find in Soviet police records into a set of variegated individual stories, each one of which is restored its own rights as a private, intimate, individual experience.

At the various levels of this inferno there are a few consolations. Work is one—solving problems, making things. But the matter that can transcend misery is sexual attraction. It needn't necessarily involve any activity, just the proximity of people belonging to different sexes, and the hope or dream of some kind of fulfillment makes it possible to endure either the Cancer Ward or the First Circle. One of the cruellest aspects of imprisonment is precisely its monastic feature, and the heavenly aspect of the First Circle of hell is the presence of women. We note that the free workers who have to deal with the prisoners receive a careful indoctrination in inhumanity. They are taught to fear, suspect, and hate them, and for the most part this indoctrination takes effect. The one point of weakness is the sex difference. Serafima and Clara each fall in love with a prisoner, and when that happens human communication suddenly becomes possible. Simochka is a simple girl with nothing in her head that the authorities haven't put there. She believes that the prisoners are enemies of the human race, and particular enemies of the Soviet Union, that they are mad dogs in the pay of imperialism and the White House, that they are capable of the most heinous crimes; but she knows also and with complete fervor that there is *one* exception to the rule: her own Gleb. It's almost a pathetic paradigm, a primitive model of true love. And even this solid, tight, reliable vessel of human feelings is frustrated in Solzhenitsyn's world. When they're deprived of women, men are also deprived of humanity, of human warmth and human dialog, and this is the tragic fate of Kostoglotov in *Cancer Ward* who has the grim choice of death by cancer, or emasculation by the hormone he must take to cure the cancer. Solzhenitsyn in his treatment of sex and love is, once again, far out of phase with the modern accent. He seems to have discovered that "normal" heterosexual love unencumbered by complex or deviation is a wonderful thing, and quite suitable for treatment in literature.

There is in the novel a steady contrast between the free people and the prisoners. With the exception of the wives of the prisoners and the women who make love to the prisoners, the free people that we meet tend to be shallow, stupid, and mean, dishonest with themselves and others, cheap and gaudy in their tastes, or, like Yakonov, thoroughly compromised in their inner being. The generalization is suggested that in Stalin's Russia all the decent people were in jail. The only people whom we hear talking sense are in jail. Anyone in the novel who ever had an honest thought or did a good deed is in jail or on the way to jail. Even loyal and convinced communists— Rubin is a case in point—are in jail. The Lyubyanka functions in the novel as a kind of evil magnet that drew into its narrow cells in successive periods the best that the country and the Party had produced: leaders of industry, engineers and architects, bourgeois politicians, almost all the leaders of the revolution; revolutionaries who fought the Bolsheviks, Bolsheviks opposed to Stalin, Bolsheviks loyal to Stalin—all somehow found their way into the interrogation rooms of the Lyubyanka. The little interrogation table at which Gerasimovich and his wife have their meeting concentrates for a moment the long history of the prison and of the Soviet Union itself:

> This crude little table had a story richer than many human lives. For many years people had sat behind it, sobbed, shuddered in terror, struggled with devastating sleeplessness, spoken proud, angry words, or signed scurrilous denunciations of those close to them. Ordinarily they were not given either pencils or pens—only for rare handwritten statements. But the prisoners had left marks on the warped surface of the table, strange, wavy or angular graffiti, which in a mysterious way preserved the subconscious twistings of the soul.

Sympathy for the imprisoned, we might say, is the novel's dominant recurring emotion, and the reader is at last ready, almost, to agree with Professor Chelnov, "that only the prisoner really has an immortal soul, but the free man may be denied it for his vanity." The prisoners enjoy other advantages over the free people. They are free to think, to discuss ideas, to know at least a part of the truth. The prisoner has lost everything and therefore has nothing to fear; and the lower he sinks in the prison hierarchy the less he is afraid. But fear governs the lives of the people who live in "freedom." No matter that they've compromised themselves, and discredited themselves: the free people still are not free, but live in as much of a trap as the prisoners themselves. The successful writer Galakhov must choose carefully the topics he will treat and carefully select the details to emphasize; Yakonov lives in dread of a return to prison; Roitman is afraid he'll be attacked as a Jew; we are certain that the prosecutor Makarygin and his family will be in deep trouble as the result of his *son-in-law's* arrest; Major Shikin is obliged to conceal his brutish inefficiency from his superiors by "redoubled vigilance" and constant interrogations; Oskolupov is afraid of Sevastyanov; Sevastyanov is afraid of Abakumov; Abakumov lives in terror of Stalin, who could shoot him without reason and even without notice; and Stalin himself in his stuffy quarters, old and half sick, is afraid of conspirators, afraid of his doctors, afraid of his enemies, and he doesn't trust his friends. The enormous machine that he has fashioned for purposes of "security" functions only to produce an atmosphere of terror which he himself breathes.

Over it all presides the morose, brooding figure of Stalin himself, the "gloomy giant" who rules half the world. Solzhenitsyn's experiment in the genre of historical fiction is more than a portrait of Stalin; it is an attempt to capture, in the character and ambience of a single human being, the sense and spirit of a particular age. Solzhenitsyn undertakes no less a task than to recreate Stalin himself. And it is a savage and searing portrait. It has often been compared to Tolstoy's operation upon Napoleon in *War and Peace,* but the two portraits are very different, both in their purpose and in their technique. In the first place the Napoleon of *War and Peace* is a kind of abstraction in the sense that he is an episode in Tolstoy's historical argument, indeed an object lesson in Tolstoy's polemic with the historians of the War of 1812. Tolstoy has an additional purpose: the effect of his realism is always to puncture myths (as Eichenbaum has pointed out); "You thought that Napoleon was a great driver of history's wheel," he seems to say to the reader, "but observe how petty and insignificant he really was." Solzhenitsyn, on the contrary, expounds no theory of history, and isn't trying to prove anything in his portrait of Stalin. At the time he wrote only the most ignorant could still believe in Stalin's genius, and the crimes he had perpetrated were already widely known. There was no myth left to puncture. Solzhenitsyn's purpose is rather to examine the psychic makeup of one of history's great criminals. To explore the rubbish of his mind; to follow its halting lucubrations; to invade its privacy. Solzhenitsyn likes to expose what's hidden from the normal view, to turn up the inside of the cup, to tear the veils from the Cancer Ward or the *sharashka;* and in his portrait of Stalin he penetrates a whited sepulcher that within was full of dead men's bones and of all uncleanness.

By introducing Stalin as he pads about in his musty little underground—his windowless cell—Solzhenitsyn provides the reader with a viscerally satisfying sense of moral superiority to the Ruler of Half the World, the Father of Western and Eastern peoples, the Leader of All Progressive Humanity, the Wise Father and Teacher, the Caesar of all Caesars, for whom we feel scorn as for a moral idiot.

Stalin is not exactly stupid, but banal and narrow. His one outstanding trait is a chronically festering *amour-propre.* What most repels you in that little underground study is the unmistakable aroma of suppurating ego. The technique used to reveal the man is a kind of inner monolog, punctuated but not really interrupted by the interview with Abakumov. In his meditations Stalin recalls occasions when his comrades had laughed at him; and the Red general Tukhachevsky had even accused him of making a mistake. Those comrades and that general had long since been murdered; but there are still dangers lurking in the shadows, and he needs new purges and more blood. Nothing helps his megalomania. He thinks that he alone is the mover of history. What would they have done without me? What will they do when I'm gone? He wallows onanistically in the sickening phrases of the adulatory *Brief Biography of Stalin,* already sold in five million copies. But that's not enough. No. Ten million would not be enough: there should be a copy for absolutely everyone. But would that be enough?

Another method of the portrait is the mimicking of Stalin's language, particularly his writing style. Stalin the orthodox seminarian, as Trotsky long ago pointed out, developed a style which is a weird miscegenation of content and form: communist ideas couched in a quasi-religious, catechetical style. We all remember those drearily repetitive questions and answers: "Was the policy of the Right opposition in accord with the teachings of Lenin? No, the policy of the Right opposition was not in accord with the teachings of Lenin." And when in the novel we come upon Stalin writing his famous article on Linguistics, we find him answering implied questions in the dogmatic fashion: "The superstructure was formed by the base for the purpose of . . ."; "language was formed for the purpose of. . . ." Another characteristic of his style was the endless catalog, and here Solzhenitsyn mimics the interminable Stalinist itemized list:

> This man's name was endlessly inflected by the world's newspapers, was uttered by thousands of announcers in hundreds of languages, cried out by speakers at the beginning and the end of speeches, sung by the tender young voices of Pioneers, and proclaimed by bishops. This man's name was baked on the lips of dying prisoners of war, on the swollen gums of camp prisoners. It had been given to a multitude of cities and squares, streets and boulevards, schools, sanatoriums, mountain ranges, canals, factories, mines, state and collective farms, battleships, icebreakers, fishing boats, shoemakers' artels, nursery schools—and a group of Moscow journalists had proposed that it be given also to the Volga and to the moon.

And an example of the same stylistic quirk from Stalin's own prose:

> Whatever language of the Soviet nations we take: Russian, Ukrainian, Belorussian, Uzbek, Kazak, Georgian, Armenian, Estonian, Latvian, Lithuanian, Moldavian, Tatar, Azerbaidzhanian, Bashkir, Turkoman. . . .

Then there are those artless repetitions, each one a superfluous hammer blow on the nail already driven in; and the fixed dogmatic formulas, which once formulated, baffle and terrorize anyone disposed to ask a question. For instance, that Stalinist speech tag so widely imitated by writers in all fields: "It's clear to everyone." When a statement is probably false or palpably insupportable, in the style of that period it could acquire *ex cathedra* sanction by use of the rubric "It is clear to everyone." Or, if the statement involves a violently absurd slander on an individual, or a group of people, or a whole nation, the nail that drove the slander home might very well be "The whole world knows." Solzhenitsyn invites us to observe Stalin developing one of these crystal clear points: "It's clear to everyone," he writes. "Well, now we need here something that's clear to everyone," he thinks. "But what is clear?" he asks himself. "Nothing is clear," he answers, and he can't cope with the knotty problem. There are no philosophers left to whom he might turn for help; they're all dead. At such a moment, ironically enough, he thinks he might call Beria. "But hell," he thinks, "Beria doesn't know anything."

In the passage which reveals Stalin working out the ideas for his famous 1950 article on linguistics we have a magnificent example of what might be called "intellectual mimicry"—done with fierce satiric intent—as we trace the man's lame and halting dialectic, supported at frequent intervals by the crutch of dogma. We experience his heavy-handed efforts to manipulate the Marxist concepts, only to come out at last with the ultimate ineptitude so crushing to any writer who values language—the idea that it is a "tool of production—like lathes, like railroads, like the post office. After all, it is a means of communication."

Since Solzhenitsyn's art is closely involved with historical reality, it is quite legitimate to ask a question as to the historical authenticity of Stalin's portrait in *The First Circle*. It is generally agreed that Tolstoy in his portrait of Napoleon warped historical truth in order to reduce the stature of Napoleon. Has Solzhenitsyn performed a similar operation? We might ask what evidence, what materials did Solzhenitsyn use in constructing his portrait? It is clear that a prime source for Stalin's intellectual personality was Stalin's own writings. I would suggest that another principal source was Khrushchev and the de-Stalinizers in the Party who supported Khrushchev, and in that sense the portrait might even be considered a brilliant political act, an intended contribution to the de-Stalinization program of the fifties. If we compare the portrait of Stalin with Khrushchev's famous "secret speech" of 1956 we find that certain character traits appear in both: Stalin's belief that he was absolutely necessary ("What will they do without me?"), his consent to the glorification of his own person, and his enjoyment of the adulation in *The Short Biography*.

Both documents purport to reveal certain intellectual limitations: Khrushchev maintained that Stalin as a strategist was practically illiterate, that he didn't even know how to read maps, and that he used a kind of school-boy's globe when making his military decisions. The idea of his utter and foolish belief in Hitler is common to both Khrushchev's speech and the literary portrait. Solzhenitsyn used other sources as well. For instance, stories of the low opinion the Party intellectuals had of Stalin were current among the Party opposition and are to be found in Trotsky's biography of Stalin. No doubt some of these stories were still remembered even during the forties and fifties, and many communists who knew Stalin well may still have been alive at that time and in Stalin's camps, where Solzhenitsyn certainly had opportunity to meet them. Certain minor physical details of the portrait, we now know, came from stories that circulated in the literary community. Stalin had "greasy fingers that left marks on books," says Solzhenitsyn, no doubt drawing upon the story he had heard that Demyan Bednyi[2] left a note in his diary to the effect that "he didn't like to lend books to Stalin because of the dirty marks left on the white pages by his greasy fingers"; and here an authentic historical detail acquires a mighty symbolic force.[3]

We might also ask another question: what independent evidence is there as to Stalin's psychological makeup and intellectual level? Svetlana Allilueva in her *Twenty Letters to a Friend* provides much evidence on the narrowness and intellectual limitations of her father. She tells us of his anti-Semitism, his suspicion of intellectuals, and his notion that the reading of Michael Arlen's *The Green Hat* led to his wife's suicide. But Svetlana gives us this information only in passing and I think inadvertently. There's interesting evidence as to the quality of Stalin in Milovan Djilas's *Conversations with Stalin,* a fascinating document which reveals in the man a frightening combination of crudity, ignorance, and shrewdness, at the same time emphasizing his moral and intellectual poverty. We hear his coarse jokes; observe his crude domination of his entourage, whom Djilas describes as "courtiers" rather than advisers; and listen to his obvious and cliché opinions about literature, all expressed with absolute dogmatism. And beside his labors over linguistic problems in the fictional work we may set Djilas's story of Stalin's rather elementary interest in the question of Slavic languages. Djilas writes: "He used to ask me to tell him what the Serbian words were for certain things. Of course the great similarity between Russian and Serbian was apparent. 'By God,' Stalin exclaimed, 'there's no doubt about it: the same people.' "[4] Evidence from many sources indicates that Solzhenitsyn's fictional penetration of the "study" at Kuntsevo has revealed a human being remarkably like the real Stalin.

There's one historical puzzle, however, upon which neither Khrushchev nor Djilas sheds any light, and that is the mysterious question how such a man managed to hold supreme power in Russia for almost twenty-five years. But where historical evidence has failed, Solzhenitsyn's fictional portrait offers an interesting speculation. Just as the Midas touch turned everything to gold, says Solzhenitsyn, so Stalin turned everything to mediocrity. A mediocre man himself, he could tolerate no one outstanding around him, and used any means to lower the general level of accomplishment. In Stalin and his entourage we see exemplified something like what Hannah Arendt calls the *banality of evil*. From Stalin through Abakumov and down to Rusanov, the system is dominated by disgustingly average human beings governed by the most ordinary feelings: vanity, ambition, greed, jealousy, fear of rivals, fear of prisoners, fear of superiors, and so forth. Stalin is a banal nonentity, whose only ambition is to be revered as truly great, and so he must remove physically the dangerous rivals that surround him—and there will always be someone to remove. Once such people have shut themselves into a narrow dogmatic system, where they allow no light to enter, then the most horrible crimes may receive a kind of perverse logical justification. Once he is firmly locked in, it only remains for a man to do his duty, and they are all devoted to doing their duty. What I'm suggesting is that the function of Solzhenitsyn's art in its human context is to penetrate the closed system, to let the light shine into it.

The chapter entitled *fonoscopija* is a critical one for the novel's moral argument, for it is in that chapter that the prisoner Rubin, who still considers himself a member of the Communist Party, agrees with his jailers to help them run down the criminal. Rubin is one of the best examples of the "captive mind" that we meet in Solzhenitsyn's works. His natural human feeling, his instinctive sympathy for helpless victims of the terror like himself, is smothered by what he calls the "dialectic of history," whose perverse logic frustrates every clear thought, and any human impulse. We recall that Rubin hears the voice of Volodin on the tape provided by the secret police: it is a distraught and terror-stricken voice, but the voice of a man who still has the courage to do something decent, and Rubin is deeply moved as he listens to it. But the voice is effectively shut off by the perverse logic of Rubin's dialectic, with its set of fixed formulas that are divorced from reality. *If* the Soviet Union is the most progressive nation; and *if* these dull and despicable policemen represent the Soviet Union *at this stage of history,* and *if* they are engaged in the pursuit of someone who *could* harm the Soviet Union; then it *follows* that one must give up one's human feelings and work with the abhorred policemen, which is what Rubin agrees to do. Rubin is impaled on the triple prong of a syllogism: USSR = Progress; Police = USSR; ∴ Police = Human Progress. But in that syllogism the major premise, the minor premise, and the conclusion all are false, and the responsibility of Rubin, as of so many others who reasoned in that way, for all the human victims, is driven home to us as the chapter ends with the names of the five human beings—the suspects—who are threatened with destruction, each an individual life with its own right to existence: Petrov, Syagovityi, Volodin, Shchevronok, Zavarzin.

DEMING BROWN

The Art of Andrei Siniavsky

The imprisonment of Andrei Siniavsky in 1965 stilled, in mid-career, the most original and enigmatic voice in contemporary Soviet literature. At the time of his arrest he was known in the USSR solely as a gifted, liberal literary critic and scholar. Abroad he was known as Abram Tertz, a mysterious Russian author—possibly not even a resident of the Soviet Union—who had written a brilliant, devastating critique of socialist realism, two short novels (*The Trial Begins* and *Liubimov*), six short stories, and a small collection of aphorisms (*Unguarded Thoughts.*)

As Siniavsky he had written (sometimes collaborating with A. Menshutin) reviews and essays on contemporary Soviet poetry, several articles in literary histories and encyclopedias, and a superb introduction to a collection of Pasternak's poetry. He had coauthored, with I. Golomshtok, a book on Picasso. Nearly all of these writings were remarkable for their intellectual discipline, liveliness, erudition, and aesthetic sensitivity. At the same time these writings, though often controversial in their liberal bias, were well within the prevailing ideological limits.

As Tertz, on the other hand, he was both the advocate and the practitioner of what he called, in his essay *On Socialist Realism,* a "phantasmagoric art," a literature of the grotesque which strove to be "truthful with the aid of absurd fantasy." Such an art was not without precedent in Russian literature. The strain of the grotesque and fantastic, stemming primarily from Gogol, had been prominent in the nineteenth century. It had been even more pronounced in the first

From *Slavic Review*, XXIX, No. 4 (December 1970), pp. 662-81. Reprinted by permission of the *Slavic Review* and the author.

two decades of the twentieth century, in such writers as Sologub, Bely, and Remizov, and it was prominent during the early years of the Soviet period, in the prose fiction of Zamiatin, Olesha, and others. With the imposition of socialist realism as official doctrine in the early 1930s the use of the grotesque and the fantastic as artistic devices was suppressed. (One genre—science fiction—was somewhat exempt.) Only in the late fifties, in such a work as Dudintsev's[1] *A New Year's Tale*, did they begin timidly to reappear. Tertz's advocacy of such means, if not altogether heretical, was well in advance of the times. It was understandable that one who held such views might, if he were a Soviet citizen, wish to mask them under a pseudonym.

Until Siniavsky was unmasked by purely extraliterary means no one suspected on the basis of the texts alone that he was Tertz. The fine literary intelligence and sophistication of Siniavsky are paralleled by the creative inventiveness of Tertz, but there the similarity between the two ends. Siniavsky had mastered two quite distinct voices and had managed to keep them separate. This article will be concerned almost exclusively with the Siniavsky who wrote as Tertz. But it should be kept in mind that a writer who is adroit enough to sustain two independent literary personalities may also be capable of launching and maintaining still others. Siniavsky-Tertz is an exceedingly complex thinker and artist.

Siniavsky's direct pronouncements on the fantastic in literature are few. His article on science fiction, published in a Soviet journal in 1960, urges Russian writers of this genre to be less "practical" and "earthly" and to give more rein to their imaginations. In the context of the times the article is at most mildly unorthodox, and it develops no real theory of the fantastic. *On Socialist Realism*, his genuinely bold and daring theoretical essay published abroad under the pseudonym Tertz, is almost totally devoted to demonstrating the bankruptcy of the official literary ideology of the past quarter-century. Only at the very end of this essay, as if in an ironic afterthought, does he explicitly advocate a "phantasmagoric art," and he does not elaborate on its principles. For his view of the fantastic, then, one must see what is implicit in his fiction and in his critique of socialist realism.

On Socialist Realism is a carefully reasoned indictment of the theory and practice of Soviet literature. Siniavsky's polemic strategy is to describe and seemingly accept the ideological premises on which this state-controlled literature is based while he simultaneously— through example, paradox, and arguments based on the history of Russian literature—undermines the whole concept of socialist realism by reducing it to absurdity. This basic strategy, however, is augmented by such a profoundly ironical treatment of the ideological premises underlying socialist realism that considerable doubt arises as to whether the author accepts even these premises. For the sake of argument Siniavsky accepts the teleological notion that history has a direction, goal, and Purpose, and that it is a function of literature to serve this Purpose—the attainment of communism. He then proceeds to show that the literary models that have been arbitrarily selected as methodological guides for this purposeful literature—the nineteenth-century Russian realists—are ill-suited to this function. The method of "realism," he argues, is inapplicable to the kind of heroic mythmaking that the building of communism requires. A more suitable model, he suggests, would be eighteenth-century Russian neoclassicism, which was rigid and stable, affirmative, expansive, and devoid of the poisonous subtlety of doubt and irony that are inherent in nineteenth-century realism. In Siniavsky's opinion Mayakovsky was the only Soviet artist who had understood that literature which truly serves the Purpose must not aspire to be realistic: Mayakovsky relied on hyperbole.

Siniavsky's essay is more than just a literary argument. It is a savage attack on Stalinism, among other things, and an examination, with copious illustrations from Soviet cultural history, of the problem of ends and means. The essay is so loaded with sarcasm, moreover, that it is often impossible to determine whether an assertion is serious or tongue-in-cheek. At times, he seems to burlesque his own ideas. The ostensible purpose of the essay is to find a viable Communist literary *aesthetic*, but Siniavsky comes very close to saying that this is *ethically* impossible. One could interpret his last-minute advocacy of a "phantasmagoric art," for example, as a statement of desperation: since it is impossible to write "realistically" in Soviet society (i.e., to tell the truth), let us stop fooling ourselves and frankly resort to fantasy. If this interpretation were correct, *On Socialist Realism* would best be considered a kind of Swiftian modest proposal. And perhaps that is what it is.

On the other hand, there is no evidence in Siniavsky's writings to indicate that he is a conscious disbeliever in communism (which would in fact make a "Communist art" inimical in his view) or that he thinks that all avenues to the truth in Soviet literature are closed. What seems to disturb him is that socialist realism demands in the writer a pose of certainty, a dogmatic self-assurance which a truly intelligent and sensitive writer must find impossible to maintain. It is this feeling, I believe, that leads Siniavsky to espouse, at the close of his essay, a "phantasmagoric art with hypotheses instead of a Purpose and the grotesque instead of a depiction of ordinary life." Truth in art, he seems to imply, can only be reached, if at all, through guesses, indirection, tentative exaggeration, and distortion, and through the language of metaphor.

Siniavsky's art, then, is based on an ironic understanding of his own uncertainty and confusion, a lack of teleological confidence in orderly and purposeful processes, and a fascination with the bizarre and the irrational. By dealing in opposites and incongruities and by creating ironic analogies, he seems to be bent on conjuring up actuality rather than describing it. Although there are patterns in his writings taken as a whole, his work at first produces an effect of extreme fragmentation, of polyphony without harmony. His apparently undisciplined and illogical swarms of impressions suggest an artistic personality that is intricate without being integrated. And it is true that some of his works—one thinks of the stories "You and I" and "Tenants" and of several passages in *Unguarded Thoughts*—seem hopelessly chaotic and abstruse. As a rule, however, his writings are not as disjointed and obscure as they at first appear to be. One suspects that his excesses come from the fact that he is an enemy of artificial coherence, of intellectual and artistic systems that sweep contradictions under a rug.

All of Siniavsky's fiction has contemporary Russian settings. Soviet mores and linguistic peculiarities, Soviet institutions, mental habits, and attitudes are essential to its fabric. The problems and conflicts he depicts are recognizably those of contemporary Soviet civilization. *The Trial Begins*, for example, is set in Moscow at the time of Stalin's death and tells of specific events and places with considerable—if impressionistic—accuracy. There are allusions, in several of the stories, to actual public events and personages, and many of the details of Soviet life are set down with fidelity. Siniavsky is therefore a "realist" in the sense that his works tangibly reflect the Soviet environment. At the same time, however, "plausible" characters, objects, and occurrences frequently blend into "implausible" ones, in violation of the laws of nature or commonly accepted principles of cognition. His method of shifting back and forth between the real and the grotesque and fantastic can perhaps best be called surrealism.

The most prominent surrealistic element in Siniavsky's fiction is the supernatural. In "The Icicle," for example, the hero—an ordinary Muscovite—suddenly becomes clairvoyant. He is cursed with the ability to see both backward and forward in time so that he "lies adrift in the

waves of time and space." He can read minds, foresees the circumstances of his own death, and, since souls are transmigratory, he lives
simultaneously with his and others' past and future incarnations. In
Liubimov the hero is magically endowed with the power of mass hyp-
nosis, which enables him to delude the populace of a provincial town
into believing, for instance, that he has turned mineral water into
spirits, a tube of toothpaste into a fish, a river into champagne. With
these powers he becomes the local dictator for a time, and improvises
an illusory utopian state. The novel abounds in supernatural tricks and
creatures, ghosts, spells, and folk magic, so that, in distinction to "The
Icicle," it has many of the qualities of a fairy story or folk tale, and in
fact seems in part to be a conscious exploitation and parody of that
genre. A third and still different use of the supernatural is found in
"Pkhentz," whose hero is a creature from outer space, a cactuslike
vegetable who manages to exist on earth by disguising himself as
a man.

Siniavsky's friend Alfreda Aucouturier has testified to his fondness
for "authentic accounts of witchcraft and magic" and has stated that
"he believes in the power of fantasy to attempt by a trick to offer an
explanation of reality, while simultaneously recording a mystery."[2] At
the same time, she does not state flatly that he believes in the supernatural, and there is on record no statement from Siniavsky himself to
this effect. The question is moot, but whether or not Siniavsky does
"believe in ghosts," it is certain that his use of the supernatural in his
fiction is rational, calculated, and sophisticated. Its employment is
largely a matter of artistic strategy, in the tradition of Bely and Sologub. And like these two writers he sometimes makes it difficult to
distinguish between patently supernatural phenomena and purely
psychological ones, between demonic happenings on the one hand and
dreams, delusions, and hallucinations on the other. The story "Tenants," for example, consists entirely of a monologue which appears to
be the ravings of a dipsomaniac writer who thinks he sees a woman
turned into a rat, who fancies he can transform himself into a glass,
and whose world is populated by sprites and spirits. He argues that
industrialization has so polluted streams, rivers, and lakes that water
nymphs have fled to the cities:

> What a lot of them perished! Countless numbers. Not en-
> tirely, of course—after all, they are immortal beings. Nothing
> to be done about that. But the brawnier specimens got stuck
> in the water mains. You've probably heard it yourself. You turn
> on the kitchen tap, and out of it come sobs, various splashings,

and curses. Have you thought whose antics these are? The
voices are those of water nymphs. They get stuck in a wash-
basin and it's murder the way they sneeze![3]

This story, then, may be the psychological portrait of a fevered imagination. But there is also much evidence to support the notion that the
narrator is actually a goblin who has possessed the drunken writer, and
that the story is this devil's monologue, in which case the tale would
be basically supernatural.

Whatever the orientation of this particularly puzzling story, there are
others, devoid of the supernatural, in which the fantastic element
comes purely from the psychological derangement of the individual
characters. Such is the case in "You and I," a story of divided personality, and in "Graphomaniacs," whose dominant note is paranoia. In
still others a fantastic effect is created through the detailing of normal
workings of the imagination and the unconscious—dreams and reveries
that have no particular pathological significance. Thus in *The Trial
Begins* the prosecutor Globov and his idealistic schoolboy son Seryozha
attend a symphonic concert. The music stimulates contrasting private
fantasies in them. For Seryozha:

> The music was like his private image of the revolution. The
> flood drowned the bourgeoisie in a most convincing way.
> A general's wife in evening dress floundered, tried to scram-
> ble up a pillar and was washed away. The old general swam
> with a vigorous breast-stroke, but soon sank. Even the musi-
> cians were, by now, up to their necks in water. Eyes bulging,
> lips spitting foam, they fiddled frenziedly, randomly, below the
> surface of the waves.
> One more onslaught. A lone usher, riding on a chair, swept
> past. The waves beat against the walls and lapped the portraits
> of the great composers. Ladies' handbags and torn tickets
> floated among the jetsam. Now and then, a bald head, white
> like an unripe watermelon, slowly floated up out of the sono-
> rous green depth and bobbed back out of sight.

Globov, on the other hand, thinks in images of authoritarian power:

> He, too, was fascinated by the flood, but he understood it
> better than Seryozha. What struck him was that this surge of
> music wasn't left to its own devices; it was controlled by the
> conductor.
> The conductor built dams, ditches, aqueducts, canalizing the
> flood; at the sweep of his arm one stream froze, another flowed
> forward in its bed and turned a turbine.

Globov slipped into a seat in the front row. Never had he sat so close, never had he realized how hard was the conductor's work. No wonder! Think of having to keep an eye on all of them, from flute to drum, and force them all to play the same tune.

The reveries of both Seryozha and Globov are presented in grotesque patterns of imagery. In neither of them, however, is there an indication of mental illness. Rather, their thoughts are metaphorical expressions of their personalities.

Whether dealing with the supernatural, with hallucination and delusion, or with the normal subconscious, Siniavsky makes extensive use of subjective, introspective modes of narration. His first-person narrators are usually engaged in confessing or complaining to an unspecified audience that seems to be unsympathetic or uncomprehending. Sometimes his narrators appear to be mumbling to themselves. Moreover, these subjective voices often switch barely perceptibly, and sometimes imperceptibly, so that the reader cannot always be certain of the narrator's identity. This combination of subjective narration and ambiguity concerning the narrator emphasizes the aura of the fantastic.

Much of what *seems* fantastic in Siniavsky is in fact simply grotesque. He distorts his material in order to find new angles, fresh emphases, unusual perspectives. The "unreality" of much of *The Trial Begins*, for example, comes from its technique of montage, its kaleidoscopic juxtaposition of scenes and characters to reflect the atmosphere of confusion that surrounded the demise of Stalin. A similar distortion for the purpose of intensifying thematic concepts and epitomizing feverish psychological states is found in the story "At the Circus." Like his predecessors in the writing of ornate prose—such as Bely, Remizov, Zamiatin, and Pilniak—Siniavsky makes special use of shapes, shadows, and reflections. In *The Trial Begins*, the beautiful, self-centered, and depraved Marina gazes at her reflection in the display window of a beauty shop:

There she saw herself as in a distorting mirror. People walked across her, trolley-buses drove past, and flasks of scent and pyramids of colored soap drove through them.

"All these beauty preparations only spoil your skin," she thought as she looked sulkily at her image. But her face, smudged with shame and temper, trodden by the shadows of the passers-by, remained beautiful enough.

In this scene the world is not unreal or fantastic, but merely "strange." Much in the manner of Iurii Olesha (who, however, scrupulously avoided the supernatural), Siniavsky portrays a "different" order of reality and suggests that things are not what they seem. He does this also by means of caricature, hyperbole, and downward comparisons, and by deliberately depriving phenomena—such as sex—of their conventional romantic overtones.

Despite his formal similarities to the Russian symbolists, he is much less interested than they were in using art as an approach to metaphysics. For one thing, he seems too earthy and ironic by nature to commit his art to such solemn purposes. The absurd for him tends to be a source of satire, not of metaphysical speculation. At the same time, he is obviously in earnest when he uses the bizarre and the illogical as a device for exploring the world of common experience. He employs the unreal and the unusual to speak vividly and arrestingly about the real and the usual—to examine actual psychological states, spiritual and moral problems, historical and cultural essences. But his art is one of impressions and fragments rather than consistently unified generalizations, and this, I believe, is why he writes in *On Socialist Realism* of the importance of "hypotheses." In his view, art can only pursue the truth indirectly; the image is a kind of tentative proposition.

Siniavsky is a self-consciously *literary* writer. His works are peppered with allusions, both overt and covert, to a wide variety of literary schools and figures, chiefly Russian and West European of the nineteenth and twentieth centuries. The temptress Marina in *The Trial Begins* is said, at thirty, to be of a "Balzacian age."[4] Lyonya Tikhomirov, the mesmerizing young dictator in *Liubimov*, liberates the prisoners in the local jail and exhorts them to remember: "The word 'man' has a proud ring!"—Siniavsky's sarcastic reference to Gorky's much-abused line from *The Lower Depths*. There are zany misquotations and puns, such as one in which the title of Gogol's *Dead Souls* emerges as "The Dead Smother." Siniavsky's most brilliant literary allusions, however, are in his parodies. A long apostrophe to Soviet railroads in "The Icicle," for example, is an exact parody of Gogol's famous apostrophe to the Russian troika. *Liubimov* is largely patterned on Saltykov-Shchedrin's *History of One Town*, and this novel also has long passages of calculated, purple Gogolian rhetoric. In *The Trial Begins* there are numerous parodies of the jargon used in Stalinist literary criticism.

To a certain extent Siniavsky's abundant literary references and parodies are simply a clever writer's game, a form of exuberant play. As a rule, however, these exercises also have a satiric purpose and constitute serious literary commentary, for the subject of much of

Siniavsky's fiction is literature itself. *The Trial Begins* is, among other things, a story about socialist realism: in its prologue the narrator is given an assignment to depict a group of characters and events in the prescribed official manner; the body of the story is his defiantly unorthodox response to the assignment; the epilogue describes his punishment. The novel as a whole is an implicit demonstration of the absurdity of socialist realism: the very nature of the characters and events with which the narrator is dealing—contemporary Soviet citizens in contemporary circumstances—is such that the formula does not work. Although *Liubimov* is not as neatly programmatic as *The Trial Begins*, it too is extensively concerned with literary problems as such. It is, in part, a novel about novel writing, a novel which talks to itself. Within its loose and elaborate structure there are two primary narrators, whose styles clash, who interrupt one another and quarrel over strategy, fumble, and sometimes cancel each other out. His main narrator, a good-natured, pedantic philistine with literary pretensions, is given to confusion, false starts, and Sterne-like confessions to the reader (he dislikes the fantastic!) through which the author himself engages in wry and sophisticated spoofing of novelistic techniques and devices.

In other works Siniavsky is more specifically concerned with the conditions under which literature exists in the Soviet Union. "Tenants" features a devastated, drunken writer—by no means a uniquely Soviet phenomenon, but under conditions which suggest that this peculiar society has caused his downfall. "Graphomaniacs" is, indirectly, about censorship. Its hero is a writer who has not published, surrounded by writers who are also unpublished:

> But do you know what we owe it to? To censorship. Yes, censorship is the dear old mother who's cherished us all. Abroad, things are simpler and harsher. Some lord brings out a wretched book of *vers libre,* and immediately it's spotted as crap. No one reads it and no one buys it, so the lord takes up useful work like energetics or stomatology. . . . But we live our whole lives in pleasant ignorance, flattering ourselves with hopes. . . . And this is marvelous! Why, damn it, the state itself gives you the right—the invaluable right—to regard yourself as an unacknowledged genius. And all your life, all your life you can—

In this situation of frustrated creativity, where everyone is possibly a stifled genius, the hero develops the paranoiac conviction that successful, *published* writers have plagiarized his works.

Literature traditionally examines itself, and fiction that is concerned with literary problems and conditions per se is not, of course, unusual. There is special significance, however, in Siniavsky's overt preoccupation with problems of writing, with the psychology of art and the principles of creativity. His concern epitomizes the situation of a post-Stalinist literature that is trying to reassert and, to a great extent, remake itself, that is rediscovering techniques and approaches to artistic expression from which it has been cut off for more than three decades. More than any other contemporary Soviet writer, Siniavsky represents a return to the devices and interests of the 1910s and 1920s.

In the structure of his works and in his stylistic devices Siniavsky most strikingly resembles such early twentieth-century writers as Bely, Remizov, Pilniak, and Zamiatin. His chief structural characteristic is a fondness for abrupt transitions and the scrambling of chronology, settings, and characters. Scenes and dialogues shift rapidly and sometimes barely perceptibly, without apparent bridging or connection. At times this gives his narratives a jerky, staccato quality. In most cases, however, passages that seem merely to be randomly juxtaposed turn out, on closer inspection, to be related thematically. *The Trial Begins*, for example, is a carefully constructed progression of scenes that are connected to each other not so much through their characters and the development of plot as through recurrent imagery and the ironic association of ideas. But even in this novel—Siniavsky's most tightly knit and symmetrical work—there are authorial digressions, direct apostrophes to the reader, and flights of rhetoric that are strongly reminiscent of the loose and discursive structures of Bely and Pilniak. In other works the narrators seem to be purposely unidentified or, at best, calculatedly unreliable or poorly individualized. The narrator of "At the Circus," for example, is omniscient, but sometimes gives the illusion of being confused and uncertain of his facts. The narration in "You and I" is shared by two halves of the same personality: they address each other, the point of view shifts constantly between them, but at times they are indistinguishable. In "Tenants," written in the form of a conversation in which only one side is recorded, the narrator lacks a consistent identity. It should be emphasized that these are not innovations in Russian literature: Gogol and Dostoevsky used similar techniques, and they became the stock in trade of writers in the first decades of the twentieth century. But they have been almost totally absent from Soviet literature for the past thirty years.

Siniavsky's most ambitious and, on the whole, most successful experimentation with narrative structure is in the novel *Liubimov*. Its basic form is that of a historical chronicle, recorded by an eyewitness scribe. This scribe, Savely Proferantsov, is subjectively involved as a participant in the events he records and is, moreover, a bumbling, self-conscious stylist. He is particularly fond of and confused by the writing of footnotes. It is through the medium of these footnotes that a second narrator appears—the ghost of Samson Proferantsov, an eccentric nineteenth-century liberal intellectual. Samson's voice is first heard as the usurper of Savely's footnotes: he takes them over to criticize the way in which Savely is writing his chronicle, and a quarrel ensues between the notes (Samson) and the text (Savely). A few pages later Samson again intrudes himself into the notes, then leaps into the text to propose that he and Savely finish the story together by writing it "in layers." From here on, despite Savely's violent objections, his spectral collaborator periodically takes over the narration at will. In contrast to Savely's halting, clumsy, and bemused prose, Samson's is elegant in the finest nineteenth-century tradition. But there is yet a third voice, for occasionally the author becomes his own narrator, in passages of sharp and witty commentary. The existence of these three voices, which clash and yet amalgamate, is fundamental to both the thematics and the structure of the novel. They offer a variety of perspectives on the fantastic events that take place and enhance the novel's narrative interest by providing a change of pace.

Liubimov is also Siniavsky's most versatile display of narrative devices and tricks, most of them, it would seem, tongue-in-cheek. Here again the footnotes play a prominent part. In describing the Soviet government's ineffectual attempt to bomb the revolutionary town of Liubimov, for example, Savely portrays the approaching airplanes in the text itself and the town in the footnotes, alternating rapidly between the two in an awkward attempt to create a cinematic effect through the typography of the printed page. And when he is stumped over the problem of narrating two simultaneous events, Savely again trots out his footnotes to handle one of them. There are also numerous digressions in which Savely discusses his notions of literature and takes the reader into his confidence to talk over his methods of writing and his compositional difficulties. This mixture of candor and ineptness produces a good-natured spoof of bad writing.

In his approach to characterization also, Siniavsky is reminiscent of Bely and Zamiatin. His characters are intentionally flat and two-dimensional. There is very little concrete description of them, a minimum of biographical detail, and little, if any, growth and development. Their distinguishing marks, as a rule, are a few carefully highlighted,

often grotesque physical, mental, or verbal traits that serve as leit-
motivs. Despite their lack of "roundedness," they are made vivid and
striking by caricaturelike details of appearance, gesture, speech, and
behavior. They are important not as individuals but as types, as per-
sonifications of elements, forces, and problems—they all "stand for
something." In *Liubimov* each of them represents—although not in a
rigidly allegorical fashion—aspects of the Russian national character,
or particular traits of Russian political, cultural, or social behavior.
The Trial Begins is a kind of symbolic organism, each of whose inter-
locking or carefully juxtaposed characters stands for a cardinal phenomenon in the Moscow society of 1953.

Siniavsky makes extensive use of heavily laden images and symbols.
At a soccer game in *The Trial Begins* a particularly aggressive attempt
to score a goal becomes a metaphorical commentary on the novel's
theme of sexual frustration and that of ends and means. When the goal
is scored and then disallowed, additional symbolic meanings accrue
that are related to the novel's themes of creativity, sterility, and abortion. In both *The Trial Begins* and *Liubimov*, the KGB agents Vitya
and Tolya dream of creating a "psychoscope"—a remotely operated
mind-reading machine that resembles, in its general conception, fantastic instruments of thought control that serve as symbols in works
of Zamiatin, Leonov, and Olesha. In the story "The Icicle" an icicle
hanging menacingly above a Moscow sidewalk becomes the symbol of
inescapable fate whose power transcends even that of the hero's
clairvoyance and, as an ironic reminder of the ultimate freezing of the
planet, of the absurdity of the "march of history." Like those of
Zamiatin and Pilniak, Siniavsky's symbols tend to be either exceedingly
primordial or supermodern, and his imagery to be ominous and violent.
(Marina's announcement to Globov that she has had an abortion produces in her husband the effect of an atomic bomb exploding.) In
common with the prose fiction of the Russian symbolists, however,
Siniavsky's writing contains many prominent images whose associations
are neither limited nor absolutely clear. In "At the Circus," for example, the circus symbol and the character named Manipulator suggest a multiplicity of meanings, some of them contradictory. Likewise,
the pathetic, alienated, nonhuman hero of "Pkhentz" invites a wide
variety of interpretations.

Ultimately it is Siniavsky's prose style that brings him closest to the
"ornamental school." Whole passages resemble, in their texture and
devices, the prose of Bely, Remizov, and Pilniak and hark back to the
stylistic father of them all—Gogol. The ingredients are various. Siniav-

sky has, first of all, an extremely sensitive ear for contemporary Soviet speech and can both reproduce and parody it with great fidelity. The characters in *Liubimov*, especially the hero Lyonya Tikhomirov, speak in clichés and use heavily the political and ideological jargon of Soviet newspapers. The language of "Pkhentz" is current pseudo-intellectual urban slang, larded with bureaucratese and, like that of the narrator Savely in *Liubimov*, with archaic, high-flown, bookish expressions. Hackneyed slogans in *The Trial Begins* and *Liubimov* are burlesqued and ironically distorted to add symbolic overtones and satiric nuances. In *The Trial Begins* Stalin speaks like Jehovah and his presence is always described in Biblical language. Many of the works, most notably *Liubimov*, contain passages of brilliantly idiosyncratic, Gogolian *skaz*.

Another characteristic that attaches Siniavsky to the ornamental tradition is his proclivity for mixing first-, second-, and third-person narration. In "Tenants" and "You and I" the narration alternates between first and second person, and "You and I" culminates in a bewildering mixture of the two. "At the Circus" combines all three persons. Moreover, Siniavsky is capable of achieving great variety and complexity within the confines of a single mode. "Pkhentz," written in first person, combines reported dialogue, narrative monologue, and interior monologue. In the two novels Siniavsky's interior monologue closely resembles that of Bely and Pilniak, especially when it conveys fragmented, semicoherent thought and impressionistic representations of speech.

A hallmark of "ornamentalism" is exuberant verbal experimentation. Siniavsky indulges in this with gusto, sometimes to create ironic effects, but often seemingly for the sheer fun of it. In the novels there are rhetorical passages whose syntax is so carefully balanced that the author seems to be proclaiming facetiously, "Here, readers, is prose rhythm." English, French, and German words are frequently inserted, producing a comic incongruity. There are numerous ridiculous and grotesque puns—to show stream-of-consciousness associations in the private fantasies of characters, to convey satiric authorial double meanings, and sometimes, apparently, just for the hell of it. There is much alliteration, sound repetition, and word repetition, at times for rhetorical effect and at others purely for decoration. Like Bely, Remizov, Zamiatin, and Pilniak—and Gogol before them—Siniavsky plays games with the letters of the Cyrillic and Roman alphabets, fascinated by their shapes and associations. The voluptuous Marina in *The Trial Begins* notices that the profile of her torso resembles the letter S. In the same novel a letter tries to squirm away from a secret police search:

> [The detective] ran his hand over the first page and, presumably by way of censorship, scooped up all the characters and punctuation marks. One flick of the hand and there on the blank paper was a writhing heap of purple marks. The young man put them in his pocket.
>
> One letter—I think it was a "z"—flicked its tail and tried to wiggle out, but he deftly caught it, tore off its legs, and squashed it with his fingernail.

In the person of Savely, the naïve narrator of *Liubimov*, Siniavsky makes sport of his own creative processes:

> You write and don't understand what's happening to you, and where all these words come from, which you have never heard and haven't thought of writing, but have suddenly emerged from the pen and swum, swum over the paper like some kind of ducks, some kind of geese, some kind of black-winged Australian swans. . . .
>
> At times you write in such a way that terror seizes you and the fountain pen falls out of your hands. I didn't write this! Honest, it wasn't I! But you read it over, and you see that it's all correct, that this is the way it was. . . . Lord!

But for the erudite Siniavsky, inspiration is obviously only partly a fortuitous matter. His vocabulary—at all levels—would seem to be enormous. He has an impressive command of colloquial, vulgar (including scatological) language, he exploits fully and ironically the stale hieratic words of official propaganda and ritual, and he is a master of archaisms and the ecclesiastical lexicon.

His language, moreover, is exceedingly figurative, with bizarre tropes that frequently develop, as do those of Mayakovsky, into elaborately extended metaphors. Whole stories, such as "At the Circus," are based on a central metaphor (a restaurant, sexual activity in a bathhouse, religion, society, and life itself are portrayed as a circus). In contrast to Solzhenitsyn, for whom the image is a direct quintessence, an epigram, Siniavsky assiduously exploits his images for their secondary and tertiary meanings. There is a multiplicity of meanings, for example, in the fact that the hero of "Pkhentz" is not an earthling but a cactus-like vegetable who subsists on water. Not only is he an alien, he is also cleaner and, in his physical and mental purity, intrinsically superior to the filthy human race. His estrangement is something like that of the artist Siniavsky, whose lack of dogmatic self-assurance compels him to communicate by means of ironic indirection:

> How could they understand me, when I myself am quite un-
> able to express my inhuman nature in their language. I go
> round and round it, and try to get by with metaphors, but
> when it comes to the main point—I find nothing to say.

In his oblique manner Siniavsky does, of course, have "something to say." In sum, he is saying, like Dostoevsky, that the world is more complex and mysterious, good and evil less tangible, human nature more intricate, human behavior less rational, than we generally suppose them to be. And he is likewise saying that the human situation is more pathetic and absurd than the official Soviet literature of mandatory affirmation can show it to be. One of his major themes is alienation, the estrangement of the individual not only from society at large but also, at times, from his immediate neighbors, his family and sexual partners, and even from himself. The collective is hostile and confusing, one's intimate associates (especially those of the opposite sex) disgusting and irritating. Life itself is a desperate and lonely muddle, governed by weird and incomprehensible, mischievous, and malevolent forces. This theme is not totally consistent throughout all of Siniavsky's fiction, of course, and the emphasis on its various aspects fluctuates from story to story. In *Liubimov*, for example, it is lightened by a vein of rollicking satire, and in such works as *The Trial Begins* and "Graphomaniacs" it is narrowed and localized by the element of civic protest. Nevertheless, the portrait of the individual as a victim, isolated from his fellow men by suspicion, incomprehension, and fear and powerless to shape his destiny, is a consistent one. Siniavsky seems particularly fascinated by Jewish characters and the phenomenon of anti-Semitism; his choice of a Jewish pseudonym—Abram Tertz—is in keeping with his preoccupation with those whom the world crazily singles out for abuse.

The atmosphere of alienation is emphasized by Siniavsky's use of the grotesque. To his bewildered and suffering characters, the ordinary world seems strangely predatory, ugly, and distorted. The divided, paranoiac hero of "You and I" feels that his fellow guests at a dinner party are transvestites, "clicking their knives and forks and thereby communicating with each other in a secret code." The lonely hero of "Pkhentz," who has a number of plantlike arms which he conceals by strapping them tightly to his body, is, in human terms, deformed; in his eyes, however, the human female figure is repulsive and terrifying. In *The Trial Begins*, the mutual isolation of nearly all the characters is underlined by a myriad of grotesqueries. A banquet of secret police starts with animated conversation; as the drinking increases the participants all fall discreetly silent.

It is tempting to interpret Siniavsky's theme of alienation, in its various forms, in terms of the opposition between the individual and the centralized, omnipotent state. Surely, much of the psychic disaffection in *The Trial Begins* is shown to be attributable to the personality of Stalin and to the ponderous, corrupt, inhumane machine that he created. The maladjustment of the hero in "Graphomaniacs" is triggered by the ubiquitous state censorship of literature. One could conclude that the hero of "At the Circus" turns criminal in protest against the deadening routine of a rigidly controlled social system. The nervous, suspicious, conspiratorial atmosphere of the police state permeates the fantasy of "The Icicle" and "You and I." And the hero of "Pkhentz" is a creature who has fallen into a conformist society where individualism is suspect, and who must therefore conceal his identity: he is, metaphorically, an "internal émigré." But despite this sampling of evidence from the stories, it would be erroneous to conclude that Siniavsky is attempting to demonstrate that alienation is exclusively, or even primarily, the product of the Soviet political and social system. More likely, the Soviet scene simply provides material-at-hand, to be used in conjuring up a more generalized vision of the contemporary human situation.

At the center of Siniavsky's art, one suspects, there is a fierce ethical consciousness, a thirst for moral certainty, and a deeply frustrated idealism and sense of what is rational and just in human affairs. He exaggerates, and arranges observed and imagined data into ugly and ridiculous patterns, to express his dismay and ironic wonderment at the gulf between human pretensions and human actuality. As an artist he is motivated by the associative powers of metaphor and hyperbole, but as a moralist and satirist he uses them to startle and shock. To a certain extent Siniavsky's world of fantasy is private and closed, like the "third world" of Olesha and the darkly grotesque one of Sologub, but like theirs it also has an intrinsic moral relevance.

The Trial Begins is a systematic exploration of the problem of ends and means, with tightly interwoven references to ideology and religion, sex, politics, art, and history. As a kind of fictional counterpart of the essay *On Socialist Realism* it presents a society in which authoritarian means have so corrupted the pursuit of the Glorious Purpose that the Purpose itself has become perverted. Every character in the novel has either been infected with the falsity and brutality of this way of life or has been psychologically traumatized by it. Even the innocent and idealistic schoolboy, Seryozha Globov, who asks callow and honest—and therefore excruciatingly difficult—questions of his elders, and who is ultimately imprisoned for his naïve rebellion, can only conceive of a revolutionary utopia in which "any man who hurts another man's feelings will be shot." *Liubimov* is a similarly ironic treatment of misguided idealism, in which a village bicycle mechanic, suddenly given magic powers, sets up a benevolent dictatorship based on deception, which rots and crashes under its own weight.

Although Siniavsky's writings are not explicitly anti-Marxist (they stress heavily, in fact, the element of determinism in history), they debunk the notion that the course of history is "scientifically" measurable and predictable. We have seen that in *The Trial Begins* and *On Socialist Realism* he calls in question the smug assumption that everything can be justified in terms of the Purpose. He seems to be making further sport of the activist Leninist notion of historically aware volition in "The Icicle," where the hero is given the occult ability to foresee the future but is unable to do anything about it, despite the urgings of a colonel of the secret police, who is anxious to speed up the inevitable victory of communism. The hero says that the colonel "was evidently confusing me with God."

At the same time, Siniavsky is acutely conscious of history. Although *Liubimov* is set in the Soviet period, the novel so resounds with references to the Russian past and the Russian cultural tradition that it becomes a kind of fantastic, impressionistic historical compendium. A word might be said here about the frequent interpretations of this novel, in Western reviews and commentaries, as a parabolic satire on the Revolution or an allegorical history of Russian communism. The trouble with such interpretations is that they simply do not withstand close scrutiny. It is true that the novel makes many specific allusions to developments and figures in Soviet history—including Lenin —and that it treats ironically many Soviet policies, slogans, institutions, prejudices, phobias, and patterns of behavior. There are likewise Aesopian or metaphorical treatments of topics that relate to the Soviet experience. But neither the direct nor the figurative references are comprehensive or systematic. Attempts to read this novel as a kind of *Animal Farm* are doomed to failure; the evidence is too random and fragmentary. On the other hand, as an examination of the Russian national character that *includes* the Soviet experience and draws heavily upon it, *Liubimov* does suggest some historical conclusions: the arrogant attempts of individuals to meddle with the natural, and unchartable, course of history culminate in disaster. And one of the reasons is that the human race—as illustrated in this instance by the Russians— is ultimately too intractable and primordially perverse to tolerate such interference.

In *Liubimov* and elsewhere Siniavsky's observations about the Russian national character are so numerous, varied, and often contradictory that it is impossible to make a consistent composite of them. If one were to extract from *Liubimov*, for example, a catalogue of Russian qualities, the most prominent of them would probably be backwardness, indolence, irresponsibility, drunkenness, superstitiousness, and deceptiveness. Such an exercise would be pointless, however, for *Liubimov* is obviously a work of hyperbolic satire, in which one might well expect to find a low estimate of human nature. But there is another source—*Unguarded Thoughts*, which is not fiction—in which Siniavsky makes similarly uncomplimentary remarks about his countrymen. Under duress at his trial, Siniavsky seemed partially to disavow the views expressed in *Unguarded Thoughts* when he testified that this was "not entirely" the author speaking. Nevertheless, these views must be considered as representing the general cast of his thought. Here is one of his observations:

> Drunkenness is our most basic national vice, and more than that our *idée fixe*. The Russian people drink not from need and not from grief, but from an age-old requirement for the miraculous and the extraordinary—drink, if you will, mystically, striving to transport the soul beyond earth's gravity and return it to its sacred noncorporeal state. Vodka is the Russian muzhik's White Magic; he decidedly prefers it to Black Magic —the female. The skirt-chaser, the lover take on features of the foreigner, the German (Gogol's devil), the Frenchman, the Jew. But we Russians will surrender any beauty (consider the example of Sten'ka Razin) for a bottle of pure spirits.
>
> Together with our propensity for theft (the absence of firm faith in actual, concrete ties), drunkenness gives us a certain wanderer's familiarity and places the *lumpen* in a suspicious position in the eyes of other nations. As soon as the "centuries-old principles" and the class hierarchy crumbled and were replaced by amorphous equality, this devious nature of the Russians pushed up to the surface. Now we are all devious (who among us does not feel something knavish in his soul and fate?). This gives us unquestionable advantages in comparison with the West, and at the same time it gives the life and strivings of our nation the stamp of inconstancy, frivolous irresponsibility. We are capable of putting Europe in our pocket or of loosing an interesting heresy there, but we simply are incapable of creating a culture. As with a thief or a drunkard, one must be prepared for anything from us. It's easy to knock about, to direct us by administrative measures (a drunkard is

> inert, incapable of self-direction, he drags along in the direc-
> tion they pull him). And one should also keep in mind how
> difficult it is to rule this wavering people, how oppressive this
> direction is for our administrators!

In other passages of *Unguarded Thoughts* there are mitigating
statements of admiration and praise, but most of Siniavsky's profound brooding over the Russian national character has a similarly
somber hue. What is important, however, is not the degree of praise
or censure but the quality of the meditation that underlies it. Siniavsky's thought has a Dostoevskian intricacy and spiritual charity; his
deep concern over Russia's failings is the concomitant of an equally
deep love of Russia. In an age in which the official image of the New
Soviet Man is tinged also with prominent vestiges of Russian chauvin-
ism, Siniavsky's painful efforts to understand his countrymen in their
true complexity are remarkable for their tonic, demythologizing flavor.

Because of its aphoristic nature, *Unguarded Thoughts* presents few
fully developed ideas, and many of the entries are exceedingly cryptic.
They do serve, however, to mark out areas of Siniavsky's concern that
are also treated in his fiction. One of these is sex, which he treats with
a candor that is never found in works published in the Soviet Union.
Siniavsky is not an erotic writer. Sterility and impotence, and the ugly,
perverse, and spiritually destructive features of sex are so heavily emphasized that sex as an aspect of love is almost totally excluded. In the
novels and stories Siniavsky employs sex not for its own intrinsic interest but as a device for characterization and thematic emphasis. In *The
Trial Begins,* as we have seen, sexual imagery is brought to bear on
the question of ends and means. The theme of abortion (including a
grotesque fantasy involving the transformation of human fetuses into
fish to increase the food supply) complements the novel's image of the
state as a deadening institution that inhibits creativity. Similarly, Vitya
and Tolya, a pair of secret police who crop up periodically in the
novel, are presented as a homosexual couple. The emasculating effects
of state servitude are suggested in the character of Karlinsky, a "liberal" but corrupt lawyer who, at the culmination of an elaborate campaign to seduce the beautiful and narcissistic Marina, proves impotent.
And the presumptuous futility of Lyonya, the young dictator in *Liubimov,* is underlined when he turns out to be an impotent husband,
masochistically tormenting himself as his wife Serafima regales him
with the details of her past affairs.

In other works—notably "At the Circus"—Siniavsky portrays sexual
activity as a nasty romp, inane and repulsive. To a certain extent he

seems to do this to stress a general atmosphere of alienation. But in *Unguarded Thoughts* he expresses such a frank and explicit loathing of sex (although also, characteristically, a sinful appreciation of its charms) that his use of it in fiction seems not merely an aesthetic matter but one of conviction. In one passage he argues that the basic attraction of sex is its quality of shameful defilement, its re-enactment of the Fall. Women are not only enigmatic (in sexual activity woman "becomes a priestess, guided by dark forces"), they are physically disgusting (there is even something repulsively libidinous in the way they eat sweets). Sex is a joyless burden: "If only one could become a eunuch, how much one could accomplish!" These and many other observations in *Unguarded Thoughts* do not necessarily indicate a striking abnormality in Siniavsky. But they do show a highly developed sense of the dichotomy between the flesh and the spirit.

In *Unguarded Thoughts* it is evident that Siniavsky is a profoundly religious thinker who believes in God with a visceral faith that seems to be based largely on wonder at the beauty of nature and the mystery of creation. He is distressed over modern man's lack of intellectual humility and, like Dostoevsky, he mistrusts refined, abstract philosophizing. At the same time, he maintains a small, Dostoevskian reservoir of intellectual doubt. He asks, mischievously:

> Lord, let me know something of You. Affirm that You hear me. I don't ask a miracle, just some kind of barely perceptible signal. Let, say, a bug fly out of that bush. Let it fly out right now. A bug is a most natural thing. No one will suspect. And it will be enough for me to be able to guess that You hear me and are letting me know it. Just say it: yes or no? Am I right or not? And if I am right, then let a train whistle four times from beyond the forest. There's nothing difficult in that—to whistle four times. And then I shall know.

Despite his intellectual's love of paradox (God is "unknowable and recognized everywhere, inaccessible and nearer than close, cruel and kind, absurd, irrational and utterly logical"), he values the simple and intuitive faith which he attributes to the ordinary Russian. At the same time, his faith is not so solemn as to prevent ironic or blasphemous treatment of religion. (*Liubimov,* for example, is full of comic references to the very same folk belief that he extols in *Unguarded Thoughts.*) He is preoccupied with death, but not morbidly so: his numerous remarks about death emphasize its finality and stress the importance of a life of dignity on earth.

In his criticisms of the quality of contemporary life—its excessive materialism, frantic complexity, blind reliance on scientific progress, hostility to quiet contemplation, and inhibition of sincere communication between individuals—there is an implicit longing for some other, spiritually purer culture. Only the dim outlines of this hypothetical superior culture can be deduced: his only utopia, *Liubimov*, is a negative one. Surely it would not be modeled along Western lines: Siniavsky is unmistakably opposed to capitalist ethics, and he suggests that the liberal concept of "freedom of choice" is an illusory one. If he believes in the goal of communism, his acceptance of it is undoubtedly qualified by strong ethical reservations. He seems to believe that man's nature is so sinful that it is not amenable to institutional measures. His ideal culture, then, would be governed by a charitable acceptance of human imperfectibility. It would also embody large elements of the Russian cultural tradition, for despite his satiric treatment of Russians, he obviously views his cultural heritage with nostalgia and feels that Russians as a nation have a uniquely profound—if tragic—understanding of life. All of this would suggest that Siniavsky is ultimately a conservative with strong neo-Slavophile tendencies.

Any summary of Siniavsky's personal philosophy based on his fiction, his literary criticism, and his motley collection of aphorisms is bound to do him an injustice. One can speak with some assurance about his art, but not about his beliefs. As a true ironist, he is so inconsistent and self-contradictory that his convictions are bound to elude a firm definition. One suspects, moreover, that his is a voice that has been muffled before its maturity. We can only hope that when he has served his prison sentence a way can be found for him to resume his career as a creative writer, to pursue the truth with the aid of his marvelous imagination.[5]

ELLENDEA PROFFER

The Master and Margarita

In the late twenties Bulgakov decided to write a story about the Devil in Moscow. *The Black Magician, The Consultant with a Hoof* were among the titles he considered.[1] The story (*povest*) was to follow the usual satirical pattern,[2] except for the series of chapters entitled "The Gospel According to Woland." In these drafts the story of the New Testament is parodied—told entirely from the point of view of the Devil. The story had already turned into a novel when Bulgakov burned it along with some other works in 1930.[3] Bulgakov rewrote it, and by late 1933 what was to be Part One of the novel had taken shape. In July of 1934 he added another major character—Margarita.[4] Margarita (the Master's love is left unnamed in the story told to Ivan in Chapter Thirteen) came after Bulgakov had married Elena Serge-evna Shilovskaya, and also after the ban was lifted on *Days of the Turbins* (*Dni Turbiny*).[5]

Although he wrote many other works during this time, for twelve years *The Master and Margarita* dominated his imagination:

> I am adapting *Dead Souls* for the screen and I'll bring the completed thing with me. Then the fuss with *Bliss* will start. Oh, so much work I have to do! But through my head wander my Margarita and the cat and the magic flights. . . .[6]

He worked on the novel sporadically and read it to his friends,[7] but he was too involved with events in the theater to give all of his attention to it. When *The Cabal of Hypocrites* proved a critical failure in 1936, Bulgakov, bitter about the theater's handling of the play, began to write *Theatrical Novel* (*Teatralny roman*). In 1937, when he diag-

From the author's dissertation *Mikhail Bulgakov,* Indiana University, 1970. Reprinted by permission of the author.

nosed his illness as neurosclerosis, he immediately put aside *Theatrical Novel* and resumed work on *The Master and Margarita*. He had carefully estimated the number of months left to him and told his wife that he would probably die in 1939 (he was only three months off). Since he was still involved in writing plays to make a living, he did not have time to complete two unpublishable novels—and he considered *The Master and Margarita* his major work. He completed the basic writing of the novel and began to rewrite passages and polish the language in 1939. By this time he was blind, so he dictated corrections to Elena Sergeevna and had her read the passages back to him. When he had completely finished the rewriting, the typescript of the novel was bound. But after the novel was already bound, Bulgakov was still debating whether to add an epilogue or not. He finally decided to add it, and he dictated the epilogue, which was then pasted onto the last page of the bound copy.[8] These facts are emphasized because one of the critical theories about *The Master and Margarita* is that Bulgakov did not finish the novel and that he eventually would have changed certain scenes. The novel was written, corrected, finished, and bound before Bulgakov died.

The very existence of *The Master and Margarita* came as a shock to most readers and critics of Russian literature when it was published in 1967. Considering the efficiency of the Soviet literary "underground," it is incredible that the manuscript did not circulate until it had been submitted to a publisher. For twenty years it was known only to a handful of Bulgakov's friends, all of whom were quite discreet. And the work itself is a strange one. What historian of Soviet literature could predict that a beleaguered and ailing writer, working all through the worst purges of the 1930's, would produce a novel containing a singular mixture of elements—realistic and fantastic, religious and satiric—for which there could not be even the remotest possibility of publication? And now that this unexpected work has appeared, what do we call it? What is its genre? What are its literary antecedents, traditions, and conventions? *The Master and Margarita* is probably the most "unsoviet" novel ever written in the Soviet Union (except perhaps for *Doctor Zhivago*); but it is not just an anomaly in Soviet literature—it would have been unusual in any country, especially during the thirties. It is like a technicolor extravaganza in the time of black and white film.

It is Bulgakov's unusual blend of elements which makes it difficult to find analogous works in any literature. For example, novels such as Kazantzakis's *The Last Temptation of Christ* and Sienkewicz's *Quo*

Vadis contain descriptions of biblical times, and deal with Pontius Pilate, but unlike Bulgakov's work they do not unite the retelling of a sacred story with the considerably more profane one of modern life. On the other hand, when we look to Soviet satirical novels such as Kataev's *The Embezzlers,* Ilf and Petrov's *Twelve Chairs,* and Ehrenburg's *The Adventures of Julio Jurenito* in search of a genre model, we discover that they contain little or nothing of the blend of the fantastic, the mystical, and realistic elements characteristic of Bulgakov.

Only in the 1960's did works offering a combination of fantasy and satire come into fashion again in the West—along with witches, astrology, flowers, and black humorists. Barth's *Giles Goat-Boy,* Heller's *Catch-22,* Vonnegut's *Player Piano,* and Grass's *Tin Drum* all have something of the spirit of *The Master and Margarita*—but they tend to emphasize the grotesque aspects of a given reality without incorporating supernatural events. Curiously enough, there is a certain propriety in the fact that *The Master and Margarita* was not published until the 1960's.

Obviously, the genre of the work presents the critic with many problems. One cannot say, as one could of Bulgakov's other works, that the author was writing an "epic novel" (*White Guard—Belaya gvardiya*), a "satiric melodrama" (*Zoya's Apartment—Zoykina kvartira*), a "tragedy" (*Last Days—Poslednie dni*), and so on. In the case of *The Master and Margarita* Bulgakov was not thinking in terms of set genres, he was writing a work which united all of his talents and concerns—a novel the genre of which he invented himself.

The term "Menippean satire" is used by Northrup Frye, Gilbert Highet, and others in the West, but it has rarely been applied to Russian literature.[9] In 1929, however, the ingenious Russian formalist critic M. Bakhtin published his *Problems of Dostoevsky's Poetics,* in which he deals at great length with the characteristics of Menippean satire in general. While his definition seems tailored to fit Dostoevsky's works, for the most part it agrees with the definitions of Frye and Highet. For example, they all agree that in Menippean satire the author usually deals in the fantastic; he uses a mixture of the serious and the comic, the dramatic and the narrative. Realistic sections (such as Trimalchio's dinner in the *Satyricon*) alternate with fantastic ones. The authors almost always reveal what tradition they are writing in by quoting from or referring to previous works of satire. Bakhtin's characterization of Menippean satire contains fourteen separate (and numbered) points,[10] but not all of these are logically distinct, so several have been combined in the following summary. In each numbered section a few of the ways in which *The Master and Margarita* fit the definition of the genre are suggested:

1. Menippean satire breaks away from traditional time-space considerations and is "not bound by any demands of external real-life verisimilitude."[11] *The Master and Margarita* takes place in three days, but the Devil stops the clock at midnight for his ball. The Pilate story is told by the Devil, dreamed by Ivan Bezdomny, and written by the Master.

2. Heroes are often legendary and can be actual historical figures. Pilate and Christ are both.

3. Mystical and religious elements are often portrayed in a coarse and comic way; the ultimate questions are discussed in the most incongruous circumstances. Woland's religious discussion with Berlioz and the treatment of the figure of Ha-Nozri fulfill this requirement of the genre.

4. The philosophical and the fantastic are united. This is true of the story of Pilate and the fate of the Master, and of the Devil's role in deciding their fates.

5. There is portrayal of unusual states of mind—dreams and insanity, especially schizophrenia. Ivan is supposedly schizophrenic, and the Master is near madness. Pilate is near a breakdown. There are several important dreams (Nikanor Ivanovich, Margarita, Ivan, Pilate).

6. Scandal scenes are typical. More than anyone since Dostoevsky, Bulgakov uses these—for example, the various scandals caused by Koroviev, Behemoth, and Azazello.

7. All types of social and philosophical targets are satirized. Topical satire is evident in the sections dealing with the writers' union, the literary world, foreign currency, Muscovite love of luxury, bribe-taking, and bureaucracy in general. The Communist "philosophy" is satirized in the conversation between Woland and Berlioz.

8. Ironies and paradoxes proliferate; for instance, the Devil does good, and Berlioz tells the Devil that God does not exist.

9. There is a mixture of stylistic levels; note, for instance, the difference between the consciously elevated style of the Pilate chapters and the other styles in the novel.

It should be clear from this summary how many features of *The Master and Margarita* match the characteristics of Menippean satire. However, the novel does not fit the category as neatly as some critics suppose. The blend of satire, realism, and fantasy with philosophical concerns and intervention by other-worldly personages—all this is typical of Menippean works. However, the love story of the Master and

Margarita does not seem to fit the pattern, nor does the story of Pilate —told as it is—seem to belong in a Menippean work. It is a sacred myth retold from a new point of view, not retold satirically, but treated realistically. An even more important way in which *The Master and Margarita* does not appear to fit the category is in its structure. Menippean works tend to be episodic. Characters are picked up and then dropped, adventure succeeds adventure, and building of suspense is impossible. The typical picaresque structure is some sort of journey taken by the protagonists; along the way they meet many people and have many adventures. Structure is, therefore, linear, and the characterization of all but the protagonists is superficial.

Bulgakov the craftsman excelled at suspense-building, and episodic form would not have allowed the Bulgakovian plot ironies and mystifications. Although there are various episodes in *The Master and Margarita,* they are far from unrelated—strings that a Menippean author would have left hanging Bulgakov weaves into an Easter basket. Thus the first chapter of the novel is the cause and explanation of all that follows. The three different worlds of the novel (the theater world, the literary world, and the fantastic world) become intertwined when Berlioz, Ivan, and Woland sit on a bench together.

Woland, of course, is the figure who introduces the Pilate story and leads us to the novel's fantastic events; Ivan is the writer who goes to Griboyedov and then to the asylum—where he meets the Master and hears of Margarita; Berlioz is the roommate of Stepa Likhodeev—the manager of the Variety Theater where Woland does his act, and Berlioz and Likhodeev share Apartment No. 50 which is where the ball and other fantastic events occur. By something akin to geometric progression the hundreds of characters in the novel develop through the activities of these three. Everyone is in some way linked to everyone else. All of the main characters are also connected to Pontius Pilate: Berlioz gives a lecture on Christ's nonexistence while telling Bezdomny how to rewrite his poem about Pilate; Woland tells them that he was present at Pilate's interview with Christ and proceeds to tell them the story; Ivan meets the Master who has written a novel about Pilate; in the first chapter in which she appears Margarita reads a fragment of the Master's novel, and Azazello meets her and gains her confidence by quoting the same fragment to her; Margarita, as a witch, wrecks Latunsky's apartment because he had written a nasty review of the Pilate novel; after the ball, the Devil brings the Master back to Margarita—and also presents him with a copy of the novel—which the Master had previously burned; the resourceful Aloysius Mogarich reads Latunsky's pernicious review of the Pilate novel and then writes a denunciation of the Master for harboring illegal literature, causing the Master to be put into prison—all so that Mogarich could get his apartment; when the Master and Margarita are led after death to where the suffering Pilate sits, Woland tells the Master that Yeshua and Pilate have read the novel—and the Master is to finish it with one sentence. And, finally, in the epilogue Ivan dreams about Pilate.

The careful structural integration extends to minor figures and motifs. Take Berlioz's head. It is chopped off in Chapter Three; in Chapter Nineteen Margarita sits next to some men who are discussing how Berlioz's head was stolen from his coffin that morning, during a funeral procession; in Chapter Twenty-Three Margarita finds out who stole it and why; Berlioz's head appears at Satan's ball where Woland drinks out of the skull (after explaining to Berlioz that the Devil *does* exist, and furthermore, is living in Berlioz's old apartment—and that one receives one's desserts in accordance with one's beliefs); and finally, in Chapter Twenty-Seven the twelve apostolic detectives are searching for Berlioz's head.

Another example of the attention paid to even small links in this circular chain of cause and effect is Annushka Chuma. Annushka is the old woman who spills the sunflower oil in Chapter Three—thus causing Berlioz to slip under the trolley. In Chapter Twenty-Four she appears again, and we discover that she lives in the same apartment house as Berlioz. As Woland and company leave Berlioz's apartment, they drop a diamond horseshoe which she picks up.[12] Azazello returns for it, takes it from Annushka, and after warning her not to take other people's property, "rewards" her with two hundred rubles. In Chapter Twenty-Seven she is arrested for trying to spend dollars—the rubles have changed into foreign currency.

It can be seen from all this that in *The Master and Margarita* characters do not enter and then disappear forever as in Menippean works, and that Bulgakov is very interested in tracing the further events in each character's life. The epilogue, while making fun of readers who ask "and then what happened to them," does nevertheless answer that question.

The novel does not shift its setting as much as one would expect a Menippean work to do. The action of the novel takes place in only two basic locations—Jerusalem and Moscow. In the Moscow narrative the action unfolds chiefly in three places: the Variety Theater (four chapters), the asylum (five chapters), and the apartment building 302-A (seven chapters). The other locations (Griboyedov, the cellar apartment, Margarita's mansion, Patriarchs' Ponds, Sparrow Hills, the Pashkov roof, and the fairy landscape) are used only once or twice each.

The Pilate story is unlike anything in other Menippean fiction. We read it with fascination even though we know the plot. It turns out, of course, that we do not know the fine points of the plot, and that the story is not the story of Yeshua's crucifixion, but of Pilate's crime. As the novel progresses, the story of Pilate is brought closer to the reader. The first chapter is twice removed—the Devil relates it to Berlioz and Ivan; the second chapter is presented as Ivan's dream; and the third and fourth come from the Master's novel. Finally, we meet Pilate as he sits in his torment: we had seen him as a character in the Master's novel, and now he is a character in the novel we are reading.

Since the reader knows the "what" of the Pilate story from the Bible, he can concentrate on the why and the how. The reader is interested in the changes made, the new interpretations of historical characters. While staying true to the main ideas of the plot (Yeshua and Judas both die), Bulgakov creates suspense by introducing a series of mysterious people and events. Under the layer of myth Bulgakov constructs a complicated network of political intrigues, deceptions, and charades. The story of Pilate is not a parody of the New Testament (that would fit in better with Menippean satire)—it is a retelling of a myth from the point of view of the executioner, and it is a retelling which is realistic, not satiric.

In *The Master and Margarita* all of Bulgakov's themes and talents are brought together. Here is the realistic and somewhat lyrical author of *The White Guard*, the gay and mocking feuilletonist of *The Adventures of Chichikov* (*Priklyucheniya Chichikova*), the satirist of *Theatrical Novel*, and the creator of the tragic *Last Days* (*Poslednie dni*). All of Bulgakov's customary themes come up: *tyomnye lyudi* ("dark people"), doctors and hospitals, dreams and hallucinations, food, acts of violence, spies, human nature and money, bureaucrats, the housing problem, writers and writing, love stories, the theater world, the subtleties of politics, the nature of history, the artist versus the state, and the law of justice.

More than any of Bulgakov's other works, *The Master and Margarita* deals explicitly with philosophical questions. Throughout the novel the author examines sources of evil and its gradations—from Ryukhin, who does not believe a word of anything he has ever written, to Pilate, who lets his "insolent office" stifle his conscience. While the novel is concerned with broad philosophical problems, it does not seek to solve them all—but simply to give them form. Bulgakov had a horror of dogma, and nothing could be more alien to him than proposing moral "solutions" à la Tolstoy. As a practicing ironist, Bulgakov could never surrender himself to any one creed—religious or political. What should be is never what is, and there are many problems ideologies cannot solve or explain.

Ironies of inversion proliferate in the novel: the Devil does good, Soviet citizens are just as susceptible to the charms of money as their prerevolutionary counterparts were, Berlioz assures the Devil that Jesus does not exist, Pilate the executioner ends by pretending the crucifixion never took place, the sane Ivan is cured in an insane asylum, and Barrabas the murderer is freed while the peaceful Ha-Nozri is killed. And dramatic irony permeates the Pilate chapters. When the reader sees Pilate's first words to his secretary ("So the accused is from Galilee"), he knows who is about to enter. The reader is sensitive to the double-edged irony in Jeshua's statements about the inaccuracy of what Matthew writes down on his parchment. When Jeshua says that he fears the "confusion" resulting from the misinterpretation of his speeches will last a long time, the reader draws the conclusion himself.

One reason for the use of dramatic irony in the Pilate section is that the narrator, so visible in the satiric parts of the novel, disappears in these chapters. In the rest of the novel this narrator is the chief purveyor of irony. Every time the narrator (located somewhere between Gogol's and Dostoevsky's) intervenes to "explain" what "really" happened, the omniscient narrator tradition is parodied and his "common sense" explanations strike us as ludicrous. The narrator and most of the characters are unable to accept the idea that they must foresake their usual methods when dealing with the unusual. The narrator changes personality often—sometimes he is the friendly reporter, as in Chapter One ("and as was discovered later"); at other times he is the cranky storyteller, irritated by his own digression about whether Griboyedov read *Woe from Wit* at his aunt's house, now Massolit, or not ("But the devil knows, perhaps he did read it—that's not important" p. 128).[13] Then there is the lyrical first-person narrator who hungrily describes Griboyedov's menu in Chapter Five (which ends with an address to the reader: "But enough, you're getting distracted, reader! Follow me!). This lyric narrator is also responsible for the highly eccentric first three pages of Chapter Nineteen—the beginning of Part II. The *za mnoy* ("Follow me!") of Chapter Five is repeated here, as the narrator characterizes himself by exclamations and breezy observations:

> Follow me reader. Who told you that real, true, eternal love is not to be found in the world! Just cut out the liar's vile tongue!
> Follow me, my reader, and follow only me, and I will show you such a love! (p. 275)

The narrator starts the next paragraph with "No!" and goes on to say the Master was mistaken when he said that Margarita had forgotten him, because: ". . . That could not be. She, of course, had not forgotten him." Here the narrator coyly "reveals the secret" of the beloved's name. He also describes her life and the location of her mansion. Here he cannot resist flaunting his inside knowledge—the house is located near the Arbat: "A charming place! Anyone can confirm this himself if he wishes to visit this garden. Let him come to me, I'll tell him the address, point out the way. The mansion is still standing to this day" (p. 275).

On the next page he slips into a role like that of Dostoevsky's narrator in *The Brothers Karamazov*. He exclaims: "Gods, my gods! What did that woman need?!" (p. 276). He goes on asking a series of questions and finally answers them himself: "I don't know, it's unknown to me" (*Ne znayu, mne neizvestno*). Finally, he reveals his identity: "And even my heart, that of an honest narrator [*pravdivogo povestvovatelya*], but an outsider, aches. . . ." This exuberant narrator, this outsider (*postoronny chelovek*), seems to disappear during the fantastic events. The next time we see him it is some thirteen chapters later in Chapter Thirty-Two, but although his rhetorical skill is unimpaired, the exuberance has changed to a contemplative sadness:

> Gods, gods! How sad the evening earth! How mysterious the mists over the bogs! Whoever has wandered in these mists, whoever suffered deeply before death, whoever flew over this earth burdened beyond human strength knows it. The weary one knows it. And he leaves without regret the mists of the earth, its swamps and rivers, and yields himself with an easy heart to the hands of death, knowing that it alone can bring him peace. (p. 476)

The humorous narrator of the epilogue seems to be a combination of all the other narrators of the story. When he is discussing the rumors and what the eventual fates of the characters connected with the

Variety were, he favors expressions like *vsyo-taki* ("however"); *da, krome togo* ("and besides"); *da, delo tut* ("but the point is"), *nu vot chto* ("but here's the point"), and he once again brings himself in as a witness: "The writer of these true lines himself, personally, while going to Theodosia, heard the story on the train . . ." (p. 484). This narrator believes all of the explanations given by the police and repeats them without questioning them. However, when discussing how Bezdomny and Nikolay are tormented when there is a full moon, his tone changes. At first it is the same: "Yes, years have gone by, and the events truthfully described in this book have receded and dimmed in memory. But not for everyone, not for everyone" (p. 494). The repetition of "not for everyone" (*ne u vsekh*) marks the beginning of the change. The new narrator seems to be very close to Bezdomny himself—everything is seen from his point of view. By the last two pages, the narrator has disappeared completely.

As should be evident, the narration of the novel is extremely complex, and deliberately so. As in *The White Guard*, Bulgakov does not even try to create suspension of disbelief by means of a transparent narrator who can give the reader the effect of immediacy or reality. Bulgakov was generally against affectations, and he felt that the transparent narrator was not merely an affectation—but a lie on the part of the writer. Obviously *someone* tells any story, *someone* selects the material and arranges it in a manner calculated to affect the reader in a certain desired way. In art the world is inevitably seen through the eyes of some artist. And artists become artists because they have an unusual way of looking at the world—so why pretend that the story tells itself? Bulgakov enjoyed his narrators[14] as much as he enjoyed his characters—in *The Master and Margarita* one narrator was his alter ego, one was a gossipy, somewhat dense townsman, and another was a kind of "official" reporter.

The three narrators (or three sides of the same one) are marked by different styles—as are the different strands of the novel which they narrate. Briefly, the styles involved are: 1. the feuilletonistic style of the "Moscow life" strand, characterized by parodies of administrative clichés, substandard colloquial expressions, and detailed description of humans, less so of places; 2. the exotic lexicon and rhetorically balanced prose of the Pilate sections—in which the descriptions are very realistic—involving sight and smell to a much higher degree than the "Moscow life" strand; 3. the realistic-cinematic style of the fantastic chapters devoted to Margarita's flight, bathing in the magic stream, the ball, and the flight of the Master and Margarita to the other world;

here the scene itself is stressed in minute detail and large panoramas are described.

The mixture of stylistic levels is very great, but Bulgakov manages them with great ease. The reader is not jarred by the switches from one to another. In some of his early satiric works Bulgakov had trouble combining the satirical with his naturalistic descriptions, especially in *The Fatal Eggs (Rokovye yaitsa)*. In *The Master and Margarita* he seems to have solved that problem by means of the stylistic variations —the reader becomes accustomed to the changes in the style of the satire and can accept the bloody shooting of Maigel with little sense of shock (by this time the reader has been exposed to the death of Berlioz and to the decapitation of Bengalsky). In general, most of the problems of sympathy and naturalistic detail which came up in Bulgakov's other satiric works are solved here by the size and nature of the novel—which permits the combination of a considerable number of disparate styles and themes. Bulgakov is not writing a comedy or a short story—both of which have built-in limitations—he is writing that most indefinable of all things, a novel. The sense of freedom he experienced in writing *The Master and Margarita* is shown by the salmagundi of styles, themes, and settings.

In *The Master and Margarita* Bulgakov felt free to create wildly imaginative characters and place them in equally imaginative surroundings, to risk his talent on retelling a sacred myth, and to describe that most literary of all characters, the Devil. All of this points to a certain relaxation and sense of play on the part of the author. There is a carnival atmosphere pervading the novel—the Lord of Misrule has come to Moscow to turn things upside down. Masquerades, mystifications, metamorphoses, operatic characters, and biblical figures are all framed against the Moscow of the thirties. The sumptuousness of Satan's ball emphasizes the quotidian nature of life outside in the city. Bulgakov lovingly describes the splendor of the ball—just as he lovingly describes the food and the crystal glasses and white tablecloths throughout the novel—whether at Griboyedov, Woland's, or the cellar. The description of the exotic willow grove on an island full of mythological creatures (Chapter Twenty-One) is one of Bulgakov's most magical descriptions, and it serves as a lovely prelude to the meeting of Margarita and Woland.

Magic pervades the novel—except for the chapters set in Jerusalem. In the Moscow narrative we are shown that magical forces are behind the strange events, but in the Jerusalem narrative only realistic explanations of events are suggested. The myth becomes realistic and the quotidian fantastic.

Magic first comes up when Woland introduces himself to Berlioz as a specialist in black magic and says that he has come to Moscow as a consultant—to examine a manuscript of the necromancer Herbert Aurilachs. Traditional magic motifs are scattered through the novel: the ball takes place on Good Friday when the dead traditionally rise from their graves; observing magical custom, Margarita is washed in blood and attends the ball naked, as do the other women; Annushka spills sunflower oil—the sunflower is a magic flower; Margarita covers herself with Azazello's cream, a typical magic ointment; Azazello himself was the fallen angel who taught men magic and women how to paint their faces.[15]

Much of the violence in the novel takes place in the world of magic, in connection with Woland's band; but three of the most striking (the beating of Yeshua, the death of Judas, and the crucifixion itself) are outside this world of magic. There are an unusual number of violent incidents in the novel: two decapitations, one explosion, a shooting, and murders by choking, stifling, poisoning, and stabbing, to name but a few. These come up at the ball, which is attended chiefly by criminals of one sort or another. But not all of the violent acts are committed by the criminals. Margarita herself scratches Behemoth on the car, digs her nails into Aloysius Mogarich's face, and gleefully destroys Latunsky's apartment. Since fire is the Devil's element, it is highly appropriate that Behemoth and Koroviev burn various buildings before they say farewell to Moscow; destroyed by fire are the Torgsin store, Griboyedov, the Master's cellar apartment, and, of course, apartment house 302-A.

At the center of this carnival of magic and destruction is the Prince of Darkness himself. In the first chapter Woland is very similar to Goethe's Mephistopheles[16]—even down to the reference to Kant, who was a contemporary of Goethe. But as the novel progresses, Woland reveals himself to be more than just a literary borrowing from Goethe. In both works the Devil figures play similar roles—but Bulgakov's Woland is not the witty drinking companion of Faust who tempts "so that man will strive." He is, rather, Lucifer the fallen angel—solemn, majestic, and only occasionally witty. Bulgakov's Devil is closer to Marlowe's version of Mephistopheles—a tormented figure who carries his suffering with him. Woland comes to Moscow as Lord Satan with a retinue, not alone as a scholar (as he does in *Faust*). Woland himself does not take part in all the undignified pranks—he lets the unholy

triumvirate of Behemoth, Koroviev, and Azazello do most of the devil-
ment. He is indulgent with regard to Behemoth's lies and tricks, and
sometimes he reveals a sense of humor—but his humor is ironic, not
gay. Woland maintains a certain regal distance—his retinue of demonic characters treats him like a Master, and Margarita herself is awed
by him and his power. The Mephistopheles of *Faust*, however, is a
worldly tempter who seems more human than hellish.

It is Lucifer, not Mephistopheles, who sneers at Matthew's desire
for a world without shadows or evil. Although Woland does not go to
the lengths Mephistopheles does to tempt Faust, he does test the Muscovites by offering them the opportunity to do something petty or base.
The emphasis is on free choice (it should be noted that the Devil is
markedly absent in the story of Pilate). Characters are not pressured into
making a morally wrong choice—they are simply presented with the opportunity. Woland enters the world of the "Soviet" Muscovites—supposed believers in sharing the wealth, hard work, and disdain for
superfluous luxuries. When he examines them in a mass grouping (the
Variety show), Woland sees that they are as avaricious, selfish, and
luxury-loving as they always were. They do, however, show compassion
(when Bengalsky is decapitated) and are not any worse than people anywhere:

> "Well, now," replied the magician reflectively. "They're peo-
> ple like any others, but thoughtless . . . but they do show
> some compassion occasionally. They're overfond of money, but
> then they always were. . . . Humankind loves money, no mat-
> ter if it's made of leather, paper, bronze or gold. They're
> thoughtless, of course, but then they sometimes feel compas-
> sion too. . . . They're ordinary people—in fact, they remind
> me very much of their predecessors, except that the housing
> shortage has ruined them. . . . (pp. 159-60)

Koroviev and Behemoth test the people in the Torgsin store—and find
that although the manager is officiously indifferent to the fate of a
starving citizen (as portrayed by Behemoth), the customers are touched.
Other characters fail the tests and are punished—Varenukha, Bengalsky, Annushka Chuma, and so on. Maigel the informer does not even
need a test; he has already made the wrong choices in life—and he is
killed because he is an informer.

Margarita's reign as Queen of Satan's Ball is her supreme test. Koroviev tells her that if she does her job well, she will be in a position
to ask something of the Devil in return. But she has to go through several more tests after the ball. Woland makes no move to ask her what

she would like as payment, and Margarita debates whether she should ask him first. Because she is proud, she decides not to ask. Woland, aware of her thoughts, is pleased when she prepares to leave having asked nothing of anyone. He tells her that she was right not to ask, and that now she may request one favor of him. Just as Margarita is about to ask for the return of the Master, the desperate voice of Frieda echoes in her mind and she asks that they stop giving Frieda the handkerchief she used to stifle her baby.[17] Margarita, who was touched by Frieda's pleas at the ball, explains to Woland that she wasted her one request in this way because she had given the woman definite hope and could not live in peace if she did not fulfill her promise. As it turns out, Margarita as Queen can accomplish this absolution herself, so the Devil allows her another request. Margarita has passed all of the tests, and the Master is returned to her.

All of these "tests" lead to an understanding of the relevance of the epigraph to the novel: ". . . So who are you, finally?—I am a part of that power, which eternally wants evil and which eternally accomplishes good."[18] In *The Master and Margarita* the Devil is a force which spurs men to action, who in testing or tempting man forces him to choose between good and evil—so that man does not simply experience "unconditional repose." The story of Pilate deals with a moral decision which is far more serious than any found in the Moscow narrative. Pilate's decision determines whether a man lives or dies. However, the Devil is completely absent from the Pilate chapters. Bulgakov, as a satirist, believed that the faults lie not in the stars, but in men themselves. If the Devil had an active role in the Pilate story, Pilate's decision could be seen as "fated" or "predetermined." What Bulgakov wanted to emphasize was the fact that Pilate could have made another choice—and did not do so.

Pilate is guilty of cowardice—the worst sin, as Yeshua is supposed to have said. However, Yeshua himself never mentions cowardice—Arthanius *ascribes* the remark about its being the worst sin to Yeshua, but as far as the reader knows Yeshua said nothing of the sort. As we know, Arthanius regularly lies to Pilate. The remark does come up again when Pilate dreams about talking to Yeshua, but it is Pilate himself who mentions it. When Pilate is freed, Woland quotes the phrase about cowardice—and says that the dog Banga is not guilty of it. But the word cowardice seems to be a kind of shorthand for something else. The immediate cause of Yeshua's death is Pilate's cowardice, but the basic reason is that Pilate makes a separation between personal morality and professional morality. As soon as he puts on his Procurator's cloak he loses his humanity and *becomes* his "insolent office." Pilate is blindly obedient to his Emperor—he has made a god of a man. Yeshua gently tries to make Pilate see the nature of earthly power. The philosopher agrees that his life may be hanging by a thread, but he points out that it is not Pilate who has strung it; and it can be cut only by the one who has suspended it. But it is too late for Pilate to learn from Yeshua.

Pilate represents the highest level of evil in the novel. This concern with degrees of evil is one of the unifying principles of *The Master and Margarita*. There are many levels of evil: Bezdomny's false poetry, Berlioz's smug dogmatism, Annushka's avarice, Varenukha's surliness, Likhodeev's woman-chasing, the bartender's lies, Maigel's spying, the destructive hypocrisy of Latunsky, and finally, Aloysius Mogarich's denunciation of the Master. All of these Muscovite evils are rather banal. At Satan's ball we are shown people who are guilty of worse sins—poisoners, debauchees, child murderers. But it is not merely the existence of all these levels of evil which Bulgakov emphasizes—he shows the *consequences* of evil acts, no matter how trivial they are. One man's decision, by virtue of a repeating cause-and-effect series, can affect many people. Latunsky writes a vicious review of the Master's novel; Mogarich reads it and denounces the Master—and the Master is imprisoned. On a very ordinary day two thousand years before Latunsky, one Procurator of Judea reviews a normal case and decides that the accused party is indeed guilty of speaking against the Emperor Tiberius. The Procurator offers the High Priest Caiaphas the choice (customary at holiday time) of freeing either the murderer Barrabas or the vagrant Ha-Nozri. Caiaphas chooses to let Barrabas live and is, therefore, given an infamous sort of immortality, as is Pilate. The acts of men, locked in a chain of causation, are always interdependent, and each in turn always generate new effects.

For most of the characters, political morality is the only morality. If the rules of political morality change, they change with them. The critics who attacked the Master's novel are an example of this. The critics may think that they believe what they are doing to the Master's novel is politically moral, but the Master detects a falseness in their articles which indicates that there is a difference between what they actually believe and what they write. Pilate is the clearest example of the narrow devotion to political morality which ignores the personal sense of right and wrong. Pilate can be defended on the ground that he was simply doing his job—any other Procurator would have made the same choice. But Pilate knows what he does and is aware that he is sending a harmless "madman" to death. Pilate is punished severely for stifling his conscience and following the dictates of his office. The striking autonomasia of the first Pilate chapter (*prokurator* is repeated 82 times) reinforces the idea that Pilate has *become* his office. Like the Master's critics, he is too cowardly to risk ruining his career (p. 311). This sort of "professional" cowardice is found in minor characters as well—such as the poet Ryukhin, who writes political poems and does not believe in any of them. The implication is that the moral attitudes of a Pilate are in no way different from the moral attitudes of a Latunsky—it is only their position in life that makes a difference.

The novel insists again and again that earthly power is fleeting— one can die at any moment, and all these allegiances to state or empire come to nothing. The empire crumbles and is remembered only by historians; political dogmas come and go, but the concepts of good and evil remain curiously the same. In the end the fame of Yeshua far exceeds that of the Emperor Tiberius.

This attitude leads to an implied theory, or nontheory, of history: history does not really develop, it simply continues. Bulgakov deliberately juxtaposes Jerusalem to Moscow and shows their similarities, not their differences—even though they are two thousand years apart. All of the examples above demonstrate that the same moral questions are raised in both narrative lines. However, this is not the only way in which the Moscow and Jerusalem narratives are connected. The impression that all of the strands are bound together results from formal as well as philosophical parallels. For example, a comparison of the chronology of the two sections shows that the events in both Moscow and Jerusalem take place at the same time of year and in the same week. The Moscow narrative begins on Wednesday at sunset, the Jerusalem narrative on Friday morning (with the events of Wednesday and Thursday reported). When Margarita enters the novel and meets Azazello it is Friday noon (the same Friday on which Woland's magic act takes place). Satan's ball takes place Friday night —and as mentioned before the dead can leave their graves on Good Friday. We already know that it is spring from the opening pages; therefore, we must conclude that the ball, like the crucifixion, takes place on Good Friday. Satan conveniently stops the clock at midnight, so that when Margarita leaves the ball it is early Saturday morning. The last installment of the Pilate story also ends early Saturday morning.

The cities are also linked by the weather. There are violent storms in Jerusalem after the crucifixion and in Moscow on Saturday at sunset as the Devil is preparing to leave. The two descriptions are so similar as to make the parallel between the cities unquestionable:

> *The darkness which had come* from the Mediterranean *shrouded* the *city* hated by the Procurator. The hanging *bridges* connecting the Temple with Anthony's dreaded tower *disappeared.* The abyss that had descended from the heavens engulfed the winged gods over the Hippodrome, the crenellated Hasmonaean *Palace,* the bazaars, the caravansaries, the alleys, ponds. . . . The great city of Yershalayim *had vanished as though it had never existed on earth.* (p. 378)
>
> This *darkness which had come* from the West *shrouded* the huge *city.* The *bridges* and *palaces* had *disappeared.* Everything *had vanished as if it had never been on earth.* (p. 456)

The exact parallels are italicized. Both passages are in prominent positions—the first is the opening paragraph of a chapter, the second the closing paragraph of a chapter. The Jerusalem passage is very specifically about Jerusalem. The names of buildings are mentioned, as is the name of the city itself. The Moscow description contains no such specific references—it could describe either city equally well.

Motifs from the Pilate story are repeated in the Moscow narrative, suggesting parallels between people and events, through space and time. Most of the motifs that are repeated occur originally in the very first Pilate installment—it is particularly rich in sensuous imagery. There are many such motifs—roses,[19] dogs, yellow and black combinations, the blood-red cloak, and the peculiar exclamation "O gods! gods!" (*o bogi, bogi.*) But the most important of these unifying motifs are the sun and the moon.

Sunlight is used to link Jerusalem and Moscow; both cities have buildings with golden roofs which reflect the sun. It seems significant that in Jerusalem there are golden idols and roofs which reflect the sun, and that in Moscow the churches of the Kremlin and the domes of Novodevichy monastery do the same. The glittering idols appear in Ivan's *dremota* (doze): "He saw a city . . . with roofs flashing in the sunlight . . . with bronze statues which glowed in the sunset . . . (p. 424). Margarita is also fascinated by the idols; she says:

> "Do you know . . . that just as you were going to sleep last night I was reading about the darkness that came in from the Mediterranean . . . and those idols, ah, those golden idols! For some reason they give me no peace. (p. 457)

The mist from the Mediterranean is mentioned in the first lines of Chapter Twenty-Five, and the reference to the idols occurs a page later:

> Other shimmering flashes called up from the abyss the palace of Herod the Great facing the temple on the Western hill; as they did so, the golden statues, eyeless and terrible, flew up into the black sky and stretching their arms toward it. Then the fire from heaven would be quenched again and great thunderclaps banished the gilded idols into the darkness. (pp. 378-79)

The sun is often used in the traditional manner, as a good sign: "The May sunshine shone on us. And quickly, quickly this woman became my secret wife" (p. 179). A variation on this motif is the sunset-sunrise opposition; the dawn usually signifies something good—the Devil operates at night, and Rimsky, for example, is saved from Hella by the cock's crow signaling the coming of dawn. When the Master and Margarita are freed and approach their home for eternity, the narrator says: "The Master and Margarita saw the promised dawn" (p. 482).

References to the sun occur both at the beginning of the novel and near the end—as the Devil arrives in Moscow and as he is leaving:

> His gaze halted on the upper stories, whose panes threw back a blinding, fragmented reflection of the sun which was setting on Mikhail Alexandrovich forever. . . . (p. 15)

> . . . The city spread but beyond the river with fragments of sun glittering from the thousands of West-facing windows, and on the onion domes of Novodevichy monastery. (p. 472)

The symmetrical repetition of this imagery reinforces the other parallels between beginning and ending (Bezdomny and Pilate, the "absurd notion of immortality" mentioned by Pilate).

The sun plays a large part in creating the atmosphere of the Pilate sections—Bulgakov uses it to evoke the exotic Middle-Eastern heat. But chiefly these sections emphasize the fact that Pilate is a tortured and sick man, living in a city and climate he detests, almost driven insane by the heat and his hemicrania. While the sun does not seem to bother such characters as Ha-Nozri, Matthew, or the centurion Krisoboi, it is the constant tormentor of Pilate.

The sunlight motif recurs most frequently in the first half of the novel, but the moonlight motifs increase in number and significance in the second half. Both the Pilate narrative and the Moscow narrative take place at the same time of month, and both have a full moon for much of their action. Some of the references to moonlight (*pri lune*) are general, while others are specifically to the full moon (*polnaya luna*)—always a time of the supernatural in magic and mythology.

The moon, like the sun, appears very early in the novel and is also used at the end.[20] The first important reference to the moon is at the end of Chapter Three, when as Berlioz dies: "One more time, and for the last time, the moon flashed, but was already shattering into pieces, and then it became dark" (p. 61). This description is "doubled" near the end of the novel when Bezdomny is walking to the bench on which he and Berlioz had sat that first evening: ". . . When Berlioz, long forgotten by everyone, saw the moon shattering into pieces for the last time in his life" (p. 494). This kind of symmetrical "doubling" is very typical for Bulgakov.

In the last Pilate section, we are told that the Passover feast is in progress. Judas notices the moon:

> Judas saw that two gigantic five-branded candlesticks had been lit . . . above the temple. . . . They seemed like ten huge lamps that burned over Jerusalem in rivalry with the single lamp climbing high above the city—the moon. (p. 307)

Bulgakov later repeats this in the Moscow narrative:

> [Ivan] cannot control what happens at the springtime full moon. As soon as it draws near, as soon as that heavenly body begins to reach that fullness it once had when it hung in the sky high above the two five-branched candlesticks, Ivan Nikolaevich grows uneasy . . . (p. 381)

In the chapters concerning Azazello's cream and the ball ("Krem Azazello" and "Veliky bal u satany"), it is emphasized that all of the fantastic events take place in the light of the full moon. The ball is called the "spring ball of the Full Moon, or the Ball of the One Hundred Kings" (p. 319). Woland himself explains to Margarita that "The night of the full moon—is a holiday night" (p. 349).

While other characters (notably Ivan in the Epilogue) are sometimes associated with the moon images, in the main body of the novel there is a particularly large number of references to the moon in connection with Pilate and the Master. The Master visits Ivan at night and "The unknown Master began to get agitated, and in anguish began wringing his hands, looking at the moon" (p. 216). The Master is returned on the night of the ball, and just after Margarita requests his return the moon appears: "In the distant heights a full moon came out—not the morning but the midnight moon (p. 360)." However, the returned Master apparently thinks he is having hallucinations: "But for some unknown reason he got depressed and anxious, got up from his chair, wrung his hands and turning to the distant moon, trembling, began to mutter: 'There is no peace for me in the moonlight. . . . Why have you disturbed me? Oh, gods, gods! . . .'" (p. 369).

Pilate gazes at the moon, just as the Master dies in the asylum. Pilate then dreams of the blue path of moonlight, a dream which foreshadows his eventual fate:

> The couch was in semidarkness, shaded from the moon by a column, but a ribbon of moonlight stretched from the staircase to the bed. And the moment the Procurator lost contact with surrounding reality, he immediately started out along the gleaming road and went up and up, directly toward the moon. . . . There had been no execution! None! This was the charm of this journey upwards on the staircase of the moon. (pp. 402-3)

Pilate's complaint that there is no peace for him in the moonlight almost exactly corresponds to the Master's similar statement (quoted above); however, Pilate makes a connection between his moonlight torture and what he has done that day as part of his job: "And at night, in the moonlight. I have no peace! . . . Oh gods. . . . You also have a bad duty, Mark. As a soldier, you punish . . ." (p. 494).

When Margarita and the Master get their first glimpse of Pilate himself, the moon imagery dominates again:

> The moon flooded the small plateau with bright green light, and Margarita soon discerned in the wasteland an armchair and the white figure of a man sitting in it . . . The moon helped Margarita well, it was brighter than the best electric light, and Margarita saw that the sitting man, whose eyes seemed blind, rubbed his hands with short, quick movements and stared at the disk of the moon with his unseeing eyes. She saw now that next to the massive stone chair, glittering with strange sparks in the moonlight, there lay a dark, huge, sharp-eared dog, looking at the moon with the same troubled eyes as his master. . . . (pp. 478-79)

Woland explains that "in the moonlight he gets no peace" (p. 479), and that the Procurator always says the same things when the full moon comes to torment him with insomnia:

He says that even in the moonlight he has no peace, and that
he has a bad job. He says this always, when he is not sleeping,
and when he sleeps he always sees the same thing: a path of
moonlight. And he wants to climb it and talk to the prisoner
Ha-Nozri because he had not said all that he wanted to say.
. . . But alas, for some reason he never succeeds in getting on
that road. . . . (p. 479)

In the epilogue everyone is tormented by the full moon. Bengalsky
(master of ceremonies at the Variety) kept the "unpleasant, painful
habit of falling into a state of anxiety every spring during the full
moon" (p. 490). Nikanor Ivanovich "alone with only the company of
the full moon—got terribly drunk" (p. 492). Ivan gets irritable, loses
his appetite, and cannot sleep when the moon begins to reach the
fullness it had when it "hung high above the two five-branched candle-
sticks" (p. 494). Going home he takes a route which goes by both the
oil shop (where Anna bought the oil Berlioz slipped on) and Margarita's apartment house. In the garden of this house is Nikolay Ivanovich, also condemned to regret in the moonlight that he did not go off
with Natasha. In Ivan's dream at the end of the book, he sees the
moonlight path Pilate always dreamed of (p. 497). The dream changes
and the Master and Margarita appear from the moonlight path:

> Then the beam of moonlight froths up, and a torrent of light
> gushes out of it and overflows in all directions. The moon is
> mistress of all, the moon plays, dances, gambols. Then a
> woman of incomparable beauty emerges from the stream and
> walks toward Ivan, leading by the hand a bearded man. (pp.
> 497-98)

Margarita kisses Ivan on the forehead and then

> recedes, recedes, withdraws with her companion to the
> moon. . . .
> And then the moon bursts into frenzy, it tumbles streams of
> light upon Ivan, it splashes light in all directions, a moonflood
> fills the room, the light sways, rises, washes over the bed. And
> it is then that Ivan Nikolaevich sleeps with a blissful face. (p.
> 498)

Near the end of the novel the Master says he has overcome the fear
which had enveloped him, but not because of any treatments at the
clinic: ". . . I am not afraid, because I've already experienced everything, they frightened me too much, and they can't frighten me anymore" (p. 460). When the Master advises Margarita to leave him so

that she will not ruin her life, she calls him a "skeptical, unhappy man" (p. 460).

When the reader first hears the Master's story it may not be absolutely clear just where he spent the three months which elapse between the knock on the door and his entrance into the asylum (after finding that someone else has his apartment). Later we discover that Aloysius Mogarich had written a denunciation of the Master. This *donos* ("denunciation") was inspired by the reading of Latunsky's attack; and anyway Mogarich wanted the Master's living quarters. His charge was that the Master possessed illegal literature (p. 365). The Master has been to prison where, he says, hunger and cold became his constant companions. When he says "they broke me" (p. 369), he does not mean the critics; and when he says bitterly, "I have suffered too much because of it" (p. 370)—that is, the novel—he is not referring to his wounded ego.

But his fear came before his arrest. He tells Ivan specifically that it was *not* the articles on his novel that caused it:

> —And then came the third state: fear. Don't misunderstand me, I was not afraid of the articles; I was afraid of something else which had nothing to do with them or with my novel. I started, for instance, to be afraid of the dark. I was reaching the stage of psychological illness. . . I felt, especially just before going to sleep, that some very cold, supple octopus was fastening its tentacles around my heart. I had to sleep with the light on. (p. 184)

Earlier in this same chapter he says that the failure of his novel seemed to have withered his soul, that something began to happen to him, that he was sunk in depression, and that the psychiatrist had probably figured it out a long time ago. Whether it was that the Master (who lived, after all, in the Soviet Union of the thirties) expected arrest at any moment or whether it was simply a breakdown, the reader can never be certain. The total impression of all this is similar to the impression of a sick, hopeless Pilate—both he and Pilate have given up the struggle and long for peace.

The sunlight and moonlight motifs have a larger significance for the novel as a whole. The key to the frequent repetitions of both motifs can be found in the words of Satan himself, who chides Matthew for his monochromatic view of things:

> You spoke your words, as though you do not acknowledge the existence of shadows or of evil. Think now: where would your

good be if there were no evil, and what would the earth look like without shadow? Shadows are thrown by people and things. There's the shadow of my sword. But shadows are also cast by trees and living beings. Do you want to strip the whole globe by removing every tree and everything alive to satisfy your fantasy of naked light? You are stupid. (pp. 452-53)

This passage is Bulgakov's restatement of ideas found in the prologue to *Faust*. In the prologue the Lord is identified with the sun and lives in everlasting light (see further the naked light mentioned above). The angels point out that on earth there is no such unchanging light, but an alternation of day and night, light and dark. This theme recurs in Goethe's work and comes to have a more specific meaning: Faust longs for the light and wishes never again to suffer darkness and longing; Mephistopheles says of the Lord that "He dwells in eternal light; us [the devils] he has consigned to darkness, and you human beings have only day and night." The Devil is pointing out that unless a man is presented with the opportunity of doing evil, good cannot triumph. Untested goodness is merely inertia.

This corresponds to one of the central ideas of *Faust*—the Devil is necessary to keep man striving. In the world of Faust, it does not seem to matter whether a man does bad or good—as long as he acts. As the angels carry Faust (who has certainly erred) up to Heaven they say:

> *Er findet sich in einem ew'gen Glanze,*
> *Uns hat er in die Finsternis gebracht,*
> *Und euch taugt einzig Tag und Nacht.* (Lines 1782-85)

Goethe's theory of polarities,[21] which underlies *Faust*, emphasizes that moral concepts are only one facet of the whole, of which both immorality and amorality are a part. Action is all that matters—whether good or bad. Although this theory may explain why the Master received not light but peace, it is not the philosophical idea which underlies Bulgakov's novel. Woland assures Margarita at one point that: "Everything will be as it should—this is what the world is built upon" (*Vsyo budet pravilno, na etom postroen mir*)—(p. 480). But the world we are shown is not *pravilno:* Latunsky flourishes while the Master is destroyed; the gentle philosopher is killed and the murderer Barrabas is set free—and Pilate's punishment does not negate the crucifixion.

All of these examples of thematic and formal parallels help to explain why it is that *The Master and Margarita* seems a unified novel in spite of its clear separation into two narrative strands. The actual story of Pontius Pilate only takes up four chapters of the novel (two in Part I, two in Part II), but its themes and motifs gradually reticulate. By the end the plexus has come to dominate the Moscow narrative, and the major themes and motifs of the Pilate story all come together in Ivan's dream in the Epilogue. The Master's novel about Pilate has played a major role in *The Master and Margarita*. Although the first two chapters of the Master's novel are presented as being told by Woland and dreamed by Ivan, we assume since the style is the same, that it is all part of the Master's novel. There are, however, other mystifications concerning the Master's novel.

In Chapter Thirteen the Master tells Ivan what the last words of his novel are to be: ". . . The fifth procurator of Judea, the knight Pontius Pilate" (p. 176). But the purported last words of the final section from the Master's novel are not exactly the same: "The fifth procurator of Judea, Pontius Pilate" (p. 416). Since Bulgakov was unusually careful about such repetitions, we must conclude that the Master's real novel does not end there. In Chapter Thirty-Two we find out that the novel is not finished when Woland tells the Master that "they" have read the novel and "They said only one thing, that it was unfortunately unfinished" (p. 479).

Woland has taken the Master and Margarita to see Pilate himself sitting in the moonlight. Yeshua has asked that Pilate be freed, and Woland tells the Master to tell Pilate that he is free. Woland turns to the Master and says, "Well now you can finish your novel with one sentence." But the sentence used is not the one that the Master has planned: "Free! Free! He awaits you!" (p. 480).

But the ending the Master had originally planned *does* appear in the novel—both at the end of Chapter Thirty-Two (which was meant to be the final chapter of *The Master and Margarita*), and at the end of the Epilogue which *is* the end of *The Master and Margarita*. In both places the lines end: ". . . The fifth procurator of Judea, the knight Pontius Pilate." In this way we are apprised that the novel the Master wrote is the one we have just read—and that its title is *The Master and Margarita*.

Notes

Introduction

1. There are at the present writing three acceptable histories of Soviet Literature: Gleb Struve, *Soviet Literature, 1917-1950*, Norman, Okla., 1951 (the most complete for the period covered). A revised edition of this work is in preparation; Vol. I has appeared: *Russian Literature Under Lenin and Stalin*, Norman, Okla., 1971; Edward J. Brown, *Russian Literature Since the Revolution*. New York, 1963, revised and enlarged, 1969; and Johannes Holthusen, *Russische Gegenwartsliteratur*, Vol. I, 1963, Vol. II, 1969.

2. Vladimir Markov's *The Longer Poems of Velimir Khlebnikov*, University of California Press, Berkeley, 1962, helps to put Khlebnikov in proper perspective. Yury Tynyanov's article *"Promezhutok,"* written in 1923 and published in his *Arkhaisty i novatory*, Moscow, 1929, contains excellent criticism of Khlebnikov, Mayakovsky, Esenin, and many other poets of the early period.

3. A distinguished collection of works about Pasternak is Donald Davie and Angela Livingstone, eds. and trs., *Pasternak, Modern Judgments*, New York, 1969.

4. *Anna Akhmatova: sochineniya*, by G. P. Struve and B. A. Filippov, eds., New York, 1965.

5. Wiktor Woroszylski, *The Life of Mayakovsky*, tr. from the Polish by Bolesław Taborski, New York, 1971. A Czech scholar, Zdenek Mathauser, has produced a book and several interesting articles on Mayakovsky. These deal principally with the influence of the Russian avant-garde on his work. See Zdenek Mathauser, *Umeni poezie; Vladimir Majakovski a jeho doba*, Prague, 1964.

6. Patricia Blake's essay was published as the introduction to the collection of materials edited by her: *Vladimir Mayakovsky, The Bedbug and Selected Poetry*, New York, 1960.

7. *Osip Mandelshtam, Collected Works in Three Volumes,* G. P. Struve and B. A. Filippov, eds., New York, 1967.
8. See also the study by Elizabeth Klosty Beaujour, *The Invisible Land; a Study of the Artistic Imagination of Iurii Olesha,* New York, 1970. A translation of a part of Arkady Belinkov's work on Olesha appeared in *The Russian Review,* October 1971, pp. 356-68.
8. See also the study by Elizabeth Klosty Beaujour, *The Invisible Land.* A ed., New York, 1963.
9. There is an excellent study of this poet: Simon Karlinsky, *Marina Cvetaeva, Her Life and Art,* Berkeley, 1966.

A Note on Soviet Poetry

1. There are two useful anthologies which contain selections from Soviet poets in translation: Vladimir Markov ed., and Merrill Sparks tr., *Modern Russian Poetry,* New York, 1967, and Dmitry Obolensky, *The Penguin Book of Russian Verse* (with translations into prose).

On a Generation That Squandered Its Poets

1. Ilya Lvovich Selvinsky (1899-), the leader of a modernist group of poets known as "constructivists." Nikolay Aseev (1889-1963) was a poet close to the futurist movement—ed.
2. When we say "private" we certainly do not intend to detract from the value of their work as poetic craftsmanship. The poetry of Evgeny Baratynsky or of Innokenty Annensky, for instance, might be called "private."
3. Leonid Nikolayevich Andreev (1871-1919), a writer of short stories and plays pessimistic in content and symbolic in manner—ed.
4. A nearly untranslatable Russian word which suggests "mores," "convention," the "established way of life," the "daily grind," "middle-class values," and so forth—ed.
5. *Komi,* an aboriginal non-Russian minority who live north and east of the Ural mountains and speak a language belonging to the Finno-Ugrian group—ed.
6. Pyotr Yakovlevich Chaadaev (1794-1856), author of a famous "philosophical letter" which was highly critical of Russian culture and Russian life—ed.
7. Nikolay F. Fyodorov (1828-1903) was a Russian philosopher who maintained that the resurrection of the dead should become a major project of Christendom—ed.
8. The title of an early collection of poems—ed.
9. Bela Kun (1886?-1940?), Hungarian Communist, head of the short-lived Hungarian Soviet government in 1919—ed.
10. These are all prominent poets of the first three decades of the nineteenth century—ed.

Akhmatova and Mayakovsky

1. M. V. Nesterov (1862-1942), an outstanding Russian painter who, in his earliest period, dealt with religious themes—ed.
2. Fyodor Ivanovich Tyutchev (1803-1873), a lyric poet.

The Unshackled Voice: Anna Akhmatova

1. The worst years of the purges in the 1930s, when Yezhov was head of the NKVD, and when Akhmatova's husband was shot and her son imprisoned.
2. Tsarskoe Selo, a country palace built for Catherine the Great and surrounded by country houses; also a small town where Akhmatova often stayed.

Modern Russian Poetry: Velimir Khlebnikov [Excerpts]

1. Stoglav (literally The Hundred Chapters), a collection containing the decisions of a sixteenth-century Church Chronicle—ed.
2. Russian literary scholars of the early part of the century—ed.
3. Premier of the Provisional Government in 1917, under whose rule counterfeiting was not uncommon—ed.
4. A. S. Griboyedov (1795-1829), a dramatist, author of Woe from Wit. Ermolov was the commander of Russian armies in the Caucasus, on whose staff Griboyedov worked—ed.
5. Syllabo-tonic is the technical name for the traditional metrical system of Russian nineteenth century poetry—ed.
6. This article was written in 1919—ed.
7. Emilio Filippo Tommaso Marinetti (1876-1944) was an Italian poet who founded the futurist movement in literature (1911)—ed.
8. A. E. Kruchonykh (1888-1968), one of the most active members of the futurist group, and a close collaborator of Khlebnikov—ed.
9. L. V. Shcherba (1880-1944), a Russian linguist, professor at the University of Leningrad—ed.
10. Having accepted such a definition of poetry, we can term the method of research resulting from it expressionistic.
11. Franz Saran, a German philologist who specialized in problems of rhythm and meter—ed.
12. Hans Sperber, a German linguist who emphasized the importance of emotional factors in the development of language—ed.
13. Compare the hyperbole used in everyday parlance: "That's quick: one foot here, the other there."
14. The pun is not translatable: "ostavatsya s nosom" actually means "to be cheated"—ed.
15. Polotsky, Simeon (1629-1680), a Russian cleric and literary man, one of the earliest poets—ed.

16. Lomonosov, M. V. (1711-1765), a Russian scientist and poet, a pioneer in the development of modern metrics—ed.
17. Derzhavin, G. R. (1743-1816), and Nekrasov, N. A. (1821-1877), were poets and, in their time, innovators in verse form—ed.
18. Hanslick, Eduard (1825-1904), author of *Vom Musikalische-Schönen* (Leipzig, 1854)—ed.
19. Vyacheslov Ivanov (1866-1949), another leading symbolist poet—ed.
20. A. M. Peshkovsky (1873-1933), a Russian linguist and a specialist in the problems of syntax—ed.
21. A. A. Fet (1820-1892), one of the leading lyric poets of the nineteenth century—ed.
22. O. M. Brik (1888-1945), a leading theoretician of the Russian formalists—ed.
23. Literally "obese clouds," where an etymological relationship of "obese," and "cloud" is suggested by phonetic similarity—ed.
24. *Molnienosna*, literally, *hearing* lightning.
25. Josef Zubaty (1885-1931), a Czech linguist, interested in problems of comparative grammar—ed.
26. I. F. Annensky (1856-1909), a Russian poet who belonged to the "decadent" movement—ed.
27. See his article "Zvukovye povtory" (*Sound repetitions*) in *Poetika* (Petrograd, 1919).
28. Elena I. Guro (1877-1913), a poet and a member of the Cubo-futurist group—ed.
29. Franz von Stuck (1863-1908), a German painter who specialized in allegorical subjects—ed.
30. F. F. Fortunatov (1848-1914), a Russian linguist, interested in comparative linguistics—ed.
31. V. K. Tredyakovsky (1703-1769), a poet and theoretician of verse, one of the creators of the metrical system in use during the late eighteenth and the nineteenth century—ed.

V. V. Khlebnikov

1. The formalist Organization for the Study of Poetic Language, founded in 1915 in Petrograd—ed.
2. *Modern Russian Poetry* (*Noveyshaya russkaya poeziya*), Moscow, 1919. See above, pp. 58-82.
3. Both early futurist publications.
4. V. V. Kamensky (1884-1961), a poet who belonged to the futurist group.

On Khlebnikov

1. *Budetlyanin*, an almost exact translation into Russian of the word "futurist"—ed.

2. Fyodor Ivanovich Tyutchev (1803-73), a Russian poet who lived abroad 22 years, mainly in Munich, where he met Heine and Schelling. He was somewhat influenced by German Romantic poetry—ed.

3. Yakov Karlovich Grot (1812-93), an outstanding Russian philologist who wrote the influential, standard work *Russian Orthography* (1885)—ed.

4. Nikolay Nikolaevich Strakhov (1828-95), philosopher, critic, journalistic ally of Dostoevsky, friend of Tolstoy, and author of *Reminiscences and Fragments* (1892) about Tolstoy—ed.

5. Aleksandr Petrovich Sumarokov (1718-77), and Lomonosov, Mikhaylo Vasilevich (1711-65), both poets and theorists of Russian versification who laid the foundations for modern Russian literature within the framework of Neoclassicism—ed.

6. Pushkin's first long poem (1820), a romantic epic featuring characters from the early period of Russian history—ed.

7. Nikolay Ivanovich Lobachevsky (1792-1856), great Russian mathematician, creator of non-Euclidian geometry—ed.

8. Dmitry Vladimirovich Venevitinov (1805-27), a philosophical poet, friend of Pushkin, leader in the twenties of a society called the Lovers of Wisdom, devoted to German Idealistic philosophy.

9. Pyotr Andreevich Vyazemsky (1792-1878), poet and intimate friend of Pushkin.

The Poetry of Pasternak

1. R. M. Glière (1875-1956), prolific composer, conductor, and teacher. His pupils included Prokofyev and Khatchaturyan—ed.

2. Tretyakov and Chuzhak were leaders of the "Lef" group associated with Mayakovsky.

3. M. I. Tsvetaeva (1894-1941), a modern lyric poet who lived for many years in the emigration, then returned to the U.S.S.R. in 1938, where she committed suicide—ed.

4. Vera Fyodorovna Komissarzhevskaya (1864-1910), actress and producer of many plays—ed.

Views and Reviews: Postscript on Pasternak

1. Boris Pasternak, *I Remember; Sketch for an Autobiography*. Translated by David Magarshack (New York, 1959), pp. 121-22.

2. See Edmund Wilson, et. al., "Legend and Symbol in *Doctor Zhivago*," *The Nation*, 25 April 1959.

3. Edmund Wilson, *The New Yorker*, 15 November 1958, p. 216.

4. Pantheon edition of *Doctor Zhivago*, translated by Max Hayward and Manya Harari, pp. 284-85.

5. Ibid., p. 406.

6. Ibid., p. 291.
7. Ibid., p. 164.
8. Ibid., p. 467.
9. F. Stepun, "B. L. Pasternak," *Novy Zhurnal*, March 1959, p. 202.
10. Nils Ake Nilsson, "Pasternak: 'We Are the Guests of Existence,'" *The Reporter*, 27 November 1958, p. 35.
11. John Strachey, "The Strangled Cry," *Encounter*, December 1960, pp. 36-37.

On Reading Mandelstam

1. "O svobode v poezii," *Vozdušnye Puti*, II (1961), 228.
2. *Zvezda*, 12 (1958), 122.
3. None other than the poet Akhmatova, the author assures me—ed.
4. *Peterburgskie zimy* (New York, 1952), p. 118.
5. *Očerki po istorii russkoj sovetskoj poezii* (Moscow, 1936), p. 60.
6. "*Preodolevšie* simvolizm," *Russkaja Mysl*, 12 (1916), 43.
7. This poem appears on page 59 of Vol. I of the Inter-Language Literary Associates edition of Mandelstam's poetry.
8. *Vozdusnye Puti*, II (1961), 94.
9. *Tekuščaja literatura* (Moscow, 1930).
10. "Put' k setke," *Literaturnyj Kritik*, 5 (1933), 116.
11. *The Prose of Osip Mandelstam*, Princeton University Press, 1965. Second printing, with corrections, 1967.
12. Since this was written a collection of his letters has been published in Volume III of the I.L.L.A. edition of Mandelstam's works.

Osip Mandel'štam and His Poetry

1. A similar call for "hardness," "clarity," or "concreteness" in poetry was made by poetic groups in other countries as well, the English imagists or the Italian Hermetists, for instance. Hardness could refer to the subjects chosen or to the use of certain euphonic devices or—more importantly—to a more direct relation between language and reality after the Symbolist "rien, que la suggestion" (Mallarmé).
2. The numbers refer to the numbers of the poems in O. Mandel'štam, *Sobranie sočinenij*, I (Washington, 1964).
3. See Pape, W., *Wörterbuch der griechischen Eigennamen*, 3. Aufl. Braunschweig 1911, p. 1494 or Pauly's *Real-Encyklopädie der classischen Altertumswissenschaft*. Zweite Reihe. Neuter Halbband, Stuttgart 1934, p. 91ff.
4. This metaphor is perhaps connected with the Greek image of bees playing on the lips of great poets, see Pauly's *Real-Encyklopädie*, dritter Band, Stuttgart 1899, p. 447.
5. See my paper *Life as Ecstasy and Sacrifice. Two poems by Boris Pasternak* in Scando-Slavica V, 1959.
6. Taranovsky, K. *Stichosloženije Osipa Mandel'štama* (*s 1908 po 1925*

god) in International Journal of Slavic Linguistics and Poetics V, 1962, p. 123.

7. Another explanation which demands a more detailed examination is the impact of tradition, of the verse created by Puškin and the generation of Romanticism. It may have kept back the development of a free verse in Russia. Although Symbolist poets and their successors are exploring new verse forms, they seem to hesitate to change to a completely free verse form; a feature very striking on comparison with the simultaneous development of European poetry. An examination of the problems of free verse in Russia is indeed much needed.

A Look Around: The Poetry of Andrey Voznesensky

1. P. Levi, "Versions of Voznesensky" (*The Guardian,* Manchester, 5 August 1966), a review of A. Voznesensky, *Selected Poems,* trans. with introduction by H. Marshall, London, 1966.

2. For similar reservations felt by Soviet critics see I. Grinberg, "Postoyannaya izmenyayemost" (*Voprosy Literatury,* 2, Moscow, February 1965, pp. 33-4) and St. Rassadin, "Pokhozhe na vsyo nepokhozhe" (*Voprosy Literatury,* 4, Moscow, April 1965, pp. 56-72).

3. A. Voznesensky, *Antimiry* (*Izbrannaya lirika*), Moscow, 1964.

4. *Ibid.,* pp. 8 and 35.

5. J. P. Sartre, *L'être et le néant,* Paris, 1943, p. 276.

6. A. Voznesensky, *op. cit.,* pp. 6 and 33.

7. *Ibid.,* p. 152.

8. *Ibid.,* p. 150.

9. *Ibid.,* p. 105.

10. J. P. Sartre, *op. cit.,* p. 325.

11. My proposal as to how this motif may be considered a coherent part of Voznesensky's imagery might answer the criticism of the apparent gratuitousness of this image made by St. Rassadin, *op. cit.,* p. 60: "The symbolic (and as a symbol very hazy) image of a motor cycle which occurred in 'Triangular Pear' wanders now from poem to poem, and the real (if indeed real) meaning of the symbol has long worn away. There remains only a pretension to symbolism,—all the more superficial for being so insistent."

12. A. Voznesensky, *op. cit.,* p. 42.

13. *Ibid.,* p. 42.

14. *Ibid.,* pp. 5 and 146.

15. Notes about himself given by Voznesensky in reply to a questionnaire (*Voprosy Literatury,* 9, Moscow, September 1962).

16. A. Voznesensky, *op. cit.,* p. 20.

17. *Ibid.,* p. 30.

18. *Ibid.,* p. 139.

19. *Ibid.,* p. 98.

20. *Ibid.*, p. 132.
21. *Ibid.*, pp. 3 and 145.
22. *Ibid.*, p. 161.
23. *Ibid.*, p. 17.
24. *Ibid.*, p. 18.
25. *Ibid.*, pp. 10 and 176.
26. *Ibid.*, pp. 10 and 176.
27. *Ibid.*, p. 76.
28. *Ibid.*, p. 109.
29. *Ibid.*, p. 121.
30. C. M. Bowra, *Poetry and Politics, 1900-1960*, Cambridge, 1966, p. 117.
31. A. Voznesensky, *op. cit.*, p. 189.
32. *Ibid.*, p. 190.
33. *Ibid.*, p. 190.
34. *Ibid.*, p. 163.
35. *Ibid.*, p. 195.
36. *Ibid.*, p. 193.
37. *Ibid.*, p. 193.
38. *Ibid.*, p. 198.
39. *Ibid.*, p. 144.
40. *Ibid.*, p. 199.

Gorky in the Soviet Period

1. Gorbachov, *Contemporary Russian Literature*, 36. Gorky's anti-Bolshevik articles are now available in English in *Untimely Thoughts* (trans. and ed. by H. Ermolaev).
2. Zamyatin's memoir of Gorky, originally published in French translation in *La Revue de France* (August 1, 1936), was included in *Litsa* and is now available in English in *A Soviet Heretic*.
3. Gorbachov, *Contemporary Russian Literature*, 33-35.
4. Mirsky, *Contemporary Russian Literature*, 120.
5. S. Balukhaty and K. Muratova, *M. Gorky: Spravochnik* (*M. Gorky: A Reference Guide*), 75-76.
6. A. N. Tolstoy, *Chetvert' veka sovetskoy literatury. Doklad na yubileynoy sessii Akademii Nauk SSSR 18 noyabrya 1942 goda* (A Quarter of a Century of Soviet Literature: Report Read at the Jubilee Session of the Academy of Sciences of the U.S.S.R. on November 18, 1942), 9.
7. For some inconsistencies and fluctuations in Soviet accounts of the circumstances of Gorky's death see, for example, G. Herling, *Da Gorki a Pasternak: Considerazoni sulla letteratura sovietica*, 7-41.
8. Something toward this end was done by the poet Khodasevich, Gorky's friend, in his reminiscences of their life together at Sorrento. See *Sovremennye Zapiski* (*Contemporary Annals*), Vol. LXIII (1937), Vol. LXX (1940). Cf. also Gorky's letters to Khodasevich in *Novy Zhurnal* (Nos.

29-31, 1952) and their English version in *Harvard Slavic Studies*, Vol. I (1953). This period in Gorky's life has also been vividly described in the "autobiography" of Nina Berberova (Khodasevich's wife at the time), *The Italics Are Mine* (1969).

Two Adams and Eve in the Crystal Palace: Dostoevsky, the Bible, and We

1. It is true that the futuristic novels of H. G. Wells (who strongly influenced Zamyatin) are not without satirical overtones. But whereas in Wells satire is a subsidiary and dispensable element, in *We* it is inalienable and essential.
2. Introduction to Eugene Zamiatin, *We*, trans. Gregory Zilboorg (New York: Dutton, 1959), p. viii ("Dutton Everyman Paperback").
3. *Zamyatin, a Soviet Heretic* (London, 1962), p. 56.
4. *Zamiatin, My* (New York, 1952), pp. 84-85. For the quotations from the text of *My*, I have drawn upon the translation by Gregory Zilboorg (see note 2 above), with minor modifications.
5. It is also interesting to compare Dostoevsky's rebel who swears he will never "bring a single brick" to the building of the Crystal Palace (F. M. Dostoevsky, *Sobranie sochinenii* [Moscow, 1956], IV, 152) to Zamiatin's latter-day rebels, who by their apostasy have "lost their rights to be the bricks . . . of the United State" (Zamiatin, p. 128).
6. Zamiatin, p. 13.
7. Dostoevsky, p. 152.
8. *Ibid.*, p. 158.
9. Zamiatin, pp. 37 ff.
10. Dostoevsky, p. 155.
11. Zamiatin, pp. 59-60. Richards (pp. 60-64) takes cognizance of this correspondence but not of the others.
12. The words are actually pronounced by the "lame schoolteacher," but they are an admiring description of Shigalovism, and evidently have Shigalov's approval.
13. Dostoevsky, VII, 423, 424.
14. *Ibid.*, p. 442.
15. *Zamiatin*, p. 9.
16. *Ibid.*, p. 111.
17. *Ibid.*, p. 56.
18. *Ibid.*, p. 25.
19. *Ibid.*, p. 66.
20. *Ibid.*, p. 74.
21. *Ibid.*, p. 56.
22. *Ibid.* The fact that R-13 is referring to O-90, while the reader (and no doubt D-503) have quite another "Eve" in mind is characteristic of Zamiatin's compounded ironies.

23. *Ibid.*, p. 121.

24. *Ibid.*, p. 96. Ironically, this Guardian Angel is, in fact, a *fallen* angel, for it is S-4711 that the hero is referring to. Since Satan, too, was once an angel, Zamiatin is being faithful to religious as well as literary tradition here.

25. The use of the Roman alphabet for the nomenclature of Zamiatin's characters made punning difficult in Russian. His excellent command of English makes that language appear to be the likeliest candidate, although it is true that the play would also have been valid in French (*Satan, serpent*) or German (*Satan, Schlange*). The reader may wonder why Zamiatin did not try to slip in symbolic hints of the Genesis story in the other names. The answer is that he seems to have done exactly this. Thus, the *phonetic* value of Eve's initial in English is rendered by the Cyrillic "И," which, in turn, is the conventional *written* equivalent of the English letter "I." Hence an identity of sorts between I-330 and her mythological archetype. If this seems a little far-fetched, it will be noted that the letter of the poet R-13 phonetically rendered in Russian is "P," the graphic equivalent of which in our alphabet is, of course, also "P." Since Zamiatin's poet was almost certainly a kind of avatar of Pushkin (see note 38 below), the initial once again fits the archetype. When it came to encoding the mythic name of the hero, Zamiatin encountered a special problem, since all the men in the United State had to have *consonantal* names. Unable to use Adam's first letter, Zamiatin simply used the second one.

26. Zamiatin, p. 122.

27. *Ibid.*, p. 50.

28. It does not follow, of course, that whenever Zamiatin's plot diverges from Genesis we must look for irony. There are important narrative elements in *We* which are quite unrelated to the story of Eden. The myth is, after all, only one strand—though a very important one—in Zamiatin's plot.

29. Zamiatin, p. 101.

30. *Ibid.*, p. 111.

31. *Ibid.*, p. 142.

32. D-503 tries to free his fellow men by turning his spaceship "Integral" over to the insurgent enemy.

33. Zamiatin, p. 184.

34. *Ibid.*, p. 183.

35. This may also have been suggested by Dostoevsky, whose underground hero was a symbolic forty years old.

36. Zamiatin, pp. 185-86.

37. *Ibid.*, p. 193.

38. What, for instance, are we supposed to make of the hints which Zamiatin drops with regard to R-13? His status as the country's greatest poet, his somewhat negroid features, and his ebullient character—to say nothing of

the fact that he composes hymns of praise to his country, but fights for individual freedom and eventually falls victim to the regime—all this cannot fail to remind the Russian reader of Pushkin. But it cannot be said that this identification, even if valid, helps illuminate the novel as a whole. More than anything, it seems like a private joke. Symbol hunters will also note the use of the seasonal cycle (spring fever at the beginning, autumnal resignation and defeat at the end), as well as water imagery (dripping faucets, bubbling fountains), which is clearly connected with the motif of freedom and revolt. Here, too, however, the artistic effectiveness of these symbols may be questioned.

Islanders

1. *Islanders* is no more anti-British than *The Fires of St. Dominic* is anti-Spanish, nor are the many works set in tsarist and Soviet Russia to be considered specifically antitsarist or anti-Soviet. In many instances Zamyatin poses a conflict between (in his terms) Energy and Entropy, the Entropy being social, religious, or political as the particular case may be.
2. The classic statement on the subject is Edmund Wilson's "Philoctetes: The Wound and the Bow," in his *The Wound and the Bow: Seven Studies in Literature* (New York, 1947), pp. 272-95.
3. This definition of alienation is my own and is derived from literary and philosophical works too numerous to mention. For an introduction to the problem of alienation, discussed from a wide range of philosophical viewpoints, see Eric and Mary Josephson (eds.), *Man Alone: Alienation in Modern Society* (New York, 1959).
4. This and similar references to *Islanders* are to the text found in Volume III of Zamyatin's *Sobranie sochinenii* (Moscow, 1929).
5. Edward J. Brown, "Zamjatin and English Literature," in *American Contributions to the Fifth International Congress of Slavicists* ('s-Gravenhage, 1963), II, 29.
6. Uncle Pavel, Bazarov, and Mme. Odintsova pay little attention to the natural world. When they are on the literary stage there are no lyric descriptions of nature by the author. Such descriptions by the supposedly objective narrator do occur, however, in the presence of Katya and Arkady. They love the natural world and respond to it, just as they respond to each other. They have children and will apparently lead happy, productive lives. Pavel, Odintsova, and Bazarov do not respond to the natural world, are childless, isolated, and sterile. At the novel's end, Bazarov dies, and Pavel and Odintsova may be considered spiritually dead.
7. See especially Seymour L. Gross, "Nature, Man, and God in Bunin's 'The Gentleman from San Francisco,'" *Modern Fiction Studies*, IV (1960), 153-63.
8. This image occurs also in *The Flood* (*Navodnenie*).

The Pioneers: Pil'nyak and Ivanov

1. "Snega," *Rasplyosnutoe vremya. Rasskazy* (Moscow-Leningrad, 1927): first quotation on p. 121, second on p. 117. The story "God ikh zhizni" is also in this collection, pp. 99-101. "Tselaya zhizn'" can be found in *Prostye rasskazy. Sobranie sochinenii,* v (Moscow-Leningrad, 1929), 16-26. Some of these "primitive" stories can be found in English translation in *Tales of the Wilderness,* transl by F. O'Dempsey, London, 1924.
2. *Zavoloch'e, Sobranie sochinenii,* IV (Moscow-Leningrad, 1929), 69-164. Excerpt in *Krasnaya nov',* as "Gibel' Sverdrupa," No. 3 (1925), pp. 113-124.
3. *Materialy k romanu, Krasnaya nov',* No. 2 (1924), p. 77.
4. *Golyi god* (Petersburg-Berlin, 1922), p. 132. The only English translation of this novel is the bowdlerized and inaccurate one by A. Brown (*The Naked Year,* London, 1928).
5. *Ibid.,* pp. 153-54.
6. Quoted by Evgenii Zamyatin, "Aleksandr Blok," in *Litsa* (New York, 1955), p. 25. Many of the peasant poets—notably Esenin, Klyuev, and Klychkov—adopted a profoundly anti-intellectual stance and hailed Lenin and the Bolsheviks as a direct expression of the popular will because they had destroyed civilization. Cf. Georgii Ivanov, *Peterburgskie zimy* (New York, 1952), pp. 228-30. The attitudes of the intellectual toward the peasantry and the "soil" in this century offer possibilities for a fascinating study, which has not yet been undertaken; nor has the peasantry as a literary theme—myth would be the better term—in the writing of the last seventy or eighty years been investigated. For an interesting survey of the image of the peasant in Russian literature (chiefly of the nineteenth century), see Donald Fanger, "The Peasant in Literature," in *The Peasant in Nineteenth Century Russia,* ed. Wayne S. Vucinich, Stanford, 1968, pp. 231-62.
7. For a good survey of Eurasianism, cf. S. I. Gessen, review of *Evraziiskii vremennik,* IV (Berlin, 1925), in *Sovremennyya zapiski,* XXV (Paris, 1925), 494-508. Gessen traces the changes in the movement in the direction of greater moderation. Gleb Struve has a useful account of it, with an extensive bibliography, in *Russkaya literatura v izgnanii* (New York, 1956), pp. 40-49. For a literary version by a member of the Pil'nyak "school," cf. Nikolai Ognyov, *Evraziya, Krasnaya nov',* No. 1 (1923).
8. Leon Trotsky, *Literature and Revolution,* New York, 1957, Chap. II.
9. A. K. Voronskii, at a conference organized by the Agitation-Propaganda Department of the Central Committee in February, 1922, to discuss what was to be done with private publishing houses. As quoted by A. G. Dement'ev, "A. Voronskii—kritik," in *A. Voronskii. Literaturno-kriticheskie stat'i,* compiled by G. A. Voronskaya and A. G. Dementev, ed. by L. Shubin (Moscow, 1963), p. 6. At the time, many privately owned pub-

lishing houses and journals operated under the protection of the law; they were the source of much of the "bourgeois" literature of which Voronskii complained.

10. "Literaturnye siluety. Pil'nyak," *Krasnaya nov'*, No. 4 (1922), pp. 252-69.

11. *Ibid.*, p. 255. The reference is to the writer Vasilii Rozanov (1856-1919).

12. *Ibid.*, p. 267.

13. *Ibid.*, pp. 255-56.

14. *Ibid.*, p. 255.

15. *Ibid.*, p. 266.

16. B. Pil'nyak, *Materialy k romanu, Krasnaya nov'*, No. 1 (1924), pp. 3-27; No. 2 (1924), pp. 63-96. Quotes from the work will be identified in parentheses in the text by part (I or II) and page number. The "novel" that eventually emerged from these "materials" was *Machines and Wolves (Mashiny i volki)* (Moscow, 1924).

17. A. Voronskii, "Literaturnye siluety. Bor. Pil'nyak," p. 258.

18. Andrei Kozhukhov is the terrorist-hero of a novel by Mikhail Stepnyak Kravchinskii (1851-95), which is set in the late 1870's and deals with the Russian revolutionary movement. It was first published in 1889 in English, under the title *The Career of a Nihilist* (Kravchinskii himself was a revolutionary who spent a large part of his life in emigration) and was later translated into Russian, partly by the author, under the title *Andrei Kozhukhov*. See the discussion below of Pil'nyak's fondness for literary borrowings.

19. "Mesto Pil'nyaka," in *Boris Pil'nyak. Stat'i i materialy* (Leningrad, 1928), p. 20.

20. Andrei Belyi, *Peterburg*, Part 2 (Berlin, 1922), p. 87.

21. V. Bryusov, "Lyublyu ya linii vernost' . . . ," (1899), *Polnoe sobranie sochinenii i perevodov*, II, *Tertia Vigilia* (St. Petersburg, 1914), 71.

22. "O Pil'nyake," *LEF*, No. 3 (1925), pp. 126-36; quotation from Belyi on p. 128. Shklovskii dislikes Pil'nyak's sensationalism, but his main objection is that Pil'nyak "has canonized the chance manner of his first piece, *Bare Year*, creating things from manifestly crumbling pieces" (p. 127).

23. Cf., e.g., A. Voronskii, "Pisatel', kniga, chitatel'," *Krasnaya nov'*, No. 1 (1927), pp. 226-39.

24. *Novyi mir*, No. 6 (1926), p. 184. The editors expressed agreement with Voronskii, considered it a "manifest and gross error" to have published the work and, in No. 1 (1927), printed Pil'nyak's apology ("Pis'mo v redaktsiyu," p. 256).

25. Letter to Gor'kii, beginning of June 1926, in *M. Gor'kii i sovetskaya pechat'. Arkhiv A. M. Gor'kogo*, x, Book 2 (1965), 38. The writer Fyodor Gladkov asserted that Pil'nyak had read the story to Voronskii, who gave his approval. He also said that the editors of *New World* had not bothered to look at it because it was by an established writer and because Voronskii had given it his blessing (letter to Gor'kii, May 5,

1926, in *Gor'kii i sovetskie pisateli. Literaturnoe nasledstvo*, LXX [Moscow, 1963], 79).

26. Voronskii to Gor'kii, *Arkhiv*, p. 38. Gor'kii reacted with the remark that he could not "understand your incident with Pil'nyak" (quoted from an unpublished letter dated July 24, 1926, in the Gor'kii archive in an editorial note to Gladkov's letter to Gor'kii, *ibid.*, p. 80).

27. Gladkov, *ibid.* The relatively permissive policy toward literature began to change perceptibly around 1925, and Voronskii, as the leading spokesman for that policy, found himself increasingly isolated. Finally in 1927 he was dismissed as editor of *Red Virgin Soil.* For a fuller account of these developments, see the book from which this selection is taken, *Red Virgin Soil: Soviet Literature in the 1920's*, Princeton, 1968, esp. Ch. V.

28. There has recently been a quickening of interest in Pil'nyak in English-speaking countries. For a good representative sample of his work, cf. *The Tale of the Unextinguished Moon and Other Stories*, trans. by Beatrice Scott, New York, 1967; and *Mother Earth and Other Stories*, trans. and ed. by Vera T. Reck and Michael Green, New York and Washington, 1968.

29. "Literaturnye siluety. Vsev. Ivanov," *Krasnaya nov'*, No. 5 (1922), p. 258.

30. *Ibid.*, p. 255.

31. "Literaturnye siluety, Bor. Pil'nyak," *Krasnaya nov'*, No. 4 (1922), pp. 255-56. "Andreevism" refers to the writer Leonid Andreev (1871-1919).

32. "Iz proshlogo," *Prozhektor*, No. 6 (1927), p. 20.

33. "Literaturnye siluety. Vsev. Ivanov," p. 258.

34. *Partizany, Krasnaya nov'*, No. 1 (1921), p. 26.

35. *Bronepoezd 14-69, Krasnaya nov'*, No. 1 (1922), p. 89.

36. *Golubye peski, Krasnaya nov'*, Nos. 3 (1922)-3 (1923).

37. *Mimesis: The Representation of Reality in Western Literature* (Garden City, New York, 1957), pp. 86 ff.

38. "Kak sozdayutsya kurgany," *Krasnaya nov'*, No. 4 (1924), p. 3.

39. *Ibid.*, p. 8.

40. "Bog Matvei," *Krasnaya nov'*, No. 3 (1927), p. 124.

41. *Partizany*, p. 40.

42. *Ibid.*, p. 31.

43. See, e.g., G. Gorbachov, *Sovremennaya russkaya literatura* (3d ed.; Moscow-Leningrad, 1931), pp. 229-46. Voronskii's reappraisal is seen in "O knige Vsevoloda Ivanova 'Tainoe tainykh,'" *Mister Britling p'yot chashu do dna* (Moscow, 1927), esp. p. 160. Voronskii here remarks Ivanov's chronic pessimism and his inability to reconcile the concept of blind fate and vital, spontaneous creation.

44. Cf., e.g., Aleksandr Fadeev's novel *The Rout* (*Razgrom*), published in 1927, for a "proletarian" treatment of these themes.

Through the Wrong End of Binoculars:
An Introduction to Jurij Oleša

1. Olesha, Yu., *The Wayward Comrade and the Commissars*, N.Y. 1960, p. 12. On some occasions the translation has been revised.
2. *ibid.* p. 13.
3. *ibid.* p. 79.
4. *ibid.* p. 42.
5. *ibid.* p. 39.
6. *ibid.* p. 101.
7. *ibid.* p. 104. It is interesting to note that Venjamin Kaverin in his *Unknown Artist* (*Chudožnik neizvesten*) often uses similar devices to present his characters, for instance: "Shpektorov's profile floated by in the dim glass of a shop window, bisected by the blind, reflecting the shoulders and heads of the two detached figures, leaving their now elongated, now foreshortened legs far behind them." (See Y. Olesha. *Envy*. V. Kaverin, *The Unknown Artist*. London 1947, p. 150.) Other examples: "He pointed at the show-case of a cinema: Elizabeth Bergner's melancholy face peered through the half-open door of a car, reflected in the glossy asphalt polished smooth by the tyres"; "A man holding a plasterer's shovel came out of an open doorway, the misty frame of which was reflected momentarily in Archimedov's glasses—the mouths of people talking and drinking, arms stretched out towards tumblers, a restless outline by the telephone, a waiter caught in action with a tray swaying over his head—all the elements of a vision, like an interrupted dream." (*Ibid.* p. 150).
8. *Ibid.* p. 115.
9. *Ibid.* p. 89. Cf. in Vladimir Nabokov's *The Gift* a more elaborate use of this device: "As he crossed toward the pharmacy at the corner he involuntarily turned his head because of a burst of light that had ricocheted from his temple, and saw, with that quick smile with which we greet a rainbow or a rose, a blindingly white parallelogram of sky being unloaded from the van—a dresser with mirror across which, as across a cinema screen, passed a flawlessly clear reflection of boughs, sliding and swaying not arboreally, but with a human vacillation, produced by the nature of those who were carrying this sky, these boughs, this gliding facade." (Nabokov, V., *The Gift*, New York 1963, p. 14 (*Popular Library*).
10. Olesha, Yu. *op. cit.*, p. 59.
11. *Ibid.* p. 58.
12. Oleša, Ju., *Izbrannye sočinenija*, M. 1956, p. 344.
13. *Ibid.* p. 310.
14. Olesha, Yu. *Envy*, p. 24.
15. *Ibid.*

16. *Ibid.* p. 55.
17. *Ibid.* p. 101.
18. *Ibid.* p. 95.
19. *Ibid.* p. 57.
20. *Ibid.*
21. *Ibid.* p. 39.
22. *Ibid.* p. 113.
23. *Ibid.* p. 126.
24. *Ibid.* p. 58.
25. *Ibid.* p. 81.
26. *Ibid.* p. 14.
27. *Ibid.* p. 36.
28. *Ibid.* p. 103.
29. *Ibid.* p. 21.
30. *Ibid.* p. 43.
31. *Ibid.* p. 42.
32. *Ibid.* p. 50.
33. *Ibid.* p. 89.
34. *Ibid.* p. 27.
35. *Ibid.* p. 125.
36. *Ibid.* p. 50.
37. *Ibid.* p. 127. A. Voznesenskij stresses the metamorphosis as an important principle of modern art in his *40 liričeskich otstuplenij iz poemy Treugol'-naja gruša*, M. 1962, p. 101. On the metaphor as "une forme magique du principe d'identité" in French surrealism, see, for instance, Raymond, M., *De Baudelaire au surréalisme*, Paris 1952, p. 286. On materialized metaphors in German expressionism, see Sokel, W., *The Writer in Extremis*, N.Y. 1964, p. 46ff. (*McGraw-Hill Paperbacks*).
38. *Ibid.* p. 81.
39. Oleša, *Izbr. soč.* p. 345.
40. *Ibid.*
41. *Ibid.* p. 41.
42. Čechov, A. P., *Polnoe sobranie sočinenij*, T. 13, M. 1948, p. 215.
43. *Godošnik na Sofijskija universitet. Istoriko-filologičeski fakultet.* T. XXXVIII, Sofija 1942, p. 19f.
44. Čechov, A. P., *Polnoe sobr. soč.*, T. 9, M. 1948, p. 87.
45. Cf., for instance, Vladimir Majakovskij's article *Dva Čechova* of 1914 Majakovskij, V., *Polnoe sobranie sočinenij*, T. 1, M. 1955, p. 301.
46. See, for instance, his letter to Apollon Majkov, dated December 23, 1868 (with its passage which comes close to Oleša's: "As a matter of fact this [the fantastic] is genuine, true realism!" Dostoevskij, F. M., *Pis'ma* II, M. & L. 1930, P. 150), and the wellknown letter to N. N. Strachov from 1869 (*Pis'ma*, T. 2, p. 169f). Of course, Gleb Struve is right when he points out the parallel between Kavalerov and Dostoevskij's *Man from the Underground* as well as certain other parallels with Dostoevskij's

works. (See Yu. Olesha. *Envy*. V. Kaverin. *Unknown Artist*, London 1947, p. VII).

47. Poe, E. A., *The Complete Poems and Stories*. Vol. II, N.Y.: 1946, p. 664.
48. Gogol, N., *Taras Bulba and Other Stories*, N.Y. 1962, p. 238 (*Washington Square Press*).
49. *Ibid.* p. 241.
50. *Grani* 32, 1956, p. 95.
51. Zamjatin, E., *Lica*, N.Y. 1955, p. 237.
52. See below.
53. Quoted from Drew, E., *Poetry. A Guide to its Understanding and Enjoyment*, N.Y. 1959, p. 31.
54. *Ibid.* p. 30.
55. Dostoevskij, F. M., *Polnoe sobranie chud. proizvedenij*, T. XIII, M.-L. 1930, p. 82.
56. Quoted from Balakian, A., *Surrealism. The Road to the Absolute*, N.Y. 1959, p. 55.
57. Bergson, H., *La Pensée et le Mouvant*, 5me éd. Paris 1934, p. 170.
58. See, for instance, his article entitled *Bergson's Theory of Art* in *Speculations*. Ed. by Herbert Read, p. 141ff (*Harvest Books*).
59. Sklovskij, V., *Voskresenie slova*, 1914, n. p.
60. Oleša, Ju., *Izbrannye sočinenija*, p. 267.
61. *Ibid.* p. 268.
62. Cf. Porebina, Gabriela, *Aleksander Woronski. Poglady estetyczne i krytycznoliterackie* (*1921-1928*), Wrocław, Warszawa & Kraków 1964, p. 122 (Polska Akademia nauk. Oddział w Krakowie. Prace Komisji Słowianoznawstwa. Nr. 6).
63. Voronskij, A., *Iskusstvo kak poznanie žizni* in *Krasnaja nov'* nr. 5 (15), 1923, p. 350.
64. Voronskij, A., *Iskusstvo videt' mir*, M. 1928, p. 84.
65. *Ibid.* p. 83. Cf. Pasternak's words about Leo Tolstoj: "All his life at any given moment he possessed the faculty of seeing things in the detached finality of each separate moment, in sharp relief, as we see things only on rare occasions, in childhood, or on the crest of an all-embracing happiness, or in the triumph of a great spiritual victory." (Pasternak, B., *I Remember. Sketch for an Autobiography*, N.Y. 1960, p. 69). Tolstoj can, of course, provide us with many interesting examples of "the device of detachment" and "removing the veils." It would, however, be going too far to discuss here his use of these devices, which partly have a different purpose compared to Oleša.
66. Quoted from Edel, L., *The Modern Psychological Novel*, N.Y., 1964, p. 95 (*The Universal Library*). Joyce's epiphanies have at the same time a more complex background and purpose, see Chayes, Irene, *Joyce's Epiphanies* in *Joyce's Portrait. Criticism and Critiques*, N.Y. 1962, p. 204-21 (*Goldentree Books*).
67. Hulme, T. E., *Speculations*, p. 159.

68. Olesha, Yu., *The Wayward Comrade*, p. 57.
69. *Ibid.* p. 48.
70. *Ibid.* p. 128.
71. Giraudoux, J., *Bella,* Paris 1926, p. 220f.
72. Olesha, Yu., *The Wayward Comrade*, p. 46.
73. *Ibid.* p. 40.
74. *Ibid.* p. 114.
75. *Ibid.* p. 25.
76. Oleša, *Izbrannye soč.,* p. 260.
77. *Ibid.* p. 286.
78. Cf. a French novel from 1911, in which this expression has the same magic tone: "Blériot a traversé La Manche! . . . Brusquement, nous sommes sortis de l'hypothèse et nous avons palpé le fait. La fantome est devenu chair! Nous étions bien sûrs que l'air était conquis! (Kistemaeckers, H., *Lord Will Aviateur,* Paris 1911, p. 254; quoted from Bergman, P., *"Modernolatria" et "Simultaneità,"* Uppsala 1962, p. 19).
79. Cf. V Doroševič's sketch about the popularity of bicycles in Odessa as early as in the 1890's in his book *Odessa, odessity i odessitky,* Odessa 1895, p. 48. In France the new sport was called "La religion nouvelle" and was described in numerous novels and stories (See Bergman, *op. cit.* p. 14).
80. Olesha, *The Wayward Comrade,* p. 12.
81. Oleša, *Izbr. soč.,* p. 291.
82. Apollinaire, G., *Le Poète Assassiné,* Paris 1947, p. 97.
83. Balakian, *op. cit.* p. 54.
84. Oleša shared Zamjatin's interest in H. G. Wells, see *Literaturnaja Moskva. Sbornik vtoroj,* M. 1956, p. 723f.
85. See his sketch *Mysli o Čapline (Izbr. soč.* p. 436) and his play *A List of Blessings.*
86. Balakian, *op. cit.* p. 51.
87. In the dramatization of *Envy,* entitled *Conspiracy of Feelings,* Andrej Babičev too is occasionally able to see the world around him from Kavalerov's point of view. On one occasion, for instance, he says: "Look at that blue basin. Beauty. Over there is a window, and if you will please bend down, you can see the window dancing in the basin" (quoted from Barry Levin's translation in *Yury Olesha: His Times and His "Conspiracy of Feelings,"* Cambridge, Mass. 1962.) This change, as compared with *Envy,* is perhaps to be explained by the fact that Oleša—influenced, as it seems, by the criticism against his *Envy*—here tried to make Andrej a somewhat more positive character, a representative of the new age, who "knows how to be even a poet of sausage" (See *Gos. Bol'šoj dram. teatr,* programme for 1931-32, Moskva 1931, p. 16).

The Theme of Sterility in Olesha's Envy

1. Report has it that a Soviet librarian in 1956, not long after the Soviet Union opened its doors to Western tourists, complained that she was tired of hearing from her American visitors that *Envy* was the greatest Soviet novel. In his history of Soviet literature Edward J. Brown refers to Olesha's writings as "among the most significant artistic productions of the twentieth century" (*Russian Literature since the Revolution* [New York and London, 1963], p. 84).

2. A listing of the Russian critical literature is to be found in *Russkie sovetskie pisateli—prozaiki*, III (Leningrad, 1964), 348-67. Several of the better articles published in this period are mentioned in the footnotes of the present article. There has been almost no Soviet criticism of Olesha since his partial rehabilitation in 1955. The only piece worthy of mention is the excellent introduction, by B. Galanov, to Iurii Olesha, *Povesti i rasskazy* (Moscow, 1965), pp. 3-16. In the literature published outside the Soviet Union there are three significant treatments of the novel by Gleb Struve: *Soviet Russian Literature* (Norman, Okla., 1951), pp. 98-105; "Introduction," in Y. Olesha, *Envy* (London, 1947), pp. i-xv; and "Pisatel' nenuzhnykh tem," *Novyi zhurnal*, XXV (1951), 140-46.

3. See V. Polonskii, "Preodolenie 'Zavisti,' " *Novy mir*, No. 5, 1929, 191-92; Struve, "Pisatel' nenuzhnykh tem," p. 141.

4. See Polonskii, pp. 191-92; and Struve, *Soviet Russian Literature*, pp. 104-5.

5. See, for example, Erich Fromm, *The Forgotten Language* (New York, 1951). Recently I discovered that my friend and colleague Robert Maguire has analyzed Olesha's *Envy* from a somewhat similar point of view. The interested reader may consult Professor Maguire's forthcoming book, *Red Virgin Soil: A Study of Soviet Literature in the 1920s* (to be published by Princeton University Press, 1967).

6. *Envy* is not a work which can be effectively summarized; besides, it is short and readily available in English. In addition to the translations of P. Ross (London, 1947) and Anthony Wolfe (in Philip Rahv, ed., *Great Russian Short Novels* [New York, 1951], pp. 635-771), the novel is published in a paperback edition under the spurious title of *The Wayward Comrade and the Commissar*, trans. Andrew R. MacArthur (New York, 1960).

   All quotations are translated by the present author from the Russian, from Iurii Olesha, *Povesti i rasskazy* (Moscow, 1965), pp. 17-120.

7. Friedrich Engels argued that "the modern individual family is founded on the open and unconcealed domestic slavery of the wife." Under communism Engels would take women out of the home and place them in productive industrial life, which "demands the abolition of the monogamous family as the economic unit of society." Housekeeping would then

become a "social industry." Quoted from Engels, *The Origin of the Family, Private Property and the State* (New York, 1942), pp. 61-73. Alexandra Kollontai, the noted Soviet feminist, popularized such views in the Soviet Union in the 1920s.

8. See Rufus W. Mathewson, Jr., *The Positive Hero in Russian Literature* (New York, 1958), pp. 243-44, esp. n. 31.

9. The opening scene of the novel, in which Andrei is in the toilet, may possibly be regarded as the very scene in which this child of his sterility is born. His spirit of "joy of life" (*zhizneradost'*), which infuses this passage, is quite appropriate, in Soviet mythology, for creative activity.

10. See Struve, "Introduction," in Olesha, *Envy*, pp. v-vii.

11. In his reminiscences Olesha mentions his own youthful interest in sports, especially in soccer; see "Iz zapisnykh knizhek 1954-1956," *Izbrannye sochinenia* (Moscow, 1956), p. 461. See also his recently published memoirs, *Ni dnya bez strochki* (Moscow, 1965), pp. 109-16.

12. Olesha's stories "The Cherry Stone," "Love," "Aldebaran," and "Natasha" show similar figures. See my article "The Philosophical Tales of Jurij Oleša," in *Orbis Scriptus: Dmitrij Tschižewskij zum 70. Geburtstag*, ed. Dietrich Gerhardt *et al.* (Munich: Wilhelm Fink Verlag, 1966), pp. 349-54.

13. See D. Tal'nikov, "Literaturnye zametki," *Krasnaia nov'*, No. 6, 1928, pp. 238, 244. See also Struve, "Introduction," in Olesha, *Envy*, pp. vii-viii; and "Pisatel' nenuzhnykh tem," p. 143.

14. See Olesha's sketch "Ia smotriu v proshloe," in *Izbrannye sochineniia* (Moscow, 1956), pp. 284-91, based on reminiscences of childhood.

15. Fictional narrators tend to win the reader's sympathy or at least sneaking affection; thus, an "inside view can build sympathy for even the most vicious character" (Wayne Booth, *The Rhetoric of Fiction* [Chicago, 1961], p. 378).

16. Since the much abused term "expressionistic" appears several times in this study, it may be well to provide a definition. I call a symbol "expressionistic" when it takes on a fantastic form which is designed, through its sheer fantasticality, to reinforce a symbolic meaning or to uncover more strikingly a hidden symbolic truth.

17. Sigmund Freud, "Medusa's Head," *International Journal of Psycho-Analysis*, XXII, No. 1 (Jan. 1941), 69-70.

18. See Struve, *Soviet Russian Literature*, p. 106. Olesha himself wrote an article on Chaplin, "Mysli o Chapline," in *Izbrannye sochinenia* (Moscow, 1956), pp. 436-39. In his play, *Spisok blagodeianii* (1931), a Chaplinesque figure appears.

19. See *The Collected Papers of Otto Fenichel*, 2d series (New York, 1954), pp. 11-14.

20. Reinhard Lauer, "Zur Gestalt Ivan Babičevs in Olešas 'Zavist'," *Die Welt der Slaven*, VII (1962), 45-54.

21. In 1927, when *Envy* appeared, this reference to "bookkeepers" no doubt

suggested the capitalist entrepreneurs who flourished under the New Economic Policy. Thus, in Valentin Kataev's novel *The Embezzlers* (*Rastratchiki*) two bank clerks embezzle funds which they spend in a picaresque whirl over Russia.

22. This myth is illustrated in such tales as that of the Golem of Prague, Mary W. Shelley's *Frankenstein*, and Karel Čapek's *R.U.R.* For Olesha's admiring comments on the last-named work, see his *Ni dnya bez strochki*, pp. 237-39.

23. Fantasies of a woman with a penis are found in psychoanalytic literature. Géza Róheim has analyzed the figure of the witch in European folklore as such a figure; see his "Aphrodite, or the Woman with a Penis," *Psychoanalytic Quarterly*, XIV, No. 3 (July 1945), 361-75. In Róheim's interpretation the Sphinx, whose riddle Oedipus solves, is also a castrating mother figure; see his *Riddle of the Sphinx* (London, 1934).

24. *Ni dnya bez strochki*, p. 106.

25. *Ibid.*, pp. 298-99.

26. Late in the novel Olesha does suggest, in a physical description of Valia, that she is rather earthy and that she belongs to the contemporary world as much as to the romantic world of Kavalerov's dreams. In this he seems to be pointing to a synthesis of idealism and materialism, akin to the synthesis proposed in "The Cherry Stone" (see note 27). But Valia's presence in the novel is too slight to permit the reader to accept her reality as convincing, and the attempt to give her reality comes too late to be effective.

27. Such a synthesis is suggested not in *Envy* but in Olesha's stories, especially "Love," "The Cherry Stone," and "Aldebaran." See my article, "The Philosophical Stories of Jurij Oleša," p. 352. In "The Cherry Stone" we have a symbol of sterility in the concrete skyscraper which Fedia learns is to be erected under the Five-Year Plan. But still the cherry stone which he has planted will germinate and grow into a tree, for the planners have remembered to provide the new building with a garden. So life will persist in spite of the threat of technology.

Isaac Babel: A Critical Romance

1. N. N. Sukhanov (1882-?) a revolutionary journalist; editor, with Maxim Gorky, of the magazine *New Life* in 1917. He is the author of *Notes on the Russian Revolution*.

Zoshchenko's Unfinished Novel: Before Sunrise

1. The most extensive Western study of Zoshchenko to my knowledge is Rebecca A. Domar's useful article, "The Tragedy of a Soviet Satirist: The Case of Zoshchenko," in *Through the Glass of Soviet Literature*, ed. Ernest J. Simmons (New York, 1953). Miss Domar cites all the official

Soviet attacks on *Before Sunrise*, but does not discuss it herself, except to imply disapproval of its frankness in sexual matters. Gleb Struve, in *Soviet Russian Literature, 1917-50* (1951), discusses *Before Sunrise* succinctly and with discernment, but in my opinion underestimates its literary value. The best brief study of Zoshchenko is McLean's Introduction to *Nervous People and Other Satires* (New York, 1963)—ed.

Four Novels

1. Mikhail Sholokhov, *The Silent Don*, trans. Stephen Garry (New York, 1946), p. 552.
2. Serial publication accounts in part for the bombshell effect the novel had. Apparently there was a widespread expectation that Gregor would be "converted," or at least brought to a positive acceptance of the new regime. Such a resolution, of course, would violate all that had gone before. The somewhat grudging Soviet acceptance of the novel has taken two forms: first, that socialist realism is broad enough to encompass all the complexities of social struggle even when the outcome is tragic for individuals engaged in it; second, that Gregor's tragedy is that of a willful individualist who "has cut himself off from the people," and therefore must die (L. I. Timofeev, *Sovremennaya literatura* [Moscow, 1947], p. 311).
3. A. Lunacharsky, "Mysli o kommunisticheskoi dramaturgii" *Pechat i revolyutsiya*, No. 2 (1921).
4. See Leon Trotsky, *Literature and Revolution*, trans. Rose Strunsky (London, 1925), pp. 240-45, for his discussion of tragedy.
5. *Pervyi vsesoyuznyi s'ezd sovetskikh pisatelci, 1934; stenograficheski otchet* (Moscow, 1934), p. 680.
6. See Appendix, pp. 333-34.
7. Yu. Yuzovsky, "Osvobozhdennyi Prometei," *Literaturny kritik*, No. 10 (October, 1934), pp. 113-39.
8. I. Altman, "Dramaturgicheskie printsipy Aristotelya," *Literaturny kritik*, No. 10 (October, 1935), pp. 52-74.
9. The title of one of the plays under discussion, Vishnevsky's *Optimistic Tragedy*, gives the game away.
10. Leonid Leonov, *Road to the Ocean*, trans. Norbert Guterman (New York, copyright 1955, by A. A. Wyn, Inc., formerly L. B. Fischer Publishing Corp.), p. 4.
11. Leonov is sometimes called "Dostoevskyan." The remark of one of Kurilov's colleagues suggests that his solitude has its origins in a rebellion against God similar to Ivan Karamazov's: "Atheism means ignoring God. But you negate him, fight against him, disrespectfully take the universe away from him." (*Ibid.*, p. 463.)
12. *Ibid.*, p. 100.
13. *Ibid.*, p. 99.

14. Leonov emphasizes this point by his extraordinary frankness about the dirt, disorder, and breakdown of Soviet life, and the vanity, dishonesty, and selfishness of the people Kurilov encounters. The present is indeed imperfect if not unbearable.

15. Leonov, *Road to the Ocean*, p. 453.

16. *Ibid.*, p. 362.

17. *Ibid.*, p. 262.

18. I. I. Grinberg, "Geroi sovetskogo romana," in *Obraz bolshevika* (Leningrad, 1938), pp. 3-93. This book, an obvious response to the purge trials, is concerned with proving that loyalty to the Party of Lenin and Stalin is the noblest of *human* virtues. The qualities of Leonov's questioning individualist Bolshevik, Kurilov, prompt the speculation that if he had been real, he might well have ended in the dock with Bukharin, Radek, and others, from whose mold he seems, in some respects, to have been cast. Grinberg's definition of the monolithic Bolshevik "new man" contrasts sharply with Kurilov. It has the additional virtue of standing for hundreds of other such pronouncements. "The Bolshevik, the hero of our literature and of our epoch, is a man who is changing the world, an active man, strong-willed, whose actions are full of a high Leninist-Stalinist ideology, a man who grows in struggle, a man for whom the happiness of the whole people is a vital matter, the happiness of our beautiful and happy motherland, for the defense of which he has given, is giving, and is ready to give all his strength, abilities, and talents." (*Ibid.*, p. 79.)

19. Grinberg may be right in one sense. It is possible that Kurilov's extraordinary capacity for speculation and fantasy are a "falsification" of the literal human reality. It may be that by humanizing the Bolshevik, Leonov has sentimentalized him out of all recognition. It seems more likely that Leonov has dramatized his own idiosyncratic terms for making peace with the painful, disorderly revolutionary reality, and has projected them into the figure of the political commissar.

20. Leonov, with Marx clearly in mind, says of the inhabitants of Ocean: "The people stood more erect, seemed more assured—whether because each one was aware of his neighbor at his side and did not fear him, or because the clean air of the new time did not contain the bacillus of falsehood. . . . I expected them to boast of the perfection of their social order and I should not have condemned their pride, but actually they took no notice of the social order. Here, man's natural state had at last been attained—he was free, he was not exploited, and he rejoiced in the work of hand and brain. But although everything was in reach—bread, work and fate itself—we often saw people with careworn faces. We understood that sadness dwelt among them, and that they, too, knew tragedy, though of a kind more worthy of man's dignity." (Leonov, *Road to the Ocean*, p. 365.)

21. Grinberg, "Geroi sovetskogo romana," in *Obraz bolshevika*, p. 19.

22. *Ibid.*, p. 18.

23. See *ibid.*, p. 25.
24. Quoted in *ibid.*, p. 23.
25. A recent Soviet novel had this to say on the question: "Great historical events are accompanied not only by general excitement, finding expression in elation or dejection of the human spirit, but also by suffering and deprivations far from the ordinary and beyond the power of man to prevent. For one who recognizes that the events taking place are part of the general movement of history, as well as for one who is consciously guiding the course of history, this suffering does not cease to exist any more than physical suffering ceases to exist when the disease causing it is known. But such a person reacts differently to the suffering than one who does not appreciate the historical significance of events, knowing only that life today is harder or easier, better or worse, than it was yesterday or will be tomorrow. For the former, the logic of history lends meaning to his suffering; for the latter, the suffering seems to have been imposed only to be suffered, as life itself seems to have been granted only to be lived." (Konstantin Fedin, *No Ordinary Summer* [Moscow, 1950], pp. 9-10.) The belief that there are political inoculations against the destructive effects of suffering is undoubtedly one of the positive sources of Soviet morale.
26. Alexei Tolstoy, *Road to Calvary*, trans. Edith Bone (New York, 1946), p. 350.
27. *Ibid.*, pp. 351-52.
28. *Ibid.*, p. 353.
29. *Ibid.*, p. 355.
30. *Ibid.*, p. 877.
31. *Ibid.*, p. 884.
32. *Ibid.*
33. *Ibid.*, pp. 884-85.
34. It is comforting to discover that Grinberg is in complete disagreement with my evaluation of the two halves of the novel. He finds a lack of ideological clarity in the first two parts, and condemns them, therefore, as bad writing. In those sections of Part III which were published by the time he wrote his article, he found vast improvement on all levels. (Grinberg, "Geroi sovetskogo romana," in *Obraz bolshevika*, pp. 80-86.)
35. An episode is revealing: "There was not much to learn, but these things were noted: Razvalikhin drinking and gathering all the rotters around him and keeping the better comrades out of things. Pavel reported all this to the Bureau. The other comrades . . . were all for reprimanding Razvalikhin severely, when Pavel surprised them by saying: 'I am for expelling him without the right to apply for membership again.' Everybody thought this much too severe, but Pavel said again: 'This scoundrel must be expelled.'" (Nikolai Ostrovsky, *The Making of a Hero* [New York, 1937], pp. 377-78.) He was.
36. Consider this passage: "He was in a constant hurry to *live;* not only in

a hurry himself, but anxious to urge others on too. . . . Often a light could be seen in his window late into the night, and people there gathered round a table—reading and studying. In two years they had worked through the third volume of *Capital,* and had gained an understanding of the delicate mechanics of capitalist exploitation." *Ibid.,* p. 377.

37. Oddly enough, this is not necessarily so in wartime, when the enemy is tangibly present on Soviet soil and every blow against him is a socially useful act. The literature reflects this *relaxation* of attitude and exhibits a greater concern with the heroism and the human problems of the humble, non-Party citizens. There is no large body of war literature, partly because there was little time to write during the war, and partly because Zhdanovism ruled it out shortly after the war. But novels like Simonov's *Days and Nights,* Panova's *Train,* or Leonov's *Chariot of Wrath* exhibit a more than minimal concern with the problems of being human, and a consequent diminution of the political strain. Nation, army, state, or people are the objects of primary allegiance, not the Party, since they are the institutions that conduct the struggle.

38. See *Chto delat?* (Moscow, 1947), pp. 55-56 and 191.

39. *Literature and Art* (New York, 1947), p. 61.

Solzhenitsyn's Cast of Characters

1. V. G. Belinskij, *Polnoe sobranie sočinenij* (13 vols). M., 1953-57, I, 287.
2. Demjan Bednyj (1883-1945), a prolific Soviet poet whose work consists for the most part of rhymed editorials and propaganda pieces.
3. Nadezhda Mandelshtam, *Hope Against Hope: A Memoir.* (Translated from the Russian by Max Hayward. New York: 1970, p. 26.
4. Milovan Djilas, *Conversations With Stalin.* Translated by Michael B. Petrovich. New York: 1962, p. 79.

The Art of Andrei Siniavsky

1. V. D. Dudintsev (1918-   ), a Soviet novelist and writer of short stories; author of the novel *Not By Bread Alone* (1956), a critical study of industrial bureaucracy in the Soviet Union—ed.
2. Alfreda Aucouturier, "Andrey Sinyavsky on the Eve of His Arrest," in Leopold Labedz and Max Hayward, eds., *On Trial: The Case of Sinyavsky (Tertz) and Daniel (Arzhak)* (London: Collins and Harvill, 1967), p. 343.
3. Professor Assya Humesky has suggested to me that this passage may be a reference to a popular parody of the prologue to Pushkin's *Ruslam i Liudmila* which circulated in the Soviet Union in the 1920s as an ironic protest against the new regime's attacks on romanticism.

    In quoting from the works of Siniavsky I have used the following translations, altering them occasionally on the basis of my own interpretation of the original Russian: Abram Tertz, *Fantastic Stories* ("You and I" and "The Icicle," trans. Max Hayward, "Graphomaniacs," "At the Circus," and "Tenants," trans. Ronald Hingley) (New York: Pantheon Books, 1963); "Pkhentz," trans. Jeremy Biddulph, in Peter Reddaway, ed., *Soviet Short Stories*, vol. 2 (Baltimore: Penguin Books, 1968), pp. 214-63; Abram Tertz, *The Trial Begins*, trans. by Max Hayward (New York: Pantheon Books, 1960); "Thought Unaware" [*Unguarded Thoughts*], trans. Andrew Field and Robert Szulkin, *The New Leader*, July 19, 1965, pp. 16-26.

4. This may also be a reference to Lermontov, who uses the same term in *A Hero of Our Times*.

5. The author wishes to express his indebtedness to three of his seminar students, whose interpretations are reflected in this article: Ray J. Parrott, Jr. ("Pkhentz"), Susan Wobst ("At the Circus"), and the late Guy W. Carter (*Liubimov*).

The Master and Margarita

1. A. Vulis, "Posleslovie," *Master i Margarita* in *Moskva*, No. 11 (1966), pp. 1-60. Vulis says the idea came to Bulgakov from reading Le Sage's *Le Diable boiteux*, but there are no genuine parallels between the two works. Bulgakov's work apparently was begun in 1928 or soon before.

2. The traveler who comments on the customs of a country is a traditional satirical device used by Montesquieu, Swift, Le Sage (the traveler is also a devil), and many others.

3. See Bulgakov's letter to the Soviet government, March 28, 1930.

4. Vulis, "Posleslovie," p. 128.

5. It is interesting that in Anna Akhmatova's poem *Khozyaika*—which is about Elena Bulgakova—she refers to her as a *koldunya*. Elena Sergeevna also made a black cap with a yellow "M" on it which Bulgakov wore while dictating the revisions to his novel.

6. This is from a letter to Popov on June 26, 1934. Quoted in B. Brainina, ed., *Sovetskie pisateli*, III, pp. 98-99.

7. Vitaly Vilenkin, a historian and teacher at MXAT, described these readings to me when reading parts of his (as yet unpublished) memoirs of Bulgakov.

8. Elena Sergeevna Bulgakova still has the original bound typescript, a small book about 10" x 7". She did debate whether to publish the epilogue or not—but only briefly, because it was Bulgakov's last decision.

9. See Northrop Frye, *Anatomy of Criticism* (New York, 1968) and Gilbert Highet, *The Anatomy of Satire* (Princeton, 1962).

In his "Afterword" to the *Moskva* publication Vulis devotes half a page to describing the novel as Menippean satire. However, the best Soviet Bulgakov critic more or less dismisses this suggestion (see V. Lakshin, "Roman M. Bulgakova 'Master i Margarita,' " *Novy mir*, No. 6

(1968), 284-311), and the other important Soviet critics have largely ignored the problem. See, for example, L. Skorino, "Litsa bez karnaval-nyx masok," *Voprosy literatury*, No. 6 (1968), 24-43; I. Vinogradov, "Zaveshchanie mastera," *Voprosy literatury*, No. 6 (1968), 43-76; P. Palievskij, "Poslednyaya kniga M. Bulgakova," *Nash sovremennik*, No. 3 (1969), 116-20.

The material on Menippean satire and certain other parts of this chapter were printed in Ellendea Proffer, "Bulgakov's 'The Master and Margarita': Genre and Motif," *Canadian Slavic Studies*, III, 4 (1969), 615-28.

10. M. Bakhtin, *Problemy poetiki Dostoevskogo* (Moscow, 1929; republished, 1963), pp. 150-62.

11. *Ibid.*, p. 152.

12. In *Faust*, Mephistopheles is repeatedly called "the cavalier of the horse's foot."

13. M. Bulgakov, *Master i Margarita* (Frankfurt/M., 1969). This text is used for all quotations.

14. Recall that his biography of Molière was rejected because of the unconventional narrator used.

15. H. F. Wedeck, *Dictionary of Magic* (New York, 1956), p. 61—and there are more details in M. Rudwin, *The Devil in Legend and Literature* (Chicago, 1931), pp. 253-54. Different demonologists assign the demons different roles. In Milton's *Paradise Lost* Azazel is Satan's standard-bearer (I, 533-36), and Behemoth is mentioned only in passing (VII, 471). E. M. Butler, *Ritual Magic* (Cambridge, 1949) makes Azazel the Prince of Air (p. 161). E. Langton, *Essentials of Demonology* (London, 1949) says Azazel is a Fallen Archangel (pp. 130-32) and M. D. Conway, *Demonology and Devil Lore* (New York, 1881) makes him Devil of the Desert (II, 131).

16. Vulis ("Posleslovie") is totally wrong when he concludes that the name Woland was chosen—after the elimination of Asmodeus and others—because it has "absolutely no literary associations" (p. 125). Woland is the name Mephistopheles uses in the Walpurgis Night scene in *Faust*, Part I (line 4023).

17. This parallels the drowning of the baby in *Faust*—by Gretchen. Frieda is also a "Faustian" name.

18. This is from the first scene with Faust and Mephistopheles as a traveling scholar:

> FAUST: *Nun gut, wer bist du denn?*
> . . MEPHIST: *Ein Teil von jener Kraft,*
> *Die stets das Böse will und stets das*
>   *Gute schafft.*
>   (lines 1336-38)

19. The smell of attar of roses torments Pilate; the Master and Margarita love roses, and at the ball Margarita smells of attar of roses after being

washed in blood. Roses are mentioned three times on the opening page of the first Pilate chapter, three more times later in the chapter. The reader, therefore, remembers where he has seen roses before when the Master tells Margarita that roses are what he loves. It seems important, but inexplicable, that Pilate hates roses and the Master loves them. There is a reason for this, and it is to be found in *Faust*. In the closing scene the angels fight the devils for possession of Faust's soul. The angels scatter roses—which burn those who hate and bless those who love. Pilate is tortured by the roses because he does not believe that people are good and is filled with hate for Jerusalem and its inhabitants.

20. It should be pointed out that Lakshin, *op. cit.* (*Novy mir*, p. 288) correctly mentions the references to moonlight and sunlight, and he sees part of their role in the parallels between Moscow and Jerusalem. Also, Bulgakov does similar things in his play *Don Quixote*. Don Quixote himself is called the "Knight of the White Moon," and there are important speeches on its symbolic meaning.

21. On polarities, see Ronald Gray, *Goethe* (Cambridge, 1967), p 20. On *Faust* and Bulgakov, see Rold Schroder, "Bulgakows Roman 'Der Meister und Margarita' im Spiegel der Faustmodelle des 19. und 20. Jahrhunderts," *Der Meister und Margarita* (Berlin, 1968), pp. 393-428. This article promises information about *Faust* and Bulgakov, but much of it is tangled up in pointless discussions of everything from Thomas Mann to *The Life of Klim Samgin*. And on the cane with the black poodle's head which Woland carries, see Barbara A. Woods, "Goethe and the Poodle Motif," *Fabula*, I, Heft ½ (Berlin, 1957), pp. 59-75.